THE TIMETABLES™ OF
AFRICAN-AMERICAN HISTORY

*A Chronology of the Most Important People and Events
in African-American History*

SHARON HARLEY

SIMON & SCHUSTER
050220
New York   London   Toronto   Sydney   Tokyo   Singapore

SIMON & SCHUSTER
Rockefeller Center
1230 Avenue of the Americas
New York, New York 10020

The Timetables of African-American History is a trademark of Simon & Schuster Inc.
The Timetables of African-American History is part of a best-selling series of books,
including *The Timetables of Science, The Timetables of History, The Timetables of Technology,
The Timetables of Jewish History,* and *The Timetables of American History.*

SIMON & SCHUSTER and colophon are registered trademarks
of Simon & Schuster Inc.

Designed by Irving Perkins Associates
Manufactured in the United States of America

3 5 7 9 10 8 6 4 2

Library of Congress Cataloging-in-Publication Data

Harley, Sharon.
The timetables of African-American history : a chronology of the
most important people and events in African-American history /
Sharon Harley.
p.   cm.
Includes index.
1. Afro-Americans—History—Chronology.   I. Title.
E185.H295   1995
973'.0496073—dc20   94-22571   CIP
ISBN 0-671-79524-4

INTRODUCTION

Growing public interest in the unique historical experiences of African Americans has produced an enormous demand for more scholarly and popular publications about the integral roles African Americans have played in the history of the United States. As a result of this demand, a plethora of monographs, anthologies, encyclopedias, biographical dictionaries, and even textbooks focusing on historical and contemporary black experiences have materialized during the past three decades. Ironically, what these texts reveal is how much more there is to know and learn about the historical experiences of Africans and African Americans.

Before we can begin to understand and appreciate the complexity of the African-American experience, we must resurrect historical figures, events, and activities, and make them more widely known. *The Timetables of African-American History* is a major effort to chronicle significant events, figures, and movements in the historical and contemporary lives of African Americans from 1492 to 1992 in a succinct, easily readable format. The format is designed to give the reader a greater sense of the interconnections of events and how together they form the larger story of the African-American past. An exploration of these events and movements should advance the reader's knowledge of the field of African-American history and foster a new understanding of the events and forces that shaped the lives of all Americans.

The book presents information about major events and individuals in the African-American experience in the following categories: General History; Education; Laws and Legal Actions; Religion; Literature, Publications, and the Black Press; the Arts; Science, Technology, and Medicine; and Sports. I selected these categories because they represent areas in which there appears to be the greatest popular interest and documented information. Placing information chronologically in selected subject areas makes thousands of facts related to the historical experiences and contemporary lives of African Americans in the United States covering a period of five hundred years

accessible to readers and enables them to appreciate developments over time.

The placement of events into particular categories was not a simple process. In many cases a single entry might readily be placed into two or more categories. For instance, it was decided to place almost all entries about schools in the Education category even if they had legal or religious implications, and all entries dealing with religion, including religious publications, were placed in the Religion category.

To save space we have abbreviated quite liberally (for example, US refers to the United States) and used "black" as opposed to "African American"; the latter is the more widely accepted racial designation of black people in the United States today. Non-black persons generally have been identified by an asterisk except when context makes their racial or ethnic designation obvious.

This chronology should become an invaluable resource for historians, the general public, teachers, and young readers. By indicating what happened and when, this book documents the presence and contributions of African Americans in various, largely unknown aspects of the American heritage. The information presented in *The Timetables of African-American History* is sure to inform as well as to delight its readers as they discover new and exciting facts about the contributions of African Americans to major events and developments in the United States. For readers already knowledgeable about the key events and people listed, this volume will acquaint them with more obscure individuals and events in the lives of black Americans. This is not to imply that every event and individual of probable importance to the African-American and non–African-American community has been included but to reveal to the reader an array of important individuals and events.

A project of this magnitude would by impossible to complete without a very dedicated research team. I want to begin by expressing my heartfelt gratitude to the exceptional project leader, La'Tonya Rease Miles, who had the unenviable task of coordinating the overall project and keeping the research/editorial team on task. At various points over the course of this project, the *Timetable* benefited from the able research assistance of Laura Gaither, Ashaki Goodall, Jeanne McCarty, Thembi McWhite, David Orr, Marc Powers, Mona Shah, Deb Taylor, and Jennifer Watson. The research and critical editing skills of Tish Crawford and Craig Seymour greatly minimized the errors that might have existed in a project of this size; where errors remain, I take full responsibility. Of course, the project might not have existed were it not for the vision of Simon & Schuster editor Bob Bender and his assistant Johanna Li. My involvement as editor was facilitated by the faith that both Bob and literary agent Carla Glasser had in my ability to complete such a formidable task.

The book is dedicated to my young daughter Ashley, for her early interest in African and African-American people and events (at age four she became fascinated with Nelson Mandela and insisted that I take her to hear him speak in Washington, D.C., just after he was released from prison in South Africa) and who periodically comments about how hard her mother works. I hope *The Timetables of African-American History* will help her and the book's many readers to capture the grand vistas of the African-American experience and to better appreciate the wealth of events and individuals who have constituted that experience. If it meets these goals, it will have been well worth the work.

Sharon Harley
University of Maryland at College Park

	A. **General History**	B. **Education**	C. **Laws and Legal Actions**	D. **Religion**
1492	Pedro Alonzo Niño, navigator of the *Santa Maria,* arrives with the explorer Christopher Columbus* African servants, slaves, and explorers come to the Western Hemisphere with the first Spanish and French explorers			
1501			The Spanish throne officially approves the use of enslaved Africans in the Americas	
1502	Portugal lands its first cargo of enslaved Africans in the Western Hemisphere Diego Mendez is a member of the crew on the *Capitana* when Christopher Columbus* makes his last voyage to the Western Hemisphere			
1513	When Vasco Núñez de Balboa* discovers the Pacific Ocean, 30 Africans are with him; these Africans help Balboa build the first ship to be constructed in the Western Hemisphere			
1517	In order to encourage Spanish emigration to the Americas, Bishop Bartolomeo de las Casas,* conquistador, persuades the Spanish Crown to allow each Spanish settler to import 12 enslaved Africans to the Americas; this is the formal beginning of the Atlantic slave trade; when Bishop las Casas dies in 1566, he leaves behind a book, *History of the Indies,* that remains unpublished for over 300 years; in the book, the Bishop expresses regret over his decision to enslave Africans Archduke Charles* of Spain grants monopoly of the African slave trade to Florentine merchants			
1518	King Charles I* of England grants an *asiento,* or commercial license, to individuals who then import			

	A. **General History**	B. **Education**	C. **Laws and Legal Actions**	D. **Religion**
1518	African slaves to Spanish-American colonies, free of customs duties			
1519	Approximately 300 Africans are with Hernando Cortés,* captain of the Spanish expedition, when he sets out to conquer Mexico			
1526	Africans accompany Spanish colonizer Lucas Vásquez de Ayllón* on his expedition northward on the Florida peninsula; a settlement, San Miguel, is erected within the borders of what is present-day Georgetown, SC; the colony lasts only one year, as over half of the Spanish die; the Africans eventually revolt, set fire to the settlement, and settle among Native Americans; these Africans are the first non–Native Americans to live permanently in the Western Hemisphere			
1527	Africans accompany Spanish explorer Pánfilo de Narváez* on his expedition that is shipwrecked, leaving only four survivors, in southwestern Florida; this expedition continues with Narváez's successor, Álvar Núñez Cabeza de Vaca*			
1538	Estevanico, "Little Stephen" (d Mexico, Apr 1539), explorer and guide for the Franciscan missionary Marcos de Niza,* leads an expedition from Mexico through the American Southwest territory and claims to have sighted the "Seven Cities of Cibola" of the Zuni, a Native American group, in present-day Arizona and New Mexico Africans and Spaniards establish settlements from what is present-day Florida to California, and as far north as present-day Kansas Escaped slaves set up the Gracia Real de Santa Teresa de Mosé settlement near present-day Florida,			

	A. **General History**	B. **Education**	C. **Laws and Legal Actions**	D. **Religion**
1538	the first black settlement on the continent; the Spanish king gives liberty to all slaves who cannot reach the settlement			
1539	Africans accompany Spanish explorer Hernando de Soto* on a journey to the Mississippi River			
1540	An African with Spanish explorer Hernando de Soto's* expedition settles among Native Americans in the territory of present-day Alabama			The Roman Catholic Church in Spain has established three Brotherhoods of the True Cross of Spaniards by this year, two of which are dedicated to the Christian conversion of blacks and Native Americans in the Americas
1550	European merchants and leaders of African coastal kingdoms make slave trading agreements			
1562	Great Britain enters the Atlantic slave trade after Sir John Hawkins* carries enslaved Africans from Portuguese Africa to Latin America and sells them to Spanish planters			
1565	Africans accompany Pedro Mendez,* Spanish settler, in founding St. Augustine, FL, the oldest permanent US city founded by Europeans			
1600	By this date, 900,000 enslaved Africans are brought to Latin America (by 1700, 2,750,000 will be added)			
1608				Gov. Quirogy* reports to the Spanish crown that certain slaves in the free black settlement of Gracia Real de Santa Teresa de Mosé near St. Augustine, FL, have become Christians
1618	The English government grants monopolies to several slave trading companies			
1619	Twenty Africans, three of them women, arrive in Jamestown, VA, on a Dutch ship and are sold as indentured servants; indentured servitude acts as			*Voodoo*, the word and the religious system, arrives in British North America when the first Africans land in Jamestown, VA

	A. **General History**	B. **Education**	C. **Laws and Legal Actions**	D. **Religion**
1619	forerunner to slavery in English colonies			
1621	The Dutch West India Company is chartered, initiating Dutch merchants into the Atlantic slave trade; the charter grants a transatlantic trade monopoly for 24 years			
1623	William Tucker, of Jamestown, VA, is the first black child born in English colonies			Anthony, son of Isabel and William, free blacks, is the first black in the English colonies to be baptized, Jamestown, VA
1624	The Dutch import Africans to serve on Hudson Valley farms, New Amsterdam France enters the Atlantic slave trade		The Virginia court rules that John Philip is qualified to give court testimony against blacks because he was baptized in England in 1612 and thus is Christian	
1626	Dutch West India Company exports 11 male slaves to New York			
1630	Hugh Davis,* a Virginian, is sentenced to be whipped "before an assembly of Negroes and others for abusing himself to the dishonor of God and shame of Christians, by defiling his body in lying with a Negro"		Massachusetts enacts a law protecting enslaved Africans who flee owners because of ill treatment	
1634	Enslaved Africans are imported to Maryland and Massachusetts	French Catholics provide education for all laborers, regardless of race, in Louisiana		
1638				A group of citizens petition Dominie Everardus Bogardus,* Dutch Minister in New Amsterdam colony, for a "school master to teach and train the youth of both Dutch and blacks in the knowledge of Jesus Christ"
1639	New England seamen enter slave trade when Capt. William Pierce* sails to the West Indies and exchanges enslaved Native Americans for Africans		The first Virginia legislative enactment making reference to blacks states: "All persons except Negroes are to be provided with arms and ammunition or be fined at the pleasure of the governor and council"	
1640			In *Re Sweat*, the Virginia court rules that a black servant woman and Robert Sweat* be whipped pub-	

	A. **General History**	B. **Education**	C. **Laws and Legal Actions**	D. **Religion**
1640			licly because Sweat has impregnated her	
			The General Virginia Court decides the *Emmanuel* case, which involves a black man who, along with six white servants, participates in a conspiracy to escape; when recaptured, the whites are all sentenced to extra years of service while Emmanuel is whipped, branded with an "R," and required to wear shackles for one year	
1641	Mathias De Sousa, former indentured servant is elected to serve in the Maryland General Assembly		Earliest recorded appearance of a black in a New England court, for an unnamed offense	John Winthrop* reports that the first slave to be baptized in New England is a woman from Dorchester, MA
			The Massachusetts Body of Liberties outlaws bond slavery (a term used interchangeably for chattel slavery in the British colonies) except in the cases of "just wars" and "strangers" who are voluntarily or involuntarily sold into slavery; consequently, Massachusetts becomes the first US colony to recognize slavery as a legal institution	
			The Virginia court rules in favor of John Graweere, an indentured servant who petitioned the court for permission to purchase his child's freedom from the owner of the child's mother	
			A Virginia law authorizes branding both white and black runaway servants	
			In *Re Negro John Punch*, the Virginia court mandates an extra year's service for two white men and lifetime servitude for John Punch for running away	
1642			Virginia passes a fugitive slave order penalizing those who assist runaway slaves	
1643			New England Confederation declares that mere certification by a magistrate is sufficient evidence to convict an escaped	

	A. **General History**	B. **Education**	C. **Laws and Legal Actions**	D. **Religion**
1643			slave; this intercolonial agreement paves the way for future fugitive slave laws in the US	
1644	Antony van Angola and Lucie d'Angola marry on Manhattan Island, NY— the first recorded marriage of blacks in the colony		Eleven African indentured servants petition the Council of New Netherlands when they are denied their freedom after 18 years of service to the Dutch West India Company; the council rules in their favor and awards them a parcel of land in what is present-day Greenwich Village, NYC	
1645	First known record of African slaves in New Hampshire Two Massachusetts slave merchants raid an African village, killing 100 persons; two blacks are brought to Massachusetts and sold; a local magistrate indicts the merchants for murder and man-stealing and orders that the slaves be returned to their Guinea home			
1646	Gov. Theophilus Eaton* of the New Haven, CT, colony frees his slaves, John Wham and his wife; this is the earliest account of free blacks in New England, as recorded in the *Public Records of the State of Connecticut*		A Massachusetts statute taxes black slaves as individuals (their masters have to pay)	
1648			The Council of New Netherlands passes a resolution that opens slave trade to Brazil and Angola	
1649	As of this year, 300 African slaves are in Virginia			
1650			Connecticut legally recognizes the legal institution of slavery	
1651	Anthony Johnson imports five servants into Virginia and thus qualifies to receive a 250-acre land grant along the Puwgoteague River, VA; other blacks join him and attempt to launch an independent black community; at its height the settlement reaches 12 black homesteads			

	A. **General History**	B. **Education**	C. **Laws and Legal Actions**	D. **Religion**
1652	All blacks and Native Americans who live with or are servants of the English settlers in Massachusetts are required to undergo military training due to an "ever-present Indian danger"		Rhode Island enacts the first law against slavery in North America; slavery is limited to 10 years	
1654			Anthony Jansen, a free New York mulatto, successfully sues a white man for unlawful bondage and receives compensation for his work	
1656			Massachusetts bars blacks and Native Americans from military service because colonists fear black and Native American uprisings	
1657			Virginia statute authorizes the establishment of a colonial militia to track down runaway servants	Quaker leader George Fox* advocates religious instruction for blacks and Native Americans
1658	Several blacks and Native Americans burn their masters' homes in Hartford, CT		A Virginia statute requires all masters to cut the hair of captured runaways "close above the ears"	
1659			Virginia statute imposes reduced import duties on merchants who bring slaves into the colony	
1660			Virginia statute holds servants who run away with slaves liable for the loss of any slaves A Connecticut law bars blacks and Native Americans from military service	The duty of Christianizing slaves as well as Native Americans in the New World is urged upon the Council for Foreign Plantations by King Charles II* of England
1661			Following the dwindling supply of indentured servants, the Virginia legislature legally recognizes the institution of slavery in order to maintain needed labor on tobacco plantations In order to encourage the slave trade, the Virginia Assembly offers exemptions from local duties to Dutch ships bringing in Africans	
1662	King Charles II* of England charters the "Company of Royal Adventurers trading to Africa" to sup-		Virginia legislature enacts a law declaring that the status of the mother determines whether children	

	A. **General History**	B. **Education**	C. **Laws and Legal Actions**	D. **Religion**
1662	ply 3,000 enslaved Africans annually to the West Indies		are slaves or free; Christians who fornicate with blacks are to pay double fines

Virginia and Maryland pass laws prohibiting interracial marriage | |
| **1663** | Major slave conspiracy takes place in Gloucester County, VA, involving enslaved blacks and white indentured servants who plan to rebel and overthrow their masters; the plot is betrayed; Gloucester County citizens display the heads of the rebels from chimney tops and declare the day a ''holy day''

Settlers are offered 20 acres for every black male slave and 10 acres for every black female slave brought into the Carolina colony | | Maryland legally recognizes the institution of slavery; passes law enslaving all imported Africans; freeborn English women who marry black slaves are enslaved, as are the children of such unions | |
| **1664** | Boston, MA, traders begin to import slaves directly from Africa; this stimulates the entry of other New England merchants into the slave trade | | New York and New Jersey legally recognize the institution of slavery | |
| **1667** | A sermon book by Adrian Fischer* describes the slave holiday ''Pinkster Day,'' the name given to Pentecost Sunday | | Virginia repeals earlier statute enfranchising blacks who convert to Christianity

Virginia statute provides that baptism will not affect the bondage of slaves | |
| **1668** | | | Virginia enacts statute that denies equality before the law to freed blacks | |
| **1669** | | | North Carolina enacts a law that grants slave owners absolute power and authority over enslaved blacks

A Virginia act provides that slave owners will not be held liable for killing their slaves

In *Re Franck Negro,* a Massachusetts court finds a black man not guilty of conspiring to assist someone in escaping from prison; this case marks one of the first times that | |

14

	A. **General History**	B. Education	C. **Laws and Legal Actions**	D. **Religion**
1669			blacks successfully participate in the legal system	
1670			A Massachusetts law declares that the status of the mother determines whether children are slave or free Virginia law declares that all non-Christians imported to its territory are to be slaves for life; removes voting rights from recently freed slaves and indentured servants	
1671	As of this year, 2,000 African slaves are in Virginia		A Maryland legislative act declares that slaves who convert to Christianity retain their slave status Louisiana Creoles (persons of mixed Spanish or French and African ancestry), *not* mulattoes, black Africans, or black Americans, are exempt from paying poll tax	
1672	King Charles II* of England establishes the Royal African Company which soon dominates the Atlantic slave trade		Virginia enacts a law that provides for a bounty on the heads of "maroons" (black fugitives who form communities in the mountains, swamps, and forests of the southern colonies) Virginia legislature forbids Quakers from admitting blacks to their meetings	
1675	As of this year, there are 100,000 African slaves in the West Indies, compared to 5,000 in the North American colonies			Missionary John Eliot* sends a letter to the Boston General Council arguing that repression and slavery are contradictory to the teachings of the Bible
1676			In *Re Negro Sebastian,* a black servant in Massachusetts is found guilty of rape and ordered hanged; his master requests leniency, and Sebastian instead receives 39 lashes and is required to always wear a rope around his neck	
1678	Royal African Company is granted exclusive rights to trade between the Gold Coast (the West			

	A. **General History**	B. **Education**	C. **Laws and Legal Actions**	D. **Religion**
1678	African Coast) and British colonies in the Americas John Endicott* of Boston, MA, sells a Spanish mulatto to Richard Medlicott,* a Virginian, stipulating that she is to serve for no more than 10 years even though lifetime servitude is legally recognized in Virginia			
1680			In order to curb runaways, a Massachusetts law prohibits the captain of any "ship, sloop, ketch, or vessel" weighing more than 12 pounds from entertaining blacks on board without a permit Virginia enacts a law prohibiting slaves from carrying arms of any type, revolting, or leaving the grounds of their owner without a pass; defiance is punishable by death	
1681	John Saffin,* Boston, MA, merchant, begins smuggling Africans into Massachusetts through Rhode Island		Maryland passes a law that declares children of white servant women and black slaves free, and reverses its 1663 law A black woman is indicted for burning down a building in Roxbury, MA; she is later burned at the stake	
1682			South Carolina legally recognizes the institution of slavery A Virginia law reduces all non-Christian bondsmen/women to permanent slave status regardless of future conversion to Christianity A Virginia law sanctions punishment for any slave who remains on a plantation other than his or her owner's for more than four hours without permission A New York ordinance requires black and Native	Instructions are sent from the British crown to colonial governors instructing them to do all within their power to "facilitate and encourage the Conversion of Negroes and Indians" to Christianity

	A. **General History**	B. **Education**	C. **Laws and Legal Actions**	D. **Religion**
1682			American slaves to carry a valid pass and prohibits them from leaving their masters' homes on Sundays; free blacks and Native Americans are exempt from this ordinance	
1685			A New York ordinance prohibits more than four black and Native American slaves from meeting and also prohibits them from carrying firearms	Morgan Godwin,* an English minister who spends several years in Virginia, decries the priorities of the colonists in a published sermon, ''Trade Preferr'd Before Religion and Christ Made to Give Place to Mammon''
1686			England provides the death penalty for any master in the colonies who willfully kills his servant or slave In an effort to lessen the resentment of white workers, a New York ordinance prohibits blacks from working as porters A South Carolina act fines those who buy or sell goods to slaves or servants A South Carolina statute fines any servant who is absent from work an additional 28 days of work for each day missed (the penalty is reduced in 1717) South Carolina laws impose stiff penalties for interracial sexual relations between servants (slaves are not mentioned)	
1688	Germantown, PA, Quakers sign the ''Germantown Mennonite Resolution Against Slavery''; the first official written protest against slavery in North America			
1690	Isaac Morrill* is arrested for allegedly attempting to organize black and Native American slaves to flee to Canada and later return to		In a Pennsylvania case, a white woman and a black man are charged with having a ''bastard child''; the woman receives 21 lashes	

	A. General History	B. Education	C. Laws and Legal Actions	D. Religion
1690	attack English settlers, Newbury, MA		whereas the man is ordered to never again touch a white woman A South Carolina act declares that "no slave shall be free by becoming a Christian" Several Connecticut towns institute 9:00 PM curfews for blacks and Native Americans, forbidding them from leaving their hometowns without a pass or permit	
1691			A Virginia law is expanded and its ban on interracial marriages clarified—whites who marry blacks, mulattoes, or Native Americans are to be banished; free white women who mother interracial children are required to pay a fee to church wardens, and the children become wards of the church until age 30 A Virginia law prohibits whites from freeing blacks or mulattoes without also providing, within six months, transportation out of the colony for the newly freed persons A New York ordinance prohibits blacks from working as cart drivers without a license	
1692	Sarah Good,* Sarah Osborne,* and Tituba, a slave, are the first persons accused of witchcraft in Salem Village, MA; their trials serve as the catalyst for the infamous witchcraft trials that follow		The Virginia House of Burgesses enacts the Runaway Slave Law, making it legal to kill a runaway slave in the course of apprehension	
1693			A Massachusetts law prohibits buying or receiving goods from blacks or Native Americans when there is suspicion that the goods are stolen Massachusetts forbids any innholder, taverner, common victualler, or retailer	Quaker George Keith* begins promoting religious training of slaves as preparation for emancipation Cotton Mather,* a Puritan minister, organizes a Society of Negroes in Massachusetts, which meets,

	A. General History	B. Education	C. Laws and Legal Actions	D. Religion
1693			from selling liquor to any apprentice, servant or black, except by special permission of their owner A Philadelphia, PA, "presentment" (formal statement presented to an authority) permits whites to "take up" any black found without a pass	with the permission of each master, every Sunday evening to pray, sing, and listen to sermons; this is the earliest recorded account of blacks organizing for religious meetings
1695		Rev. Samuel Thomas* begins teaching slaves in the first known school for blacks in the US, Goose Creek Parish, Charleston, SC		
1696			Both mulattoes and Creoles in Louisiana are exempt from capitation tax (blacks still have to pay)	Pennsylvania Quakers importing slaves are threatened with expulsion from the Society of Quakers
1697			British Parliament expresses the view that blacks are highly valued property, and 10 members of the Court of King's Bench agree that slaves are merchandise that can be regulated under the Navigation Acts	
1698	Slave trade opens to any ship flying the British flag		A Massachusetts act provides that all slaves be considered "real estate"	
1700	Fewer than 1,000 blacks are in the New England colonies Enslaved population in the English North American colonies reaches 28,000 (with 23,000 in the South) Boston, MA, becomes the slave trading center for the New England colonies Samuel Sewall,* a prominent Boston merchant, and the Boston Committee of Massachusetts openly oppose the slave trade Samuel Sewall* publishes *The Selling of Joseph,* an antislavery pamphlet; it is the first direct attack on slavery in New England		Rhode Island and Pennsylvania legally recognize the institution of slavery	

19

	A. General History	B. Education	C. Laws and Legal Actions	D. Religion
1701				The Society for the Propagation of the Gospel in Foreign Parts is established in London to do Christian missionary work among blacks and Native Americans in the North American colonies (operates through branches of established churches)
1702			A New York act allows for slaveholders to punish (not murder or dismember) their slaves; prohibits slaves from testifying except in conspiracy cases involving slaves; prohibits slaves from striking free Christians A Connecticut law obliges a slave's last owner to provide for that slave's care; this law ostensibly provides protection for elderly slaves or those considered "of little use"	First missionary for the Society for the Propagation of the Gospel in Foreign Parts, the Rev. Samuel Thomas,* is sent to South Carolina to offer religious instruction to slaves Rev. Cotton Mather* writes *Magnalia Christi Americana*, in which he criticizes Puritan slaveholders who "deride, neglect, and oppose all due means of bringing their poor Negroes unto our Lord"
1703			A Boston, MA, act establishes a 9:00 PM curfew for Native Americans, blacks, and mulattoes in response to national uprisings and disturbances Rhode Island prohibits householders from entertaining black or Native American servants in their homes after 9:00 PM	
1704		Elias Neau,* a French immigrant, opens the Catechism School for black slaves in New York City with help from the Society for the Propagation of the Gospel in Foreign Parts; by 1708 he is instructing more than 200 pupils		
1705	A black trumpeter gives a customary New Year's Day salute to Judge Samuel Sewall* in Boston, MA; this incident, which Sewall records in his diary, is among the earliest references to black musicians		The Virginia Assembly decrees that "no Negro, mulatto, or Indian" can hold civil, military, or ecclesiastic office or serve as a witness in court; condemns them to lifelong servitude unless they have been either Christians in their native land or free men in a Christian country; also declares that all mulatto children are indentured servants until age 31	Rev. Samuel Thomas,* missionary, reports that he has brought 1,000 slaves under Christian instruction in Goose Creek Parish, SC

	A. **General History**	B. **Education**	C. **Laws and Legal Actions**	D. **Religion**
1705			A Virginia statute establishes a fine against female indentured servants who have illegitimate children by blacks or mulattoes; if the woman is free and white, she is also subject to a fine *or* five years additional service	
			A Virginia law relegates all black, mulatto, and Native American slaves to the status of "real estate," liable as payment for debts	
			A Massachusetts law provides that any black or mulatto who strikes a white person be "severely whipped at the discretion of the justices before whom the offender was convicted"	
			A New York statute provides for reimbursement when a slave is executed according to judicial decree	
			Massachusetts laws are passed to prohibit interracial marriage	
			A Massachusetts act imposes a duty tax on blacks imported into the US and requires that slaves be registered at an import office	
1706			A New York act is passed to encourage the baptism of slaves, although a slave's baptism does not entitle freedom	Rev. Cotton Mather,* in his tract *The Negro Christianized,* uses scriptural verse and logical arguments against those who deny blacks their humanity
			A New York law that prohibits slaves from testifying for or against a free person in any case is passed	
1707			A South Carolina law requires militia captains "to enlist, traine up and bring into the field for each white, one able slave armed with a gun or lance"	English minister Isaac Watts* publishes *Hymns and Spiritual Songs* that becomes especially popular among blacks
1708	Black slaves in the Carolinas outnumber white inhabitants, both free and bonded, for the first time		A Connecticut law imposes a penalty not exceeding 30 lashes for any black "who disturbed the peace, or who attempted to strike a white person"	
	Slaves serve as cowboy patrols to help protect Charleston, SC, from Native American attacks		A New York statute makes it a capital offense for a	

	A. **General History**	B. **Education**	C. **Laws and Legal Actions**	D. **Religion**
1708	Slaves in Long Island, NY, kill seven whites; four slaves are executed; this rebellion results in a new law allowing justices "to sentence [slave] rebels to be executed in any way or manner they might think most likely to secure public tranquility" Gov. Joseph Dudley* of Massachusetts informs the Board of Trade that "the Negroes . . . brought in from the West Indies are usually the worst servants they have," thereby increasing the value of Africans, particularly those from the African Gold Coast		black, mulatto, or Native American to kill a free white person A New York statute states that a slave can be arrested only when a warrant is issued by a justice of the peace A South Carolina act allows for the emancipation of slaves who "in actual invasion" capture or kill an enemy upon providing proof "by any white person"	
1709	Slave market is erected at the foot of Wall Street, NYC		A New York ordinance requires masters to tend to their slaves' physical needs; prohibits the willful killing, deliberate mutilation, or maiming of slaves	A group of clergymen in North Carolina complains that slaveholders do not allow their slaves to be baptized for fear that a Christian slave might be freed by law
1710	Thomas Fuller, an "illiterate" slave who possesses such extraordinary arithmetic abilities that he is able to answer difficult math questions in minutes, b (d 1790)			
1711	The Rhode Island Friends Society (a Quaker group) dismisses a woman from their group because she treats her slave inhumanely A group of maroons (fugitive slaves who live primarily in bands) lead a raid against a predominantly white community, South Carolina		Pressured by the Mennonites and Quakers, the Pennsylvania colonial legislature outlaws slavery; the British Crown overrules it	The bishop of St. Asaph, Dr. Fleetwood,* preaches a sermon before the Society for the Propagation of the Gospel in Foreign Parts in which he outlines the duty to instruct blacks in the Christian religion; the sermon is printed and dispersed to plantations
1712	Slaves of the West African Carmantee and Pappa nations revolt, New York City; 21 blacks are executed for participation in the revolt; authorities close the Catechism School after learning that blacks involved in the revolt are students there; the revolt discourages religious instruction of blacks, and stricter importation laws are passed in Massachusetts and Pennsylvania		A Rhode Island act imposes a duty tax on imported blacks and requires traders to register slaves at the Naval Office The preamble of the Rhode Island Act of 1712 disapproves of the African slave trade because it discourages the use of white servants Pennsylvania passes the first colonial legislation	

	A. **General History**	B. **Education**	C. **Laws and Legal Actions**	D. **Religion**
1712			prohibiting the slave trade	
			A Massachusetts law prohibits the importation of Native American indentured servants and enslaved Africans due to increasing numbers of conspiracies and uprisings	
			A New York act bans blacks, mulattoes, and Native Americans from home ownership	
			A New York statute establishes as a statutory offense slaves killing other slaves	
			The New York legislature enacts a law that declares the status of the mother determines whether children are slave or free	
			A South Carolina slave code requires all slaves to carry a pass when traveling away from their owner's plantation, and all slave property is liable to forfeiture	
			Rhode Island law provides that ship captains who fail to register imported Africans are subject to imprisonment	
			A South Carolina act imposes stiff penalties on runaways, including flogging and the death penalty	
			A New York statute prohibits any person from harboring slaves and makes liable for the payment of the assessed value of the slave any person caught harboring a slave; blacks, Native Americans, and mulattoes are forbidden to carry firearms	
1713	England assumes a dominant role in the slave trade with the Treaty of Utrecht—takes over the right to issue *asientos* from Spain and agrees to deliver 144,000 slaves to Spanish colonies			Rev. E. Taylor* of the Church of England is sent to South Carolina as a missionary; he meets opposition from slaveholders when he provides religious instruction to slaves
1715	Blacks comprise 24.2% of the total Virginia population		New Hampshire forbids the sale of liquor to any apprentice, servant, or black except by special	Francisco Xavier de Luna Victoria is the first black bishop in America (Panama)

	A. General History	B. Education	C. Laws and Legal Actions	D. Religion
1715	Slaves are used to help the Carolina militia fight the Yamassee, a Native American group		permission of that person's owner	
			North Carolina legally recognizes the institution of slavery, passing an antimiscegenation law, and outlawing meetings of slaves	
			Maryland enacts laws designed to further guard against interracial marriage (new laws are also enacted in 1717 and 1728)	
			In order to deter economic self-sufficiency, a New York act forbids blacks, Native Americans, and mulattoes from selling oysters in New York City	
1716			A South Carolina law stipulates that only white men professing Christianity can vote	
1717			The South Carolina legislature enacts an antimiscegenation law	
			At the insistence of New London, CT, citizens, the Connecticut legislature enacts several laws that prohibit free blacks and mulattoes from residing in any town in the colony and forbids them from purchasing land or establishing businesses without consent; home ownership by free blacks already living in the colony is now considered illegal	
1718			A bill entitled An Act for Encouraging the Importation of White Male Servants and the Preventing of the Clandestine Bringing of Negroes and Mulattoes fails in the Massachusetts House of Representatives	
			A New Hampshire law imposes the death penalty for any master who willfully kills black or Native American slaves or indentured servants	
			A Rhode Island law is enacted that states if a slave is found in a free black's	

	A. **General History**	B. **Education**	C. **Laws and Legal Actions**	D. **Religion**
1718			home, both will be whipped	
1720	Several slaves are burned alive and others are banished after they are implicated in a revolt near Charleston, SC		A New York law requires blacks to carry lighted lanterns on the street after nightfall	
1721			Delaware enacts an anti-miscegenation law A South Carolina statute limits voting rights to free white Christian men	Earliest recording of a black baptism in Pennsylvania
1722			A New York ordinance prohibits gambling among slaves A South Carolina act declares that slaves can no longer hire themselves out and prohibits slaves from working for themselves under any condition A South Carolina law requires slave owners who manumit slaves to provide transportation out of the colony for the newly freed person; freed persons are required to depart within one year or forfeit emancipation A South Carolina act makes slave escape punishable by death Slave testimony is permitted in all noncapital cases in South Carolina White justices in the Carolinas are authorized to search blacks for firearms	
1723	Boston, MA, slaves are accused of setting a dozen fires in one April week During the French and Indian Wars in America, Army musician Nero Benson serves as a trumpeter in Captain Isaac Clark's* company, Framingham, MA		A Connecticut law establishes fines against anyone who entertains black or Native American slaves after 9:00 PM Black, Native American, and mulatto slaves in Massachusetts are forbidden to remain on Boston Common after sunset The Virginia Assembly enacts laws to limit the increase of free blacks to those who are either born free or manumitted by legislature; free blacks are	Rev. William Guy* of St. Andrew's Parish reports baptizing a black man and woman, South Carolina Rev. Brian Hunt* of St. John's Parish reports having a slave among his communicants in South Carolina Society for the Propagation of the Gospel in Foreign Parts missionaries extends beyond South Carolina into other colonies, renewing the fears of many slaveholders that Christian

	A. General History	B. Education	C. Laws and Legal Actions	D. Religion
1723			denied the right to vote and forbidden to carry weapons The Virginia legislature imposes a duty on the importation of liquor and slaves The Maryland Assembly passes a law to suppress the meetings of slaves on Sunday to curb independent religious meetings among blacks Massachusetts slaveholders petition the state legislature for a law to restrain slaves in response to nightly disturbances; the House of Representatives appoints a committee to regulate slaves and to restore peace	conversion will lead to the freedom of slaves
1724			The city of Boston, MA, enacts several articles directed toward blacks, Native Americans, and mulattoes (non-whites); the articles require non-whites to remain inside their masters' homes between one hour after sunset and one hour before sunrise; all free non-whites are required to indenture their children between the ages of 4 and 21 to English slaveholders; free non-whites are forbidden to entertain slaves Louisiana enacts its comprehensive Black Codes: the legal status of blacks is that of "moveable property of his master"; children born of black parents follow the mother's condition; slaves are forbidden to carry weapons; neither freeborn blacks nor slaves can receive gifts from whites; slaves face death if they strike or kill their owners or any member of their owners' families	William Black,* a minister in Accomako, VA, informs the bishop of London that he has baptized about 200 slaves since his arrival and instructed slaves in their owners' homes Virginia offers a tax break to slaveholding colonists if they instruct and baptize their slaves A document encouraging Christian education of Native American, black, and mulatto children is circulated in Virginia
1725			Pennsylvania enacts an antimiscegenation law	
1727	Benjamin Franklin* organizes the Junto, a benevolent association in Philadelphia, PA, that opposes slavery			Bishop Edmund Gibson* of the Society for the Propagation of the Gospel in Foreign Parts outlines in two pastoral letters the

	A. **General History**	B. **Education**	C. **Laws and Legal Actions**	D. **Religion**
1727	Blacks and Native Americans attempt an uprising in Middlesex and Gloucester counties, VA; plot is discovered			duty of missionaries in the conversion of blacks to Christianity
1728			Massachusetts legislature compels ship captains to provide, under oath, a complete list of all Africans aboard their vessels or risk a fine	
1729	The governor of Louisiana, Étienne de Périer,* orders an armed band of slaves to exterminate the Chouchas, a Native American group; this is the first instance where armed blacks defend the colony Disputes over slavery cause Carolina to divide into separate colonies; North Carolina, settled primarily by less wealthy Quaker and Scotch-Irish farmers, is one of the most active antislavery states in the South The Chickasaw, a Native American group, allegedly incites and inspires the Bambara, enslaved Africans from the Senegal basin in West Africa, who attempt to massacre whites and start their own colony, New Orleans, LA; the plot is betrayed		Massachusetts and Rhode Island require every slaveholder to post a bond to guarantee that his or her slave, after emancipation, will not become a public charge	The Crown Attorney* and Solicitor General of England,* in reply to an appeal from several colonies, declare that baptism in no way changes the status of slaves A slave is baptized by Dr. Timothy Cutler,* a member of the Society for the Propagation of the Gospel in Foreign Parts, Boston, MA
1730	A slave conspiracy, involving over 200 slaves, is discovered in Virginia; it arises after rumors spread among slaves that whites had suppressed orders from King George II "to sett all those slaves free that were Christian" The Natchez, a Native American group, massacre whites in New England and spare 106 blacks		A Connecticut law provides for a penalty of 40 lashes for any black, Native American, or mulatto who attempts to defame or defames any white person The New York General Assembly enacts legislation to fine any person who entertains slaves in his home Virginia law orders white males to carry arms to church in response to discovered slave conspiracies	Rev. J. Usher* of the Society for the Propagation of the Gospel in Foreign Parts reports 30 blacks and Native Americans in his New England congregation
1732			Rhode Island Assembly repeals its duty tax on black slaves A Virginia law prohibits blacks, slave or free, from giving testimony "except at a trial of a slave for a capital crime"	

27

	A. **General History**	B. **Education**	C. **Laws and Legal Actions**	D. **Religion**
1733			Spanish decree promises escaped English slaves freedom in Florida	
1735	Free black military officers lead black troops in a war against Native Americans, Louisiana		A coroner's jury tries Dutch burgher John Van Zandt* for whipping his slave to death outside his quarters, NY; Van Zandt asserts that the slave was killed "by the visitation of God" A South Carolina law orders the death penalty for fugitive slaves who resist capture with a stick or other instrument A South Carolina act requires slaves to wear "Negro cloth," which includes "checked cottons, scotch plaids, garlix or calico" A South Carolina act requires a newly freed person to depart the state within six months after manumission; freed blacks who return within seven years are to be reenslaved The South Carolina legislature permits slave testimony in all criminal trials of slaves A Georgia law bans the importation of slaves and prohibits the use of slaves within the colony	
1736	Emanuel Manna Bernoon, a free black, opens the first catering business in Providence, RI; Bernoon and his wife later establish a highly successful oyster house in Providence (d Rhode Island, 1769)			Earliest recorded baptism of a black in New Jersey
1737			In a rare court case, James, an indentured servant in Massachusetts, petitions for his freedom after the death of his mistress and wins; typically, indentured servants, particularly blacks, are not granted their freedom White coopers (barrel makers) in New York City petition the colonial assembly about the "great number of [blacks] enter-	The Society for the Propagation of the Gospel in Foreign Parts extends its missionary work: Rev. P. Stoupe* baptizes four blacks at New Rochelle, NY; Rev. Charles Taylor,* a schoolmaster, keeps night school for the instruction of blacks in Newburgh, NY; Dr. Timothy Cutler* reports four black slaves among those admitted to his church in Boston, MA

	A. **General History**	B. Education	C. **Laws and Legal Actions**	D. **Religion**
1737			ing their trade''; Lt. Gov. George Clarke* supports the petition	
1738	Fugitive slaves seek refuge in Georgia with the Creeks, a Native American group, and in Florida with the Spanish			The General Association of the Colony of Connecticut allows the baptism of infant slaves

Moravians establish a mission exclusively for blacks, Bethlehem, PA |
| **1739** | The first major slave uprising in South Carolina begins about 20 miles west of Charleston at Stono; slaves kill two warehouse guards, secure arms and ammunition, and flee south, hoping to reach Florida; they march to the beating of two drums and kill all whites who attempt to interfere; armed whites eventually capture all but a dozen rebels | | | Rev. Samuel Seabury* of New London, CT, baptizes two blacks |
| **1740** | New York slaves are accused of trying to poison the water supply

Two New Jersey slaves are killed for barn burning | A South Carolina act prohibits teaching slaves to write | The South Carolina legislature passes a slave code that forbids slaves from raising livestock, provides that animals owned by slaves be forfeited, and fixes severe penalties for slaves who made ''false appeals'' to the governor on the grounds that they are in bondage illegally

A South Carolina law determines all slaves to be ''chattel'' | The religious revivals of the 1740s bring blacks into the Methodist and Baptist churches offering ''Christianity to all'' |
| **1741** | The earliest known ''Negro election day'' occurs, Salem, MA, May 17; during this festive mock election blacks hold a parade and dress in fantastic costumes; the central figure is the ''governor'' who leads the parade

Arsonist acts prompt reports of a slave conspiracy in New York City; with no direct proof or evidence, citizens believe that black and white conspirators in tend to burn the city and kill white citizens; massive white backlash leads to the execution of 31 slaves and 5 whites

Boston, MA, blacks attempt to escape to St. Augus- | | | Bishop Sicker,* the secretary of the American Church for Negroes, reports seeing a register sheet 33 pages long in that church; this sheet is filled with baptism records of blacks |

	A. **General History**	B. **Education**	C. **Laws and Legal Actions**	D. **Religion**
1741	tine, FL, in a stolen boat; they are captured at Barnstable Bay and sent to jail A conspiracy by blacks to burn Charlestown, MA is discovered			
1743	The British government supplies the governor of South Carolina with three regular infantry companies in order to protect that colony and Georgia from possible slave uprisings In the October 24 issue of the *Boston Evening Post*, a runaway slave musician is mentioned in an advertisement as being able to "play well upon a flute, and not so well on a violin"			The Society for the Propagation of the Gospel in Foreign Parts opens a school in Charleston, SC, to train blacks for Christian missionary work (closes in 1763) The first known black Baptist, identified as Quassey, is listed as one of 51 members of a Newton, RI, church The Protestant Episcopal Church in Maryland publishes a book of sermons and dialogues for use by slaveholders to teach their slaves to be obedient
1744		Anglican missionaries establish a school for blacks, South Carolina	Virginia amends its 1705 law declaring that blacks cannot serve as witnesses in court cases; instead it admits "any free Negro, mulatto or Indian being a Christian" as a witness in a criminal or civil suit involving another black, mulatto, or Native American	
1745				The French Code Noir mandates that slaveholders enlighten their slaves concerning Christian principles
1746			Blacks, mulattoes, and Native Americans in Boston, MA, are forbidden to keep hogs because they allegedly will be tempted to steal from their masters, "spend time away from their masters, and possibly plot together"	Blacks and whites worship together at First Baptist Church in Philadelphia, PA—the city's first Baptist church
1747			South Carolina Assembly commends soldiers for "faithfulness and courage in repelling attacks of His Majesty's enemies"; it subsequently makes provisions for utilizing black recruits in the event of danger or emergency and authorizes the enlistment of no more than half of all able-bodied slaves ages 16 to 20	Presbyterians begin religious instruction of blacks

E. Literature, Publications, and The Black Press	F. The Arts	G. Science, Technology, and Medicine	H. Sports	
				1741
				1743
				1744
				1743
Lucy Terry (later Prince) (b 1730; d 1821), a slave, writes "Bar's Fight," a commemorative poem recreating the Deerfield Massacre; this poem is the first known to be written by a black person in the US and is not published until 1895				**1746**
				1747

	A. **General History**	B. **Education**	C. **Laws and Legal Actions**	D. **Religion**
1748				
1749			A Georgia law repeals prohibitions on importation of enslaved Africans; also helps to protect slaves from cruel treatment and being hired out	
1750	Slave population reaches 236,400 in the English colonies (more than 206,000 living south of Pennsylvania) Blacks comprise 20% of the NYC population		Georgia repeals its earlier ban and legally recognizes slavery A Rhode Island law forbids selling liquor to any Native American, mulatto, or black servant	Anglican minister Thomas Bacon* delivers a series of sermons that address slaveholders and slaves concerning the importance of the religious instruction of slaves Dr. Thomas Cutler* of the Society for the Propagation of the Gospel in Foreign Parts baptizes five black children in Boston, MA
1751		Associates of Dr. Thomas Bray* establish a school in Georgia for the education of blacks and Native Americans; Bray sets up a similar school in North Carolina	A South Carolina law prohibits slaves from learning about poisons and other medicines, and prohibits them from becoming doctors	The Bishop of London* sends Dr. Thomas Bray* to Maryland to convert blacks; his mission extends into other colonies
1752	Eighteen slaves are at Mount Vernon, VA, when Gen. George Washington* acquires the estate; under Washington, the number of slaves on the estate grows to 200		Maryland enacts its first manumission statute	
1753			A Massachusetts law provides that any black, Native American, or mulatto servant convicted of deliberately breaking street lamps be publicly whipped	
1754	Blacks comprise 40% of the total Virginia population			John Woolman,* one of the founders of the Quaker sect in the US, begins a campaign against slavery with the publication of *Some Considerations on the Keeping of Negroes,* an exhortation to

E. Literature, Publications, and The Black Press	F. The Arts	G. Science, Technology, and Medicine	H. Sports	
	Phillip Bazadier, military trumpeter, b Guadaloupe; known as the bugler-trumpeter of the Clarendon Horse Guards and the Light Horse Company and as a prominent musician who performs at public events and balls (d Wilmington, NC, 1848)			**1748**
				1749
				1750
				1751
				1752
	Scipio Moorhead, painter, b; one of the earliest black painters, Moorhead is only known through Phillis Wheatley's poem, "To S.M., a Young African Painter, on Seeing His Works"; none of his paintings survive	Benjamin Banneker (b Ellicott, MD, 1731; d 1806), astronomer, philosopher, mathematician, and inventor, constructs the first striking clock with all parts made in America; two years in the making, this wooden clock is so accurate that it keeps perfect time for 40 years, unfailingly striking each hour		**1753**
				1754

	A. **General History**	B. **Education**	C. **Laws and Legal Actions**	D. **Religion**
1754				fellow members of the Society of Friends to consider manumitting their slaves on grounds of morality
1755	A Maryland census records slightly more than 1,800 free blacks (4% of the black population) in the state, 80% of whom are mulattoes; this is the earliest count of free blacks in the South		A Georgia law increases the number of slaves permitted on a plantation and reduces the penalties for a slave's murder	
1756	Blacks serve in the French and Indian War from 1756 to 1763			
1758		Philadelphia, PA, provides schools for black children	Blacks are forbidden to work in any handicraft in the entire Georgian colony (in order to encourage white tradesmen to settle there)	Rev. John Wesley* baptizes the first black Methodist First black Baptist church in the US, African Baptist or "Bluestone" Church, is erected on the William Byrd* plantation near Bluestone River in Mecklenburg, VA The Philadelphia [PA] Yearly Meeting of the Society of Friends votes to exclude buyers or sellers of slaves from membership; societies in other cities adopt similar condemnations of slavery
1759			Blacks, mulattoes, and mestizos are forbidden to serve as constables in Georgia	
1760	US black population reaches 325,806			Quaker policy on slavery is not uniformly adopted; one group in Rhode Island actively continues the slave trade, and a few in the Carolinas and Virginia refuse to relinquish slaves
1761			A Georgia law excludes black males from voting, restricting voting to white men	
1762			A Virginia law excludes black males from voting, restricting voting to white men	Providence, RI, Baptist Church records 19 black members

E. Literature, Publications, and The Black Press	F. The Arts	G. Science, Technology, and Medicine	H. Sports	
				1754
				1755
				1756
				1758
				1759
Briton Hammon's *A Narrative of the Uncommon Sufferings, and Surprizing Deliverance of Briton Hammon, a Negro Man-Servant to General Winslow, of Marshfield, in New England: Who Returned to Boston, After Having Been Absent Almost Thirteen Years* is published in Boston by Green and Russell				**1760**
Poet Jupiter Hammon (b Oyster Bay, NY, 1711; d 1800), pens *An Evening Thought: Salvation by Christ with Penitential Cries,* his first volume of poetry	Barzillai Lew (b Groton, MA, 1743; d Dracut, MO, 1821), one of the first black fifers and drummers for the US Army, serves in Thomas Farrington's* Company of Groton, MA, during the French and Indian War			**1761**
				1762

	A. General History	B. Education	C. Laws and Legal Actions	D. Religion
1763	Louis XV* decrees that all Louisiana "mixed" bloods who can claim descent from a Native American and white ancestor outrank those mixed bloods who have only white and African ancestors The citizens of the Mosé settlement move to Cuba when Florida is given to the English Slaves who work as chimney workers in Charleston, SC, protest their working conditions			
1764	Slave ship captains and merchants oppose efforts to raise the price of sugar and molasses, declaring them essential to the Massachusetts slave trade Abijah Prince, a free black, owns 100 acres of land in Guilford, VT	Rhode Island College is founded; later renamed Brown University, after the Brown brothers,* wealthy New England shippers who made a substantial profit from the African slave trade, Providence, RI	A South Carolina case holds that a free black may bring a civil suit in chancery court	
1765	Ninety thousand blacks and 40,000 whites populate South Carolina		Georgia allows free black immigrants to settle in the colony and offers free mulattoes restricted rights, excluding voting and seats in the General Assembly Jenny Slew (b c1719), a mulatto woman, files suit in Massachusetts claiming that she has been unlawfully kidnapped and enslaved; the court awards Slew her freedom, four pounds, and court costs	
1766	Gen. George Washington* orders that one of his slaves who is recaptured after running away be sold in the West Indies for molasses, rum, limes, tamarinds, sweet meats, and liquor A Rhode Island merchant landowner owns 238 slaves—an unusually high number for a New England slaveholder			The first Methodist congregation in New York welcomes blacks; slaves are among the original members
1767			A Massachusetts bill that would have banned slavery and the importation of slaves fails passage in the legislature	

1763

Newport Gardner (b Occramer Marycoo, 1746), one of the first black American music teachers, begins to write music at age 18

1764

1765

1766

Phillis Wheatley, one of the first known black poets in the U.S. and the first published black author in North America. (MSRC)

Phillis Wheatley (b c1753; d 1784) writes "A Poem by Phillis, a Negro Girl, on the Death of Reverend George Whitefield," her first work; the poem is not published until 1770

The earliest reference to a Negro dance appears in a New York newspaper, the *New York Journal*, when an article refers to a "Negro Dance, in Character," performed by a Mr. Tea on Apr 14

Peter Hill, later to become a famous clockmaker, b Burlington Township, NJ, Jul 19 (d Burlington Township, NJ, 1820)

1767

	A. General History	B. Education	C. Laws and Legal Actions	D. Religion
1768	The *New London* [CT] *Gazette* is the first newspaper to use a stereotyped picture of a fugitive slave dressed in a short skirt with a bundle on his head and carrying a stick in his hand; this type of advertisement later becomes popular in the South		A black man convicted of rape is sentenced to death in Worcester, MA, while a white man is sentenced to sit on the gallows for the same crime	
1769	Spain gains control of Louisiana; more than one-half of the black population is mulatto		Thomas Jefferson* unsuccessfully presses for a bill in the Virginia House of Burgesses to emancipate slaves A slave named James sues Richard Lechmere* of Cambridge, MA, for assault and battery and "imprisoning and holding the plaintiff in servitude"; the Inferior Court of Common Pleas rules against the slave, but the Suffolk Superior Court later settles the case by compromise	
1770	Crispus Attucks (b 1723), runaway slave and seaman, is the first American killed by British soldiers in the Boston Massacre, Mar 5	Quakers led by Anthony Benezet* open a school for blacks in Philadelphia, PA	Georgia forbids slaves "to assemble on pretense of feasting," etc., and commands any constable to break up any such meeting Georgia slave code declares that any "slave, free black, mulatto, mestizo, or Indian (not in amity with the government) could be executed if he should attempt to rape or rape any white person"	
1771			A bill passed by the Massachusetts Assembly to end all importations of Africans fails to win the governor's assent Mary and William Butler, the grandchildren of a slave and a white woman, sue for their freedom in a Maryland court, claiming descent from a free white woman; a lower court grants them freedom, but the Court of Appeals reverses the decision	The first Christian burial in California is that of Ignacio Ramirez
1772	Aaron, US patriot, participates in the burning of the British cutter *Gaspee* in Rhode Island		Lord Mansfield* hands down a decision against slavery in the *Somerset* case in England, freeing all slaves who join British forces; it is an attempt to encourage slaves to run away; the case stimulates	Blacks receive membership into the First Baptist Church of Boston, MA Rev. Chauncey Whittlesey* of New Haven, CT, has from 20 to 30 blacks in a total membership of 450–500

E. Literature, Publications, and The Black Press	F. The Arts	G. Science, Technology, and Medicine	H. Sports	
				1768
	Contemporary sources cite some of the first theatrical performances of ''Negro songs'' in the US; Lewis Hallam* the Younger sings ''Dear Heart! What a Terrible Life I Am Led'' in his role as Mungo in Bickerstaffe's* comic opera *The Padlock* in New York City; in the following years Charles Dibdin* and Joseph Tyler* attract attention as singers of Negro songs in plays and between acts			**1769**
James Albert Ukawsaw Gronniosaw's *A Narrative of the Most Remarkable Particulars in the Life of James Albert Gronniosaw, an African Prince, as Related by Himself* is published	Robert Munford's* comedy of elections in Virginia is written; its cast of characters includes the first black in American theater Blacks are among Englishman William Tuckey's* church choir when they give the first musical performance of George Frideric Handel's* *Messiah* in the colonies			**1770**
	One of the first positive usages of black dialect in a drama is used in a play by an anonymous author called *The Trial of Atticus, Before Justice Beary, for a Rape* when Caesar, a comic, makes a brief appearance			**1771**
				1772

	A. **General History**	B. **Education**	C. **Laws and Legal Actions**	D. **Religion**
1772			requests for legislative action against slavery in New England A white man sells two free mulatto children and their Native American mother into slavery; the woman sues for freedom, and a Massachusetts court declares the sale illegal The Virginia House of Burgesses enacts a prohibitive duty on slave imports and requests the crown to accept this curtailment of slavery; the crown vetoes the bill	Blacks and whites worship together at the first Methodist meeting houses in Baltimore, MD
1773	Pennsylvania slave trade is stifled after a 20-pound tax is imposed on every imported slave Jean Baptiste Point du Sable (b Saint Domingue, 1745; d St. Charles, MO, 1818), businessman, purchases the house and land of Jean Baptiste Millet* at Old Peoria Fort, IL Fourteen newly imported Africans flee together from a Virginia slave merchant		Massachusetts slaves petition the legislature for their freedom; there are records of at least eight other petitions during the Revolutionary War period Leicester and other Massachusetts towns instruct their legislative representatives to work against slavery and the slave trade Georgia slaves are forbidden to drive cattle	One of the first known black Baptist churches in the US is founded at Silver Bluff, SC (although the cornerstone of the present church building claims 1750 as the founding date); freed slave George Leile (b 1750; d Jamaica, 1820) is the church's first minister (David George is later ordained) Rev. Andrew Bryan (b Goose Creek, SC, 1732; d Georgia, 1812) and Rev. George Leile organize the first black Baptist church in Savannah, GA Rev. Isaac Skillman* asserts that slaves should rebel against slaveholders Presbyterian minister Samuel Hopkins* and Dr. Ezra Stiles* send letters to New England churches urging them to oppose the slave trade Rev. Samuel Hopkins* and Dr. Ezra Stiles* train 30 to 40 blacks to be sent to Africa to spread the Gospel among the peoples of Africa; the onset of the Revolutionary War prevents the missionaries from going to Africa
1774	Massachusetts blacks enlist in the Minutemen companies Rhode Island population contains 3,761 blacks—6.3% of the total population	Quakers open another school for black children, Philadelphia, PA Benjamin Franklin* opens a school for black children, Philadelphia, PA	Massachusetts General Assembly passes a measure prohibiting the importation of slaves; Gov. Thomas Gage* suspends the law the next day	The English Society of Friends votes for the expulsion of members who engage in the slave trade Philadelphia [PA] Yearly Meeting of Society of Friends forbids Quakers

1772

1773

Phillis Wheatley's *Poems on Various Subjects, Religious and Moral* is published; it is the first book written by a black in North America and the second published by a woman in North America; *Poems* is better received in England than in the US; the Lord Mayor of London* presents Wheatley with a copy of *Paradise Lost* in recognition of her work

---

1774

Nicholas Cresswell,* an Englishman traveling in Maryland, makes one of the earliest references to the banjo, which he reports being used by slaves at a ''Negro Ball''

	A. General History	B. Education	C. Laws and Legal Actions	D. Religion
1774	Bacchus, a Virginia house servant, forges a pass under the assumed name John Christian and heads for the coast to board a vessel to England but never makes it; a number of other blacks successfully use this ploy to gain freedom during the Revolutionary years Thomas Jefferson* describes the abolition of slavery as one of the goals of the colonists and accuses Great Britain of blocking efforts to end the slave trade		Continental Congress bars the importation of slaves after December 1, 1774 Rhode Island enacts a law freeing slaves henceforth brought into the colony but not those already there A New York act grants freedom to slaves who serve three years as soldiers Virginia legislation orders an end to further slave importation Boston, MA, blacks petition Gov. Thomas Gage,* offering to fight for the British in exchange for emancipation; the proposal is not accepted Connecticut bans the importation and sale of slaves Georgia legislature requires slaves "sent out for hire" to wear a public badge	from buying or selling slaves and requires them to prepare their enslaved for imminent emancipation; the penalty for resistance is disownment
1775	An unknown slave guides Daniel Boone's* expedition to Kentucky The midnight rides in Massachusetts of Paul Revere* and William Dawes* alert the Minutemen, many of whom are black volunteers, that the British troops are coming Black patriots, including Lemuel Haynes, join Ethan Allen* and the Green Mountain Boys* in the capture of Fort Ticonderoga, NY Black soldiers, among them Salem Poor, Barzillai Lew, and Cuff Whitmore, distinguish themselves at the Battle of Bunker Hill; soldier Peter Salem (b Framingham, MA, 1750; d Framingham, 1816) is credited with shooting and killing British Maj. John Pitcairn* Prince Hall (b Bridge Town, Barbados, 1735; d Boston, MA, 1806) and others apply to the Grand Lodge of England for a warrant to establish an independent black lodge, which they		Maryland slaveholders petition Gov. Robert Eden* for arms to protect themselves against possible slave uprisings The Massachusetts Committee of Safety, also known as the [John] Hancock* and [Joseph] Warren* Committee, decides that only free blacks (and not slaves) may serve in the Revolutionary Army Shortly after he takes command of American troops, Gen. George Washington* issues an order forbidding officers to recruit blacks for enlistment in the military Virginia opens the militia to all free males; many slaves pass themselves off as free and sign up The Continental Congress rejects Edward Rutledge's* proposal to discharge all blacks from the US Army The Continental Congress authorizes the Continental Navy to send ships to sea to defend against the British fleet, Oct. 13; both free and enslaved black sailors are	Philadelphia Quakers organize the Pennsylvania Society for the Abolition of Slavery, the first abolition society in the US; Benjamin Franklin* is elected president and helps to organize a Society for the Relief of Free Negroes Unlawfully Held in Bondage Of the estimated half million slaves in the US, less than 5% are members of formal American churches

E. **Literature,**
Publications, and
The Black Press   F. **The Arts**

G. **Science,**
Technology,
and Medicine   H. **Sports**

1774

1775

Barzillai Lew serves as a
fifer in Captain John
Ford's* Company of the
Twenty-Seventh Regiment
of Massachusetts during the
Battle of Bunker Hill

	A. **General History**	B. **Education**	C. **Laws and Legal Actions**	D. **Religion**
1775	name the African Lodge No. 1, Boston, MA		permitted to serve the following day	
	A free black posing as a runaway slave dupes Lord Dunmore* of Virginia into believing that Norfolk's Great Bridge is inadequately guarded, and American patriots subsequently force Dunmore's troops back to their fort; the first shots are fired in the South during this altercation, known as the Battle of the Great Bridge		Lord Dunmore,* royal governor of Virginia, issues a proclamation offering freedom to all male slaves who join the British forces; approximately 800 blacks respond and are officially called the "Ethiopian Regiment"	
	It is decided at a Virginia convention that all runaway slaves who return to their masters within ten days will be pardoned		Gen. George Washington* reverses his stance and orders recruiting officers to accept free blacks into the Revolutionary Army	
	At least 100,000 slaves run away from their masters during the Revolutionary War		It is decreed in Georgia that any master or overseer who permits his or her slaves to beat drums, blow horns, or play any other loud instruments will be fined	
1776	Spain joins France as an ally of the US, sending black troops from Spanish-controlled Louisiana to join with the US revolutionary forces; the Louisiana troops include companies of free blacks and slaves commanded by black officers		Continental Congress approves Washington's action permitting free blacks to enlist in the Revolutionary Army	First African Baptist Church is organized, Williamsburg, VA
	Thomas Hubey* is hanged for conspiring to overthrow Gen. George Washington* and restore British rule; his plot is exposed by Phoebe Francis, a servant		South Carolina legislation authorizes the death penalty for slaves who defect to the British	Philadelphia [PA] Yearly Meeting directs local meetings of Friends to disown any Quaker who resists final pleas to free slaves
	The British hang Nathan Hale,* an alleged US spy; the hangman is Bill Richmond, loyalist slave, who later becomes a heavyweight boxing champion in Europe		The Declaration of Independence is approved and signed in Philadelphia, PA; a section that alleges King George III* forced the slave trade and slavery on the colonies is removed at the insistence of representatives from Georgia and South Carolina	Blacks form the Harrison Street Baptist Church, Petersburg, VA
	Prince Whipple and Oliver Cromwell are with Gen. George Washington* when he crosses the Delaware en route to an attack on the British in Trenton, NJ; Whipple is the bodyguard to Washington's aide, Gen. William Whipple,* in New Hampshire		The Second Continental Congress resolves "that no slaves be imported into any of the Thirteen United Colonies"	
	Marquis Marie Joseph de Lafayette* praises black soldiers for successfully covering Gen. George		Delaware's constitution prohibits the importation of slaves	
			Virginia law opens militia service to *all* free males	

E. **Literature,**
  Publications, and
  The Black Press   F. **The Arts**

G. **Science,**
  Technology,
  and Medicine   H. **Sports**

1775

1776

Upon receipt of her poem
praising him, Gen. George
Washington* invites Phillis
Wheatley to his Cambridge,
MA, headquarters to thank
her

G. **Science,**
  Technology,
  and Medicine   H. **Sports**

E. **Literature,**
  Publications, and
  The Black Press   F. **The Arts**

	A. **General History**	B. **Education**	C. **Laws and Legal Actions**	D. **Religion**
1776	Washington's* retreat to Long Island, NY; blacks also help cover Washington's retreats at Trenton and Princeton; still, many rebel leaders oppose integration of forces, and two all-black companies are formed Peter Salem fights at Saratoga and Stony Point, and serves until the end of the war Margaret Corbin (or "Captain Molly") takes up arms during the Revolution; she is wounded during an attack on Fort Washington, NY			
1777	Ty, an American patriot, leads a raiding party of 20 black and white troops who capture two British naval captains Soldier Jack Sisson facilitates the capture of British general Richard Prescott* by crashing a door open with his head, Newport, RI Agrippa Hull (b Northampton, MA, 1759; d 1848), a free black, enlists in the Revolutionary Army; for the duration of the war he serves as a private in the Massachusetts Line brigade Edward Hector, a soldier who served in the Third Pennsylvania Artillery, is awarded $40 for his brave service at the Battle of Brandywine	New Jersey opens public schools for black children	Several Boston slaves address a petition to the Massachusetts legislature, pointing out the inconsistencies between conditions of slavery and the principles of the American Revolution A Virginia law provides that no black may enlist in the Revolutionary War unless he provides a certificate of freedom Vermont is one of the first states to abolish slavery in its constitution North Carolina reenacts colonial law prohibiting private manumissions unless granted by the court for meritorious service New York law extends suffrage to black males	Richard Allen (b Philadelphia, PA, Feb 14, 1760; d 1831), slave, converts to the Methodist denomination; Allen's master allows him to conduct prayers in his house; Allen and his brother eventually purchase their freedom
1778	Seven hundred black troops fight under Gen. George Washington* at Monmouth Court House, the last great battle in the North Gen. George Washington* sends officers to enlist a black battalion consisting of over 300 former slaves to fill depleted ranks in Rhode Island; the troops are compensated equally with their white comrades-in-arms and promised freedom after the war; in the Battle of Rhode Island, they hold off 1,500 British troops		The Rhode Island General Assembly authorizes the enlistment of slaves as militia troops; blacks who serve for the duration of the war will be declared free The Massachusetts state constitution prohibits blacks, Native Americans, and mulattoes from voting South Carolina law authorizes the use of blacks, free or not, as navigators in the state navies	Baptists decide that slave marriages should be respected

1776

1777

William "Bill" Richmond (b Staten Island, NY, Aug 5, 1763; d London, England, Dec 1829) is taken by Gen. Earl Percy,* commander of the British forces occupying New York, to England to box against British soldiers

1778

Jupiter Hammon's 21-stanza poem "To Miss Phillis Wheatley" is published

Scipio Brown (b c1757; d RI, Feb 16, 1834) enlists in Col. Christopher Greene's* and Jeremiah Olney's* black regiment in Rhode Island to serve as a drummer during the American Revolution

	A. **General History**	B. **Education**	C. **Laws and Legal Actions**	D. **Religion**
1778	Quamino Dolly, an aged slave guide, leads British troops as they capture Savannah, GA John Chavis (b c1763), future clergyman, enlists in the Revolutionary Army Over 3,000 blacks, enslaved and free, have fought in the Revolutionary War by this year			Maryland Quakers make slaveholding an offense warranting disownment from the group
1779	Austin Dabney (b 1760) is the only slave patriot to fight in the successful Battle of Kettle Creek, GA, and achieves fame for his efforts A committee of the Continental Congress reports that South Carolina can provide little manpower in the war effort because the militia is needed at home to suppress slave rebellions Pompey, slave, is largely responsible for Anthony Wayne's* capture of the Stony Point Fort, NY; Pompey obtains the British password and helps Americans overpower the British lookout; many black spies and undercover agents serve during the Revolutionary War More than 500 Haitian free blacks accompany French forces at a Savannah siege, GA The Louisiana regiment of the US Army, the majority of whom are black troops and officers, captures Mobile, AL, and Pensacola, FL; six black officers are decorated for bravery British Commander-in-Chief Henry Clinton* officially promises freedom to the slaves who flee their masters and join the British militia, although both sides have been recruiting black troops Jean Baptist Point du Sable establishes a trading post at the mouth of the Chicago River and becomes a suc-		US Congress approves a proposal authorizing the use of slaves as soldiers, but representatives from South Carolina reject the proposal Twenty slaves petition the New Hampshire legislature to abolish slavery Virginia law permits blacks to serve in its navy	Rev. Andrew Bryan begins preaching to both blacks and whites in Georgia Rev. George Leile preaches to enslaved and free black Baptists during the three years the British occupy Savannah, GA

E. Literature,
Publications, and
The Black Press

F. The Arts

G. Science,
Technology,
and Medicine

H. Sports

1778

1779

E. Literature,
Publications, and
The Black Press

F. The Arts

G. Science,
Technology,
and Medicine

H. Sports

	A. **General History**	B. **Education**	C. **Laws and Legal Actions**	D. **Religion**
1779	cessful trapper, trader, miller, cooper, and husbandman			
1780	Two blacks aid in the capture of British spy Maj. John Andre* in New York		Pennsylvania passes gradual emancipation law and repeals law prohibiting racial intermarriage, becoming the first state to do so Maryland is the only southern state to authorize slave military enlistments The Massachusetts constitution abolishes slavery Paul Cuffe (b Cuttyhunk, MA, Jan 17, 1759; d 1817) and other black taxpayers of Massachusetts protest to the state legislature against "taxation without representation," demanding the right to vote; the case is eventually decided in their favor	Blacks begin worshiping in the gallery of the all-white First Baptist Church, Richmond, VA First African Baptist Church is founded in Richmond, VA Former slave Richard Allen becomes a Methodist minister; Bishop Francis Asbury* gives Allen assignments and allows him to travel with white ministers The Methodist church declares that slavery is contrary to biblical teaching and hurtful to society; requires traveling preachers to emancipate their slaves The "Second Awakening" sweeps across the US; this religious movement is characterized by revival camp meetings that usually take place in tents in the woods; during the services large numbers of mostly interracial worshipers sing spirituals and "shout"
1781	James Armistead (b 1760), former slave, is hired by British Gen. Charles Cornwallis* to spy on Americans but actually is an American patriot counterspy Black soldiers defend Col. Christopher Greene* near Points Bridge, NY, until they are killed Saul Matthews, Virginia slave and US spy, supplies crucial information about British defenses and leads the successful raid that forces Gen. Charles Cornwallis* to abandon his position at Portsmouth, VA Nicholas, a free black patriot, rides to Dover, DE, to alert US troops that the British are coming Maroon attacks on plantations and an uprising in Williamsburg, VA, are reported		Several Virginia slaves are condemned to death for "feloniously and traitorously" waging war against Virginia; two dissenting justices argue that since slaves are not citizens and owe no allegiance to the country, they cannot be guilty of treason; Gov. Thomas Jefferson* approves a reprieve that the Virginia House and Senate members sign Maryland law declares that all free men are subject to the military draft South Carolina prohibits free blacks from testifying in court, overturning *John Mayrant v. John Williams* case of 1764 The New York general assembly authorizes the enlistment of slaves in the Revolutionary Army	

1779

1780

		James Derham (b Philadelphia, PA, 1762) obtains a license to practice medicine during the 1780s; Derham becomes the first black man licensed to practice medicine in the US	

1781

	A. **General History**	B. **Education**	C. **Laws and Legal Actions**	D. **Religion**
1781	Maryland colony raises 750 black troops to be incorporated with other troops Los Angeles, CA, is founded by 44 settlers, of whom at least 26 are blacks			
1782	Approximately 5,000 fugitive slaves leave for England after British forces withdraw from Savannah, GA Great Britain and the US sign a preliminary peace agreement; the British refuse to agree to return fugitive slaves to their masters Slave population in Virginia reaches 260,000; because of restrictive emancipation laws in Virginia, the free black population reaches only 2,800 Deborah Gannet, a black woman disguised as a man, serves in the Fourth Massachusetts Regiment for 17 months and is later cited for bravery		Virginia enacts laws allowing private manumissions but denying free blacks the right to vote or carry weapons A New York statute frees blacks who join the British ranks prior to Nov. 30	David George (b near Essex County, VA, 1742; d Sierra Leone, 1810), slave exhorter from Silver Bluff, SC, sails with British troops to Nova Scotia, where he establishes a Baptist church In order to curb voodooism, the Louisiana governor issues an order banning the importation of blacks from the French West Indian Island of Martinique
1783	Continental Congress declares an end to the Revolutionary War; approximately 10,000 blacks have served in the continental armies (5,000 as regular soldiers) Gen. George Washington* chooses Fraunces Tavern, NYC, a famous black-owned restaurant, as the site for his retirement banquet and farewell to his troops The Black Regiment of Revolutionary War soldiers is deactivated at Saratoga, NY Several thousand blacks immigrate to Great Britain following the Revolutionary War; many others immigrate to Canada or migrate to Native American settlements or to swamps in Florida The Society for the Propagation of the Gospel in Foreign Parts ceases operation		A Virginia law grants freedom with the permission of their masters, to all slaves, who served in the Revolutionary War The Massachusetts Supreme Court abolishes slavery; blacks in taxable categories are granted suffrage New Hampshire law abolishes slavery Maryland law disfranchises blacks Theodore Sedgwick* argues before the court of Great Barrington, MA, for the freedom of Elizabeth "Mum Bett" Freeman, who is struck on the arm by a shovel when her mistress attempts to hit Freeman's sister; the court awards Freeman her freedom and orders her former master to pay 30 shillings in damages	Silver Bluff Church, SC, is revived under Rev. Jesse Peler five years after it was disassembled Newport, RI, African Union Society begins holding religious services in members' homes Strong testimonials in favor of emancipating enslaved Africans are voiced at a Methodist conference in Virginia

1781

1782

"Negro Jig" is included in James Aird's* *Selection of Scotch, English, Irish, and Foreign Airs;* although it is not certain whether "Negro Jig" is composed by a slave, its inclusion in Aird's book shows the continuing influence of Negro music in the colonies

1783

James Derham purchases his freedom from Dr. Robert Dow,* a Scottish physician, for the sum of 500 pesos; Derham has previously performed several medical services while assisting Dr. Dow

	A. **General History**	B. **Education**	C. **Laws and Legal Actions**	D. **Religion**
1783	Peter Williams (b New Brunswick, NJ, c1780; d 1823), a slave, asks the members of the John Street Methodist meeting house in New York to purchase him; the congregation agrees and hires him as a sexton; Williams repays the church in two years			
1784	The Philadelphia Society reorganizes into the Pennsylvania Abolition Society	A Rhode Island emancipation bill requires all black children to learn to read and write	The US Congress narrowly rejects Thomas Jefferson's* proposal to exclude slavery from all western territories after 1800 Connecticut (again in 1797) and Rhode Island pass gradual emancipation laws A Connecticut law "provide[s] that no Negro or mulatto child should be held in slavery beyond the age of 25 years" North Carolina legislature frees Edward Griffin, Revolutionary War soldier, commending his meritorious service A New York statute provides for the care of slaves whose masters' properties have been confiscated or forfeited in the war Rhode Island law abolishes slavery	Virginia Quakers require members to free their slaves There is only one Quaker slaveholder in the state of New York (he frees his slave in 1787) Methodist Episcopal Church Conference in Baltimore, MD, adopts rules requiring members to free their slaves or face excommunication; Rev. Richard Allen attends Bishop Porteus,* formerly of the Society for the Propagation of the Gospel in Foreign Parts, publishes a plan for the conversion of slaves to Christianity Rev. Harry Hosier, the first American black minister of the Methodist Episcopal Church, travels with Bishop Francis Asbury* and Rev. Thomas Coke* filling ministerial appointments in New England and the South Rev. George Leile establishes the first Baptist church in Jamaica The oldest black Catholic community in the US is established in St. Augustine, FL, by escaped slaves
1785	New York Manumission Society is organized; Federalists John Jay* and Alexander Hamilton* serve as president and vice president, respectively		New York's Council of Revision fails to approve bill for gradual emancipation because the bill denies political and civil rights to free blacks Delaware Assembly rejects a bill for the gradual abolition of slavery A petition for gradual emancipation is rejected in the Virginia House of Burgesses	General Committee of Virginia Baptists condemns slavery as "contrary to the word of God" Methodist conference at Baltimore, MD, suspends the rule requiring gradual manumission Blacks form a separate Baptist church in Williamsburg, VA Lemuel Haynes (b West Hartford, CT, 1753; d 1833)

E. Literature,
  Publications, and
  The Black Press   F. The Arts

G. Science,
  Technology,
  and Medicine   H. Sports

1783

1784

1785

	A. General History	B. Education	C. Laws and Legal Actions	D. Religion
1785			A Louisiana ordinance aimed at curbing the activities of quadroon women forbids them from wearing jewels and feathers, orders them to wear their hair in a kerchief, and forbids them from attending balls New York slaves who served in the Revolutionary Army are emancipated	is ordained a minister in Litchfield County, CT; he preaches to white congregations in Torrington, CT John Marrant (b New York, 1755), missionary to Native Americans, publishes *A Narrative of the Lord's Wonderful Dealings with John Marrant, a Black*, London Due to increased racial segregation, black Methodists in Baltimore begin withdrawing from meeting houses and form a Colored Methodist Society; from this Society emerges Sharp Street Methodist Episcopal Church and Bethel African Methodist Episcopal Church—the first black Methodist churches in the South
1786	Importation of new slaves ends in all states but South Carolina and Georgia Slaves constitute 7 percent of the total New York State population A group of ex-slaves who call themselves the King of England's Soldiers wage guerrilla warfare against slaveholders along the Savannah River in Georgia and South Carolina North Carolina increases the duty on every imported slave Free blacks Moses Sash, Tobias Green, and Aaron Carter join others in staging Shays's Rebellion to protest the Massachusetts government's lack of concern about farmers' harsh living conditions		The Virginia legislature frees James Armistead in recognition of his spying services for General Lafayette* The Georgia legislature frees Austin Dabney to prevent his master from reaping benefits from Dabney's military fame	Rev. Richard Allen is invited to preach at St. George's Methodist Episcopal Church, Philadelphia, PA Ushers at St. George's Methodist Episcopal Church, PA, attempt to remove Absalom Jones (b Sussex, DE, 1746; d Philadelphia, PA, Feb 13, 1817) and others after a confrontation over segregation in the church First year in which Methodists distinguish between black and white members in church census; there are 1,890 blacks in a total membership of 18,791
1787	Free blacks of Newport, RI, establish the African Union Society to promote a return to Africa Pennsylvania Society for the Abolition of Slavery is reorganized as the Pennsylvania Society for Promoting the Abolition of Slavery, the Relief of Free Negroes Unlawfully Held in Bond-	Boston, MA, blacks, led by Masonic organizer and abolitionist Prince Hall, petition the legislature for equal school facilities for blacks New York Manumission Society opens a school for blacks in New York City, the African Free School (schools are eventually transferred to city authorities)	Continental Congress adopts Northwest Ordinance, which prohibits slavery in the Northwest Territory and all land north of the Ohio River US Constitution is adopted; it states that the importation of slaves will not be prohibited before 1808 and considers one slave	Rev. Richard Allen and Absalom Jones, a Methodist lay minister, found the Philadelphia Free African Society, the first black mutual aid group; in 1791 the group votes to align themselves with the Church of England (Episcopalians), although Allen remains with the Methodist denomination

E. **Literature,
Publications, and
The Black Press**   F. **The Arts**

G. **Science,
Technology,
and Medicine**   H. **Sports**

1785

1786

In New York a music
teacher known only as
"Frank the Negro" is said to
have instructed "about
forty scholars"

1787

Ottabah Cugoano's
*Thoughts and Sentiments on
the Evil of Slavery in London*
is published

Jupiter Hammon's *Address
to the Negroes of the State of
New York* is published; in
the work, Hammon calls for
slaves to be obedient to
their masters

	A. **General History**	B. **Education**	C. **Laws and Legal Actions**	D. **Religion**
1787	age, and for Improving the Conditions of the African Race	There are at least seven schools for blacks in Philadelphia, PA The Presbyterian Synod of New York and Pennsylvania urges its members to educate their slaves	equal to three-fifths of one [white or free] person in congressional apportionment; demands that fugitive slaves be returned to their masters South Carolina enacts temporary prohibition on slave imports Rhode Island responds to Quaker petitioning and forbids its citizens from participating in slave trade Mary Butler, the daughter of Mary and William Butler, who sued for their freedom and lost in 1771, sues for her freedom and wins, establishing a precedent in Maryland that liberalizes the rule of descent	St. George's Methodist Episcopal Church in Pennsylvania inaugurates a policy of segregation; black members, including Absalom Jones and Rev. Richard Allen, withdraw and conduct their own religious services as part of the activities of the Free African Society Slave minister Jesse Peters (also called Jesse Galphin) becomes pastor of the newly organized Springfield Baptist Church of Augusta, GA
1788	An antislavery society is established, Delaware Dick Pointer, a slave, single-handedly fights off a Native American attack at Fort Donnelly, VA, until the town garrison comes to his rescue	A New Jersey legislative act requires that slaveholders teach their slaves to read	A New York statute makes it illegal to sell any slave imported into the state and also frees any such slaves who are ''improperly imported''	Rev. Andrew Bryan establishes the First African Baptist Church in Savannah, GA, and becomes its first pastor; he is assisted by Rev. Jesse Peters; soon after, Bryan is arrested and flogged for his religious pursuits Rev. Lemuel Haynes begins preaching to white congregations in Rutland, VT; he ministers there until 1818
1789	The Providence [RI] Society for Abolishing the Slave Trade is formed Caesar Tarrant, a slave, pilots the schooner *Patriot* when it captures the British brig *Fanny;* the Virginia legislature grants Tarrant his freedom later in the year for his service	Massachusetts free blacks initiate a school for free blacks assisted by white philanthropic and state appropriations Quakers organize the Society for the Free Instruction of Orderly Blacks and People of Color, Philadelphia, PA	All southern states entering the Union after this date, except Tennessee, exclude blacks from voting Delaware law forbids its citizens from engaging in the slave trade Connecticut shippers are prohibited from engaging in the slave trade anywhere	Missionary John Marrant publishes *A Sermon; Preached on the 24th Day of June, 1789, Being the Festival of St. John the Baptist, at the Request of the Right Worshipful the Grand Master, Prince Hall* The Baptist church reaches its most advanced position as an antislavery body when it condemns slavery and recommends using local missions to influence its abolition nationwide
1790	First federal US census shows approximately 757,208 blacks in the US (19.3% of the population); 59,557 are free There are 7,684 slaves and 586 free blacks in Charleston, SC	The Pennsylvania Society appoints a committee to supervise instruction of free black youth and to encourage their school attendance	The US government signs a treaty with the Creek nation that provides for the return of runaway slaves The US Congress limits naturalization to white aliens Quakers and the Pennsylvania Abolition Society pe-	Throughout the North, free blacks, scorned by racial segregation in churches, begin to form separate all-black congregations The African Baptist Church is established in Lexington, KY

E. **Literature,**
   Publications, and
   The Black Press   F. **The Arts**

G. **Science,**
   Technology,
   and Medicine   H. **Sports**

1787

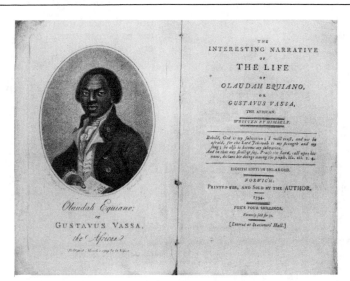

The Interesting Narrative of the Life of Olaudah Equiano
provides a rare and detailed account of life in West Africa prior to
the transatlantic slave trade and also details the Middle Passage.
(LC)

First known protest against
slavery written by a black
person is published; little is
known about Othello, the
author

1788

Olaudah Equiano's *The In-*
teresting Narrative of the Life
of Olaudah Equiano or Gusta-
vus Vassa, the African, Written
by Himself is published

Benjamin Banneker pre-
dicts the solar eclipse of
1789

1789

Joseph Mountain's *Sketches*
of the Life of Joseph Mountain,
a Negro, Who Was Executed at
New Haven, on the 20th Day
of October, 1790, for a Rape,
Committed on the 26th Day of
May Last is published in
New Haven, CT

1790

	A. **General History**	B. **Education**	C. **Laws and Legal Actions**	D. **Religion**
1790	Blacks constitute only 2 percent of the population of New England As of this year all New England colonies have abolished slavery Jean Baptist Point du Sable makes the first permanent settlement in what is now present-day Chicago, IL The Virginia Abolition Society organizes in Richmond Charleston, SC, free black men establish the exclusive Brown Fellowship Society; membership, which costs $50, is limited to 50 persons		tition the US Congress to use its constitutional powers to abolish slavery; petitions evoke angry debate and attacks on Quakers by congressmen from the Deep South Mulattoes in Sumter County, SC, petition the state legislature for relief from acts of discrimination All blacks in Boston, MA, are freed; Boston is the only city in the US that has no slaves	Rev. Andrew Bryan's First African Baptist Church in Savannah, GA, numbers 225 full communicants and 350 converts, many of whom do not have their masters' permission to be baptized *A Journal of the Rev. John Marrant, from August the 18th, 1785, to the 16th of March, 1790,* is published in London
1791	François-Dominique Toussaint-Louverture (b May 20, 1743; d 1803) leads approximately 100,000 Haitian slaves in successful revolt against their French masters Vermont enters the Union as a free state Following the suppression of a Louisiana revolt by blacks, 23 slaves are hanged and three white sympathizers are deported Newport Gardner, a slave in Rhode Island, wins $2,000 in a lottery and purchases his freedom and that of his family Thomas Jefferson* writes a letter to scientist and inventor Benjamin Banneker; in the letter Jefferson expresses hope that blacks improve their condition, and he declares that blacks have a natural right to freedom and education		Free blacks in Charleston, SC, petition the state legislature, protesting laws restricting their freedom The US Congress excludes blacks and Native Americans from peacetime militia	Absalom Jones and Rev. Richard Allen begin to hold regular Sunday services; with the aid of Benjamin Rush,* they organize The African Church, Philadelphia, PA The First African Baptist Church of Williamsburg, VA, is admitted into the Dover Baptist Association, a predominantly white organization
1792	Kentucky enters the Union as a slave state According to a Spanish census, 449 of the 1,600 residents in Texas are black		The second US Congress passes a bill which provides that the militia can be called out to enforce the laws of the Union, suppress insurrections, and repel invasions; it restricts enlistment to white male citizens A Virginia statute imposes a penalty of six months' imprisonment on whites who marry blacks; blacks receive	Georgia passes an act that protects the religious ceremonies of whites yet forbids blacks to assemble for worship Rev. Josiah Bishop is named pastor of First Baptist Church in Portsmouth, VA; he becomes the first black minister of a white congregation

1790

1791

In New Orleans, LA, the first public performance in "black face" minstrel style is performed by a company of slaves; in black face entertainment, performers cover their faces with black makeup in order to caricature blacks

Newport Gardner, one of the first black music teachers in the US, opens a music school in Newport, MA

Benjamin Banneker is appointed by Maj. Andrew Ellicott* to help survey and lay out a 10-mile square known as Federal Territory, later to become the District of Columbia

1792

Benjamin Banneker calculates ephemerides (tables showing the positions of the planets) for almanacs, which he begins to publish and distribute; he also begins publishing an annual almanac specifically for farmers

	A. **General History**	B. **Education**	C. **Laws and Legal Actions**	D. **Religion**
1792			no prison sentence for the same offense South Carolina imposes a poll tax on free blacks Delaware law disfranchises blacks	Antoine Blanc founds the first black Catholic sisterhood in the US Rev. David George is recruited to settle in Sierra Leone and to organize a Baptist church there; he writes his autobiography, *An Account of the Life of Mr. David George*
1793	Twenty-three free black men and women from Canada and some white supporters sign a petition protesting the state poll tax on free blacks in South Carolina Francisco Reyes, an Afro-Spaniard, is mayor of Los Angeles, CA; he serves for two years The New Jersey Abolition Society is formed Members of the Free African Society, including Revs. Absalom Jones and Richard Allen, organize many in the black community of Philadelphia, PA, to serve as nurses and undertakers during the yellow fever epidemic Eli Whitney* invents the cotton gin, making it possible to separate cotton fiber from its seed; the invention also ushers in phenomenal economic growth in the southern states, which, in turn, increases the demand for African slaves		The US Congress adopts the first Fugitive Slave Law, which increases the possibilities for the extradition of slaves and makes it a criminal offense to protect a fugitive slave Georgia law bans slave imports from the West Indies or Spanish Florida but remains the only state to legally import slaves from Africa Virginia passes a law that forbids free blacks from entering the state	Rev. Jesse Peters organizes and leads the First African Church of Augusta, GA (later renamed Springfield Baptist Church) An estimated one-fourth of the total Baptist membership of 73,471 is black A large number of French-speaking Haitian refugees arrive in Baltimore, MD, and begin attending service in the basement chapel of St. Mary's Seminary; these refugees establish one of the first black Catholic communities in the US General Committee of Virginia Baptists decides emancipation is a political issue that belongs in the legislature, not in the church
1794	First convention of southern and northern abolition societies organize as the American Convention of Delegates from Abolition Societies, Philadelphia, PA		The US Congress prohibits slave trade with foreign countries The French National Convention votes to abolish slavery in all French territories (the law is repealed by Napoleon* in 1802) South Carolina law prohibits free blacks from entering the state	Rev. Richard Allen and followers establish the Bethel African Methodist Episcopal Church in Philadelphia, PA Rev. Absalom Jones is ordained a deacon in the Protestant Episcopal Church Rev. Absalom Jones and followers open St. Thomas Protestant Episcopal Church, the first black Episcopal congregation, Philadelphia, PA; it is dedicated and formally received into the diocese of Pennsylvania First African Baptist Church is built for Rev. Andrew

| | | Cesar, a slave, gains such notoriety for his curative knowledge of roots and herbs that his cure for poison is published in the *Massachusetts Magazine;* the Assembly of South Carolina purchases Cesar's freedom and gives him an annuity of 100 pounds | | **1792** |

1793

1794

	A. **General History**	B. **Education**	C. **Laws and Legal Actions**	D. **Religion**
1794				Bryan's congregation in Savannah, GA, on property purchased by Bryan
1795		Rev. Richard Allen opens a day school in Philadelphia, PA Committee of Pennsylvania Society petitions the state legislature to establish schools for free blacks		The Pennsylvania diocese votes that St. Thomas African Episcopal Church may not send a clergyman or deputies to the annual meetings or interfere in any way with church government
1796	Tennessee enters the Union as a slave state, yet its constitution allows suffrage to free blacks Boston [MA] African Society, a mutual aid and charity organization, is established with 44 members Amos Fortune (b 1710; d New Hampshire, 1801) is one of the founding members of the Social Library, New Hampshire; he later begins a bookbinding business		Pres. George Washington's* commission negotiates a treaty with the Creek nation in Florida; Creeks agree to return all fugitive slaves Lucy Terry Prince is the first woman to argue a case before the US Supreme Court; the Court rules in favor of the Prince family in a dispute with a white man who attempts to steal land from them	Members of the Methodist Episcopal Church in New York (among them, James Varick) withdraw from John Street Methodist Church because of discrimination and social proscription of its black members; they begin to organize the African Methodist Episcopal Zion Church, the first black Methodist church in New York Philadelphia [PA] Yearly Meeting of Society of Friends resolves that members are to be admitted on the basis of views, not race Black parishioners from St. George's Methodist Episcopal Church in Philadelphia, PA, establish Zoar Methodist Episcopal Church which maintains its affiliation with white Methodists
1797	Hiram Lodge No. 4, Providence, RI, is the second black Masonic lodge in the US Prince Hall delivers one of the earliest recorded black antislavery orations before the African Masonic Lodge, Boston, MA Agrippa Hull is awarded a grant of land in Ohio for his military service; he requests that the land be sold to found a school for blacks		A group of North Carolina blacks present an antislavery petition to the US Congress seeking redress against a North Carolina law that requires slaves who are freed by their Quaker masters be returned to the state and to slavery; the petition is rejected A Connecticut law emancipates slaves at age 21 Fugitive slaves in Philadelphia, PA, deliver a petition before the US Congress, asking that their freedom be protected; Congress declines even to receive the petition	
1798	US Secretaries of War and the Navy issue separate directives forbidding black enlistments in the Marine Corps and on naval war-	A school for black students is established in the home of Primus Hall, a free black, Boston, MA	The US Congress debates a motion to prohibit slavery from Mississippi Territory but rejects it	

E. **Literature, Publications, and The Black Press**	F. **The Arts**	G. **Science, Technology, and Medicine**	H. **Sports**	
				1794
	For the first time in US theater, a black actor plays a role that is not a comic servant; the role is of a secondary romantic character in James Murdock's* *The Triumph of Love*			**1795**
	Joshua Johnson, the first black portrait painter in the US to gain public recognition, opens a studio in Baltimore, MD			**1796**
				1797
Venture Smith's *A Narrative of the Life and Adventures of Venture, a Native of Africa; but Resident Above Sixty Years in the United States of Amer-*				**1798**

65

	A. **General History**	B. **Education**	C. **Laws and Legal Actions**	D. **Religion**
1798	ships, contrary to a non-racial enlistment policy that has been in effect for years; some blacks slip past the ban, including William Brown on the *Constellation* and Georges Diggs, quartermaster of the schooner *Experiment* The African Masonic Lodge, the third in the country, is established in Philadelphia, PA; Rev. Absalom Jones is worship master and Rev. Richard Allen is treasurer Black US soldiers and sailors begin service in the naval war with France		Georgia law abolishes the slave trade Georgia law makes killing or maiming slaves an offense equal to killing or maiming a white person	
1799	After winning $1,500 in the lottery, Denmark Vesey (b c1767), a free black, opens a carpentry shop in Charleston, SC		Revs. Absalom Jones and Richard Allen lead Philadelphia black community in petitioning the state legislature for the immediate abolition of slavery	Methodist Bishop Francis Asbury* ordains Richard Allen a deacon Catherine "Katy" Ferguson (b c1774; d New York, 1854), former slave, begins the first modern Sunday school in New York City
1800	There are 1,002,037 blacks in the US, which is 18.9% of the total population In the North (mostly in New York and New Jersey) 36,505 blacks are enslaved The price of a "prime" field slave averages $200 Records show 951 slaves in Connecticut Gabriel Prosser (b c1776) and Jack Bowler organize a plan to lead 1,100 fellow slaves to attack Richmond, VA; after betrayal of the plot, Prosser, Bowler, and many others are executed Jean Baptist Point du Sable sells his holdings in Chicago, IL, and eventually moves to St. Charles, MO, where he purchases a stone mansion built by Pierre Rondin; this house is later sold to Alexander McNair* who becomes the first governor of Missouri while residing in the house		US citizens are barred from exporting slaves Free blacks of Philadelphia, PA, led by Rev. Absalom Jones, present an antislavery petition to Congress; Congress rejects it by a vote of 85 to 1 Charleston, SC, law bans the assembly of slaves in confined or secret places after dark South Carolina prohibits free blacks from entering the state	First African Methodist Episcopal Zion Church is built in New York City The General Conference of the Methodist Episcopal Church officially endorses racial separation but agrees to ordain black ministers In the early 19th century, Ralph Freeman, a slave from North Carolina, is ordained a Baptist minister; he baptizes, administers communion, and travels and preaches with Rev. Joseph Magee* Under Rev. Andrew Bryan's leadership, the First African Church of Savannah (GA) increases to nearly 700 members
1801		The Abolition Society of Wilmington, DE, conducts a school for black children	The New York legislature passes a bill that protects state residents against los-	The African Methodist Episcopal Zion Church is officially incorporated in New

1798

ica; Related by Himself is published in New London, CT

1799

1800

In the early 1800s "corn" songs, also known as call and response songs, are sung by slaves to accompany corn shuckings

Jacques Constantin Deburque, violinist and music teacher, b; Deburque will later direct the orchestra at the Theatre de la Renaissance for the "free colored" in New Orleans, LA (d 1861)

1801

	A. **General History**	B. **Education**	C. **Laws and Legal Actions**	D. **Religion**
1801			ing ownership of their slaves when entering and leaving the state, and prevents slave owners from leaving their slaves behind in other states; this bill also prohibits owners from leaving the state with slaves purchased less than a year earlier	York; Rev. John Mc Claskey* of the General Conference of the Methodist Episcopal Church recognizes the AMEZ church In Lexington, KY, a slave named Old Captain forms a church that eventually includes over 300 members The General Assembly of Presbyterians commissions John Chavis a missionary Rev. Richard Allen publishes the first hymnal designed for the exclusive use of blacks, *A Collection of Hymns and Spiritual Songs from Various Authors*
1802	Haitians force French government to end slavery in Haiti; François-Dominique Toussaint-Louverture is declared governor	Blacks in Western Reserve, OH, organize School Fund Society and begin establishing education centers (1802–1870)	Gov. William Henry Harrison* of Indiana Territory calls a convention at Vincennes that appeals to US Congress to suspend Northwest Ordinance and allow slaves to be brought into the territory; later an indentured servants act allows *de facto* slavery Ohio's constitution abolishes slavery	Rev. Andrew Bryan authorizes Henry Francis, an exhorter, to start the Second African Baptist Church in Savannah, GA
1803	South Carolina reopens ports to African slave trade with Latin America and the West Indies because of expanding cotton and rice production in the US Runaway slaves and members of the Five Nations (Choctaw, Chickasaw, Cherokee, Creek, and Seminole Native American groups) begin to move into Indian Territory (present-day Oklahoma) The US government purchases land from France that extends from the Mississippi River to the Rocky Mountains (becomes known as the Louisiana Purchase) Ohio enters the Union as a free state		The US House of Representatives grants protection of the rights of black seamen in foreign waters Ohio disfranchises free blacks	Rev. Henry Francis organizes Great Ogechee Colored Church in Savannah, GA The Colored Baptist Society of Alexandria (VA) is established; it later evolves into the Alfred Street Baptist Church
1804	York, a slave, serves as a guide for the Meriwether Lewis* and William Clark* expedition to the Pacific; he	Rev. Richard Allen organizes a Society of Free People of Color for Promoting the Instruction and School Education of Children of	New Jersey passes a gradual emancipation law Ohio legislature enacts the first Black Laws, restricting	Absalom Jones is ordained into the priesthood of the Protestant Episcopal Church

E. Literature, Publications, and The Black Press	F. The Arts	G. Science, Technology, and Medicine	H. Sports	
				1801
				1802
				1803
	Isaac Hazzard, musician, b; Hazzard plays for parades, leads dance orchestras, and runs a music studio; his best known pieces are "The			**1804**

	A. **General History**	B. **Education**	C. **Laws and Legal Actions**	D. **Religion**
1804	is emancipated after the expedition The Female Benevolent Society and the African Friendly Society are established, New Haven, CT The prototype of the Underground Railroad begins after Gen. Thomas Boude* purchases a slave, Stephen Smith, and brings him home to Columbia, PA; Smith's mother escapes to find him, and the Boude family takes her in; when Smith's owner follows and demands her property be returned, the Boudes refuse to surrender Smith; they later free her White delegates at the American Convention of Abolition Societies complain of declining interest in the abolition movement	African Descent in Philadelphia, PA Rev. Absalom Jones founds the second school for blacks at St. Thomas Church in Pennsylvania Rev. Lemuel Haynes is the first black in the US to receive an honorary Master of Arts degree, Middlebury College, VT	the rights and movements of blacks in the North As of this year, all states north of the Mason-Dixon Line (Maryland border—19 miles south of the 40th parallel) have laws that forbid slavery or provide for its gradual elimination	
1805	Auguste Tessier* of New Orleans, LA, holds balls twice a week that are limited to white men and free black women; these balls are the precursors to the famed Octoroon Balls		Maryland law prohibits free blacks from selling wheat, corn, or tobacco without a license	African Union First Colored Methodist Protestant Church, Inc., emerges out of the Methodist Episcopal Church Thomas Paul (b Exeter, NH, Sep 3, 1773; d 1823) organizes a Baptist congregation of free blacks in Boston, the First African Baptist Church; his congregation is later renamed Joy Street Church A group of blacks withdraw from predominantly white Asbury Methodist Church in Wilmington, DE, and build Ezion Methodist Church, with Rev. Peter Spencer as their pastor Joshua Smith and Abner Jones collaborate and publish *Hymns Original and Selected* for use by black Christians
1806	Edward Rose first leads a group of fur traders west; this group, known as Mountain Men, will become notorious for fur trapping; Rose later becomes a guide and interpreter for three large North American fur-trading companies	New York City provides schools for black children for the first time	Pres. Thomas Jefferson* urges US Congress to prohibit slave trade as soon as constitutional restriction expires (after 1807) Virginia passes a law that requires all manumitted slaves to leave the state	James Varick (b near Newburgh, NY, 1750; d New York City, Jul 22, 1827) of the African Methodist Episcopal Zion Church and two other ministers become the first blacks to be ordained in the State of New York

Miercken Polka Waltz'' and
''The Alarm Gun Quadrille''
(d 1865)

1804

William ''Bill'' Richmond
fights and loses to Tom
Cribb,* English boxing
champion, Halsham, En-
gland; it is the first time a
black American athlete
competes for a world title in
any sport

1805

1806

	A. **General History**	B. **Education**	C. **Laws and Legal Actions**	D. **Religion**
1806			within a year of manumission A Charleston, SC, ordinance prohibits teaching slaves "in any mechanic or handicraft trade"	
1807	Kentucky antislavery society, Friends of Humanity, is formed Two boatloads of enslaved Africans arriving in Charleston, SC, starve themselves to death rather than submit to slavery; this is only one example of how Africans resisted slavery Rev. Thomas Paul serves as chaplain of the African Grand Lodge No. 459, Boston, MA	Bell School, the first school for black children in Washington, DC, is established by George Bell, Nicholas Franklin, and Moses Liverpool, free blacks	The US Congress prohibits importation of new slaves into the US, effective Jan 1, 1808; this law is widely ignored British Parliament abolishes the slave trade The revised New Jersey state constitution limits suffrage to free white males Ohio legislature stipulates that blacks are allowed to settle in Ohio if they can provide $500 bonds	A division of the Union Church of Africans is incorporated at Wilmington, DE First African Presbyterian Church is founded by John Gloucester (b Tennessee, c1776; d 1822) in Philadelphia, PA
1808	The Federal ban on importation of slaves is scheduled to take effect on Jan 1; however, from 1808 until 1860 an estimated 250,000 slaves are illegally imported; the breeding and bartering of enslaved Africans continues within various territories of the US as well As of this year, there are one million enslaved Africans in the US The African Society of Boston, MA, publishes a formal antislavery statement that draws a parallel between the sentiments that drove the American Revolution and enslaved blacks' desire for freedom Peter Williams is one of the founders of the African Association for Mutual Relief in New York City Black New Yorkers hold three parades to celebrate the slave trade prohibition, New York City			General Conference of the Methodist Episcopal Church decides to delete rules on slavery from copies of its *Discipline* sent to the Deep South Rev. Absalom Jones publishes his sermon on the abolition of slavery Rev. Richard Allen publishes a pamphlet containing the confession of John Joyce, a murderer; the publication is intended to be a warning against sin
1809	Revs. Richard Allen and Absalom Jones, and James Forten, Sr. (b Philadelphia, PA, 1766; d 1842), businessman, help to organize the Society for the Suppression of Vice and Immorality		New York law sanctions marriage within the black community; married blacks were not legally recognized prior to this law	Black Baptists form the first black Baptist church in Philadelphia, PA—the First African Baptist Church Black members withdraw from Trinity Episcopal

E. Literature, Publications, and The Black Press	F. The Arts	G. Science, Technology, and Medicine	H. Sports	
				1806
				1807
				1808
	Francis "Frank" Johnson (b Martinique, West Indies, 1792; d Philadelphia, PA, 1844), wins recognition in Philadelphia, PA, as a bandmaster, composer, and performer of the keyed bugle;			**1809**

	A. General History	B. Education	C. Laws and Legal Actions	D. Religion
1809				Church in New York due to discrimination and form St. Philip's Church, which is formally received into the Episcopal diocese in 1818 Rev. Thomas Paul founds the Abyssinian Baptist Church, New York City, Jul 5
1810	There are 1,377,808 blacks in the US (19% of the total population); there are over 100,000 free blacks in the southern states (nearly 9% of the black population) There are 310 slaves in Connecticut There are 210 free blacks in Mississippi		The US Congress excludes blacks from mail carrier positions in the US Postal Service *Adelle v. Beauregard:* a Louisiana court declares that a "person of color" is presumed free; it distinguishes between persons of color and Africans, those who are slaves or have an African mother In *Maryland v. Dolly Chapple,* a court rules that enslaved blacks may testify in court regarding criminal acts in which enslaved people are victims	New York State requires slaveholders to teach all slave children biblical scriptures
1811	Charles Deslandes leads a revolt of Louisiana slaves in two parishes located about 35 miles from New Orleans; US troops suppress the revolt, resulting in more than 100 slaves killed or executed Paul Cuffe, merchant mariner, sails with a small group of blacks to Sierra Leone, underscoring his advocacy of the return-to-Africa movement	Christopher McPherson, a wealthy free black, opens a night school for free blacks in Richmond, VA; McPherson is jailed and later sent to the Williamsburg Lunatic Asylum, and the teacher is soon run out of town	Delaware forbids free blacks from entering the state and stipulates that any native-born free black who has been out of Delaware for more than six months is a nonresident	
1812	Free blacks and slaves serve in the War of 1812; they are particularly successful at the Battle of Lake Erie; the British invite slaves to join their naval service and also supply arms to Florida blacks and Native Americans Revs. Richard Allen and Absalom Jones are requested to help organize defenses for Philadelphia, PA, against the British, who recently attacked Washington, DC Georgia state troopers are sent to Florida to "extermi-		Louisiana enters the Union as a slave state; state law enables freedmen to serve in the state militia Louisiana law disfranchises blacks	Union Church of Africans is organized and incorporated, Wilmington, DE Black Methodists of Baltimore's Bethel Church claim 600 people attend their services

E. Literature, Publications, and The Black Press	F. The Arts	G. Science, Technology, and Medicine	H. Sports	
	Johnson is noted for being the first black American to give formal concerts and the first to tour widely in the US			**1809**
Benjamin Prentiss's *The Blind American Slave, or Memoirs of Boyrereau Brincho* is published in St. Albans, VT George White's *Account of Life, Experience, Travels, and Gospel Labours of George White, an African, Written by Himself and Revised by a Friend* is published in New York City			Tom Molineaux, a native-born American (d Galway, Ireland, Aug 14, 1818), fights Tom Cribb* in a controversial boxing match, Copthall Common, England; a referee allows Cribb two minutes to revive after he is knocked down, and Cribb eventually wins the match after 43 rounds	**1810**
				1811
	Black navy musicians known to have served in the War of 1812 are George Brown, a bugler on the *Chesapeake;* Cyrus Tiffany, a fifer on the *Alliance* who fought in the Battle of Lake Erie; and Jessie Wall, a fifer on the frigate *Niagara* Jordan Noble (1796–1890) serves as an army drummer during the War of 1812; a New Orleans newspaper of Noble's time carries an article referring to him as a "matchless drummer"; he is said to have "beat his drum during all and every fight in the hottest hell of		Tom Molineaux loses his second championship fight against the English title-holder, Tom Cribb*	**1812**

	A. **General History**	B. **Education**	C. **Laws and Legal Actions**	D. **Religion**
1812	nate'' the Seminole Nation and to reenslave refugee blacks			
1813	Ten to 25 percent of Admiral Oliver H. Perry's* victorious naval force in the Battle of Lake Erie, Put-in-Bay, OH, are black		The New York legislature declares Jul 4, 1827, as the date for the absolute end of slavery; allows nonresidents to enter the state with their slaves, but slaves are to be forfeited after nine months	Rev. Peter Spencer (b 1782) and several others withdraw from the Methodist denomination and organize a black independent church—African Union Church of Wilmington, DE
				Lott Carey (b Charles City County, VA, 1780; d Sierra Leone, 1828) is licensed to preach from the First Baptist Church, Richmond, VA
				Rev. Andrew Marshall, nephew of Rev. Andrew Bryan, is chosen pastor of First African Baptist Church in Savannah, GA
1814	Gen. Andrew Jackson* appeals to free blacks to fight as part of the militia in the War of 1812	The African Free School in New York City is burned	Connecticut law disfranchises blacks	The African Union Methodist Church holds its first annual conference
	Two battalions of black soldiers are with Gen. Andrew Jackson* when he defeats British troops at the Battle of New Orleans, LA; at a New Orleans ceremony, Jackson praises the troops for their service			
	Blacks participate in victories at Plattsburg and Lake Champlain, NY			
	The New York legislature authorizes the formation of two black regiments; 2,000 blacks enlist and are sent to Sacketts Harbor, NY			
	A New York act provides for two black military regiments; black soldiers receive the same pay as whites; slaves who enlist with their masters' permission are emancipated at the end of the war			

1812

the fire, and was complimented by [Gen. Andrew] Jackson* himself after the battle"

It is said that the "colored Creoles" of Louisiana who fight in the Battle of New Orleans, LA, have their own special war song, "En Avan, Grenadie" ("Go forward, grenadiers; he who is dead requires no ration"), which they sing along with "La Marseillaise" and other songs

1813

Henry F. Williams, a musician and native of Boston, MA, b; Williams performs with the Francis Johnson bands in the 1840s before leading his own bands in Philadelphia, PA; he returns to Boston as a composer, performer, arranger, and music teacher; his Thanksgiving anthem "O, Give Thanks" is very popular; several editions of his dances and marches "Rose Schottishe, Sunny Side Polka," and the "Parisien waltzes" are published

1814

	A. **General History**	B. **Education**	C. **Laws and Legal Actions**	D. **Religion**
1815	Paul Cuffe helps a group of 38 US blacks reach Africa via one of his own ships Quaker Levi Coffin* establishes the Underground Railroad after soldiers returning from the War of 1812 bring news of freedom in Canada A free black battalion fights in the defeat of the British at the Battle of New Orleans, LA Jehu Jones, a free black, purchases a hotel for $13,000 at a public auction in Charleston, SC	The African Free School reopens in new location in New York City	A New York bill requires blacks to obtain special permits in order to vote in state elections	Rev. Lott Carey helps to organize the Richmond African Baptist Missionary Society for black members of First Baptist Church, VA John Jea's *The Life, History, and Unparalleled Sufferings of John Jea, The African Preacher* is published
1816	The Seminole Wars begin with an attack on a western Florida fort containing hundreds of runaway slaves, Creeks, and Seminole; blacks and Native Americans fight against federal troops in the First and Second Seminole Wars, 1816–42 The American Colonization Society, which seeks to colonize free blacks in Africa, is organized in Washington, DC; Cong. John C. Calhoun* (SC) and Cong. Henry Clay* (KY) are among its supporters US troops attack Fort Blount on Apalachicola Bay, FL, where approximately 300 fugitive slaves and 20 of their Native American allies have sought refuge; approximately 270 black women and children are killed James P. Beckwourth (b Fredericksburg, VA, Apr 6, 1798), a former slave, signs on as a scout for Gen. William Henry Ashley's* Rocky Mountain expedition, New Orleans, LA	Rev. Daniel Coker founds Bethel Charity School for Negroes, Baltimore, MD	A Louisiana state law prohibits slaves from testifying against whites and free blacks except in cases where free blacks are allegedly involved in slave uprisings The Indiana state constitution abolishes slavery An Indiana law disfranchises blacks	African Methodist Episcopal Church, the first independent black denomination, is started at a Philadelphia conference called by the black Methodist movement (led by Revs. Richard Allen, Daniel Coker, and Stephen Hall) Rev. Daniel Coker (b Isaac Wright, Maryland, 1780; d Freetown, Liberia, 1846) is elected the first bishop of the AME church but declines the position; Rev. Richard Allen is then named the first bishop The Methodist Church lists 42,000 black members, of which 30,000 are southern slaves John Stewart (b Powhatan County, VA, 1786; d Ohio, 1823) begins missionary work with the Wyandott Native American group in the Sandusky, OH, area Rev. Morris Brown establishes a Methodist Society for black men in Charleston, SC
1817	Rev. Absalom Jones, Bishop Richard Allen, and James Forten, Sr., organize a meeting of over 3,000 free blacks at Bethel Church to oppose American Colonization Society, Philadelphia, PA		New York state enacts a gradual abolition act, effective Jul 4, 1827 Florida and Mississippi laws disfranchise blacks To curb illegal voodoo ceremonies an ordinance is	Rev. Morris Brown is ordained a deacon in the African Methodist Episcopal Church Bishop Richard Allen authorizes Jarena Lee (b 1783) to hold prayer meetings in her house, and she thereby be-

E. **Literature, Publications, and The Black Press**	F. **The Arts**	G. **Science, Technology, and Medicine**	H. **Sports**	
William, a slave, has his narrative published: *The Negro Servant: An Authentic Narrative of a Young Negro, Showing How He Was Made a Slave in Africa, and Carried to Jamaica, Where He Was Sold to a Captain in His Majesty's Navy, and Taken to America, Where He Became a Christian, and Afterwards Brought to England and Baptised*	Frank Johnson organizes the members of the Third Company of Washington Guards into his first band after the War of 1812		William "Bill" Richmond officially retires from boxing; at the end of his career he has won 12 bouts and lost 2	**1815**
	A segregated section in the upper tier of the New Orleans, LA, Opera House is established for blacks			**1816**
A Discourse Delivered on the Death of Captain Paul Cuffe, an account of Pan-Africanist Paul Cuffe's life and his pursuit for the establishment of a colony in Africa for black Americans, is published	Patrick Henry Reason, a Philadelphia, PA, engraver, b; he is known for his depiction of a chained slave who asks: "Am I not a man and a brother?"; this work is used mainly as the emblem of the British anti-slavery movement and for		Tom Molineaux tours Ireland teaching the art of boxing	**1817**

	A. General History	B. Education	C. Laws and Legal Actions	D. Religion
1817	Free blacks in Richmond, VA, meet to protest colonization A group of blacks and Seminoles attack a boat containing military supplies and kill 35 soldiers and 6 women; 6 soldiers and 1 woman are taken as prisoners, Fort Scott, GA; retired general Andrew Jackson,* recalled to active duty, pursues the attackers into Spanish Florida Mississippi enters the Union as a slave state		passed forbidding slaves to dance anywhere or anytime except in Congo Square, New Orleans, LA, on Sunday; by 1830 slaves are forbidden to dance in the square even on Sundays	comes the first black female minister in the African Methodist Episcopal Church The African Methodist Episcopal Church publishes its first official document, *The Doctrines of the African Methodist Episcopal Church,* a pamphlet that outlines the church rules, regulations, and organizational structure The New York African Bible Society is established
1818	There are 10,000 slaves in Missouri Gen. Andrew Jackson* defeats a force of blacks and Native Americans at the Battle of Suwannee, ending the first Seminole War, FL	Philadelphia free blacks establish Pennsylvania Augustine Society "for the education of people of colour" Schools for blacks receive public aid in Philadelphia, PA	Illinois state constitution abolishes slavery; Cong. James Tallmadge, Jr.* (D-NY), opposes its statehood because he feels the proposed state constitution does not contain a sufficiently strong prohibition of slavery Illinois law disfranchises blacks Connecticut is the only New England state to officially disfranchise blacks Norfolk (VA) County Court awards William Flora 100 acres of land for his service in the American Revolution	St. Philip's Episcopal Church is organized in New York City (incorporates in 1820) The African Methodist Episcopal Church reports 1,066 members Black parishioners of Bromfield Methodist Episcopal Church in Boston form a separate, all-black church originally named May Street Methodist Church (it is later renamed Fourth Street Methodist Church) Due to increased racial discrimination in Sands Street Methodist Church in Brooklyn, NY, black members establish Brooklyn African Wesleyan Methodist Episcopal Church; the church later becomes affiliated with the African Methodist Episcopal denomination As early as this year, black churches sponsor their own camp meetings Rev. Morris Brown is ordained an African Methodist Episcopal elder Bishop Richard Allen compiles the first official hymn book of the African Methodist Episcopal Church, *The African Methodist Pocket Hymn Book*
1819	Alabama enters the Union as a slave state; its constitution provides the state legis-		Federal law is enacted that authorizes the US president to send armed vessels to	Rev. Lott Carey, minister at First Baptist Church in Richmond, VA, begins ser-

				1817
	various other abolitionist causes			
	Richard Milburn, composer, b; Milburn will compose "Listen to the Mocking Bird," which he sells to a white man for a low price; 20 million copies of the song will be sold			

				1818
	Frank Johnson becomes the first black to publish sheet music in the US		William "Bill" Richmond exits from retirement to fight an "impromptu" bout with Jack Carter*; he KO's Carter in three rounds; there is no record of Richmond fighting again	
	While visiting New Orleans, LA, architect Benjamin Henry Latrobe* witnesses hundreds of dancers gathering after Sunday religious services to form a circular dance; this communal form of slave dancing occurs in the Place Congo and is perceived by many to be an African tradition that has been transplanted to the southern US			

1819

	A. General History	B. Education	C. Laws and Legal Actions	D. Religion
1819	lature with power to abolish slavery and compensate slave owners, to try slaves figuring in crimes above petty larceny, and to set penalties for the malicious killing of slaves		Africa to suppress illegal US slave trade The US Congress appropriates $100,000 for the transportation of blacks illegally imported to the US back to Africa Cong. James Tallmadge, Jr.* (D-NY), introduces an amendment to the Missouri statehood bill prohibiting the further introduction of slaves and providing for gradual emancipation Alabama law disfranchises blacks	vice with the Baptist Board of Foreign Missions The New York diocese of the Episcopal Church votes to admit a black applicant to candidacy for Holy Orders; neither he nor any of his congregations is entitled to attend the diocesan convention, and no black congregation will be granted representation Bishop Daniel Coker is sent to Liberia as a missionary from the African Methodist Episcopal Church John Fanning Watson, of the African Methodist Episcopal Church, protests the improvised singing of hymns in public places and camp meetings; this protest, which continues for years, will eventually lead the church to pass a resolution banning the singing of specially composed hymns in public places Samuel E. Cornish (b Sussex County, DE, 1795) is licensed to preach in the Presbyterian Church The Methodist Episcopal Church establishes its first official mission to Native Americans based on the groundwork laid by Rev. John Stewart, a missionary
1820	American Colonization Society sends an expedition to Africa to establish Liberia, a black republic in West Africa; the *Mayflower of Liberia*, the first ship to carry blacks from the US to Liberia, leaves New York City with 86 blacks *The Emancipator*, the first abolitionist paper in the South, is published in Tennessee The US Army is forbidden to accept blacks and mulattoes	Pennsylvania legislature grants free blacks a share of the state school fund to support separate schools Boston, MA, opens a public elementary school for black students Cincinnati, OH, opens its first school for blacks	The US Congress declares foreign slave trade to be recognized as piracy and punishable by death The US Congress authorizes citizens of Washington, DC, to elect white officials and permits them to adopt a code for governing slaves and free blacks The Missouri Compromise is enacted: Maine will be admitted as a free state, Missouri as a slave state; slavery is prohibited in the territory of the Louisiana Purchase, north of 36° 30′ Maine's constitution gives all of its male citizens the right to vote and the right to an education, regardless of race.	First copy of *Discipline* for African Methodist Episcopal Zion Church is adopted; incorporates the earliest declaration against slavery from a Methodist church First attempt to merge African Methodist Episcopal Church and African Methodist Episcopal Zion churches is made by officials of AMEZ and AME Bishop Richard Allen; the mission is not accomplished Marie Saloppe, voodoo priestess, achieves popularity during this decade; she specializes in hex removal

E. Literature,
Publications, and
The Black Press

F. The Arts

G. Science,
Technology,
and Medicine

H. Sports

1819

1820

Simeon Gilliat, renowned
slave violinist, d; Baron
Botetourt,* the royal governor of Virginia, is Gilliat's
master

John Cromwell is the leading black singing-school
master in Philadelphia, PA,
during the early part of this
decade; two of his students,
Morris Brown, Jr., and
Robert Johnson, later open
their own schools

	A. General History	B. Education	C. Laws and Legal Actions	D. Religion
1820	The African Union Meeting House, a non-sectarian self-help organization and community center, is organized in Providence, RI			Rev. Samuel E. Cornish of the Presbyterian Church serves as a missionary to slaves in Maryland
				Rev. Nathaniel Paul (b Exeter, NH, 1793; d Albany, NY, Jul 17, 1839) helps organize the Albany African Church Association, New York
				Blacks from Ebenezer Methodist Church in Washington, DC, withdraw and organize Israel Baptist Church—the first independent black church in Washington; the following year the church becomes affiliated with the African Methodist Episcopal denomination and appoints Rev. David Smith pastor
				During this decade black churches begin sponsoring sacred music concerts featuring a series of solo songs, generally following the traditions of white concerts
1821	Under the Treaty of Indian Springs, in exchange for $200,000 the Creeks give up 5 million acres of land and possession of any fugitive slaves living among them, GA		Missouri law disfranchises blacks New York restricts black male suffrage by establishing property qualifications of $250 and longer residence requirements for blacks than whites The Georgia legislature grants US veteran Austin Dabney a farm of 112 acres for his heroism in the Revolutionary War Maine law outlaws interracial marriages and nullifies such marriages already existing	African Methodist Episcopal Zion Church is formally organized at Zion Church, New York City; Rev. William Phoebus presides; Rev. James Varick is elected the first bishop Revs. Lott Carey and Colin Teague sail for Sierra Leone; they are the first US missionaries to that country Revs. Lott Carey and Colin Teague organize Providence Baptist Church in Richmond, VA Rev. Samuel Cornish establishes and pastors New Demeter Presbyterian Church in New York City John F. Cook, Sr. (b Washington, DC, c1810; d Washington, DC, Mar 25, 1855), helps organize the Union Bethel Church in Washington, DC (later renamed Metropolitan AME Church)

E. **Literature,**
   Publications, and
   The Black Press   F. **The Arts**

G. **Science,**
   Technology,
   and Medicine   H. **Sports**

1820

1821

The first all-black acting troupe, the African Grove Theatre, begins performing on Mercer Street, NYC; over the years the company will perform several Shakespearean dramas, the classics, and lighter popular melodrama; James Hewlett, renowned actor, plays Othello and Richard the Third

Frank Johnson begins an association with the elite military band, the Philadelphia State Fencibles, Pennsylvania

	A. **General History**	B. **Education**	C. **Laws and Legal Actions**	D. **Religion**
1822	Denmark Vesey, a free black carpenter, organizes a plot to seize Charleston, SC; the plan fails because a house slave betrays the plot; 139 blacks are arrested; Vesey and 47 others are executed Black American settlers from the American Colonization Society take possession of the land now known as Liberia; Monrovia, capital city of Liberia, is named for US President James Monroe*; the Society sponsors the fare of Rev. Lott Carey and 28 other colonists to Liberia	New York blacks establish The Phoenix Society, a literary and educational group		Rev. Samuel E. Cornish is ordained in the Presbyterian Church Rev. Nathaniel Paul becomes pastor of the African Baptist Church, the only black church in Albany, NY Rev. Peter Spencer publishes the *Union African Hymn Book* for the Ezion Union African Church in Wilmington, DE (it is reprinted in 1839) The entire all-black congregation from Providence Baptist Church, Richmond, VA, sails to Liberia as missionaries The African Methodist Episcopal Church begins mission activities; Rev. Charles Butler serves as the first official foreign missionary and John Boggs is the first missionary to reach Liberia
1823		Alexander L. Twilight (b Bradford, VT, 1795; d Wilburforce, OH, 1906) receives a B.A. degree from Middlebury College, VT; first known black graduate from a US college Mississippi enacts laws that prohibit teaching reading and writing to blacks and meetings of more than five slaves or free blacks	The US Circuit Court declares that the removal of a slave to a free state bestows freedom and that cruel treatment of a slave is an indictable offense of common law The Camp Moultrie Treaty provides that the US government protect the Seminoles from all persons whatsoever and prevents white persons from intruding on their lands; the Seminoles promise to prohibit fugitive slaves from joining their ranks and to return any slaves captured to their masters upon request In *Elkison v. Deliesilline*, a federal judge decides that the Black Seaman's Act, which allows for black seamen whose vessels enter harbors to be imprisoned until time of departure, is invalid	The Virginia state legislature refuses to grant a permit for a black Baptist church to be built in Richmond, VA, arguing a resistance to making blacks landowners
1824	Henry Highland Garnet (b New Market, MD, Dec 23, 1815; d Feb 12, 1882) escapes from slavery and flees to New York	Dartmouth College, New Hampshire, opens admissions to blacks The Marquis de Lafayette* visits the African Free School in New York City		Membership in the African Methodist Episcopal church reaches 9,888 The rapid organization of black Methodists in Ohio

E. **Literature,
Publications, and
The Black Press**   F. **The Arts**

G. **Science,
Technology,
and Medicine**   H. **Sports**

1822

1823

Henry Brown's *The Drama of King Shotaway* becomes the first play in US history produced by a black writer, at the African Grove Theatre, NYC

The Tailor in Distress, a comedy, features Edwin Forest in the role of a black washerwoman; he becomes the first black actor to gain the approval of a white audience in the US

Ira F. Aldridge, who studied at the African Grove Theater, New York, was renowned in Europe for his performances in Shakespeare's plays, particularly as Othello. (MSRC)

1824

William Grimes's *Life of William Grimes, the Runaway Slave, Written by Himself* is published

Ira Frederick Aldridge (b NYC, Jul 24, 1805; d Lodz, Poland, Aug 8, 1867), the first widely known black actor of tragedy and comedy in the US, goes to the British Isles to perform; Al-

	A. **General History**	B. **Education**	C. **Laws and Legal Actions**	D. **Religion**
1824				necessitates formation of a Western Conference
				The South Carolina Methodist Conference calls for a separate agency for religious instruction of slaves
				Former members of First African Presbyterian Church in Philadelphia, including Jeremiah Gloucester, establish Second African Presbyterian Church; the church closes before 1900
				Colored Union Church, a nonsectarian church, is organized in Newport, RI
1825	Abraham, aka "Sohanac" (b c1790), begins interpreting for the Seminole head chief in negotiations with the US government in Washington and begins service as the principal Seminole Negro chief			Josiah Henson (b Charles County, MD, Jun 15, 1789; d 1883), slave, serves as a minister to a group of slaves he leads from Maryland to his master's brother's plantation in Kentucky
				Sanité Dédé, voodoo priestess, reigns from 1822 to 1830, New Orleans, LA
				Theodore Wright (b 1797; d Mar 25, 1847) enters the Princeton Theological Seminary, NJ; becomes the first black graduate of a theological seminary; soon becomes pastor of the First Colored Presbyterian Church, NYC, where he serves until his death
1826	Rev. Lott Carey is elected vice-agent of the Liberia colony		South Carolina law decrees that free blacks may own real estate	The Episcopal Church ordains Peter Williams, Jr. (d Oct 17, 1840)
	Frances "Fanny" Wright* establishes Nashoba, a colony for free blacks near Memphis, TN; plagued by administrative problems and widespread disease, the colony will fail and the remaining settlers move to Haiti in 1830			
1827	Slavery is officially abolished in New York State; 10,000 blacks are freed		A Michigan act provides that all blacks must prove emancipation and pay a $500 bond before settling there	The African Methodist Episcopal Church establishes a mission in Haiti under the leadership of Rev. Scipio Bean
			A North Carolina law requires whites to list every	Rev. Christopher Rush (1777–1873) is the second

E. Literature, Publications, and The Black Press	F. The Arts	G. Science, Technology, and Medicine	H. Sports	
	dridge is educated as a free-man in the African School in New York; he makes his stage debut in a play called *Pizarro*, later studies in Scotland, plays Othello in London, and tours Ireland and the European continent King Charles, renowned dancer, d at approximately 125 years of age; in addition to dancing he was also adept at the fiddle, fife, banjo, and hollow drum			**1824**
Solomon Bayley's *Narrative of Some Remarkable Incidents in the Life of Solomon Bayley, Formerly a Slave in the State of Delaware, North America, Written by Himself* is published	Francis Johnson publishes the sheet music for *Recognition March of the Independence of Hayti*, a song written in honor of Haiti and Pres. Jean-Pierre Boyer when France recognizes the Caribbean nation's independence; this is one of the first songs with a racial theme written by a black in the US Ira F. Aldridge, actor, has an engagement at the Coburg Theatre in London, England			**1825**
Samuel E. Cornish's article, "A Remonstrance Against the Abuse of the Blacks," is printed in several newspapers	A traveler reports seeing four black musicians, William and Joseph Appo and the two Newton brothers, in the orchestra of the Walnut Street Theatre, Philadelphia, PA James Hewlett, one of the original members of the African Company, gives a representation of "Shakespeare's Proud Heroes" at No. 11 Spruce Street in NYC			**1826**
Owned and edited by John B. Russwurm (b Port Antonio, Jamaica, 1799; d Liberia, Jun 9, 1851) and Rev. Samuel E. Cornish, *Freedom's Journal*, the first African-American newspa-	Dubois Alsdorf, conductor of orchestras and brass bands, b; Aldsdorf will later become one of the first black musicians to be a member of the Musicians Protective Association			**1827**

	A. General History	B. Education	C. Laws and Legal Actions	D. Religion
1827			free black living on their property An Illinois law decrees that blacks, Native Americans, and mulattoes are incompetent to testify in court against whites	bishop elected in the African Methodist Episcopal Zion Church Under the guidance of Sarah Allen, wife of Bishop Richard Allen, the African Methodist Episcopal Church creates Daughters of Conference organizations, wherein AME women assume responsibility to provide material improvements (food, clothes, etc.) to ministers in their annual conferences Black churches begin to sponsor sacred music concerts during the mid-1820s; the African Harmonic Society of Philadelphia holds its second concert at the First African Presbyterian Church St. Philip's also sponsors a concert in New York
1828	William Lloyd Garrison,* abolitionist and writer, begins verbal attacks on slavery in the *National Philanthropist,* a periodical, Bennington, VT US Postmaster General John McLean* rules that black laborers can be used to carry bags into post offices, providing there is supervision by whites Rev. Peter Williams, Jr., organizes the African Dorcas Association, a self-help group in New York City	The Reading Room Society, a black library, is established	Col. George Brooke* and a federal district judge in St. Augustine, FL, order Native American agents to cease returning fugitive slaves to slaveholders until titles are established in court Due to pressure from various white women's groups, an ordinance forbids white men from attending balls with blacks in New Orleans, LA; this ordinance is not enforced	Rev. Morris Brown becomes the second bishop of the African Methodist Episcopal Church St. Thomas Episcopal Church, Philadelphia, PA, becomes the first black church to purchase a pipe organ to accompany the church choir; Ann Appo (b Philadelphia, PA, 1809) is hired as the church organist; later this year Appo dies The Coloured Female Roman Catholic Beneficial Society of Washington, DC, is founded
1829	Blacks attend the inaugural reception for Pres. Andrew Jackson* at the White House, Washington, DC The Pennsylvania legislature endorses the American Colonization Society In a message to the state legislature, South Carolina governor Stephen Miller* says, "Slavery is not a national evil; on the contrary it is a national benefit"	Blacks from Santo Domingo establish the St. Francis Academy for girls, Baltimore, MD Daniel A. Payne (b Charleston, SC, 1811; d 1893), later African Methodist Episcopal bishop, opens his first school in Charleston, SC Rev. Alexander L. Twilight begins five years of service as principal of the Orleans		Haitians from St. Mary's Seminary in Baltimore, MD, organize the Oblate Sisters of Providence, the first order of black nuns in the US Two planters in South Carolina request that a Methodist preacher be appointed to a full-time mission station among their slaves; Rev. William Capers is appointed superintendent of the department for plan-

1827

per, begins publication in New York City

(American Federation of Musicians local 291)

Joseph William Postlewaite, composer, b; his best known works include the "Galena Waltz," "Dew Drop Scottisch," and "Iola Waltz"

1828

Slave George Moses Horton (b Northampton County, NC, 1797; d 1883), who works as a janitor at the University of North Carolina where his master is the college president, has three of his poems published in the *Lancaster Gazette* of Massachusetts; Horton's poetry also appears in *Freedom's Journal* this year

William Whipper (1801–1885) writes "Address . . . Before the Colored Reading Society of Philadelphia"

The African Observer, an antislavery journal, begins publication in Philadelphia, PA; *The National Philanthropist,* another antislavery journal, is founded in Boston, MA

Henry Anderson (b 1800), street vendor and singer known as the "Hominy Man," gains attention for his songs, Philadelphia, PA; Anderson is one of thousands of black vendors who sing to attract customers

---

1829

David Walker's (b Wilmington, NC, 1785; d Massachusetts, 1830) *David Walker's Appeal in Four Articles Together with a Preamble to the Colored Citizens of the World, but in Particular and Very Expressly, to Those of the United States of America* is published; this antislavery pamphlet calls on slaves to revolt against their oppressors; following publication of Walker's *Appeal,* whites place a bounty on him

James Hemmenway's (b 1800) song, "That Rest So Sweet Like Bliss Above," is published in *Atkinson's Casket,* an elite Philadelphia, PA, journal

Thomas "Daddy" Rice,* also known as "the father of American minstrelsy," reaches the height of his career as an entertainer

	A. **General History**	B. **Education**	C. **Laws and Legal Actions**	D. **Religion**
1829	Three-day race riot in Cincinnati, OH; more than 1,000 blacks flee the city after whites attack them and loot and burn their homes; they settle in Canada at the invitation of the governor of Upper Canada	County Grammar School, Brownington, VT Blacks are excluded from public schools in Ohio; segregated schools are established 20 years later The African Education Society is founded to offer academic and mechanical skills training for blacks, Washington, DC		tation missions; Revs. John Honour and J. H. Massey are sent to the fields Rev. Alexander L. Twilight preaches at the local church in Brownington, VT
1830	There are 2,328,642 blacks in the US; 18.1% of the total US population, over two million, are slaves There are 3,568 Northern slaves; two-thirds reside in New Jersey The federal census reports 3,777 blacks own slaves; the majority live in Louisiana, Maryland, Virginia, North Carolina, and South Carolina Between 1830 and 1860, Virginia exports approximately 300,000 slaves to other states; South Carolina, 179,000 A number of African names appear on a list of free blacks included in the 1830 census; many slaves and free blacks retain their African names or pass on African names to their children A white mob in Portsmouth, OH, attacks black citizens Slaveholders free more than 400 slaves to Quaker	The rise of slave insurrections and subsequent white fear lead to the curtailment of educational opportunities for blacks for the next 30 years; slave codes are imposed to restrict education in the South	An Ohio law deems blacks ineligible for serving in the state militia Blacks in Portsmouth, OH, are forced to leave the state by order of city authorities The president of a Cincinnati, OH, mechanical association is tried for "assisting a colored youth to learn a trade" The Louisiana commonwealth provides that anyone convicted of publishing and distributing abolitionist literature will be "imprisoned at hard labor for life or suffer death at the discretion of the court"	At the end of the first year of activity for the Christian Plantation Mission, 417 slave conversions are recorded Rev. Edward Jones is ordained a priest of the Episcopal Church Rev. Nathaniel Paul joins the Wilberforce Community in Upper Canada (Ontario), where he organizes a Baptist church and a school Beginning this year, black preachers, slave and free, are outlawed in most southern states

Robert Voorhis's narrative, *Life and Adventures of Robert Voorhis, the Hermit of Massachusetts, Who Has Lived Fourteen Years in a Cave, Secluded from Human Society: Comprising an Account of His Birth, Parentage, Sufferings, and Providential Escape from Unjust and Cruel Bondage in Early Life and His Reasons for Becoming a Recluse, Taken from His Own Mouth by Henry Trumbull, and Published for His Benefit,* is published

George Moses Horton's *The Hope of Liberty* is published; Horton hopes that sales of the volume of poetry will generate enough money to buy his freedom

Rev. Samuel E. Cornish revives *Freedom's Journal* under the name *The Rights of All,* a newspaper published in New York City from May to September

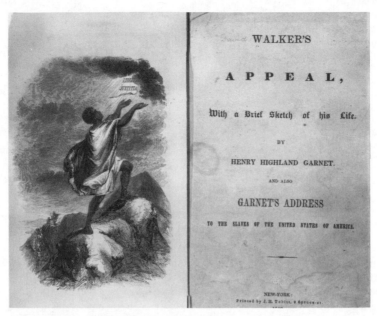

David Walker, a free-black tailor in Boston, MA, sewed copies of his militant and controversial Appeal *into sailor uniforms, hoping to reach the masses of the African-American population.* (LC)

During this decade, Peter Allen (d Goliad, TX, 1836), fifer and banjo player, serves as a musician for Captain Wyatt's* Company in Huntsville, TX

Morris Brown, Jr. (b Charleston, SC, 1812), is a choral conductor and soloist for sacred musical performances during this decade

The Negro Philharmonic Society, consisting of over 100 members, is organized by musicians in New Orleans, LA, during this decade

Joshua Johnston, the best-known black portrait artist of the nineteenth century, d; his notable works include *Portrait of a Cleric, In the Garden,* and *Benjamin Franklin and Son*

Over this decade, Jo Anderson, a slave, helps Cyrus McCormick* as he develops a reaping machine in Rockbridge, VA

Norbert Rillieux (b New Orleans, LA, Mar 17, 1806; d Paris, France, Oct 8, 1894), an instructor of applied mechanics at L'Ecole Centrale in Paris, France, publishes a series of papers on steam-engine work and steam economy that draws favorable attention in scientific circles across Europe

A. **General History**	B. **Education**	C. **Laws and Legal Actions**	D. **Religion**

1830

residents in North Carolina; while theoretical ownership is retained, the slaves are allowed virtual freedom until they are transported to free states

The first National Negro Convention meets at Bethel African Methodist Episcopal Church in Philadelphia, PA; delegates from Virginia, Delaware, Maryland, New York, and Pennsylvania consider projects to establish a college and to encourage emigration to Canada—neither is adopted

Rev. Peter Williams, Jr., urges the establishment of a settlement in northern Canada as an asylum for black American refugees

Josiah Henson, minister to slaves, escapes from slavery with his wife and children and flees to Canada

James Forten, Sr., owns a sailmaking business in Philadelphia, PA, which employs over 40 black and white laborers; he eventually acquires a fortune of more than $100,000

1831

On Aug 22, Nat Turner and five other slaves begin an uprising; over the next 40 hours they are joined by at least 60 others as they kill at least 57 whites; VA state patrols, volunteer military companies, state militia, and US forces are called in to suppress the rebels; Turner is captured on Oct 30 and hanged on Nov 11

According to a US Army survey, the Choctaw nation in southern Mississippi contains 512 blacks

The New York Committee and the New England Anti-Slavery Society, a radical abolitionist group, are formed

The first Colored Female Society is organized in Philadelphia, PA

Greenbury Logan is one of the first blacks to settle in

C. Laws and Legal Actions:

Ohio blacks are prohibited from serving on juries

Mississippi law declares that freed slaves between the ages of 16 and 50 are required to leave the state within 90 days of manumission or risk being sold back into slavery

Adams County, MS, citizens petition the state legislature to remove all free blacks from the state

D. Religion:

At the first Annual Convention of the People of Color at Wesleyan Church, Philadelphia, PA, delegates from five states resolve to study conditions of blacks, explore settlement possibilities in Canada, oppose the American Colonization Society, and recommend annual meetings; abolitionist leaders S. S. Jocelyn,* Arthur Tappan,* and William Lloyd Garrison* propose establishment of an industrial college in New Haven, CT; the convention endorses the proposal, but the New Haven community defeats it

Maria W. Stewart (b Hartford, CT, 1803; d Washington, DC, 1879), early feminist, publishes a small pamphlet, *Religion and the Pure Principles of Morality, the Sure Foundation on Which We Must Build*

E. **Literature,**
   Publications, and
   The Black Press   F. **The Arts**

G. **Science,**
   Technology,
   and Medicine   H. **Sports**

The Confessions of Nat Turner, edited by Thomas R. Gray,* is published in Baltimore, MD

Mary Prince's *The History of Mary Prince, a West Indian Slave, Related by Herself, with a Supplement by the Editor, to Which Is Added the Narrative of Asa-Asa, a Captured African* is the first slave narrative published by a black woman in the US

The Liberator, under the direction of William Lloyd Garrison,* begins publication in Boston, MA

	A. **General History**	B. **Education**	C. **Laws and Legal Actions**	D. **Religion**
1831	Texas; in four years, he will be one of a few black settlers who fight for Texas independence from Mexico; ironically, after joining the Union, Texas will become a slave-holding state, and its white residents will be notorious for intolerance of blacks A convention of blacks in New York City issues a declaration that rejects migration to Africa, asserting, "Here we were born and here we will die" Free blacks in Rhode Island petition the state for full voting rights or an exemption from taxes			African Methodist Episcopal Zion Church claims 1,689 members
1832	Twelve whites, among them William Lloyd Garrison,* organize the New England Anti-Slavery Society in the basement of the First African Baptist Church, Boston, MA William Lloyd Garrison* writes *Thoughts on African Colonization* Three hundred eighty-five freed slaves reach Mercer County, OH; they are freed at the death of Cong. John Randolph* (R-VA) who leaves them money for their transportation, land, and necessities; although Randolph's relatives cheat them of their land, the freed persons settle throughout the Ohio area There are five antiblack riots in Philadelphia, PA, between this year and 1849 The Afric-American Female Intelligence Society, a black women's literary and mutual aid organization, meets in Boston, MA One hundred forty-six blacks leave Charleston, SC, for Liberia Rhode Island blacks organize the Providence Temperance Society William de Fleurville, aka "Billy the Barber" (b Haiti	John Malvin (b Dumfries, VA, 1795), a free black, organizes the School Education Society in Cleveland, OH The Second Annual Convention for the Improvement of the Free People of Color in these United States meets in Philadelphia and focuses on the importance of education for blacks Charles B. Ray (b Falmouth, MA, Dec 25, 1807; d 1886), later prominent black leader, enters Wesleyan University, CT; northern and southern students voice objections, and Ray withdraws from the university Free blacks petition the Pennsylvania state legislature to admit their children to public school on the grounds that they pay taxes which support public education; the petition is unsuccessful At 14, Charles L. Reason (b New York, NY, Jul 21, 1818; d 1893), a former pupil, becomes an instructor at the New York Free African School Marie Bernard Couvent (b Guinea, West Africa, c 1757), a former slave, provides in her will for the "establishment of a free school	A Virginia Act prohibits free blacks from purchasing slaves other than their own parents, spouses, or children The Virginia legislature passes a law to silence black ministers except those who preach in the presence of "certain discreet white men" Seminoles sign a treaty with the US government agreeing to move into Indian territory (present-day Oklahoma); black runaway slaves who live among the Seminoles are permitted to move with them A North Carolina law outlaws black preachers and exhorters	Rev. Charles Colcock Jones* of Liberty County, GA, is the first functioning missionary of the Association for the Religious Instruction of Negroes, which is organized by local planters Despite a growing fear among whites of Christian-inspired slave rebellions, Rev. Charles Colcock Jones* publishes his sermon, "The Religious Instruction of Negroes" Rev. John Chavis's sermon *The Extent of Atonement* is published *The Life, Experience, and Gospel Labors of the Right Reverend Richard Allen* is published in Philadelphia, PA

E. Literature, Publications, and The Black Press	F. The Arts	G. Science, Technology, and Medicine	H. Sports
			1831
Chloe Spear's *Memoir of Chloe Spear, a Native of Africa, Who Was Enslaved in Childhood: By a ''Lady of Boston''* is published	The all-black acting troupe, the African Company, stops performing and disbands	Augustus Jackson, a Philadelphia confectioner, invents ice cream but does not receive a patent	**1832**

	A. **General History**	B. **Education**	C. **Laws and Legal Actions**	D. **Religion**
1832	c 1806; d Springfield, IL, Apr 3, 1868), opens the first barbershop, Springfield, IL Free blacks settle with the Cherokees at Roberts Settlement in Hamilton County, IN Maria W. Stewart begins an unprecedented public speaking tour at Franklin Hall, Boston, MA; she is the first woman in the US to engage in public political debates	for orphans of color"; L'Institution Catholique des Orphelins, or The Couvent School, as it is popularly known, opens in 1848 and is today the oldest black Catholic school in the US, New Orleans, LA Blacks establish the Library Company and the Banneker Society, literary societies, Philadelphia, PA		
1833	Black and white abolitionists organize the American Anti-Slavery Society, Philadelphia, PA; James McCrummell, Robert Purvis, Sr., James G. Barbados, Rev. Theodore Wright, and William Lloyd Garrison* are among the delegates Solomon G. Brown, a scientist, lecturer, and traveler, b; he is one of the few black chief clerks of a division in the Federal government The Female Anti-Slavery Society is organized; Lucretia Mott* is elected president; Sarah M. Douglass,* the Quaker principal of the preparatory department of the Institute for Colored Youth, Harriet Purvis, and Sarah and Margaretta Forten—daughters of James Forten, Sr.—are charter members A riot occurs in Detroit, MI, after blacks help a fugitive slave from Kentucky The Treaty of Payne's Landing is made with Abraham, a former slave, acting as interpreter for the Seminoles; this treaty required eight Seminole chiefs to go west David Ruggles (b Norwich, CT, 1810; d 1849) is employed as a traveling agent for the *Emancipator and Journal of Public Morals,* an abolitionist weekly	The Philadelphia (PA) Library Company of Colored Persons is organized; the library serves as a book repository and also sponsors lectures and concerts Oberlin College (OH), the first coeducational college, is integrated from the outset and serves as a leader in the abolitionist cause; at the start of the Civil War, blacks constitute one-third of its students Prudence Crandall,* a Quaker schoolteacher, is arrested for conducting an academy for black girls in Canterbury, CT	Alabama law makes it illegal for slaves or free blacks to preach unless in the presence of five "respectable" slaveholders and authorized by some neighboring religious society	Rev. John Malvin organizes the First Baptist Church in Cleveland, OH Rev. Noah C. W. Cannon establishes the first African Methodist Episcopal Church in Boston, MA, Bethel AME Church (known as Charles Street AME Church after 1876) At its annual conference, the African Methodist Episcopal Church passes a resolution that places education at the top of its agenda; AME ministers make a concerted effort to establish schools and encourage parents to have their children educated First Colored Baptist Church (later Nineteenth Street Baptist Church) is the first black Baptist church in Washington, DC; Rev. Sampson White is pastor (he becomes pastor of the Abyssinian Baptist Church, New York, in 1840)

1833

William Whipper writes *Eulogy on William Wilberforce*

Lydia Maria Child's* *Appeal in Favor of That Class of Americans Called Africans* is published

Ira F. Aldridge makes his debut as Othello the Moor in *Othello* at the Royal Theatre, Covent Garden, London; Othello is Aldridge's favorite and most famous role

	A. **General History**	B. **Education**	C. **Laws and Legal Actions**	D. **Religion**
1834	The National Convention of Colored Citizens meets to consider the moral and political conditions of blacks, America, Buffalo, NY A three-day, anti-abolition riot breaks out in Philadelphia, PA; white mobs wreck the African Presbyterian Church, burn homes, and attack blacks The Colored Female Anti-Slavery Society is established in Middletown, CT, and Newark, NJ David Ruggles opens a bookshop in New York City and is considered the first black American bookseller; a white mob burns the store one year later Slaves who save the Georgia capitol from fire are manumitted The British Parliament abolishes slavery in the British Empire; 700,000 slaves are liberated at a cost of 20 million British pounds sterling	First black-funded school for blacks in Cincinnati, OH, opens Black schools come under the supervision of the Public School Society in New York City, NY Prudence Crandall's school for blacks is attacked by citizens and closed by local authorities, Canterbury, CT South Carolina enacts a law that prohibits teaching free or enslaved black children	A South Carolina law forbids free blacks from becoming teachers, clerks, or salesmen	Georgia enacts a law which provides that neither slaves nor free blacks may preach or exhort at an assembly of more than seven unless they are licensed by justices The Providence Association, the earliest black Baptist association, is formed in Ohio
1835	The Fifth Convention for the Improvement of Free People of Color meets at Wesley Church (Philadelphia, PA); the convention recommends that blacks remove the word *African* from the names of their institutions and not use the word *colored* when referring to themselves The Second Seminole War begins after a US agent arrests and enslaves the wife of Osceola,* a Seminole chief; Chief Osceola is later imprisoned for six days for protesting too vigorously; the Seminoles kill the agent in retaliation; a group of Seminoles and blacks storm through Florida attacking several settlements King Phillip,* head chief of the St. John's River Native Americans, and John Caesar lead a group of blacks and Native Americans in an attack on St. John's River plantations, FL	John Malvin (d 1880), educator, calls a meeting of the State Convention of Colored Men in Columbus, OH, which establishes a School Fund Society; the Society opens schools in Columbis, Cleveland, Cincinnati, and Springfield Charles (b Louisa County, VA, 1817) and Gideon Langston are the first blacks to enter the preparatory department at Oberlin College Noyes Academy, an integrated school, is established in Canaan, NH; 14 blacks and 28 whites begin classes; the academy is destroyed by anti-abolitionists and closes after the violence North Carolina law prohibits whites from teaching free blacks	Pres. Andrew Jackson* forbids the post office to deliver abolitionist literature to the South New Orleans, LA, adopts an ordinance zoning the city's cemeteries into three sections; half for whites and one-quarter each for free blacks and slaves North Carolina repeals a voting rights provision that grants suffrage to free black males; North Carolina is the last southern state to disfranchise blacks	The Free Will Baptist Church in Providence, RI, is established In his publication, *Abrogation of the Seventh Commandment, by the American Churches,* David Ruggles condemns those who use the church to maintain black oppression

E. Literature, Publications, and The Black Press	F. The Arts	G. Science, Technology, and Medicine	H. Sports	
Jane Blake's *Memoirs of Margaret Jane Blake* is published in Philadelphia, PA	Black musicians begin performing on showboats along the Mississippi River	Les Artisans, an organization of free colored mechanics, is incorporated in New Orleans, LA; Victor Séjour (b New Orleans, LA, 1817), later a poet and dramatist, is a member		**1834**
William Boen's *Anecdotes and Memoirs of William Boen, a Colored Man, Who Lived and Died Near Mount Holly, New Jersey; to Which Is Added the Testimony of Friends of Mount Holly Monthly Meeting Concerning Him* is published		Henry Blair, an escaped slave from Maryland, is granted a patent for a device used in planting corn; he is considered the first black to receive a patent because prior to him, the race of an inventor was not recorded		
David Ruggles's first pamphlet, *Extinguisher, Extinguished,* is published		Norbert Rillieux installs the first working model of his triple-effect evaporator on the plantation of Zenon Ramon* in Louisiana; this endeavor is unsuccessful due to mechanical failure		
		Jo Anderson, slave, helps Cyrus McCormick* perfect the reaping machine		
John Greenleaf Whittier's poem, ''My Countrymen in Chains,'' is published				**1835**
Maria W. Stewart's *Productions of Mrs. Maria Stewart* is published in Boston, MA				

	A. **General History**	B. **Education**	C. **Laws and Legal Actions**	D. **Religion**
1835	William Johnson (b Natchez, MS, 1809; d 1851), barber, keeps a diary from 1835 to 1851; this only known chronological account kept by an antebellum free black is discovered in 1938 by Edwin Adams; at his death Johnson leaves more than 350 acres of farming and timber land, several small businesses, and 15 slaves William Whipper, civil rights advocate, helps found the American Moral Reform Society, an abolitionist group Ohio Anti-Slavery Convention held in Putnam, OH Blacks form a vigilance committee to prevent the kidnap of blacks and to assist fugitive slaves, New York City Antislavery pamphlets are taken from the mail and publicly burned, Charleston, SC Sally Hemings, alleged slave mistress of former US president Thomas Jefferson* and the alleged mother of at least five of his children, d			
1836	William Lloyd Garrison* is mobbed by angry white Bostonians in Massachusetts Sen. Thomas Hart Benton* (D-MO) verbally attacks abolitionists for sending petitions to the US Congress A riot occurs in Cincinnati, OH; proslavery sympathizers destroy abolitionist James G. Birney's press Rev. J. W. Lewis organizes a temperance convention in Providence, RI Robert Purvis, Sr., civil rights leader (b Charleston, SC, Aug 4, 1810; d Philadelphia, PA, Apr 15, 1898) delivers the eulogy for the memorial service of abolitionist Thomas Shipley*	After leaving Oberlin College, Charles Langston helps establish and teaches at a school for black children in Chillicothe, OH Rev. J. W. Lewis founds the New England Union Academy in Providence, RI; Lewis, along with one assistant, teaches history, geography, botany, grammar, single and double entry bookkeeping, philosophy, and astronomy Theodore S. Wright becomes the first black to receive a degree from a US theological seminary, Princeton University, NJ	The US House of Representatives passes a "gag rule" that prevents congressional action on antislavery resolutions or legislation; a stricter "gag rule" is adopted every succeeding year until 1844; the rule is overturned in 1845 A New Orleans, LA, ordinance requires free blacks and slaves jailed for more than three days to perform public work; white prisoners are exempt Arkansas law disfranchises blacks	The Methodist Church softens its opposition to slavery; it will avoid interference in civil and political relationships between slaves and slaveholders The African Methodist Episcopal Church claims 7,000 members in its four conferences John Mifflin Brown (b Cantwell's Bridge, DE, 1817), later to become the eleventh bishop of the African Methodist Episcopal Church, joins Bethel AME Church in Philadelphia, PA Rev. Jarena Lee's *The Life and Religious Experiences of Jarena Lee, a Coloured Lady* is published; this work is one of the first autobiographical texts by a black woman

E. **Literature,**
   Publications, and
   The Black Press   F. **The Arts**

G. **Science,**
   Technology,
   and Medicine   H. **Sports**

1835

Henry Blair receives a
patent for his "cotton planter" invention

	A. **General History**	B. **Education**	C. **Laws and Legal Actions**	D. **Religion**
1836	A group of black women rescue two fugitive slave women from a courtroom before they can be returned to their masters, Boston, MA John B. Russwurm, editor and colonizationist, begins service as governor of the Maryland Colony, a separate settlement established for emigrants from that state only, at Cape Palma, Liberia; he serves until his death in 1851 A group of northern abolitionists veto a move to have black ministers preach to them			A number of Providence Missionary Baptist District Associations are formed in Ohio; these organizations hold annual meetings of delegates from member churches and allowed communication between predominantly black congregations in a lonely, expanding frontier Rev. Moses Clayton (1783–1861) organizes the First Colored Baptist Church of Baltimore, MD
1837	Rev. Elijah P. Lovejoy,* an abolitionist and editor of the *Alton Observer*, a religious newspaper, is murdered by a proslavery mob in Alton, IL John Horse (b Florida, c1812; d Mexico City, Mexico, 1882) is commander of the Seminoles in their victory over American troops at the Battle of Okeechobee; later in the war the Seminoles surrender and agree to move west peaceably under the protection of the US Army Gen. Thomas Jesup* makes an agreement with the Creeks and the Florida militia that grants soldiers ownership of any unclaimed black runaways they capture Josiah Henson serves as a captain in the Second Essex Company of Colored Volunteers for one year during the Canadian Rebellion The first Antislavery Convention of American Women meets in New York; one-tenth of the members are black; Grace Bustill Douglass is elected a vice president and Sarah Forten's poem, "We Are Thy Sisters," is printed by the convention Detroit (MI) Anti-Slavery Society is formed	The Institute for Colored Youth, the first black coeducational classical high school, opens in Philadelphia, PA; heretofore high schools for blacks have been vocational/industrial	The Pennsylvania Supreme Court excludes blacks from suffrage A group of black men petition the New York State legislature for equal voting rights Michigan law disfranchises blacks	The first National Negro Catholic Congress is held in Washington, DC The first African Methodist Episcopal Zion Church in Providence, RI, is established Charles B. Ray is ordained a Methodist minister African Methodist Episcopal ministers vote to appoint missionaries to Canada and the western part of New York State

E. **Literature,
Publications, and
The Black Press**

F. **The Arts**

G. **Science,
Technology,
and Medicine**

H. **Sports**

1836

Moses Roper's *A Narrative of the Adventures and Escape of Moses Roper from American Slavery, with a Preface by the Reverend T. Price* is published

George Moses Horton's *The Hope of Liberty* is reprinted twice under the title *Poems by a Slave*

The Weekly Advocate changes its name to the *Colored American*; Rev. Samuel E. Cornish is editor, Phillip A. Bell is publisher, and Charles B. Ray is the general manager and agent for this weekly

William Whipper's essay, "Non-Resistance to Offensive Aggression," is published in the *Colored American*

Victor Séjour's first work is published in the *Revue des Colonies*

Rev. Hosea Easton's *A Treatise on the Intellectual Character and Political Condition of the Colored People of the U.S.* is published

Olaudah Equiano or Gustavus Vassa, an Autobiography of a Negro, is published

Frank Johnson, bandmaster and composer, sails to London, England, with his band and begins a series of concerts at the Argyll Rooms, becoming the first black American to win acclaim in the US and England and the first American of any race to take a musical ensemble abroad to perform in Europe; after his performance before Queen Victoria,* Johnson is presented with a silver bugle

Signor "Mr. Cornmeal" Cornmeali performs a minstrel show at the St. Charles Street Theatre in New Orleans, LA; Cornmeali did not perform in blackface as other minstrels did

Messrs. Rhodes and Little direct their company in plays and ballad operas in Philadelphia, PA; they produce *The Indian Hunter, a Sailor's Dream* and other pieces

James McCune Smith (b 1813), a physician and writer educated in New York's African Free School and at the University of Glasgow in Scotland, begins to practice medicine in New York City and eventually opens a pharmacy there; he also conducts pioneer work in the scientific study of race

	A. **General History**	B. **Education**	C. **Laws and Legal Actions**	D. **Religion**
1838	Blacks hold a meeting in Philadelphia, PA, to protest the action of the Pennsylvania Reform Convention of 1837, which denies them the right to vote	Ohio law prohibits the education of black children at the expense of the state	Pennsylvania law disfranchises blacks	Black ministers in the southern states are forbidden to conduct services, as slaves may worship only under supervision of their masters
	Abolitionist Charles Lenox Remond (b Salem, MA, Feb 1, 1810; d Dec 22, 1873) is the first black lecturer employed by the Massachusetts Anti-Slavery Society	Virginia law prohibits the return of blacks who attend schools in other states		First Bethel Baptist Church is chartered by two blacks and four whites in Jacksonville, FL
	A proslavery mob destroys Pennsylvania Hall in Philadelphia because of abolitionist meetings held there; the police offer no protection and stand by as fires and rioting destroy sections of the city			The first African Methodist Episcopal Church in Providence, RI, is established
	Frederick Douglass (b Tuckahoe, MD, Feb 14, 1817; d Washington, DC, Feb 20, 1895) escapes from slavery in Baltimore, MD; he settles in New Bedford, MA			Rev. James W. C. Pennington (b Maryland, 1809), abolitionist, pastors an African Congregational Church at Newtown, CT, for two years
	George Vashon (b Carlisle, PA, Jul 25, 1824; d Rodney, MS, Oct 5, 1878) is secretary of the first Juvenile Anti-Slavery Society in the US, Pittsburgh, PA			A group of black parishioners withdraws from white May Street Methodist Episcopal Church in Boston, MA, and organizes a separate church (known as North Russell Street Church after the Civil War)
	The fraternal organization Adelphic Union Library Association, which encourages intellectual debate and offers a lecture series, opens meetings to anyone regardless of race or sex, Boston, MA			
	Free blacks of Boston, MA, speak out against segregation on trains, steamboats, and stage coaches			
	Joshua R. Giddings* of Ohio is the first white abolitionist elected to the US Congress			
	US Attorney General Benjamin F. Butler* prepares an opinion for the Secretary of War indicating that the Constitution and laws oblige the president to use military power to reprimand fugitive slaves found only in a state of the Union, not in Indian territory			

William Whipper and other blacks begin to publish a periodical called *The National Reformer*

James Williams's *Narrative of James Williams, an American Slave; Who Was for Several Years a Driver on a Cotton Plantation in Alabama* is published in New York by the American Anti-Slavery Society

Chains and Freedom: or, The Life and Adventures of Peter Wheeler, a Colored Man Yet Living as Told by Charles Edward Lester is published in New York

An escaped slave known only as Joanna publishes *Narrative of Joanna, an Emancipated Slave of Surinam* (*from Stedman's Narrative of Five Years' Expedition Against the Revolted Negroes of Surinam*), in Boston, MA

The Memoirs of Elleanor Eldridge, one of the few narratives of the life of an early 19th-century free black woman, is published

Frank Johnson becomes the first musician in the US to introduce promenade concerts; he and his band perform Concerts à la Musard during the Christmas season, Philadelphia, PA

A. **General History**	B. **Education**	C. **Laws and Legal Actions**	D. **Religion**
1839 Abolitionists organize the Liberty Party, an antislavery political organization; Rev. Samuel Ringgold Ward and Henry Highland Garnet are among its leading supporters; the party urges boycotts and exclusion of southern crops and products		The US State Department rejects a Philadelphia, PA, black's application for a passport on the grounds that the Pennsylvania constitution does not recognize blacks as citizens	Rev. Samuel Ringgold Ward is licensed to preach by the New York Congregationalist Association
Rev. Samuel Ringgold Ward (b Maryland, Oct 17, 1817; d 1866), Presbyterian minister known as "the black Daniel Webster," is employed as a lecturer by the American Anti-Slavery Society			The First Baptist Church divides and the African Baptist Church is formed in Mobile, AL
The US government requires that the Seminoles and their black allies be shipped from Tampa Bay, FL, to the West; an agreement is later made that allows the Seminoles and blacks to remain in southern Florida			Daniel Payne, educator, is ordained by the Franckean Synod of the Lutheran Church
Spanish slave ship, the *Amistad*, is brought into Montauk, NY, by a group of Africans who revolt against their captors; Joseph Cinque, the young African leader and his fellow crewmen are captured; they are defended before the Supreme Court by former US president John Quincy Adams* and are awarded their freedom			
A group of black men organize The Iron Chest Company, a real estate firm, Cincinnati, OH			
Blacks entering the state of Iowa must present a $500 bond and proof of emancipation			
A black Frenchman leads a Native American raid against Texas settlers			
Robert Purvis, Sr., becomes president of the Vigilance Committee of Philadelphia, PA; he holds this office until 1844			
John Horse, commander and interpreter for the Seminoles, becomes a US guide and interpreter; he continues this work until 1842			

E. Literature, Publications, and The Black Press	F. The Arts	G. Science, Technology, and Medicine	H. Sports

Palladium of Liberty, a free black newspaper, is published in Columbus, OH

Rev. Samuel E. Cornish resigns from his position as editor of the *Colored American,* and Charles B. Ray becomes the sole editor

Abolitionist Theadore Dwight Weld's "American Slavery as It Is," considered by many to be the greatest antislavery pamphlet ever written, is published

Choral conductor Morris Brown, Jr., trains 150 singers to perform *Messiah,* a Handel oratorio; a string orchestra directed by Edward Roland accompanies the chorus for the performance of this musical selection

	A. **General History**	B. **Education**	C. **Laws and Legal Actions**	D. **Religion**
1839	Garrisonians take control of the American Anti-Slavery Society and press for immediate abolition of slavery; women hold significant positions of responsibility William Jay* publishes a pamphlet that reviews the Federal government's legal and financial support of slavery since 1789 Lunsford Lane (b 1803) of North Carolina makes an abolition speech before a southern audience			
1840	There are 2,873,648 blacks in the US, constituting 16.8% of population There are 172,302 free blacks in the northern states Free people of color constitute about 5% of the total population in the South There is a record high number of free blacks in Mississippi: 1,366 Charles Lenox Remond is one of four delegates chosen to attend the World's Anti-Slavery meeting in London, England Pope Gregory XVI* declares opposition to slavery and the slave trade in *The Vatican* A number of black clergymen withdraw from the American Anti-Slavery Society because they want to move from moral suasion to political pressure for abolition; the dissident clergymen form the American and Foreign Anti-Slavery Society	Henry Highland Garnet graduates from Oneida Theological Institute, Utica, NY Rev. Daniel A. Payne opens a school in Philadelphia for black children	The US House of Representatives votes not to receive antislavery petitions Indiana forbids racial intermarriage and sets fines of $1,000 to $5,000 and prison terms of 10 to 20 years for violators; clerks who issue licenses and ministers who perform ceremonies are also punishable New York and Vermont institute jury trials for the fugitive slaves; the Vermont law is overturned in 1843 and reinstated in 1850 Abolitionist Alexander Crummell (1819–1898) drafts a petition to the New York legislature demanding the removal of restrictions for black suffrage	As of this year, over 300 separate northern black churches exist (including 6 Episcopal, 3 Presbyterian, 1 Congregational, and 1 Lutheran) Two additional conferences rise from the African Methodist Episcopal Church: Canada and Indianapolis Rev. James W. C. Pennington begins as pastor of the African Congregational Church in Hartford, CT; he serves until 1847 Rev. William Miller (1775–1845), a founder of the African Methodist Episcopal Zion Church, is elected its bishop Black Baptists in the northeastern states organize the American Baptist Missionary Convention primarily due to the failure of the white-controlled General Missionary Convention of the Baptist Denomination in the US for Foreign Missions to establish an antislavery stance Revivals, gatherings of Christians who come to praise, ring-shout and "get religion," become widespread, mainly among black and poor white Baptists in the South
1841	Col. William Worth* captures a Seminole chief and subsequently forces approximately 200 Seminoles and blacks out of hiding; all are sent west; former slave	Susannah Bradshaw, educator, opens a school for black girls Rev. Edward Jones of the Episcopal Church is named	South Carolina law forbids black and white mill hands from looking out the same window	The Bethel African Methodist Episcopal Church of Philadelphia, PA, introduces choral singing amid protests from older members who prefer the tradi-

110

The *National Antislavery Standard* carries on a dispute with the *Colored American;* the former opposes "all exclusive action on the part of colored people except where the clearest necessity demands it," claiming that separate institutions merely perpetuate public prejudices

The Theatre de la Renaissance, a company of black actors, produces dramas, comedies, and comic operas during their winter season

James Hewlett, the principal actor of the African Grove Theatre, d; during his life he toured England twice and promoted himself as "The New York and London Coloured Comedian"

James W. C. Pennington's *A Textbook on the Origin and History of the Colored People,* the first book on the general history of blacks in the US, is published

	A. General History	B. Education	C. Laws and Legal Actions	D. Religion
1841	holders are told to seek compensation for their runaway slaves from the Federal government Frederick Douglass is an agent for the Massachusetts Anti-Slavery Society and makes his first antislavery speech in Nantucket, MA Boston, MA, authorities place black participants at the rear of Pres. William Henry Harrison's* funeral procession for fear of possible mob violence Slaves aboard the *Creole,* sailing from Hampton, VA, to New Orleans, LA, revolt and force the ship to dock at Nassau in the Bahamas, where a British court frees and grants them asylum The Quintuple Treaty is signed: England, France, Russia, Prussia, and Austria agree to the mutual search of vessels on the high seas in order to suppress the slave trade	principal of the Fourah Bay Christian School, Sierra Leone The New York legislature grants school districts the right to segregate their educational facilities	Blacks and whites in Atlanta, GA, are required to swear on different Bibles in court Frederick Douglass and white abolitionists successfully campaign in Rhode Island against the Dorr Constitution, which would repeal black voting power A New Orleans, LA, ordinance requires separate burial registration lists for blacks and whites	tional call and response method of singing The congregation of the First Baptist Church in Richmond, VA, sells its building to its 1,600 black members, who organize the First African Baptist Church under the leadership of Rev. Robert Ryland Rev. R. S. Sorrick,* a minister in Washington County, MD, is imprisoned for three months and eight days for preaching to slaves Rev. James W. C. Pennington is named president of the Union Missionary Society George Hogarth is named editor of *The African Methodist Episcopal Church Magazine,* Brooklyn, NY Rev. John F. Cook, Sr., becomes a licentiate in the presbyter in Washington, DC Rev. Samuel Ringgold Ward is invited to pastor an all-white Congregationalist church in New York Rev. John F. Cook, Sr., and David Carroll officially organize the First Colored Presbyterian Church, Washington, DC (later known as the Fifteenth Street Presbyterian Church); Cook becomes pastor Rev. John Raymond, abolitionist, becomes pastor of the First African Baptist Church, Boston, MA; he serves until 1845
1842	The capture of George Latimore, an escaped slave, triggers the first of several famous fugitive slave cases, Boston, MA; abolitionists raise enough money to purchase Latimore from his master White mob attacks a parade in Philadelphia, PA, commemorating the abolition of slavery in the West Indies	Augustus Wattles,* agent of the American Anti-Slavery Society, and Samuel Emlen,* New Jersey philanthropist, open Emlen Institute for Negro and Indian Boys, Mercer County, OH; the school specializes in industrial education	In *Prigg v. Pennsylvania* the US Supreme Court rules that states have no power over cases that arise from the Fugitive Slave Act (1793); thus states are prevented from either helping or hindering fugitive slaves Sen. John C. Calhoun* proposes a bill that excludes blacks from serving in the Navy (except as menial laborers) and the Army	Four black nuns, including Mother Juliette Gaudin and Mother Henriette Delille (1813–1862), establish a convent for black women, the Convent of the Holy Family, at New Orleans, LA Jordan W. Early (b Franklin County, VA, 1814) establishes a church for free people of color in New Orleans, LA

1841

Charles L. Reason's "The Spirit Voice" an 86-line ode, written to inspire the disfranchised blacks of New York to fight for their citizenship and rights to freedom, is published

Joseph Wilson's *Sketches of the Higher Classes of Colored Society in Philadelphia*, the first sociological study of northern blacks in the US by a black, is published

The Demosthenian Shield, the first black newspaper in Philadelphia, PA, is published

Ann Plato's *Essays, Including Biographies and Miscellaneous Pieces in Prose and Poetry* is published; while she is identified as a black American, her poem "The Natives of America" suggests that her father is a Native American

1842

The National Watchman, a newspaper edited by William G. Allen, begins publication in Troy, NY; Henry Highland Garnet is associated with Allen in this enterprise; it is discontinued in 1847

Lunsford Lane's *The Narrative of Lunsford Lane, Formerly of Raleigh, NC; Embracing an Account of His Early Life, the Redemption by*

Minstrelsy has become a distinct form of American entertainment; Daniel Decatur Emmett,* with four other white actors, forms a company to perform blackface minstrelsy; Edwin Christy* becomes a star in this period; earlier companies include the Virginia Minstrels, Congo Melodists, Ethiopian Serenaders, and Georgia Minstrels

	A. **General History**	B. Education	C. **Laws and Legal Actions**	D. **Religion**
1842	Irish coal miners battle with black competitors in Pennsylvania		The Louisiana General Assembly passes an act that prevents free persons of color from entering the state	Rev. Henry Highland Garnet pastors the only black church in Troy, NY
	George T. Downing (b New York, NY, 1819; d 1903), businessman and civil rights leader, establishes a summer catering business in Newport, RI		The Massachusetts joint legislative committee reports that railroad restrictions violate rights of black citizens and are prohibited	Rev. Jermain Wesley Loguen (b Davidson County, TN, 1813) is ordained a minister in the African Methodist Episcopal Church
	William Wells Brown (b Lexington, KY, c1815; d 1884), abolitionist, conveys 69 fugitive slaves to Canada via the Underground Railroad from May through December of this year		A Mississippi law requires free blacks who enter from other states to be whipped and deported within 20 days	Rev. James W. C. Pennington's *Covenants Involving Moral Wrong Are Not Obligatory Upon Man: A Sermon* is published
	The Register, a Raleigh, NC, newspaper, reports that Allen Jones, a free black blacksmith, was dragged from his home and whipped by whites for having described being tarred and feathered to the anti-slavery convention in New York; a town meeting including many prominent citizens is convened to protest and condemn this outrage as a violation of the law			Rev. Noah C. W. Cannon's *A History of the African Methodist Episcopal Church* is published
	Charles Lenox Remond delivers a speech, "Rights of Colored Persons in Travelling," before the legislative committee in the Massachusetts House of Representatives; he is the first black to speak before this state body			
	Joseph Jenkins Roberts (b 1809; d Petersburg, VA, 1876) is the first black American president of Liberia			
1843	Sojourner Truth (b Isabella Van Wageren, Hurley, NY, Nov 18, 1797; d Battle Creek, MI, Nov 26, 1883) leaves New York and begins abolitionist work; she is one of the first black women abolitionist lecturers		Massachusetts repeals the law banning interracial marriage	Rev. John F. Cook, Sr., is ordained in the Presbyterian Church
	William Wells Brown begins anti-slavery lecture career		US Attorney General Hugh Legare* declares that free blacks are neither aliens nor citizens	
	Rev. James W. C. Pennington begins service as a Connecticut representative to		Massachusetts and Vermont legislatures defy the Fugitive Slave Act by forbidding state officials to imprison or assist federal authorities in the recapture of escaped slaves	

E. **Literature, Publications, and The Black Press**	F. **The Arts**	G. **Science, Technology, and Medicine**	H. **Sports**	
Purchase of Himself and Family from Slavery and His Banishment from the Place of His Birth for the Crime of Wearing a Colored Skin is published in Boston, MA *Narrative of the Barbarous Treatment of Two Unfortunate Females, Natives of Concordia, Louisiana, by Joseph and Enoch, Runaway Slaves, As told by Mrs. Todd and Miss Harrington* is published in New York City	The Hutchinson family* tours the US and Great Britain performing antislavery songs (as well as popular ballads, temperance songs, and women's suffrage songs)			**1842**
Martin R. Delany (b Charleston, WV, 1812; d 1885) publishes *The Mystery*, an unsuccessful newspaper, Pittsburgh, PA Blacks in New Orleans, LA, begin publishing *L'Album Littéraire, Journal des Jeunes Gens, Amateurs de la Littérature*, a monthly review in French; it includes poems, stories, fables, and articles *Light and Truth of Slavery: Aaron's History of Virginia, New Jersey, and Rhode Island*	During the 1843–44 season Frank Johnson combines well-known bands and orchestras with prominent vocal artists of Philadelphia, PA, to perform in the first integrated concerts in the US	Norbert Rillieux receives a patent for a vacuum pan that evaporates saccharine juice in a more effective manner than currently being used; he receives a second patent for the vacuum pan three years later		**1843**

	A. General History	B. Education	C. Laws and Legal Actions	D. Religion
1843	the Anti-Slavery Convention in London, England			
	Free blacks establish the Grand United Order of Odd Fellows, which will become a major black fraternal organization; Peter Ogden leads the organization			
	Approval of the Webster-Ashburton Treaty: Britain and the US agree to keep ships off the African coast to suppress the slave trade there; agreement is not reached to restrict the trade within the Western Hemisphere			
	Rev. Henry Highland Garnet delivers his famous speech, "Call to Rebellion," at the National Negro Convention, Buffalo, NY; he encourages all blacks to adopt a "motto of resistance" to slavery and advocates armed rebellion			
	Blacks participate in a national political party convention for the first time at a meeting of the Liberty Party in Buffalo, NY; Rev. Henry Highland Garnet is a member of the nominating committee; Rev. Charles B. Ray is a convention secretary; Rev. Samuel Ringgold Ward leads the convention in prayer			
1844	Iowans announce that they will "never consent to open the doors of our beautiful state" to people of color because it would lead to "discord and violence"	A group of free blacks petition the Boston, MA, school committee to abolish separate schools for black children; their petition is denied		Baptists divide over sending slaveholding missionaries into the expanding Southwest
	George W. Bush (b Pennsylvania, 1790; d Washington Territory, 1863), explorer, leads white settlers into the Oregon Territory			Wood River Association in Illinois organizes the Colored Baptist Home Missionary Society; efforts result in the Western Colored Baptist convention, 1853–59
	James P. Beckwourth discovers a pass through the Sierra Nevadas to present-day California and the Pacific Ocean; the passage is later named Beckwourth Pass			Rev. William Capers reports that the Missionary Society has 68 stations, 22,063 black adults, and 80 missionaries under its auspices
	Rev. Jermain W. Loguen echoes Rev. Henry Highland Garnet's call for armed resistance to slavery			Rev. Nathan Ward, among others, petitions the African Methodist Episcopal Church at the general conference to allow female ministers; the petition is defeated

is published; the author is known only as Aaron

Moses Grandy's *Narrative of the Life of Moses Grandy, Late a Slave in the United States of America* is published

---

Archer Armstrong's *Compendium of Slavery As It Exists in the Present Day to Which Is Prefixed a Brief View of the Author's Descent* is published

After the death of musician Frank Johnson, Joseph Anderson takes over leadership of the Frank Johnson Brass and String Bands and maintains their excellence up to the time of the Civil War

Musician William Appo is commissioned by the Utica Glee Club of Utica, NY, to compose "John Tyler's Lamentation" during the 1844 presidential election campaign

William Henry "Master Juba" Lane (b New York, NY, c1825; d 1852), minstrel dancer, competes in a contest at the Bowery Amphitheatre in New York; it is advertised as a contest "between the two most re-

	A. General History	B. Education	C. Laws and Legal Actions	D. Religion
1844				Alexander Crummell, abolitionist, is ordained an Episcopal priest

White church members at the 21st General Convention of the Episcopal Church ignore all representatives from black churches

Rev. Stephen Gloucester organizes the Central Presbyterian Church in Philadelphia, PA, after a dispute with members of the Second African Presbyterian Church |
| **1845** | Frederick Douglass lectures in Great Britain on the abolition of slavery (through 1846)

In New Bedford, MA, the Lyceum excludes blacks from membership and assigns them to gallery seats; prominent lecturers Ralph Waldo Emerson,* Charles Sumner,* and Theodore Parker* boycott the museum

Robert Purvis, Sr., begins his presidency of the Pennsylvania Anti-Slavery Society; he continues until 1850

Jacob Dodson rides with Army officer John C. Frémont* from Los Angeles to Monterey, CA, to warn Gen. Stephen Kearney* of an uprising against Americans

Macon B. Allen (b Indiana, 1816; d Washington, DC, 1894) is admitted to the bar in Suffolk County, MA, and thus becomes the first black attorney in the state

Texas is admitted to the Union as a slave state

As US vice-consul, William Leidesdorff (b St. Croix, West Indies, 1810; d California, 1848) helps bring California under US rule

Pio Pico is named governor of California under Spanish rule | New York passes a law that allows for local option on separate schools and grants the same state subsidies allowed for white schools to towns that establish black schools

The Ohio Conference of the African Methodist Episcopal Church opens a manual labor school, Union Seminary, outside Columbus, OH | The Federal government makes a treaty with the Seminoles and the Creeks that provides for blacks and the Seminoles to live separately in a part of Creek country

A Texas law disfranchises blacks | Between 1845 and 1860 the black membership of the Baptist church increases from 200,000 to 400,000

White Baptists split over the issue of slavery

White northern Methodists undertake to discipline Bishop James O. Andrew* for holding slaves; southern Methodists withdraw from the Methodist Church to organize the Methodist Episcopal Church, South

The Rev. Charles B. Ray begins service at the Bethesda Congregational Church in New York City; he pastors there for over 20 years

Rev. Hiram R. Revels (b Fayetteville, NC, 1822; d Aberdeen, MS, Jan 16, 1901) is ordained a minister in the African Methodist Episcopal Church in Baltimore

Rev. Samuel E. Cornish organizes the Emmanuel Church in New York City

Rev. Elymas Rogers (b Madison, CT, Feb 10, 1815; d Jan 20, 1861) is ordained a minister in the Presbyterian Church |

1844

nowned dancers in the world, the original John Diamond* and the colored boy Juba"

1845

Frederick Douglass's *Narrative of the Life of Frederick Douglass* is published; it is the first of three autobiographies

Lewis Clarke's *Narrative of the Sufferings of Lewis Clarke, During a Capacity of More than Twenty-Five Years Among the Algerines of Kentucky, Dictated by Himself, Written by Joseph C. Lovejoy* is published

Les Cenelles, the first anthology of Negro verse in America, is published; it contains 82 poems written by 17 New Orleans, LA, poets

George Moses Horton's *The Poetical Works of George M. Horton, the Colored Bard of North Carolina* is published

Frances Ellen Watkins Harper's (b Baltimore, MD, 1825) *Forest Leaves* is published; there are no known copies of this work in existence

William Henry "Master Juba" Lane, minstrel dancer, receives top billing with a white minstrel company

Edmonia Lewis, sculptor (b Albany, NY, 1845; d 1890), will become the first black woman to study in Europe and to distinguish herself in art; she receives commissions to create busts of prominent people; her portrait busts in Roman classical style include those of Abraham Lincoln,* John Brown,* Charles Sumner,* and William Story;* among her better known works are marble statues titled *The Death of Cleopatra, The Marriage of the Madonna with Infant,* and *Forever Free*

J. Hawkins receives patent for "Gridiron"

	A. **General History**	B. **Education**	C. **Laws and Legal Actions**	D. **Religion**
1846	The Odd Fellows, a black fraternal organization, is formed		The New York legislature refuses to remove restrictions on black suffrage	From 1846 to 1861 the Methodist Episcopal Church, South, raises its black membership from 118,904 to 209,836
	James P. Thomas (b Nashville, TN, 1827; d Dec 17, 1913) opens a barbershop in his Tennessee home; over his lifetime he accumulates almost $100,000 in assets and property		Iowa law disfranchises blacks	The largest church in the Union Baptist Association is the Natchez Baptist Church, with 442 members: 380 are black
	Whig party leaders (including Samuel Seward,* Horace Greeley,* and Thurlow Weed*) support unrestricted black voting rights			Rev. Elymas Rogers begins serving as pastor of Plane Street Church in Newark, NJ; he remains there for 14 years
1847	Taxable total income of free blacks in Philadelphia, PA, is estimated at $400,000	The Missouri legislature prohibits the education of blacks	Dred Scott first files suit for his freedom in the Circuit Court of St. Louis, MO	Rev. James W. C. Pennington is named pastor of First (Shiloh) Presbyterian Church, New York City, and remains there until 1855
	Slaves replace striking white workers at the Tredegar Iron Works in Virginia	Ohio adopts a law that allows use of state funds for racially separate schools	US Secretary of State James Buchanan* declares that blacks seeking to leave the US may receive a special certificate "suited to the nature of the cause" rather than a passport; blacks are not US citizens	As late as this year, Rev. Charles Colcock Jones* of Georgia sounds warnings that American churches must give as much of their energies to black missions as they do to those overseas; otherwise the country will be in everlasting ruin
	Robert Gordon, former slave, starts a coal business in Cincinnati, OH		New Jersey law disfranchises blacks	
	William Leidesdorff launches the first steamboat to sail in San Francisco Bay, CA			The African Methodist Episcopal Church begins publication of *The Christian Herald,* a weekly magazine that is the first black periodical in continuous publication
	Liberia declares itself a sovereign state, independent from the control of Great Britain			
	Frederick Douglass is elected president of the New England Anti-Slavery Society			Rev. James P. Poindexter (b Richmond, VA, 1819) founds the Anti-Slavery Baptist Church in Ohio
	Robert Morris, Sr. (b Jun 8, 1823), one of the earliest black lawyers in the US, is admitted to the bar, Suffolk, MA			Rev. Noah Davis (1804–1867) organizes the Second Colored Baptist Church (later renamed Saratoga Street Baptist Church) in
	Gerrit Smith's* plan to create parcels from his thou-			

				1846

James McCune Smith's paper, "The Influence of Climate on Longevity, with Special Reference to Life Insurance," is published in New York

Lewis and Milton Clarke's *Narratives of the Sufferings of Lewis and Milton Clarke, Sons of a Soldier of the Revolution, During a Captivity of More than Twenty Years Among the Slaveholders of Kentucky, One of the So-called Christian States of North America; Dictated by Themselves* is published in Boston, MA

William Hayden's *Narrative of William Hayden, Containing a Faithful Account of His Travels for a Number of Years, Whilst a Slave in the South, Written by Himself* is published in Cincinnati, OH

John B. Meachum's *An Address to the Colored Citizens of the United States, Prefaced by a Narrative of the Author as a Slave in Virginia* is published

Aaron Connor leaves Frank Johnson's band and organizes his own group

Charles L. Reason writes antislavery tribute "Freedom"; this 48-stanza poem commemorates Thomas Clarkson,* a leading Quaker abolitionist, and declares liberty victorious over church- and state-supported slavery

---

1847

North Star, edited by Frederick Douglass, begins publication in Rochester, NY; cofounder Martin R. Delany serves as co-editor of this influential newspaper, and William C. Nell (b Boston, MA, 1816; d 1874) is publisher

Andrew Jackson's *Narrative and Writings of Andrew Jackson of Kentucky Containing an Account of His Birth and Twenty-Six Years of His Life While a Slave, Narrated by Himself, Written by a Friend* is published

Leonard Black's *Life and Sufferings of Leonard Black, a Fugitive from Slavery, Written by Himself* is published

Life and Opinions of Julius Melbourn; with Sketches of the Lives and Characters of Thomas Jefferson, John Quincy Adams, John Randolph, and Several Other Eminent American Statesmen is published; some believe this slave narrative is fictional; others, such as historian John

Peter O'Fake (b Newark, NJ, 1820), dance-band leader, performs with the Jullien Society in New York City

	A. **General History**	B. **Education**	C. **Laws and Legal Actions**	D. **Religion**
1847	sands of acres of land in NY fails to attract prospective black farmers because of their lack of capital and the infertility of the land itself			Baltimore, MD, with assistance from the Domestic Board of the Southern Baptist Convention
	George De Baptiste (b Fredericksburg, VA, 1814), a member of the Order of the Men of the Oppression, is a key figure in the Underground Railroad in Detroit, MI			
1848	Frederick Douglass is chosen to serve as president of the Colored Convention Movement, which advocates racial solidarity and economic development	Bensalem Sabbath School of the African Methodist Episcopal Church is instituted in Pennsylvania	Virginia postmasters are forced to inform police of the arrival of pro-abolition literature; it is turned over to authorities for burning	The general conference officially makes "Zion" part of the title of the New York African Methodist Episcopalian movement in order to avoid confusion with sister AME churches
	Frederick Douglass delivers a major address at a women's rights meeting in Seneca Falls, NY; this meeting spawns the women's suffrage movement		Illinois includes an anti-immigration provision in its constitution	A Baptist church in Georgetown, SC, has 798 black slave members, 33 white members; a Baptist church in Natchez, MS, has 380 black slave members and 62 white members
	Charles Langston is appointed deputy most worthy patriarch for the West, Sons of Temperance		A Virginia statute increases the term of imprisonment from 6 months to 12 months for whites who marry blacks	
	Ellen Craft, a mulatto woman, impersonates a slaveholder, and her husband, William Craft, acts as a servant in one of the most dramatic escapes of the period in Georgia		Slavery is forbidden in the Oregon Territory (includes the states of Washington, Idaho, and parts of Montana)	The Daughters of Zion, one of the African Methodist Episcopal women's societies, petitions the general conference to license female ministers, to no avail
	Henry "Box" Brown escapes to freedom after climbing into a box in Richmond, VA, and shipping himself to Philadelphia, PA		Ohio's "Black Laws" are reversed, giving blacks legal standing in courts and providing education for black children	Rev. Paul A. Trapier organizes and acts as first rector of the Calvary Episcopal Church, Charleston, SC, an all-black congregation
	James P. Beckwourth is the chief scout for Gen. John C. Frémont's* expedition		Wisconsin law disfranchises blacks	After withdrawing from the First African Baptist Church in 1840, a group of dissenters organize Twelfth Baptist Church of Boston (also known as Second African Baptist Church) under the pastorate of Rev. Leonard Grimes
	George Vashon is the first black attorney in the state of New York			
	Antislavery Democrats, Whigs, and Liberty Party members organize the Free Soil Party; the convention is attended by many black abolitionists; 291,263 votes are received for the "Free soil, free speech, free labor, and free men" platform			
1849	Harriet Tubman (b Mar 8, 1820; d Auburn, NY, Mar 10, 1913) escapes from slavery in Maryland; she returns 19 times to the	John Mifflin Brown is principal of the Union Seminary in Columbus, OH	Benjamin Roberts files the first integration suit in the US on behalf of his daughter Sarah who is denied admission to schools in	Rev. Morris Brown becomes pastor of an African Methodist Episcopal congregation in Charleston, SC

				1847
Blassingame, think it is authentic William Wells Brown's *Narrative of William Wells Brown, a Fugitive Slave, Written by Himself* is published				
Henry Watson's *Narrative of Henry Watson, a Fugitive Slave* is published	Robert Duncanson (b New York City, 1817; d 1872), the first black studio artist, paints *The Hudson River* mural	Lewis Temple (d 1854) of Massachusetts invents the toggle harpoon which becomes the standard harpoon of the New England whaling industry; he never receives a patent for his invention and dies penniless		**1848**
Rev. James W. C. Pennington's *The Fugitive Blacksmith; His Early Life, or, Events in the History of James W. C. Pennington . . . Formerly a*	Joseph William Braithwaite begins publishing his musical compositions; "St. Louis Greys Quick Step" will be published in 10 editions			**1849**

	A. **General History**	B. **Education**	C. **Laws and Legal Actions**	D. **Religion**
1849	South to bring out more than 300 slaves on the Underground Railroad

The Connecticut State Convention of Colored Men meets in New Haven, CT

William Wells Brown serves as a delegate to the Paris Peace Conference, France

John Horse founds the city of Wewoka in Mexico; it is later the Seminole capital that serves as a place of refuge for runaway US slaves

Joshua B. Smith (b Coatesville, PA, 1813) opens what will become a thriving catering business in Boston, MA

Rev. Stephen Smith (1797–1873), African Methodist Episcopal minister, and William Whipple own and operate one of the most successful coal and lumber yards on the East Coast, in Philadelphia, PA

The Woman's Association of Philadelphia, PA, is organized with the express purpose of raising money to support Frederick Douglass's newspaper *North Star*

At a Ohio state black suffrage meeting, a group of black women threaten to leave if they are denied participation in the discussion; it is later determined that they may participate | American Baptist Free Mission Society founds New York Central College (1849–c1860), McGrawville, NY; both blacks and whites are admitted to the student body and are appointed as faculty

Charles L. Reason serves for one year as professor of belles lettres, Greek, Latin, and French, and adjunct mathematics professor at New York Central College

John D. and Thomas T. White are the first black doctors to graduate from a medical school in the US, Bowdoin College, ME | Boston, MA; the Supreme Court of Massachusetts upholds the segregation, justifying the "separate but equal doctrine"; attorney Robert Morris, Sr., helps with the case

Maryland legislature enacts laws to override restrictions on the importation of slaves

Ohio lifts its ban on testimony by blacks in court

The California constitution outlaws slavery | Rev. Jarena Lee publishes *Religious Experience and Journal of Mrs. Jarena Lee, Giving an Account of Her Call to Preach the Gospel, Revised and Corrected from the Original Manuscript, Written by Herself* |
| **1850** | There are 3,638,808 blacks in the US (15.7% of the population); 37% of the free black population is classified as mulatto

The majority of the 1,792 free blacks listed in the New Orleans, LA, census are skilled workers; only 9.9% are unskilled laborers

Approximately 1,000 blacks live in California; 90 are women

There are 392 black women in non-slave states west of the Mississippi | Lucy Session earns a degree from Oberlin College, OH; she is possibly the first black woman to receive a college degree in the US | The Compromise of 1850 (the Clay Compromise) strengthens the 1793 Fugitive Slave Act, stating that federal officials must apprehend and return slaves who escape from slave states to free states and offers a fee for slaves apprehended; admits California into the Union as a free state; admits New Mexico and Utah with or without slavery, as their constitutions prescribe | The Union Church of Africans splits; as a result, the main body adopts the name the Union American Methodist Episcopal Church, and dissenters organize the African Union Church

Black Baptists number 150,000; the number increases to 500,000 by 1870

Rev. John Bailey Adger establishes the Second Presbyterian Church of Charleston, SC, as a branch for blacks |

Slave in the State of Maryland, United States is published in London, England; three editions are quickly sold

The Experiences of Thomas H. Jones, Who Was a Slave for Forty-Three Years, Written by a Friend as Given to Him by Brother Jones is published in Boston, MA

Henry Bibb's *Narrative of the Life and Adventures of Henry Bibb, an American Slave, Written by Himself* is published in New York City

Henry Box Brown's *Narrative of Henry Box Brown, Who Escaped from Slavery in a Box Three Feet Long, Two Wide, and Two and a Half High, Written from a Statement of Facts Made by Himself, With Remarks upon the Remedy for Slavery by Charles Stearns* is published in Boston, MA

Josiah Henson's autobiography, *The Life of Josiah Henson, Formerly a Slave, Now an Inhabitant of Canada, as Narrated by Himself,* is published; Henson is the reputed prototype for the character Uncle Tom in Harriet Beecher Stowe's* *Uncle Tom's Cabin*

William Wells Brown's *The Anti-Slavery Harp,* which includes several popular antislavery songs, is published

Minstrel dancer William Henry "Master Juba" Lane travels to England to join Pell's Ethiopian Serenaders

Rev. Daniel Payne's *Pleasures and Other Miscellaneous Poems* is published

Charles L. Reason, educator, reformer, and writer, publishes "Caste Schools," an essay appealing for equal educational opportunities

Sojourner Truth's *Narrative of Sojourner Truth, a Northern Slave, Emancipated from Bodily Servitude by the State of New York in 1828, Narrated to Olive Gilbert, including Sojourner Truth's Book of Life, and a Dialogue* is published

Over the decade 1850–60 Thomas Bethune "Blind Tom" (b Columbus, GA, 1849; d Hoboken, NJ, 1908) gains international recognition as a concert pianist

Blackface minstrel shows reach their zenith in American entertainment; these shows are performed by white men who blacken their faces with burnt cork, sing "Negro" or "Ethiopian" songs, dance, and tell jokes at the expense of slaves and other blacks

James Forten receives a patent for his "sail control" invention

Sojourner Truth (born Isabella Hurley), a slave in New York, became a gifted orator who devoted her life to abolitionist causes and equal rights for blacks. (Schomburg)

	A. **General History**	B. **Education**	C. **Laws and Legal Actions**	D. **Religion**
1850	Blacks in New York City form the short-lived American League of Colored Labourers, a union of skilled workers that promotes the commercial, mechanical, and agricultural education of blacks and maintains a fund to help black mechanics establish independent businesses; Rev. Samuel Ringgold Ward is named president			
	Rev. Henry Highland Garnet serves as a delegate to the World Peace Conference, Frankfurt, Germany			
	James Theodore Holly (b Washington, DC, 1829; d Mar 13, 1911), who will later become a clergyman, opens a bootmaking shop with his brother in Burlington, VT			
	Thomy Lafon (b New Orleans, LA, 1810; d 1893) opens a small store in New Orleans, LA; at the time of his death, his estate was worth almost half a million dollars			
	The passage of the revised Fugitive Slave Law increases the call for violent resistance to slavery among blacks			
	The Boston Vigilance Committee, which includes five blacks, organizes to resist the revised Fugitive Slave Law, MA			
1851	Lewis Hayden (b Lexington, KY, c 1815; d Boston, MA, April 7, 1889), member of the Boston Vigilance Committee, aided by Robert Morris, Sr., enters a Boston courtroom and rescues Frederic Wilkins, alias Shadrach, a fugitive slave who later escapes to Canada		Virginia enacts new laws requiring freed slaves to leave the state within a year or be enslaved again	Rev. Rebecca Jackson founds a predominantly black and female "outfamily" (or branch) of the United Society of Believers in Christ's Second Appearing (the Shakers), Philadelphia, PA; Jackson later writes a spiritual autobiography, *Gifts of Power*
	Black and white abolitionists enter a courtroom in Syracuse, NY, and rescue Jerry McHenry, a fugitive slave		Indiana includes an anti-immigration provision in its constitution	Jeremiah Asher's *Incidents in the Life of the Reverend J. Asher, Pastor of the Shiloh (Colored) Baptist Church, Philadelphia, U.S., with an introduction by Wilson Armstead* is published
	Armed free blacks resist kidnappers in Christiana, PA, and escape to Canada			

1850

Aaron J. R. Connor d; Connor, an important member of Frank Johnson's band, began to publish piano arrangements of band music and various songs after Johnson's death; among his best-known pieces are the dance compositions "Chestnut Street Promenade Quadrilles," "American Polka Quadrilles," and "The Evergreen Polka"

The Allen's Brass Band of Wilmington, NC, comprised of slaves and freed men, is active during the 1850s and 1860s

---

1851

The Illustrated Edition of the Life and Escape of William Wells Brown, written by William Wells Brown, is published

Thomas Smallwood's *Narrative of the Life of Thomas Smallwood, Written by Himself* is published

Lectures on American Slavery by Frederick Douglass is published

The *Colored Man's Journal* begins publication in New York City

The *Liberty Party Paper* merges with Frederick Douglass's *North Star*

Elizabeth Taylor Greenfield (b Natchez, MS, c1824; d 1876), the first black concert singer in the US, makes her debut for the Buffalo Musical Association and is immediately compared to Jenny Lind* and the other great sopranos of the era; Greenfield, who performs concerts in Europe and the US, is called the "Black Swan" because of her "remarkably sweet vocal tones and wide vocal compass"

The Colored American Institute for the Promotion of the Mechanic Arts and Sciences exhibits work of black mechanics in Philadelphia, PA

A. **General History**	B. **Education**	C. **Laws and Legal Actions**	D. **Religion**
1851 At the Eighteenth Annual Meeting of the American Anti-Slavery Society, Frederick Douglass breaks with William Lloyd Garrison* over the issue of moral suasion versus political participation as a strategy for abolition; Douglass joins the Liberty Party			
Rev. Henry Highland Garnet addresses several antislavery societies in England and Scotland			
Sojourner Truth delivers an unplanned fiery address (now known as "Ain't I A Woman?") at the Women's Rights Conference in Akron, OH			
Barney L. Ford (b Virginia, c1824), businessman, opens the United States Hotel in Greytown, CA			
Mifflin W. Gibbs (b Philadelphia, PA, 1823; d Little Rock, AR, 1915) is one of a group of prominent California blacks to publish a list of civil rights resolutions in the *Alto California,* the area's leading black newspaper			
Lewis Hayden and several others petition the Massachusetts legislature to erect a statue honoring American Revolution hero Crispus Attucks			
1852 Frederick Douglass delivers a speech, "What to the Slaves Is the Fourth of July?" Rochester, NY	Robert Purvis, Sr., of Philadelphia, PA, refuses to pay taxes for schools that exclude his children; local officials give in, and Purvis pays his taxes	California passes its own fugitive slave law	The *Christian Herald,* produced by the African Methodist Episcopal Church, is changed to the *Christian Recorder*
Charles L. Reason, Rev. Samuel E. Cornish, and Rev. James W. C. Pennington argue against an appropriation by the New York State legislature to assist the American Colonization Society with the emigration of blacks	Armand Lanusse (1812–1867) is the first elected principal of the Bernard Couvent Institute for Indigent Catholic Orphans, New Orleans, LA		Rev. Daniel Payne is elected bishop of the African Methodist Episcopal Church
Approximately 200 of the 3,500 blacks in Cincinnati, OH, are prosperous property owners whose total worth is $500,000	Myrtilla Miner* founds the Normal School for Colored Girls, Washington, DC		Union Baptist Church of Baltimore, MD, is founded by Rev. John Carey
	Ohio adopts a law that makes separate school facilities mandatory under certain conditions		

James Theodore Holly co-edits Henry Bibb's newspaper, *Voice of the Fugitive,* Canada's first black-owned newspaper

1851

Harriet Beecher Stowe's* *Uncle Tom's Cabin,* which portrays the plight of slaves in highly emotional language, is published; in its first year over 300,000 copies are sold

The Alienated American begins in Cleveland, OH, with William Howard Day as its editor

Martin R. Delany's *The Condition, Elevation, Emigration, and Destiny of the Colored People of the United States, Politically Considered* is published

James Watkins's *Narrative of the Life of James Watkins, Formerly a Chattel in Mary-*

Mary Ann Shadd Cary, attorney, editor, educator, and speaker. (MSRC)

1852

	A. **General History**	B. **Education**	C. **Laws and Legal Actions**	D. **Religion**
1852	Charles Langston establishes the St. Mark's Masonic Lodge in Ohio Napoleon Bonaparte* of France issues a decree against the slave trade			
1853	The National Council of Colored People is formed in Rochester, NY The first black YMCA is established in Washington, DC Armed blacks replace striking Irish workers on the Erie Railroad Sojourner Truth attends the Women's Rights Convention in New York City Charles Langston serves as the recording secretary and business agent for the Ohio Anti-Slavery Society John Jones (b Greene County, NC, 1816), a free black, campaigns against an Illinois law prohibiting the migration of free blacks into the state John Mercer Langston (b Dec 14, 1829; d Nov 15, 1897), a free black, begins studying law with abolitionist Hon. Philemon Bliss*	Sarah Douglass (b Philadelphia, PA, Sep 9, 1806; d Philadelphia, PA, Sep 8, 1882) takes charge of the girls primary department of the Institute for Colored Youth; she later initiates teaching physiology as a subject at the Institute	Rachel Parker wins her freedom in a Maryland state court Virginia imposes a poll tax on free blacks to obtain funds for their deportation to Africa	After several years of protest, St. Philip's Episcopal Church of New York obtains full voting rights in the Episcopal diocesan convention During his mission in New Orleans, Rev. John Mifflin Brown builds Morris Brown Chapel Rev. Henry Highland Garnet is the pastor of Stirling Presbyterian Church, Jamaica Rev. Henry McNeal Turner (b near Abbeville, SC, 1834; d 1915) is licensed to preach in the African Methodist Episcopal Church Dissenters from the African Methodist Episcopal Zion church form the Wesleyan Methodist Episcopal Zion Church; the two groups reunite in 1860 Black Baptists west of the Mississippi organize the Western Colored Baptist Convention (later renamed the Northwestern and Southern Baptist Convention) Levin Tilmon's *A Brief Miscellaneous Narrative of the More Early Part of the Life of Levin Tilmon, Pastor of a Colored Methodist Church, New York City* is published
1854	Anthony Burns (b Stafford County, VA, 1834; d Canada 1862), a fugitive slave, is arrested by US deputy marshals in Boston, MA; Bostonians attack the Federal courthouse attempting to rescue Burns; he is returned to slavery in Virginia in spite of an attempt by Boston citizens to purchase his freedom for	Presbyterians establish Ashmun Institute to prepare blacks for colonization in Africa; the institute receives its charter in 1866 and is renamed Lincoln University, PA Pennsylvania adopts an official provision for segregated schools	Kansas-Nebraska Act repeals Missouri Compromise of 1820 and permits admission, with or without slavery, of Kansas and Nebraska territories Elizabeth Jennings sues the Third Avenue Railroad Company; she wins $225 in damages and a court ruling that "colored per-	Rev. James A. Healy (b Jones County, GA, Apr 6, 1830; d Aug 15, 1900) is ordained a priest in Notre Dame Cathedral, Paris, France; he is the first black Catholic priest and later bishop *The Looking Glass: Being a True Narrative of the Life of the Reverend D. H. Peterson,*

130

1852

land, United States, Dictated to H.R. is published in Boston, MA

Mary Ann Shadd (Cary) (d 1893) publishes *A Plea for Emigration* to educate US blacks about emigrating to Canada

1853

William Wells Brown's *Clotel, or The President's Daughter,* the first novel by a black American, is published in London, England

Solomon Northup's *Twelve Years a Slave* is published

A Narrative of the Life and Travels of Mrs. Nancy Prince is published

Peter H. Clark becomes editor of the *Herald of Freedom,* Ohio

William G. Allen's *The American Prejudice Against Color: An Authentic Narrative, Showing How Easily the Nation Got into an Uproar, by William G. Allen, a Refugee from American Despotism* is published; the narrative details Allen's persecution from whites after he arries a white college student from Central College, NY

Narrative of the Life of William Green (Formerly a Slave), Written by Himself is published in Springfield, MA

When Mary Ann Shadd (Cary) becomes editor and financier of the *Provincial Freeman,* she is the first black woman editor of a newspaper in the US

George Walker's owner advertises his services in the *Richmond Daily Enquirer;* Walker, a slave-violinist, is a leading dance musician and according to the advertisement is "admitted by common consent, to be the best leader of a band in all eastern and middle Virginia"

The Luca "Singing Family" troupe—John Luca Jr. (b Milford, CT, 1832), Simeon Luca (b 1834), Alexander Luca (b 1836), and Cleveland Luca (b 1838)—perform at a convention in New York; they make their debut in the Old Tabernacle on Broadway performing before an audience of 5,000 for the New York Anti-Slavery Society

Black minstrel Japanese Tommy (né Thomas Dilworth) begins his career with Christy's Minstrels and later plays with other well-known groups, including Bryant's Minstrels, Sam Hague's Georgia Slave Troupe, and Charles Hick's Georgia Minstrels; Tommy, a singer, dancer, and violinist, is a dwarf

1854

Frances Ellen Watkins Harper's *Poems on Miscellaneous Subjects* is published

Thomas Anderson's *Interesting Account of Thomas Anderson, a Slave, "Taken from His Own Lips," Dictated to J.P. Clark* is published

William J. Anderson's *Life and Narrative of William J.*

Thomas Bowers (b Philadelphia, PA, 1826) is an outstanding tenor who acquires the title "the Colored Mario" because of the similarity between his voice and that of the Italian opera tenor Giovanni Mario*; under the management of singer Elizabeth Greenfield, Bowers tours with Greenfield

John V. DeGrasse, prominent physician, is admitted to the Massachusetts Medical Society

Allen M. Bland becomes an examiner in the US Patent Office; he is the father of musician James Bland

Henry Sigler of Galveston, TX, patents an improved

	A. **General History**	B. **Education**	C. **Laws and Legal Actions**	D. **Religion**
1854	$1,200; Burns is eventually bought and freed in North Carolina Frederick Douglass lectures at Western Reserve on "Claims of the Negro Ethnologically Considered" The New England Emigration Society is organized to settle ex-slaves in Kansas An abolitionist group in Milwaukee, WI, helps Joshua Glover, an alleged fugitive slave, escape from jail and eventually reach Canada George T. Downing erects the luxurious Sea Girt Hotel in Newport, RI; it is later destroyed by fire John P. Parker, inventor, erects a foundry near Ripley, OH; the foundry is still operating in 1981, although not under Parker family ownership John Mercer Langston is admitted to the Ohio bar Mifflin W. Gibbs organizes a California state convention of black men to protest disfranchisement; organizes again in 1855 and 1857 The Republican Party—created by Free Soilers, Whigs, and antislavery Democrats—is formed to oppose extension of slavery into the territories		sons, if sober, well behaved, and free from disease" may ride with whites in New York City horsecars	*a Colored Clergyman, Written by Daniel H. Peterson* is published
1855	Ann Wood, along with a group of Virginia slaves, escapes by wagon to Philadelphia, PA As of this year, 87% of employed blacks in New York City work in menial labor or unskilled jobs; this figure is representative of the economic conditions of free blacks in other Northern cities Black troops are assembled for Confederate service	After continued petitioning by abolitionists following *Roberts v. Boston,* the Massachusetts legislature ends the practice of racial separation in schools throughout the state	Philadelphia, PA, free blacks appeal to the US Congress for the right to vote Black Bostonians protest the absence of black jurors and call for equal judicial rights Maine, Massachusetts, and Michigan enact laws that forbid state involvement in the enforcement of federal Fugitive Slave Laws	James Theodore Holly is ordained a deacon in the Protestant Episcopal Church

1854

Anderson; or, Dark Deeds of American Slavery Revealed, Written by Himself is published in Chicago, IL

Thomas Jones's *The Experience and Personal Narrative of Uncle Tom Jones: Who Was for Forty Years a Slave; also, the Surprising Adventures of Wild Tom, a Fugitive Negro from South Carolina* is published in New York

Rev. Elymas Rogers writes the satirical 925-line poem "The Repeal of the Missouri Compromise Considered"

George Vashon, a well-educated attorney, reflects on Haitian subject matter in his poetry; writes "Vincent Ogé," the first narrative, nonlyrical poem by a black writer in the US; this epic poem of 139 lines is a poetic tribute to a black revolutionary

through Philadelphia, the Midwest, New York, and California

Elizabeth Greenfield gives a command performance before Queen Victoria* at Buckingham Palace, London, England

Edward M. Bannister (b New Brunswick, Canada, 1828) produces *The Ship Outward Bound,* his first commissioned painting; Bannister later becomes the first black to achieve recognition as a landscape painter

William Brady, composer and double-bassist, d; among his compositions are "Anthem for Christmas" and "Carnaval Waltz"

fishhook and later sells the patent for $625

1855

Frederick Douglass's *My Bondage and My Freedom; Part I: Life as a Slave, Part II: Life as a Freeman* is published

Rev. Elymas Rogers writes "A Poem on the Fugitive Slave Law"

John Brown's *Slave Life in Georgia: A Narrative of the Life, Suffering, and Escape of John Brown, a Fugitive Slave, Now in England* is published

Street whistler-guitarist Richard Milburn (b 1817) writes "Listen to the Mockingbird," one of the most popular songs of his time; this song is arranged and published by Septimus Winner* under the pen name Alice Hawthorne; 20 million copies are sold between 1855 and 1905; Milburn reportedly receives 20 copies of the song as payment and is credited only for writing the melody

A. **General History**	B. **Education**	C. **Laws and Legal Actions**	D. **Religion**
1855 Mary Ann Shadd Cary editor and outspoken abolitionist, gives address to and is elected corresponding member of the National Convention of Colored People, Philadelphia, PA Rev. James W. C. Pennington helps organize one of the early civil rights groups, the New York Legal Rights Association John Mercer Langston is elected clerk of Brownhelm township, Lorain County, OH; he is the first black elected to political office in the US The Liberty Party nominates Frederick Douglass for Secretary of State, the first black nominated for statewide office James Theodore Holly, representing the National Emigration Board, travels to Haiti to negotiate an emigration treaty US Congress grants George W. Bush a 640-acre tract, known as Bush Prairie, Puget Sound, Washington; Bush and his family settle there			
1856 The first black sailmaker is listed on the US Navy muster rolls Slave insurrections occur in Louisiana, Florida, Arkansas, Georgia, South Carolina, Virginia, Kentucky, and Tennessee Margaret Garner, Simeon Garner, their four children, and Simeon's parents flee from bondage in Kentucky to Cincinnati, OH; a group of slaveholders and US marshals trap the Garners at a relative's home; in a desperate act of defense, Margaret slits the throat of her baby daughter and strikes her two boys with a shovel in an effort to prevent them from returning to slavery; a court rules that Garner must return to her master;	The Methodist Episcopal Church founds Wilberforce University (later sold to the African Methodist Episcopal Church), the second collegiate institute founded for blacks Blacks in Ohio are granted control of their schools	Biddy Mason (d Jan 15, 1891) stays in California when her master returns to the South; the local court affirms her freedom, and she later becomes a prosperous landowner and community and civil rights activist A New Orleans, LA, ordinance forbids blacks and whites from playing cards or any other game together, in an effort to curtail interracial gambling	The African Methodist Episcopal Church has 20,000 members African Methodist Episcopal Conference recognizes slavery as "the highest violation of God's law" and pledges to do all it can to aid the enslaved Rev. James Theodore Holly of the Protestant Episcopal Church becomes the priest of St. Luke's Church, New Haven, CT

Samuel R. Ward's *Autobiography of a Fugitive Negro* is published

William C. Nell's *The Colored Patriots of the American Revolution* is published

William Grimes's *Life of William Grimes, the Runaway Slave, Brought Down to the Present Time, Written by Himself* is published

Charlotte Forten (b Philadelphia, PA, 1837) receives praise for her prize-winning poem "A Parting Hymn"

The Mirror of the Times, a San Francisco, CA, newspaper, begins publication; Melvin Gibbs serves as an editor

Rev. Peter Randolph's *Sketches of Slave Life; or, Illustrations of the "Peculiar Institution"* is published

In *The Key to Uncle Tom's Cabin*, Harriet Beecher Stowe* claims that the character of George Harris, Eliza's husband, is based on the personality of Lewis Clarke, ex-slave and abolitionist

Austin Steward's *Twenty-Two Years a Slave and Forty Years a Freeman, Embracing a Correspondence of Several Years While President of Wilberforce Colony* is published in Syracuse, NY

The Kidnapped and the Ransomed: Being the Personal Recollections of Peter Still and His Wife "Vina," After Forty Years of Slavery; Related to Kate Pickard, written by Peter Still, is published in Syracuse, NY

Peter O'Fake, band leader, serves as a choir director and chorister for St. Phillip's Episcopal Church in Newark, NJ

	A. **General History**	B. **Education**	C. **Laws and Legal Actions**	D. **Religion**
1856	in one final escape attempt, she throws herself and at least one child into the Ohio River; she is recaptured, separated from her family, and sold to a planter in the Deep South; hers is perhaps the most thoroughly recorded incident of slave resistance and infanticide While attacking slaveholders and those who favor proslavery legislation, Sen. Charles Sumner* (R-MA) is severely beaten on the Senate floor by a racist member of the House, Rep. Preston Brooks* (D-SC) Proslavery forces raid and sack Lawrence, KS; two years of violence follow in Kansas; eventually over 200 lives are lost			
1857		Ebenezer Don Carlos Bassett becomes principal of the Institute for Colored Youth (later renamed Cheney State College) in Pennsylvania; he holds this position until 1869 Harris-Stowe College is founded, St. Louis, MO	In *Dred Scott v. Sanford,* the US Supreme Court rules against citizenship for blacks; the Court rules that Dred Scott, a slave, cannot sue for his freedom in a free state because he is property and as such "has no rights a white man has to respect"; following the *Dred Scott* court decision, Dred Scott and his family are freed by their new owner, Taylor Blow,* May 26 Oregon includes an anti-immigration law in its constitution, barring blacks from admittance into the state Maine and New Hampshire continue to defy Fugitive Slave Laws and grant freedom and citizenship to people of African descent A New Orleans, LA, ordinance outlaws interracial brothels	The Presbyterian Church offends its southern membership by voicing displeasure of the Fugitive Slave Laws; southern members withdraw from the church Both white and black Methodist missionaries preach to whites and blacks assembled together in South Carolina
1858	William C. Nell, historian and abolitionist, organizes the first Crispus Attucks celebration, Boston, MA Thirty-four blacks and 12 whites attend John Brown's* antislavery			Rev. Hiram R. Revels is the first black pastor of the Madison Street Presbyterian Church in Baltimore, MD The American Baptist Missionary Convention passes

E. Literature, Publications, and The Black Press	F. The Arts	G. Science, Technology, and Medicine	H. Sports

Rev. James W. C. Pennington publishes *The Reasonableness of the Abolition of Slavery,* one of his few surviving sermons

John Thompson's *The Life of John Thompson, a Fugitive Slave: Containing His History of Twenty-Five Years in Bondage, and His Providential Escape: Written by Himself* is published

A Philadelphia, PA, free black, Frank J. Webb, authors *The Garies and Their Friends;* published in London, the novel deals with the caste system that blacks face

Rev. James Theodore Holly publishes his lecture, *Vindication of the Capacity of the Negro Race for Self Government and Civilized Progress,* in book form; Holly urges blacks to emigrate to "monarchial" Haiti where there is "far more security for the personal liberty and the general welfare of the governed . . . than exists in this bastard democracy the United States"

Thomas "Blind Tom" Bethune, pianist, makes his formal debut at Temperance Hall, Columbus, GA; James M. Bethune,* his master, binds Tom to an indenture contract even after Tom gains his freedom

Charles Ball's *Fifty Years in Chains; or, the Life of an American Slave* is published in New York City

Josiah Henson's *Truth Stranger than Fiction: Father Henson's Story of His Own*

William Wells Brown's *The Escape, or a Leap for Freedom* is the first play published by a black American

For his outstanding acting, Ira Aldridge is knighted in the Royal

	A. **General History**	B. **Education**	C. **Laws and Legal Actions**	D. **Religion**
1858	convention, Chatham, Canada

Abraham Lincoln* and Stephen A. Douglas* debate during the Illinois primary; Douglas, a Democrat, advocates popular sovereignty, letting states decide whether or not to exclude slavery constitutionally; Lincoln, a Republican, advocates Congressional prohibition of slavery in territories and gradual abolition of slavery in the US

Charles Langston and Oberlin College (OH) students rescue John Price, a fugitive, from slave catchers

Rev. Henry Highland Garnet is elected president of the African Civilization Society

Mifflin W. Gibbs moves to British Columbia where he establishes a store said to be the "first mercantile house there outside the Hudson Bay Company's fort"

Sojourner Truth bares her breasts before an audience to prove her sexual identity, Silver Lake, IN | | Minnesota law disfranchises blacks

After his master attempts to return him to Mississippi, Archy Lee flees but is apprehended by Sacramento, CA, authorities; the black leadership in the area, including Mary E. Pleasant, come to Lee's defense, but the state Supreme Court orders that Lee be returned to slavery; the decision is later overruled, and Lee is freed | a resolution instructing member churches to sever all ties with white Baptist associations |
| **1859** | John Brown,* militant abolitionist, tries to recruit Frederick Douglass for his planned Virginia raid, Chambersburg, PA; Douglass warns Brown that the raid is ill advised and declines to participate

John Brown* raids a Federal arsenal at Harpers Ferry, WV, in an attempt to strike a blow against slavery; five black men—Osborne Perry Anderson, John Anthony Copeland, Jr., Shields Green, Lewis Leary, and Dangerfield Newby—and 13 white men participate; a counterattack led by Col. Robert E. Lee* results in Brown's capture; Brown, Copeland, and Green are hanged at Charleston, WV | Sarah Jane Woodson Early (b Chillicothe, OH, Nov 15, 1825; d Aug 15, 1907), a graduate of Oberlin College, is the first black woman to serve on the faculty of an American university—Wilberforce University, OH

John F. Cook* organizes a school for free "children of color" in New Orleans, LA

Jeremiah B. Sanderson (b New Bedford, MA, Aug 10, 1821; d 1875), abolitionist and civil rights activist, heads the public schools for black children in San Francisco, CA | The Arkansas state legislature requires free blacks to choose between exile and enslavement

Blacks are excluded from Oregon when it enters the Union | There are 468,000 black church members in the South

There are an estimated 175,000 black Baptists in the US

Richard H. Cain (b Greenbrier County, VA, 1825; d Philadelphia, PA, 1887) is ordained a deacon in the African Methodist Episcopal Church

Rev. John Sella Martin, abolitionist, pastors First African Baptist Church, Boston, MA; he serves until 1861

The American Baptist Missionary Convention instructs member churches not to invite slaveholding ministers into their pulpits |

Life; with an Introduction by Mrs. H. B. Stowe* is published in Boston, MA

James Roberts's *Narrative of James Roberts, Soldier in the Revolutionary War and Battle of New Orleans* is published

Sally Williams's *Aunt Sally; or The Cross the Way to Freedom: Narrative of the Life of the Slave Girl and Purchase of the Mother of Reverend Isaac Williams of Detroit, Michigan* is published in Cincinnati, OH

Saxon Ernestinischen House Order

Harriet E. Wilson's *Our Nig; or, Sketches from the Life of a Free Black* is published and becomes the first novel by a black American published in the US; the book will be lost to readers for years until reprinted in 1983 with a critical essay by noted scholar Henry Louis Gates

The *Afro-American Magazine*, a literary journal, begins publication

A Narrative of the Life of Reverend Noah Davis, a Colored Man, Written by Himself is published in Boston, MA

Rev. Smith H. Platt's *The Martyrs and the Fugitive, or a Narrative of the Captivity, Sufferings, and Death of an African Family and the Es-*

The Negro (or Creole) Dramatic Company gives the first performance in an annual tradition that lasts until 1870

The Lucas and Hutchinson singing families, black and white respectively, perform together in Ohio; despite opposition to interracial concerts, the press for the most part responds favorably

Aaron J. R. Connor's composition, "My Cherished Hope, My Fondest Dream," is published in the *Anglo-African* magazine

A. **General History**	B. **Education**	C. **Laws and Legal Actions**	D. **Religion**

1859

The *Clothilde,* the last US slave-trading ship, arrives in Mobile Bay, AL

Martin R. Delaney and Robert Campbell lead the Niger Valley exploring party in Africa to find possible settlement locations for US blacks

The Sons of Hannibal, a fraternal society, is organized in Brownsville, PA

Charles Darwin's* *On the Origin of Species by Means of Natural Selection* is published; in the work he argues that all species have evolved through a long process of "natural selection" in which species with particular traits reproduce; this popular but controversial theory is applied socially to oppress people of color and is used to justify Anglo-Saxon domination and imperialism over oppressed people

Martin Delany, the first African-American commissioned as a major in the US Army, led an expedition through Liberia and Nigeria in 1859. (Schomburg)

1860

South Carolina is the first state to secede from the Union in opposition to Abraham Lincoln's election; Lincoln's Republican Party platform opposes slavery in the western territories

There are 4,441,830 blacks in the US (14.1% of the population); about four million are slaves

In southern urban areas and lower port cities in the South, a high percentage of free people of color work at skilled trades; 33% in Richmond, VA; 43% in Mobile, AL; 70% in Charleston, SC

As of this year, many southern free blacks own property: in Virginia, 1,200 rural free blacks control over 60,000 acres of land worth about $370,000; in Tennessee, free blacks own $435,000 worth of land and $250,000 worth of personal property

Attorney John Mercer Langston is elected to the Board of Education, OH

Fanny Jackson Coppin (b Washington, DC, 1837; d Philadelphia, PA, 1913) is one of 40 students selected to teach preparatory classes at Oberlin College, OH

Mary Smith Kelsey Peake (b Norfolk, VA, 1823; d 1862) is given protection from imprisonment or captivity by Union officers at Fort Monroe, VA, and becomes one of the first teachers in the South supported by the American Missionary Association

Two blacks in Worcester, MA, are named jurors— the first in Massachusetts's history

Frederick Douglass campaigns to repeal the New York State constitutional requirement that black men own $250 worth of real estate before they may vote

Methodist Protestant Church splits; the First Colored Methodist Protestant Church is formed

Rev. Anthony Burns, once a fugitive slave, is ordained a minister and pastors a church in Indianapolis, IN; later in the year he becomes pastor of the Zion Baptist Church, St. Catharines, Ontario, where he ministers to former slaves

Rev. Richard De Baptiste (b Fredericksburg, VA, Nov 11, 1831; d 1901), brother of George De Baptiste, is ordained a minister and pastors a black Baptist church in Ohio

Minister Henry McNeal Turner is ordained a deacon in the African Methodist Episcopal Church

Rev. G. W. Offley's *Narrative of the Life and Labors of the Reverend G. W. Offley, a Colored Man and Local Preacher, Written by Himself* is published

cape of Their Son is published in New York City

The *Anglo-African* magazine begins publication in New York City; Martin R. Delany's "Blake, or the Huts of America" appears in the first issue

Rev. Jermain W. Loguen's *The Reverend Jermain W. Loguen, as a Slave and as a Freeman: A Narrative of Real Life* is published in Syracuse, NY

Jane Brown's *Narrative of the Life of Jane Brown and Her Two Children; Related to the Reverend G. W. Offley* is published in Hartford, CT

William Craft's *Running a Thousand Miles for Freedom, or the Escape of William and Ellen Craft from Slavery* is published

Over this decade, Joseph William Postlewaite is identified by the press as director of at least four bands and orchestras

The Luca Family troupe disbands; Cleveland Luca, the piano accompanist, at the invitation of former President Joseph Jenkins Roberts* of Liberia, goes to Africa to teach music

An advertisement in *The Constitutionalist* of Augusta, GA, announces the sale of "four good carpenters, two plantation blacksmiths, a superior pressman—having had several years' experience in printing offices in Macon—and a first-rate ostler"

The Brooklyn Excelsiors is the first black baseball team to tour the US

A. **General History**	B. **Education**	C. **Laws and Legal Actions**	D. **Religion**
1860 Sixty black suffrage clubs from Brooklyn and Manhattan, NY, campaign against unfair voting laws Sixty-seven percent of North Carolina's slave-holding families have fewer than 10 slaves each; 72% of the total population hold no slaves Twenty-five percent of all US slaves live on plantations with fewer than 10 slaves Blacks make approximately 500 trips from Canada to the US South to bring out slaves Robert Adger (b Charleston, SC, 1837), political activist, organizes the Fraternal Society, an equal rights group for South Carolina blacks Harriet Tubman begins to appear at antislavery lectures and speaks for women's rights			
1861 The Civil War begins when Confederates attack Fort Sumter, SC, Apr 12 The Union Army officially rejects black volunteers but blacks fight in both land and sea battles Robert Smalls (b Beaufort, SC, Apr 5, 1839; d Feb 22, 1915), Union Navy pilot, watches preparations for attack on Fort Sumter and declares: "This, boys, is the dawn of freedom for our race" Clara Barton* and five black women aid wounded soldiers in the passage through Baltimore, MD Gen. Charles Halleck,* commander of the Military Department of the West, orders troops to send fugitive slaves already within their lines back to their masters Elizabeth Keckley (b Dinwiddie, VA, c1818; d 1907) begins service as the	Mary S. Peake opens the first of schools sponsored by the American Missionary Association on the first floor of Brown Cottage at Fortress Monroe, VA (later becomes Hampton Institute)	The Confiscation Act frees slaves under the Union Army's control *The Constitution of the Confederate States of America,* like the *US Constitution,* counts slaves as three-fifths of a person in taxation and representation The Secretary of the Navy* authorizes the enlistment of black slaves Cleveland, OH, law officials arrest Lucy Bagby, a fugitive slave; US marshals swear in 150 special deputies to prevent her release; a federal commissioner orders her return to her former master in West Virginia; she is eventually rescued by a Union Army officer when her owner tries to take her further south after the Civil War begins US Congress provides that a patent may be issued to a slaveholder for a slave's invention if the slave-	

E. **Literature,
Publications, and
The Black Press**   F. **The Arts**

G. **Science,
Technology,
and Medicine**   H. **Sports**

1860

1861

Frederick Douglass's editorial in *Douglass' Monthly* calls for a harsher war and says: "Let the slaves and free colored people be called into service, and formed into a liberating army, to march into the South and raise the banner of emancipation among the slaves"

Linda Brent, alias Harriet Jacobs, publishes *Incidents in the Life of a Slave Girl Written by Herself*

Osborne Perry Anderson's (b Pennsylvania, 1830) *A Voice from Harper's Ferry* is published; the book documents his eyewitness account of the raid on Harpers Ferry, WV

Edward Jones serves as editor of *The Sierra Leone Weekly Times and West African*

Israel Campbell's *Bond and Free; or, Yearnings for Freedom, from My Green Briar House; Being the Story of My*

Adah Menken (b Chartrain, LA, 1835; d Aug 1868) shocks audiences when, dressed in a body stocking, she stars as the Tartar youth in the debut of *Mazeppa;* Menken later takes the show to the western states to entertain miners and earns almost $500 per performance

During the Civil War, slaves who belong to a slaveholder named Dixie create the song "I Wish I Was in Dixie"

Against his will, Tom Bethune performs a concert for wounded Confederate soldiers who seek to preserve slavery and fight against slaves in the Union Army

Robert S. Duncanson paints *Land of the Lotus Eaters,* which wins the praise of the Duchess of Sutherland* and numerous critics of art journals

	A. **General History**	B. **Education**	C. **Laws and Legal Actions**	D. **Religion**
1861	dressmaker, personal maid, and confidante of Mary Todd Lincoln,* the First Lady of the US; she remains with Mrs. Lincoln until 1868

Sarah Parker Remond (b Salem, MA, 1826) begins service as vice president of the Salem Female Anti-Slavery Society, MA

Gen. Benjamin F. Butler* refuses to return three escaped slaves at Fortress Monroe, VA, because they are "contraband of war"

Rev. James Theodore Holly, along with 110 other blacks, emigrates to Haiti

William C. Nell is appointed a Boston post office clerk, becoming the first black person to hold a federal civilian job

Nicholas Biddle, who is stoned to death by a mob, is the first black killed in the Civil War, Baltimore, MD

Jefferson Davis* is elected president of the Confederate States of America

William Tillman, a cook on the *S. J. Waring,* is captured with his ship's crew by the Confederate ship *Jefferson Davis;* Tillman escapes, kills his captors, and helps return the schooner to New York; he reportedly receives a stipend worth more than $5,000 for meritorious service | | holder takes an oath that his or her slave actually invented the device; blacks receive their own patents after the Civil War

Secretary of State William H. Seward,* at the request of Charles Sumner,* grants a passport to Robert Morris, Jr.; the passport is worded: "Robert Morris, Jr., a citizen of the U.S."; the State Department issues a passport to Rev. Henry Highland Garnet, stating that he is a "citizen of the United States"

Gen. George B. McClellan,* Ohio Department, issues orders to suppress any black who attempts insurrection

Dr. Thomas Jinnings, a prominent physician from Charleston, SC, is arrested for "intrading himself among the white congregation" while attending a charity fair; the charges are dropped after white parishioners testify on his behalf | |
| **1862** | Without official authorization, Union general David Hunter* organizes the First South Carolina volunteers, the first all-black regiment—chiefly ex-slaves

Robert Smalls sails armed Confederate steamer, the *Planter,* out of Charleston, SC, and presents it to the Union Navy

First Kansas Colored Volunteers are repulsed and driven off by superior force | Salmon Foster,* US secretary of treasury, convinces Pres. Abraham Lincoln* that teachers and agriculture superintendents should be sent to the South Carolina Sea Islands to prepare the black population there for citizenship; his idea becomes known as the Port Royal Project; Charlotte Forten is the first black teacher hired for the mission | The US Congress bans slavery in the District of Columbia and US territories; slaveholders are compensated for their lost "property"

The US Congress approves the enlistment of freed blacks in the Army; the Enlistment Act provides that whites will receive $13 a month pay and blacks half that amount; pay is not equalized until 1864 | Four hundred members of Shiloh Baptist Church of Fredericksburg, VA, seek refuge with Union troops in Washington, DC; twenty-one of them establish Shiloh Baptist Church of Washington, DC

First North Carolina African Methodist Episcopal Church is established, New Bern, NC

Bishop Daniel Payne ordains Richard H. Cain an |

Life in Bondage and My Life in Freedom is published in Philadelphia, PA

James Wilkerson's *History of His Travels and Labors in the United States as a Missionary, in Particular That of Union Seminary, Located in Franklin County, Ohio, Since He Purchased His Liberty in New Orleans Louisiana* is published in Columbus, OH

Alexander Crummell's *The Relations and Duties of Free Colored Men in America to Africa* is published

Alexander Crummell's *The Future of Africa* is published

	A. **General History**	B. **Education**	C. **Laws and Legal Actions**	D. **Religion**
1862	of Confederate Soldiers at Island Mound, MO; it is the first engagement for black troops in the Civil War Susie King Taylor, at 14, becomes the first black American army nurse in the US First authorized black combat unit is organized: the First Regiment Louisiana Heavy Artillery Formation in New York of the Freedmen's Relief Association, dedicated to assist black slaves in making transition to freedom; groups in Philadelphia, Cincinnati, and Chicago consolidate as the American Freedmen's Aid Commission Nathaniel Gordon* of New York is found guilty and is hanged for slave trading Harriet Tubman serves as a spy, scout, and guerilla leader for the Union Army Caesar Antoine, army officer, organizes Company I, Seventh Louisiana Colored Regiment (Corps d'Afrique) A full regiment of free men of color, the First Regiment of Louisiana (later renamed the 73rd Regiment U.S.C. Infantry), enters the Civil War for the Union Elizabeth Keckley, White House seamstress, gives $200 to the Contraband Relief Association, a group founded and headed by Keckley, to assist former slaves who have come to Washington, DC Jeremiah B. Sanderson is one of the organizers of the Franchise League in San Francisco US recognizes Liberia as a free nation	Mary Jane Patterson (b Raleigh, NC, 1840; d Washington, DC, 1894) is the first black woman to receive a bachelor's degree from an accredited college in the US, Oberlin College, OH The New England Freedmen's Aid Society is organized to promote the education of blacks, Boston, MA The Morrill Act grants each state warrants for 30,000 acres per US congressional representative and senator to found industrial colleges; the provision gives a boost to predominantly black colleges LeMoyne-Owens College is founded, Memphis, TN	Pres. Abraham Lincoln* recommends a plan for the gradual compensated emancipation; Congress declares that the US should cooperate with any state that adopts abolition The US Congress forbids Union officers and soldiers to aid in the capture and return of fugitive slaves Pres. Abraham Lincoln* receives the first group of blacks to confer with a US president on public policy; he is criticized by northern blacks for urging them to emigrate to Africa or Central America The US Congress repeals the 1810 ban on black mail carriers Union Gen. David Hunter* issues a proclamation freeing slaves of Georgia, Florida, and South Carolina; Pres. Abraham Lincoln* revokes the proclamation The Secretary of War authorizes Gen. Rufus Saxton* to arm up to 5,000 slaves The US Congress ratifies the Second Confiscation Act grants freedom to all slaves whose masters support the Confederacy Pres. Abraham Lincoln* issues a preliminary Emancipation Proclamation, freeing all slaves in those states rebelling against the Union California blacks are granted the right to testify in cases where white men are defendants	elder in the African Methodist Episcopal Church Rev. Jeremiah Asher's *An Autobiography, with Details of a Visit to England, and Some Account of the Meeting Street Baptist Church, Providence, R.I., and of the Shiloh Baptist Church, Philadelphia, Pa.* is published
1863	In a Union assault on Port Hudson, LA, two black regiments (First and Third Native Guards) make six	Fannie M. Richards (b Fredericksburg, VA, Oct 1, 1841; d 1922) opens an academically rigorous	The Emancipation Proclamation goes into effect Jan 1, except in 13 parishes in Louisiana, 48 counties in	Pres. Abraham Lincoln* appoints Rev. Henry McNeal Turner as a chaplain in the army, First Regi-

E. **Literature, Publications, and The Black Press**   F. **The Arts**   G. **Science, Technology, and Medicine**   H. **Sports**

1862

During the Civil War, thousands of enslaved African Americans fled Southern plantations to join Union forces. (LC)

1863

Slave Life in Virginia and Kentucky, or Fifty Years of Slavery in the Southern States of America, By Francis Fedric,

After the passage of the Emancipation Proclamation, freedom songs that have been discreetly sung

A. **General History**	B. **Education**	C. **Laws and Legal Actions**	D. **Religion**
1863 unsuccessful charges on rebel fortification; Capt. André Callioux (b c1820) is the hero of the day despite lack of success	black private school in Detroit, MI; she teaches there until 1871 when the school is integrated	West Virginia, 7 counties in eastern Virginia, and all border states; it frees slaves in states in rebellion against the Union	ment, US Colored Troops; he is thought to be the first black to hold this position
The 54th Massachusetts Volunteers regiment charges Fort Wagner in Charleston, SC; in this battle Sgt. William H. Carney wins the Congressional Medal of Honor for bravery	With an appropriation from the Freedman's Bureau, Thomas Jefferson Ferguson (b Essex County, VA, Sep 15, 1830; d 1887) helps to establish the Albany Enterprise Academy for blacks in Ohio	The War Department authorizes Massachusetts to recruit black troops; the 54th Massachusetts Volunteers is the first northern black regiment	St. Francis Xavier Church is the first established for black Catholics, Baltimore, MD, and the oldest black Catholic church in the US
Three black regiments and a small detachment of white troops repulse a division of Texans in a battle at Milliken's Bend, LA	Benjamin W. Arnett (b Brownsville, PA, 1838; d 1906) is the first black teacher in Fayette County, PA	Blacks are officially accepted in the Union Army and Navy; the active recruitment of black soldiers begins under the title "United States Colored Troops"	
Two black infantry regiments, First and Second South Carolina, capture and occupy Jacksonville, FL, causing panic along the southern seaboard; eight black regiments play important roles in the siege of Port Hudson, which, since Vicksburg has fallen, gives the Union control of the Mississippi River and cuts the Confederacy into two sections	Bishop Daniel Payne buys Wilberforce University from the Methodist Episcopal Church for the African Methodist Episcopal Church, thereby making Wilberforce the first black-controlled college in the US	First National Conscription Act is passed; it does not exclude blacks	
Frederick Douglass, T. Morris Chester, and William Wells Brown recruit in Massachusetts, New York, Pennsylvania, and New Jersey for the 54th Massachusetts Regiment		A Mississippi act increases the penalty for permitting slaves to sell their own labor, with part payment to the master, from $50 to $500 fine and 60 days in jail	
White mobs destroy a black orphanage in New York		The Confederate Congress passes a resolution calling black troops and their officers criminals; captured black soldiers may be put to death or put into slavery	
Pres. Abraham Lincoln* sends ships to bring back 500 black settlers from Cow Island, Haiti, as colonization attempts fail		An Alabama law increases the fine for furnishing liquor to slaves from $50 to $500 or imprisonment for one to five years	
Mary Ellen Pleasant (b Virginia, Aug 19, 1814) leads a successful civil rights campaign and petition drive in California; she fights for the passage of a law guaranteeing blacks the right to testify in court		A group of free men of color from Louisiana appeal to Governor George F. Shepley* for permission to vote	
The First Kansas Colored Volunteers assist in the Union's routing of rebel		A Texas statute provides that a white person convicted of selling, giving, or lending dangerous weapons to slaves will be confined at hard labor in the penitentiary for two to five years	

an Escaped Slave, alias Charles Lee is published

In the *Anglo-African* magazine George L. Ruffin reviews William Wells Brown's *The Black Man; His Antecedents, His Genius, and His Achievements,* noting Brown's misinformation and omissions

John Anderson's *Story of John Anderson, Fugitive Slave* is published

The Story of Dinah, as Related to John Hawkins Simpson, After Her Escape from the Horrors of the Virginia Slave Trade, to London is published

by slaves now are openly sung by freedmen and freedwomen; songs such as "No More Auction Block for Me," "I Want Some Valiant Soldier," "Babylon Is Fallen," and "The Massa Run" are dated to this Civil War period

The Ninth US Regiment compose "They Look Like Men of War," the first battle hymn of black soldiers recorded during the Civil War, Camp Stanton, Benedict, MD

A. **General History**	B. **Education**	C. **Laws and Legal Actions**	D. **Religion**
1863 forces after an encounter at Honey Springs, Indian Territory Harriet Tubman leads Union troops in a raid along the Combahee River, SC Slavery is abolished in all Dutch colonies Poor white immigrants in New York City attack blacks in so-called anti-draft riots, leaving almost 1,200 people killed; the riots are spurred by a new provision that exempts from military service men who can pay $300, thereby drafting poorer men who cannot pay to avoid military service; these immigrants accuse blacks of initiating the Civil War Mary Elizabeth Bowser, servant in the Confederate White House, feigns mental illness while she garners information from conversations between Confederate president Jefferson Davis* and guests; Bowser reads dispatches as she dusts, and recites from memory everything she learns to the Van Lew* family, Union sympathizers			
1864 The First Kansas Colored Volunteers break through Confederate lines at Poison Spring, AR; the unit will sustain heavy losses when captured black soldiers are murdered by Confederate troops as opposed to being taken as POWs, the standard treatment for captured whites Sailor Joachim Pease wins the Congressional Medal of Honor John Lawson emerges as a naval hero during the Battle of Mobile Bay when he mans his duty station and keeps Union guns operative despite serious injury; he later is awarded the Medal of Honor One hundred forty-four blacks from 18 states meet	Rebecca Lee (later Crumpler) (b Richmond, VA, 1833), one of the first black female physicians in the US, graduates from the New England Female Medical College, Boston, MA Blanche K. Bruce (b Farmville, VA, 1841; d Washington, DC, 1898), future US Senator, organizes the first school for blacks in the state of Missouri, Hannibal, MO Pres. Abraham Lincoln* signs a bill mandating the creation of public schools for blacks in Washington, DC	Congress passes a bill granting black soldiers equal pay, arms, equipment, and medical services The Fugitive Slave Laws are repealed Maryland's constitution is amended to abolish slavery Free men of color in New Orleans, LA, petition Pres. Abraham Lincoln* for the right to vote The Louisiana Territory legislature, elected under the auspices of occupying Union forces, votes to abolish slavery, but denies suffrage to blacks Mary Ellen Pleasant sues the San Francisco Car Company because of rude	Rev. John Mifflin Brown is elected corresponding secretary of the Parent Home and Foreign Missionary Society of the African Methodist Episcopal Church Rev. Francis L. Cardozo (b Charleston, SC, Feb 1, 1837; d 1903) becomes pastor of the Temple Street Congregational Church in New Haven, CT Rev. Jermain W. Loguen is elected the thirteenth bishop of the African Methodist Episcopal Zion Church Rev. Henry Highland Garnet is named pastor of the Fifteenth Street Presbyterian Church, Washington, DC; he serves for two years

E. Literature,
   Publications, and
   The Black Press   F. The Arts

G. Science,
   Technology,
   and Medicine   H. Sports

1863

Publication of the *New Orleans Tribune,* the first black daily newspaper, begins in French and English

J. D. Green's *Narrative of the Life of J. D. Green, a Runaway Slave from Kentucky, Containing an Account of His Three Escapes, in 1839, 1846, and 1848* is published

George Vashon writes "A Life-Day," an allegory of southern history

James Mars's *Life of James Mars, a Slave Born and Sold in Connecticut, Written by Himself* is published

John Jones's 16-page pamphlet *The Black Laws of Illinois and a Few Reasons Why They Should Be Repealed* is published

John "Picayune" Butler, banjo player on the streets of New Orleans in the 1820s, d in New York City; his best known song is "Picayune Butler Is Going Away"

The Georgia Minstrels, the first permanent black minstrel troupe, is formed when W. H. Lee* organizes a troupe of 15 ex-slaves in Macon

	A. **General History**	B. **Education**	C. **Laws and Legal Actions**	D. **Religion**
1864	in Syracuse, NY, for a National Convention of Colored Citizens of the US; the group issues an appeal, written by Frederick Douglass, for the right to vote Sojourner Truth is appointed as counselor to freed blacks in Arlington Heights, VA Fourteen of 37 Congressional Medal of Honor winners at the Battle of Chaffin's Farm are black Benjamin W. Arnett organizes the Faith and Hope League of Equal Rights at Brownsville, Washington, DC, Uniontown, Pittsburgh, Monongahela City, and Allegheny, PA Gov. O. P. Morton* of Indiana commissions Mary Ann Shadd Cary as an army recruiting officer, making her the only officially recognized woman recruiter during the Civil War		treatment given her and other black women The Mississippi legislature approves slave marriages and declares their offspring "legitimate for all purposes" A federal law granting freedom to the enslaved wives and children of black soldiers is enacted	Rev. James Walker Hood successfully converts the congregation at Andrew Chapel in New Bern, NC, to Zion Methodism; Hood then seeks to make North Carolina "the capital of Zion Methodism in the South" New England and Maryland Friends (Quakers) organize the Baltimore Association for the Moral and Educational Improvement of the Colored People and begin work among newly freed blacks by operating a store charging wholesale prices only and conducting day, evening, and Sunday schools
1865	Slavery officially ends in Texas when Gen. Gordon Granger* arrives in Galveston with Union forces; the emancipation of blacks in Texas will later be commemorated in "Juneteenth" celebrations Pres. Abraham Lincoln* approves Martin R. Delany's plan to place a black regiment in the field and makes Delany an army major; the plan is never carried out because the war comes to an end The 62nd US Colored Troops and two white regiments fight in the last battle of the Civil War at White's Ranch, TX; Sergeant Crocket is believed to have been the last man to shed blood in the War The Civil War ends with the surrender of Confederate general Robert E. Lee* at Appomattox Courthouse 250,000 blacks have served in the Union forces; 38,000 have lost their lives	Patrick Healy becomes the first black American to receive a Ph.D. when he receives his degree from Lauvain, Belgium Rev. Francis L. Cardoza is named principal of the Avery Normal Institute, Charleston, SC Fanny Jackson Coppin is named principal of the female department of the Institute for Colored Youth, Philadelphia, PA Fannie M. Richards, Detroit's first black public school teacher, is appointed to teach at the Colored School No. 2, MI Shaw University is founded, Raleigh, NC Atlanta University is founded, Atlanta, GA Virginia Union University is founded, Richmond, VA Bowie State College (later, University) is founded, Bowie, MD	Gen. William T. Sherman* issues Field Order No. 15, which sets aside parts of South Carolina and Florida exclusively for blacks, parcelling no more than 40 acres of land for each family; most blacks will never receive their land because Pres. Andrew Johnson* will later reverse the policy US Congress ratifies the 13th Amendment which abolishes slavery The Bureau of Refugees, Freedmen, and Abandoned Lands, or the Freedmen's Bureau, is established by Congress to aid refugees and newly emancipated blacks Jefferson Davis,* president of the Confederacy, signs the Negro Soldier Law allowing the use of slaves as soldiers in the defense of the South, with consent of their masters Andrew Johnson,* the new president, announces his Reconstruction Plan:	Rev. Richard H. Cain is one of the first African Methodist Episcopal missionaries to arrive in Charleston, SC, during the Civil War Rev. Henry Highland Garnet is the first black to deliver a sermon on the abolition of slavery before the US House of Representatives The Colored Primitive Baptists in America secedes from the Primitive Baptist Churches of the South in Columbia, TN Pennsylvania Freedmen's Relief Association has 60 missionaries working among blacks and a budget of $250,000 per year Rev. Benjamin W. Arnett is licensed to preach in the African Methodist Episcopal Church at the Baltimore Annual Conference in Washington, DC

1864

1865

George Moses Horton's last work, *Naked Genius,* a volume of poetry, is published

The Colored American is the first black newspaper in the South, Augusta, GA

Charles Hicks, showman, organizes another group known as the Georgia Minstrels in Indianapolis, IN

Ira Aldridge makes his last professional visit to London, England, to play the leading role in Shakespeare's *Othello*

Nellie Brown (b Dover, NH, 1845) is the leading soprano of four white churches in Boston, MA

Hyram S. Thomas, chef, invents the potato chip, also known as the Saratoga chip, Saratoga Springs, NY

	A. **General History**	B. **Education**	C. **Laws and Legal Actions**	D. **Religion**
1865	With funds appropriated by Congress, blacks organize and operate the National Freemen's Relief Association and the National Association for the Relief of Destitute Colored Women and Children The government-chartered Freedmen's Bank opens, Washington, DC Benjamin W. Arnett organizes the Grand United Order of Odd Fellows, Brownsville, PA Alonzo J. Ransier (b Charleston, SC, Jan 3, 1834; d 1882) is one of the first blacks appointed to serve as registrar of US elections Pres. Abraham Lincoln* proposes enfranchising blacks who are either veterans or educated Pres. Abraham Lincoln* is assassinated at Ford's Theatre in Washington, DC John S. Rock of Boston, MA (b Salem, NJ, 1825; d Dec 3, 1866), lawyer and dentist, is the first black to practice before the US Supreme Court		complete abolition of slavery, repudiation of the Confederate war debts, and nullification of the ordinances of secession The first interracial jury in the US indicts Jefferson Davis* for treason; the case is set for trial in 1868 Former Confederate states issue "Black Codes," restricting rights and freedom of freedmen/women Wisconsin, Connecticut, and Minnesota deny suffrage to blacks Capt. William Bayliss,* abolitionist, is released from jail after being convicted of violating the Fugitive Slave Act in Virginia	A split in the American Union Methodist Church results in the formation of the Union American Methodist Episcopal Church (UAME) in the United States and elsewhere Bishop Daniel Payne establishes the South Carolina Conference of the African Methodist Episcopal Church Rev. Jonathan C. Gibbs (b Philadelphia, PA, 1827) pastors Zion Presbyterian Church and organizes Zion School in Charleston, SC Shiloh Baptist Association, consisting of all-black congregations in southern Virginia, is organized at Ebenezer Church, Richmond, VA
1866	Thomy Lafon gives two lots as a site for the first orphanage of the Louisiana Association for the Benefit of Colored Orphans Isaac Myers (b Baltimore, MD, Jan 13, 1835; d 1891) organizes black caulkers in Baltimore, MD, into the Chesapeake Marine Railway and Dry Dock Company, which employs at least 300 blacks Bands of southern white men begin a campaign of terror against blacks and white Republicans; these groups, among them the Knights of the White Camelia, the White Brotherhood, and the Knights of the Ku Klux Klan, use threats and sometimes physical force to return "white rule" in the South	The American Missionary Association, supported by Congregationalist churches, founds Fisk University, Nashville, TN Howard University is founded as Howard Seminary in Washington, DC The Freedman's Aid Society establishes Shaw University (later renamed Rust College) for free blacks in Holly Springs, MI Lincoln University is founded in Jefferson City, MO Sarah Woodson Early is appointed teacher of English and lady principal and matron at Wilberforce University, OH Edward Waters College is founded, Jacksonville, FL	The first Civil Rights Act declaring freed blacks to be US citizens and nullifying black codes passes in Congress over Pres. Andrew Johnson's* veto The US Congress passes the Southern Homestead Act, opening public lands in Alabama, Mississippi, Louisiana, Arkansas, and Florida to all settlers regardless of race	The African Union First Colored Methodist Protestant Church of America is established when the African Union Church merges with the First Colored Methodist Protestant Church Black Baptists of North Carolina organize the first state religious convention The First African Richmond Church in Virginia receives its first black pastor, Rev. James Henry Holmes, who has been serving as a deacon since 1855 Bishop Daniel Payne publishes *Semi-Centenary and the Retrospection of the AME Church in the United States of America*, the first historical record of the African Methodist Episcopal Church

| E. **Literature, Publications, and The Black Press** | F. **The Arts** | G. **Science, Technology, and Medicine** | H. **Sports** |

1865

			1866
The *Atlantic Monthly* publishes "Freedman's Story," written by William Parker, a runaway slave, detailing his escape from Maryland to Pennsylvania with his brother	The *London Art Journal* selects Robert S. Duncanson as one of the outstanding landscape artists of the day		At the first Jerome Handicap at Belmont Park, NY, jockey Abe Hawkins wins, riding Watson; at Saratoga Springs, NY, Hawkins wins the third Travers Stakes race and Travers Handicap riding Merrill
Rev. Richard H. Cain becomes editor of the *South Carolina Leader,* the first black newspaper in the state published after the Civil War	Basile Barés (b New Orleans, LA, 1846) performs several piano selections, including his composition "La Seduisante," at the Louisiana Fair		
	Pianist Thomas "Blind Tom" Bethune begins his first European tour		

	A. **General History**	B. **Education**	C. **Laws and Legal Actions**	D. **Religion**
1866	James P. Beckwourth is allegedly poisoned by the Crow after he tries to leave them In one of the bloodiest outbreaks of the Reconstruction Era, three days of racial violence in Memphis, TN, leave 46 blacks and 2 whites dead, 5 black women raped, and hundreds of black homes, churches, and schools destroyed by fire; tension had been building in this financially troubled city since the development of of Fort Pickering, a base for black troops; in general, whites, particularly poor whites, felt threatened by the presence of black soldiers who patrolled the city Edward G. Walker and Charles L. Mitchell (b Hartford, CT, Nov 10, 1829; d 1912) are elected to the Massachusetts House of Representatives, the first blacks elected to a state legislature After immigrating to Canada, Mifflin W. Gibbs is elected to the Common Council in Victoria, British Columbia A group of washerwomen organizes a strike and submits a formal petition to the mayor of Jackson, MS, demanding wages commensurate with the cost of living The National Labor Union is organized in Baltimore, MD; the organization supports such ideas as an eight-hour work day, workers' cooperatives, greenback monies, and equal pay for white women and all blacks; support for the NLU fails quickly	Rhode Island law ends segregated public schools Barber-Scotia College is founded, Concord, NH St. Augustine's College is founded, Raleigh, NC		Rev. James A. Healy is appointed pastor of St. James Catholic Church, the largest church in Boston, MA; he serves for nine years The Freedmen's Aid Society of the Methodist Episcopal Church is organized
1867	William Still (b New Jersey, Oct 7, 1821), abolitionist and businessman, leads a campaign against segregated streetcars in Philadelphia (begins in 1859 by exposing injus-	The Peabody Fund is established to provide endowments, scholarships, and teacher and industrial education for newly freed slaves across the nation	The US Congress passes the First Reconstruction Act, which divides the former Confederacy into five military districts; requires states to ratify "Civil War Amendments" and to	Black Baptists organize the Consolidated American Baptist Convention, the first attempt to create a black Baptist national assembly separate from white-dominated groups

| E. **Literature, Publications, and The Black Press** | F. **The Arts** | G. **Science, Technology, and Medicine** | H. **Sports** |

1866

E. Literature, Publications, and The Black Press	F. The Arts	G. Science, Technology, and Medicine	H. Sports	
When William Wells Brown's *Clotel* is published in the US, in Boston, MA, the story is altered: President Thomas Jefferson* is replaced by an anonymous senator	George L. White,* a teacher at Fisk University, Nashville, TN, tours with students—11 singers and a pianist—and a teacher chaperon to raise money for a Fisk building pro-	H. Lee receives a patent for an animal trap

W. A. Deitz receives a patent for a shoe invention | At the National Association of Baseball Players convention, delegates vote to exclude black players and teams from membership | **1867** |

	A. **General History**	B. **Education**	C. **Laws and Legal Actions**	D. **Religion**
1867	tices in a letter to the press); the campaign ends when the Pennsylvania legislature passes a law forbidding discrimination in streetcars John Mercer Langston begins serving as inspector-general for the Freedman's Bureau, Washington, DC Businessman Joshua B. Smith becomes the first black member of the Saint Andrew's Lodge of Freemasons of Massachusetts	The American Baptist Home Missionary Society establishes Augusta Institute (later Morehouse College) in Atlanta, GA Northern Presbyterians organize Biddle University (later Johnson C. Smith) in Charlotte, NC George Vashon is the first black professor at Howard University Talladega College, the first black college in Alabama, is founded by the American Missionary Association as a primary school	hold new elections for state offices; and includes voting rights for male citizens regardless of "race, color, or previous condition" in rebel states; enforcement of the act provides blacks with majority vote in most southern states, while alliances of blacks and white Republicans lead to control in border states The first legal voting by a black man is recorded in New Orleans, LA Iowa and Dakota grant suffrage to black males; Ohio rejects it A Philadelphia, PA, law forbids segregation in public conveniences	Benjamin W. Arnett is ordained a deacon in the African Methodist Episcopal Church Saratoga Street Baptist Church in Baltimore, MD, joins the Union Baptist Church Rev. John Jasper (1812–1901), a former slave, organizes the Sixth Mount Zion Baptist Church in a horse stable in Richmond, VA
1868	P. B. S. Pinchback and James J. Harris are the first black delegates at a Republican Party convention; they will participate in the nomination of Ulysses S. Grant* for president Oscar J. Dunn (b Louisiana, c1821), ex-slave, becomes Lt. Gov. of Louisiana Blacks hold the majority of seats in both South Carolina's constitutional convention and the first assembly of its new Reconstruction government The American Anti-Slavery Society dissolves Race riots in New Orleans, Opelousas, and St. Bernard Parish, LA Louisiana Democrats return to power after the Ku Klux Klan initiates a campaign of terror against the Republican party and newly emancipated blacks; the KKK threatens violence if blacks and Republicans vote Rev. Francis L. Cardozo is elected South Carolina secretary of state	Hampton Institute is opened by ex-Union officer Samuel Chapman Armstrong,* Hampton, VA Methodists establish, through the Freedmen's Aid Society, 29 schools for blacks with 51 teachers and 5,000 students in Virginia, Kentucky, Tennessee, Mississippi, Louisiana, Alabama, and Georgia George F. T. Cook (b Washington, DC, Jun 18, 1835; d Washington, DC, 1912) is superintendent of the Colored Public Schools of Washington and Georgetown and serves until 1900 Jeremiah B. Sanderson heads the Stockton (CA) school for black children until 1874 African Methodist Episcopal bishop James W. Hood is appointed an agent of North Carolina's Board of Education and Assistant Superintendent of Public Instruction John Mercer Langston founds and organizes the law department at Howard University	Congress passes the 14th Amendment, which grants blacks full citizenship and equal civil rights; it is later ratified	The American Missionary Association has as many as 532 missionaries and teachers working among blacks and a budget of $400,000 per year Delegates at the African Methodist Episcopal general conference vote to establish a Board of Stewardesses, "the first and only official organizational position for women in the denomination" Bishop Daniel Payne is elected president of the Methodist Pastors Association Olivet Baptist Church, under the pastorship of Rev. Richard De Baptiste, becomes Chicago's largest black congregation Benjamin T. Tanner begins editing the *Christian Recorder* and serves until 1884

1867

William Still's *A Brief Narrative for the Rights of the Colored People of Philadelphia in the City Railway Cars* is published

Robert Brown Elliott (b Aug 11, 1842; d New Orleans, LA, Aug 9, 1884) is an editor of the *South Carolina Leader*, a black Republican paper

William Francis Allen,* Charles Pickford Ware,* and Lucy McKim Garrison* publish *Slave Songs of the United States*, which consists of folk songs collected from slaves; this is the first collection of slave songs to be published in book form

William Wells Brown's *The Negro in the American Rebellion* is published

gram; over the next decade the Fisk Jubilee Singers perform the religious music of slaves to raise $1,500 for the construction of Jubilee Hall; the fund-raising goal is achieved in 1875

1868

The slave narrative *Behind the Scenes by Elizabeth Keckley, Formerly a Slave, but More Recently a Modiste and Friend to Mrs. Abraham Lincoln; or Thirty Years a Slave and Forty Years in the White House* is published

The *South Carolina Leader* becomes the *Missionary Record*, a newspaper that often criticizes white carpetbaggers

Frances Anne Rollins's (b 1845) *The Life and Times of Martin Robinson Delaney*, a biography, is published under the pseudonym Frank Rollins

William Henry Lewis is the first black chosen to play on Amherst (MA) College's football team

	A. **General History**	B. **Education**	C. **Laws and Legal Actions**	D. **Religion**
1868	When the Louisiana State legislature convenes, more than half of its members are black	Zionites move Rush Academy to Fayetteville, NC, and rename it Zion Hill Collegiate Institute		
	Rev. Jonathan C. Gibbs becomes the Florida secretary of state	Sarah Parker Remond, abolitionist, earns her medical degree in Florence, Italy		
	Caesar Antoine becomes a Louisiana state senator; he serves until 1872	Howard University Medical School in Washington, DC, is chartered and supported by the US government as a training institution for blacks in the medical professions; the coeducational medical school is open to both blacks and whites		
	Robert Brown Elliott is admitted to the South Carolina bar and opens the first of four law offices			
	The Republican Party platform omits the demand for black suffrage in northern states			
		Alexander T. Augusta (d 1890), the former head of what comes to be known as Freedman's Hospital, becomes the first black faculty member at a US medical school, Howard University Medical College		
		The Alabama state legislature votes to segregate its schools		
		Tougaloo College is founded, Tougaloo, MS		
		Claflin College is founded, Orangeburg, SC		
1869	After the Civil War, US Congress establishes four regiments of black enlisted men: Ninth and Tenth Cavalries and 24th and 25th Infantries; the Native Americans against whom they fight in the West call them "Buffalo Soldiers" because their hair, matted by dust and sweat, is thought to resemble buffalo fur; the 24th and 25th Infantry Regiments are formed with mostly white officers, the regiments patrol the plains and participate in the opening of the western frontier	Theophile T. Allain (d New Orleans, LA, 1917), businessman, opens schools for blacks and whites in West Baton Rouge Parish, LA		Black members of the integrated Cumberland Presbyterian Church agree to establish an all-black congregation, later known as the Colored Cumberland Presbyterian Church; it will later be known as Cumberland Presbyterian Church of America
		Fanny Jackson Coppin is appointed principal of the Institute for Colored Youth in Pennsylvania, becoming the first black woman in the US to head an institution of higher learning		The Reformed Zion Union Apostolic Church is organized at Boydton, VA, by Elder James R. Howell of New York, minister of the African Methodist Episcopal Zion Church
	The first convention of the Colored National Labor Union advocates the purchase and distribution of land for emancipated blacks	Clark College is founded in Atlanta, GA		Amanda Berry Smith (b Long Green, MD, Jan 23, 1837; d 1815) begins conducting revivals at the African Methodist Episcopal churches in New York and New Jersey; Smith will work as an evangelist and
		Centenary Biblical Institute (later Morgan State University) in Baltimore, MD, is chartered to train black ministers		
		The first student YMCA is formed at Howard University, Washington, DC		

160

E. Literature, Publications, and The Black Press	F. The Arts	G. Science, Technology, and Medicine	H. Sports

1868

''Three Years a Negro Minstrel,'' written by Ralph Keeler, one of the most prominent blacks on stage during the 19th century, is published in the *Atlantic Monthly*

Scenes in the Life of Harriet Tubman, as told by Sarah Bradford, is published

Frances Ellen Watkins Harper's epic poem ''Moses, a Story of the Nile'' is published

Lew Johnson (d 1910) organizes his first minstrel group in St. Louis, MO; Johnson becomes one of the most successful show managers

	A. **General History**	B. **Education**	C. **Laws and Legal Actions**	D. **Religion**
1869	The American Equal Rights Association, an umbrella universal suffrage organization, splits over the question of black male suffrage versus white female suffrage; the National Woman Suffrage Association and the American Woman Suffrage Association are subsequently formed	Charles B. Purvis is appointed to the medical faculty of Howard University, becoming the second black American instructor of medicine at an American university		is often called "The Singing Pilgrim" and "God's Image in Ebony"
	Rev. Hiram R. Revels is elected to the Mississippi state Senate			
	George L. Ruffin (b Richmond, VA, 1834; d 1886) is the first black to graduate from Harvard Law School, is one of the first blacks admitted to practice law in Boston, MA, and is elected to the Massachusetts state legislature			
	Ebenezer Don Carlos Bassett is the first black appointed to diplomatic service when he becomes US minister to Haiti			
	Alexander G. Clark (b Washington County, PA, 1826; d Monrovia, Liberia, 1891) becomes one of the vice presidents of the Republican state convention of Iowa			
	Robert Brown Elliott is appointed assistant adjutant-general of South Carolina; he is responsible for establishing and maintaining a state militia to protect black and white citizens from the Ku Klux Klan			
	Charles L. Mitchell, former Civil War soldier, is the first black appointed inspector of customs in Boston, MA			
	Following his election, John Willis Menard of Louisiana pleads with Congress to seat him along with his Republican running mate Lionel Allen Sheldon*; Sheldon is accepted, Menard is rejected because of alleged voting fraud			

	A. General History	B. Education	C. Laws and Legal Actions	D. Religion
1869	Louisa Rollin (b 1858; d Toledo, OH, Mar 1943), woman's suffragist, addresses the South Carolina House of Representatives asking the members to support universal suffrage for all races			
1870	Rev. Hiram R. Revels (R-MS) is chosen to fill the US Senate seat left vacant by Confederate president, Jefferson Davis,* becoming the first black US senator; his term lasts one year

Henry Adams (b. Newton Co., GA, 1843) is elected president of the Committee and the Colonization Council of North Louisiana; he serves for ten years; the committee encourages blacks to vote Republican and later takes an emigrationist position

Rev. Francis L. Cardozo is named director of the Greenville and Columbia Railroad and is elected president of the Grand Council of Union Leagues of South Carolina

Emanuel Stance (b Charleston, SC, 1848; d 1887), US Army, leads an attack against the Kickapoo (Native American group) in Texas; he receives a Medal of Honor for his service

Joseph H. Rainey (b Georgetown, SC, Jun 21, 1832; d 1887) (R-SC) is elected to the US Congress

Robert Brown Elliott (R-SC) is elected to the US Congress

Alonzo J. Ransier (R-SC) becomes South Carolina's first black lieutenant governor

The city of Detroit, MI, has its first all-black jury

Benjamin S. Turner (b near Weldon, NC, Mar 17, 1825; d Selma, AL, 1894) (R-AL) is elected to the US Congress | The American Baptist Home Mission Society establishes Benedict College in Columbia, SC

John Mercer Langston becomes dean of Howard University's Law School; he serves until 1873

Allen University is founded, Columbia, SC | The first series of Enforcement Acts are passed to control the Ku Klux Klan and guarantee civil and political rights to blacks through federal courts

The US Congress passes the 15th Amendment, which grants male suffrage regardless of "race, color, or previous condition of servitude"; the enfranchisement of men sparks a debate within the white and black communities over woman's suffrage

Mississippi and Louisiana repeal laws against interracial marriage | Black southern Methodists form a new denomination: the Colored Methodist Episcopal Church of America; two bishops—Henry Miles and Richard H. Vanderhorst—are elected at the general conference, Jackson, TN

In an effort to keep its members from converting to one of the black Methodist denominations, the Methodist Episcopal Church, South, authorizes racially separate conferences

African Methodist Episcopal bishop Daniel Payne ordains Benjamin W. Arnett an elder

The United Free Will Baptist Church is organized

Rev. Richard Henry Boyd (b Dick Gray, Richmond, VA, 1843; d Nashville, TN, Aug 23, 1922) organizes the first Negro Baptist Association in Texas |

THE FIRST COLORED SENATOR AND REPRESENTATIVES.
In the 41st and 42nd Congress of the United States.

164

E. Literature, Publications, and The Black Press	F. The Arts	G. Science, Technology, and Medicine	H. Sports	
George Vashon's "Ode on the Proclamation of the 15th Amendment" is published		T. Elkins receives a patent for a dining, ironing table and quilting frame combined	Viro "Black Sam" Small makes his wrestling debut at Owney's Bastile in New York; he is the first known black wrestler in the US	**1870**
		H. Spears receives a patent for a portable shield for infantry		
		J. W. West receives a patent for a wagon		
		Employed as a chief draftsman, Lewis Latimer (b Chelsea, MA, Sep 4, 1848; d Flushing, NY, Dec 11, 1928) makes the drawings for Alexander Graham Bell's* telephone		
		Upon graduation from the New York Medical College for Women, Susan McKinney Stewart becomes the third black female doctor in the US		
		At the annual meeting of the American Medical Association, members, arguing that their membership is personal and social rather than professional, vote to ban blacks from membership		

	A. General History	B. Education	C. Laws and Legal Actions	D. Religion
1870	Ex-soldiers in Shreveport, LA, form a secret intelligence organization called "The Committee"; for four years the Committee (approx. 500 men) travels to Mississippi and Texas encouraging freed persons to vote Rev. Henry McNeal Turner is appointed Coast Inspector of Customs and US Government Detective The Philadelphia (PA) Colored Women's Christian Association is founded; it is possibly the first black YWCA Blanche K. Bruce is elected to the Mississippi state senate Robert C. DeLarge (b Aiken, SC, 1842; d 1874) (R-SC) is elected to the US Congress Josiah T. Walls (b Winchester, VA, Dec 30, 1842) (R-FL) is elected to the US Congress Jefferson F. Long (b Georgia, 1836; d 1900) (R-GA) is elected to the US Congress			
1871	Cong. Jefferson F. Long (R-GA) is the first black to deliver a speech before the US House of Representatives James Wormley (b. Washington, DC, 1819; d Boston, MA, 1884) opens an establishment that becomes known as Wormley's Hotel, one of the most prestigious hotels in Washington, DC; the Rutherford B. Hayes* and Samuel Tilden* Compromise of 1877 is reached at this hotel The "ride-in" campaign in Louisville, KY, ends when mixed seating is permitted on streetcars; the campaign began one year earlier when black men boarded a car and refused to leave until arrested	Jeremiah B. Sanderson, Mifflin W. Gibbs, and other California blacks organize a statewide conference to work for integrated schools Bishop John Mifflin Brown of the African Methodist Episcopal Church organizes Payne Institute in Columbia, SC (later renamed Allen University) Alcorn College (later Alcorn State University) is founded, Rodney, MS; Rev. Hiram R. Revels is appointed president of the school Mary Jane Patterson is the first principal of Preparatory High School (later Dunbar High School), Washington, DC's premier school for blacks	Pres. Ulysses S. Grant* suspends the writ of habeas corpus in nine counties in South Carolina in an effort to restrain the Ku Klux Klan The US Congress enacts the Ku Klux Klan Act, designed to enforce provisions of the 14th Amendment	

The Fisk Jubilee Singers tour Europe and America, taking black spiritual music to new and larger audiences

Compositions by pianist Thomas "Blind Tom" Bethune are included in *The Complete Catalogue of Sheet Music and Musical Works*

L. Bell receives a patent for a locomotive smoke stack

A. **General History**	B. **Education**	C. **Laws and Legal Actions**	D. **Religion**
1871 (black women were permitted aboard); in *Fox v. Central Passenger Co.*, US District Court rules in favor of integrated cars			
Isaac Myers is named president of the Colored National Labor Union			
Pres. Ulysses S. Grant* appoints John Mercer Langston to the Board of Health of Washington, DC			
Mifflin W. Gibbs establishes a law practice in Little Rock, AR			
Mary Ann Shadd Cary speaks before the US House of Representatives Judiciary Committee, addressing woman's suffrage			
1872 The Republican National Convention is held in Philadelphia, PA; delegates Robert B. Elliott (chair of the South Carolina delegation), Joseph H. Rainey, and John R. Lynch deliver addresses	Charlotte E. Ray (b NYC, Jan 13, 1850) is the first black woman in the US to graduate from a university law school (Howard University Law School); using the initials C.E. to avoid sexual discrimination, she later applies for and is admitted to the District of Columbia bar, becoming the first black woman regularly admitted to practice law		Rev. Harvey Johnson (1843–1923) assumes the pastorate of the Union Baptist Church, Baltimore, MD; prior to this, Johnson served as a missionary to freed persons in Virginia from 1863 to 1868
Thomas Jefferson Ferguson, educator, author, and politician, is elected to the Albany (OH) City Council			Biddy Mason and others found the First African Methodist Episcopal Church, Los Angeles, CA
John Jones, wealthy businessman, is a member of the Cook County (IL) Board of Commissioners until 1875; he is perhaps the first black in the state of Illinois to win an important elective office	John H. Conyers is the first black midshipman admitted to the US Naval Academy, but he does not graduate		Lena Doolin Mason (b Quincy, IL, May 8, 1864) is called to preach at age seven; Mason, who becomes an evangelist in the African Methodist Episcopal Church, is credited with having influenced over 1,500 persons to convert to Christianity
P.B.S. Pinchback (b near Macon, GA, May 10, 1837; d 1921) becomes the first person in US history to be elected simultaneously to the House of Representatives and the Senate, although he is never seated due to supposed election irregularities	Rev. Jonathan C. Gibbs becomes Florida's superintendent of public instruction		
Alonzo J. Ransier (R-SC) is elected to the US Congress	Booker T. Washington (b Apr 5 1856; d Tuskegee, AL, Nov 14, 1915) enters Hampton Institute, VA		
John Mercer Langston is elected to the Freedmen's Savings and Trust Company Board of Trustees	Paul Quinn College is founded in Austin, TX; it is moved to Waco in 1877		

| E. **Literature, Publications, and The Black Press** | F. **The Arts** | G. **Science, Technology, and Medicine** | H. **Sports** |

1871

Frederick Douglass's *U.S. Grant and the Colored People* is published

William Still's *Underground Railroad,* a documentation of the activities of the Pennsylvania Society for the Abolition of Slavery, is published

Francis Ellen Watkins Harper's *Sketches of Southern Life* is published

The Fisk Jubilee Singers, soloists, and a local Boston choir of 150 voices appear at the World Peace Jubilee in Boston, MA

Student singers from Hampton Institute (VA) go on a winter tour to raise money for the school

Cleveland Luca, former soprano of the Luca Family Troupe and composer of the Liberian National Anthem, d, Liberia

T. J. Byrd receives patents for the improvement in holders for reins for horses; for an apparatus for detaching horses from carriages; and for improvement in neck yokes for wagons

Thomas J. Marshall receives a patent for a fire extinguisher

Elijah "The Real" McCoy (b 1844) receives a patent for an automatic lubricator

T. Elkins receives a patent for a chamber commode

John W. "Bud" Fowler (b Fort Plain, NY, Mar 16, 1858) becomes the first black salaried player in organized baseball and possibly the first black player in the major leagues when he joins a white team in New Castle, PA

1872

	A. General History	B. Education	C. Laws and Legal Actions	D. Religion
1872	Francis L. Cardozo is elected state treasurer of South Carolina (and again in 1874) Caesar Antoine becomes lieutenant governor of Louisiana; he serves until 1876 Richard H. Gleaves (R-SC) is lieutenant governor of South Carolina Rev. Richard Cain (R-SC) is elected to the US Congress The Freedmen's Bureau ceases operations P. B. S. Pinchback, LA state senator, is appointed acting governor of the state when Henry Clay Warmoth* is suspended because of impeachment proceedings George Washington (b Frederick County, VA, Aug 15, 1817; d 1905), pioneer, founds a settlement in Centralia, WA James T. Rapier (b Florence, AL, 1837) (R-AL) is elected to the US Congress			
1873	Slavery is abolished in Puerto Rico Mifflin W. Gibbs is appointed county attorney in Little Rock, AR, but resigns after he is elected municipal judge Lewis Hayden is elected to the Massachusetts state legislature John R. Lynch (b Concordia Parish, LA, 1847; d Chicago, IL, 1939) (R-MS) is elected to the US Congress A. K. Davis becomes lieutenant governor of Mississippi James Hill is secretary of state of Mississippi	Thomas W. Cardoza becomes Mississippi's superintendent of education The American Baptist Home Mission Society establishes Roger Williams University, Nashville, TN John Mercer Langston is vice president and acting president of Howard University until 1875 Richard T. Greener, first black graduate of Harvard University, is named professor of metaphysics at the University of South Carolina Bennett College is founded as a coeducational school in the basement of St. Matthew's Methodist Episcopal Church, Greensboro,	In the Slaughterhouse Cases, the US Supreme Court rules that the "due process" clause of the 14th Amendment grants protection of national, not state citizenship, rights Cong. Alonzo J. Ransier (R-SC) speaks forcefully in favor of the Civil Rights Act sponsored by Sen. Charles Sumner;* the bill is eventually watered down and an important clause concerning integrated education is deleted; Ransier refuses to vote for the weakened bill	Bishop Daniel Payne is elected senior bishop of the African Methodist Episcopal Church Rev. Richard H. Cain owns and edits *The Missionary Record*, an AME hymn book that contains spiritual songs, chants, liturgies, rituals, and other church ordinances

170

E. **Literature,**
  Publications, and
  The Black Press
      F. **The Arts**
G. **Science,**
  Technology,
  and Medicine
     H. **Sports**

1872

1873

Alberry Whitman's (1851–1902) *Leelah Misled* and *Essay on the Ten Plaques and Other Miscellaneous Poems* are published; Whitman, a minister in the African Methodist Episcopal Church, is known for his long narrative and melodramatic style

Edward Mitchell helps found the Providence Art Club; his studio later becomes the Rhode Island School of Design

The Original Colored America Opera Troupe produces an opera, *The Doctor of Alcantra*, in Washington, DC

	A. General History	B. Education	C. Laws and Legal Actions	D. Religion
1873		NC; Bennett will become a college exclusively for women in 1926 University of Arkansas, Pine Bluff, is founded Simmons University Bible College is founded, Louisville, KY Charles B. Purvis (b Philadelphia, PA, 1842; d Boston, MA 1929), credited with saving Howard University's medical school, remains on staff as an unpaid faculty member during the school's financial crisis Wiley College is founded, Marshall, TX		
1874	Frederick Douglass is named president of the failing Freedmen's Bank, Washington, DC; in a desperate act to save the bank, Douglass invests his own money and appeals to the US Senate Finance Committee for aid; confidence in the bank plummets, causing it to fold with 61,000 black depositors losing nearly $3 million In the absence of the Speaker of the House, Cong. Joseph H. Rainey (R-SC) becomes the first black to preside over the US House of Representatives The Boston Banneker Club, a scholarly literary society, is organized, MA Jeremiah Haralson (b Muscogee County, GA, Apr 1,1846) (R-AL) is elected to the US Congress John A. Hyman (d Washington, DC, 1891) (R-NC) is elected to the US Congress, becoming the first black congressman from North Carolina Charles E. Nash (b Opelousas, LA, May 23, 1844) (R-LA) is elected to the US Congress	The American Missionary Association organizes Straight University in New Orleans, LA (later renamed Dillard University) The American Baptist Home Missionary Society establishes Shaw University, Raleigh, NC Rev. Patrick F. Healy, a Jesuit priest, is named president of Georgetown University, Washington, DC; he serves until 1882 Black children begin attending the California public school system Alabama State University is founded, Montgomery, AL Edward Bouchet of Yale University is the first black to be elected to Phi Beta Kappa	Arkansas repeals the law against interracial marriages The Virginia legislature rearranges election districts and local government systems, thereby reducing the political power of blacks Cong. Robert Brown Elliott (R-SC) delivers a brilliant speech in favor of the Civil Rights Bill, countering and defeating Cong. Alexander S. Stephens,* ex–vice president of the Confederacy, who had delivered earlier in the day a speech opposing the bill	Rev. James Theodore Holly becomes the first black bishop in the Episcopal church when he is consecrated a missionary bishop of Haiti at Grace Church in New York City

1874

William Wells Brown's *The Rising Son* is published

William Still's *An Address on Voting and Laboring*, a pamphlet detailing Still's opposition to a Republican candidate and support for a reform candidate for the office of mayor in Philadelphia, PA, is published

Justin Holland's *Comprehensive Method for the Guitar* is published

Brown & Latimer receive a patent for a water closet for railway cars

T. J. Byrd receives a patent for an improvement in car-couplings

Elijah McCoy receives patents for a steam lubricator and an ironing table

H. Pickett receives a patent for a scaffold

E. H. Sutton receives a patent for the intervention of a cotton cultivator

Eugene Burkins receives a patent for a rapid-fire gun

	A. **General History**	B. **Education**	C. **Laws and Legal Actions**	D. **Religion**
1874	Robert Smalls (R-SC) is elected to the US Congress Blanche K. Bruce (R-MS) is elected to the US Senate, the second black from Mississippi; throughout his six-year term he is an outspoken champion of minority rights and is appointed chairman of the Select Committee to Investigate the Freedman's Savings and Trust Company			
1875	Alonzo J. Ransier is appointed collector of internal revenue for the second district in South Carolina Black women armed with clubs patrol the polling places on election day in South Carolina (and again in 1876)	State Normal and Industrial School at Huntsville, AL (later renamed Alabama State Agricultural and Mechanical College for Negroes) is founded; William Hooper Councill (1849–1909) is named principal Northern Presbyterians organize Knoxville College in Tennessee Joseph Corbin (b Chillicothe, OH, Mar 26, 1833; d Pine Bluff, AR, Jan 9, 1911) founds and is president of Branch Normal College, Pine Bluff, AR; Branch is the first black college in the state	The Civil Rights Act of 1875 gives blacks the right to equal treatment in inns, public conveniences, and public amusement places, and prohibits their exclusion from jury duty	Pope Pius IX* names Bishop James A. Healy head of the diocese comprising Maine and New Hampshire
1876	A monument is dedicated to Rev. Richard Allen, African Methodist Episcopal minister and educator, in Philadelphia, PA's Fairmont Park Rev. Henry McNeal Turner is elected vice president of the American Colonization Society Isaiah Dorman joins Gen. George Custer* and the Seventh Cavalry as an interpreter in an expedition against the Sioux Harriet Purvis is named the first black vice president of the National Woman Suffrage Association Robert Brown Elliott is elected South Carolina attorney general but is ousted one year later when Pres. Rutherford B.	Sarah A. Dicket opens a seminary for black girls in Mississippi Rev. Henry McNeal Turner becomes president of Morris Brown College in Georgia; he serves for twelve years Meharry Medical College, the first all-black medical school in the US, is established as a branch of Central Tennessee College, Nashville, TN; it becomes an independent institution in 1915 Edward Bouchet receives a Ph.D. in physics from Yale University, New Haven, CT; he is believed to be the first black to receive a doctorate in this field from an American university Stillman College is founded, Tuscaloosa, AL	In *United States v. Cruikshank* the US Supreme Court declares that the 14th Amendment provides blacks with equal protection under the law but does not add anything "to the rights which one citizen has under the Constitution against another"; the Court also rules that "the right of suffrage is not a necessary attribute of national citizenship"	The African Methodist Episcopal Church claims 200,000 members Rev. Henry McNeal Turner is elected bishop of the AME church; as bishop, he writes *The Genius and Theory of Methodist Policy* and compiles a catechism and hymnal The African Methodist Episcopal Zion Church begins foreign missionary activities in Liberia G. W. Gayles is named editor of *The Baptist Signal*, a newspaper

1874

1875

| | James Bland leaves Washington, DC, to tour as a professional minstrel; Bland, who began touring with the Black Diamond troupe of Boston, MA, will later tour with Sprague's Georgia Minstrels, the Bohee Brothers, and Haverly's Genuine Colored Minstrels | D. A. Fisher receives a patent for joiners' clamp

A. P. Ashbourne receives patents for a tool used in preparing coconuts for domestic use and a biscuit cutter

H. H. Nash receives a patent for a life-preserving stool | Of the 15 jockeys at the first Kentucky Derby at Churchill Downs in Louisville, 14 are black; Oliver Lewis wins the race riding Aristides and becomes the first black to win

Isaac Murphy (b Isaac Burns, Lexington, KY, January 1, 1861; d Feb 12, 1896), later considered one of the greatest jockeys in US history, rides his first race in Louisville, KY |

1876

| John W. Cromwell founds the *People's Advocate* newspaper, Alexandria, VA; the following year he moves the paper to Washington, DC. | Edward M. Bannister, specializing in landscapes, becomes the first black artist to win wide critical acclaim; Bannister wins a gold medal at the Philadelphia Centennial Exposition for his landscape *Under the Oaks*

John Knowles Paine is the first black composer of a symphonic work; his Opus 23 Symphony in C minor is presented in Boston, MA

The Hyers Sisters Comic Opera, the first permanent black musical comedy troupe, is organized; *Out of the Wilderness* is their first production | D. C. Fischer receives a patent for a furniture castor

T. A. Carrington receives a patent for a range | Billy Walker rides Baden Baden to victory in the Kentucky Derby |

	A. **General History**	B. **Education**	C. **Laws and Legal Actions**	D. **Religion**
1876	Hayes* removes federal troops from the state	Huston-Tillotson College is founded, Austin, TX		
	Richard T. Greener is admitted to the South Carolina bar	Prairie View A&M University is founded, Prairie View, TX		
	George L. Ruffin is elected to the Boston Common Council, MA			
	Lucy Parsons (b Waco, TX, 1853; d 1942) and her husband Albert join the Workingmen's party; Parsons is the first black woman to have a major role in the Socialist Party			
1877	Representatives of presidential candidate Rutherford B. Hayes* and Samuel R. Tilden* meet at the black-operated Wormley Hotel, Washington, DC; they reach an agreement that leads to the election of Hayes and the withdrawal of the remaining federal troops from the South	Henry O. Flipper (1856–1940), born a slave in Georgia, becomes the first black to graduate from the US Military Academy at West Point		
	Frederick Douglass is appointed marshal of Washington, DC, by Pres. Rutherford B. Hayes*	Philander Smith College is founded, Little Rock, AR		
	The American Nicodemus Town Company is founded by six black settlers in northwestern Kansas	Jackson State University is founded, Jackson, MS		
	Hon. Mifflin W. Gibbs is appointed receiver of the US Land Office for the Little Rock district of Arkansas; he serves for 12 years	Fayetteville State University is founded, Fayetteville, NC		
	John Mercer Langston is resident minister and consul general in Haiti and charge d'affaires in the Dominican Republic until 1885			
	In response to claims that it is the "Nigger Party," the Republican Party establishes the "Black and Tan Republican Party," which is separate from the all-white Republican Party			
1878	Two hundred and six blacks leave Charleston, SC, for Liberia aboard the *Azor*	Selma University is founded, Selma, AL		

1876

1877

Alberry Whitman's poem ''Not a Man and Yet a Man'' is published

William Hooper Councill founds the *Huntsville Herald;* he is the paper's editor for several years, AL

A. P. Ashbourne receives a patent for a coconut treating process

---

1878

James Monroe Trotter's *Music and Some Highly Musical People,* a collection of biographical sketches of Negro composers and musicians who specialize in non-black classical music, is published

Samuel Lucas (1840–1916), minstrel performer, is the first black man to play the title role in *Uncle Tom's Cabin*

J. R. Winters receives a patent for a fire escape ladder

	A. **General History**	B. **Education**	C. **Laws and Legal Actions**	D. **Religion**
1879	Benjamin "Pap" Singleton (b Nashville, TN, 1809; d 1892) and Henry Adams inspire thousands of blacks, who are called Exodusters, from the South to Kansas and other points west Maria "Mollie" Baldwin (b Cambridge, MA, 1856), educator and community worker, is the first woman to give the annual George Washington's Birthday Memorial Address at the Brooklyn Institute George Monroe is chosen to drive Pres. Ulysses S. Grant* along the Wanona Trail into Yosemite Valley, CA; Monroe Meadows in Yosemite is named in his honor Thomas Jefferson Ferguson is elected president of the Mass Convention of Colored Voters in Athens County, OH, one of the state's earliest postwar black caucuses Sen. Blanche K. Bruce (R-MS) presides over the US Senate for some time in February T. Morris Chester (b Harrisburg, PA, May 11, 1834; d Harrisburg, PA, 1892) is appointed a US courts commissioner in New Orleans, LA	Richard T. Greener is named dean of Howard University Law School, Washington, DC Zion Wesley Institute is organized in Concord, NC, to train black ministers; the institute moves to Salisbury, NC, in 1885 and is renamed Livingstone College Mary Eliza Mahoney is the first black in the US to receive a diploma in nursing upon graduation from the School of Nursing, New England Hospital for Women and Children, Boston, MA Florida Memorial College is founded, Miami, FL		Rev. Benjamin W. Arnett acts as chaplain for the Ohio state legislature
1880	Mary Ann Shadd Cary organizes the Colored Women's Progressive Franchise Association to promote equal rights for women; the association also supports home missionaries and training programs for youth, and establishes banks and stores for the community, Washington, DC Rev. James P. Poindexter is the first black elected to the Columbus, OH, city council		In *Stauder v. West Virginia,* the US Supreme Court rules that the exclusion of blacks from jury duty is unconstitutional	The Foreign Mission Baptist Convention of the USA and the American National Baptist Convention absorb the Consolidated American Baptist Convention and become the National Baptist Convention of the USA Rev. Richard H. Cain is named bishop of the African Methodist Episcopal Church Rev. John Jasper (1812–1901), pastor of the First African Church and the

| | | | | **1879** |

Businessman T. Thomas Fortune (b Florida, 1856; d 1928) founds the *New York Sun,* one of New York City's leading newspapers

Julia A. J. Foote's (b Schenectady, NY, 1823; d 1900) *A Brand Plucked from the Fire! An Autobiographical Sketch* is published

William Bailes receives a patent for a ladder scaffold-support

T. Elkins receives a patent for a refrigerating apparatus

W. H. Lavelette patents his variation of the printing machine, which is superior to the pioneer model being used during this time

Lewis Latimer receives a patent for an electric filament bulb

| | | | | **1880** |

William Wells Brown's *My Southern Home* is published

A. P. Ashbourne receives a patent for an invention to refine coconut oil

Barrett Lewis wins the Kentucky Derby riding Fonso

	A. **General History**	B. **Education**	C. **Laws and Legal Actions**	D. **Religion**
1880				Sixth Mount Zion Baptist Church, Richmond, VA, wins renown for his sermon "De Sun Do Move," which he delivers over 250 times
1881	Pres. James A. Garfield* appoints Frederick Douglass Recorder of Deeds for Washington, DC Blanche K. Bruce is appointed registrar of the Treasury by Pres. James A. Garfield*; he serves until 1885 Five thousand blacks leave Edgefield, SC, and relocate to Alabama in the largest mass migration from the state Rev. Henry Highland Garnet is appointed US minister to Liberia	Spelman College for Women is organized in the basement of a church in Atlanta, GA; Sophia B. Packard* and Harriet E. Giles,* of New England, found the school Booker T. Washington founds Tuskegee Normal and Industrial Institute, in Alabama Rev. Joseph Charles Price (1854–1893) represents the African Methodist Episcopal Zion Church at the London Ecumenical Conference, where he raises $10,000 for Zion Wesley Institute; he is elected president of the school the following year Morris Brown College is founded, Atlanta, GA Morristown College is founded, Morristown, TN Bishop College is founded, Dallas, TX	Tennessee enacts a law requiring racial segregation in railroad cars, initiating a segregation policy that will spread to most Southern states; the law becomes the precedent for what will be known as "Jim Crow" laws The Rhode Island legislature repeals a law banning interracial marriage  *Booker T. Washington, founder of Tuskegee Institute. (UPI/ Bettmann)*	
1882	Thomas Boyne receives the Congressional Medal of Honor for bravery in two New Mexico battles while serving in Troop C, Ninth US Cavalry James E. O'Hara (b NYC, 1844; d New Bern, NC, 1905 (R-NC) is elected to the US Congress	The Colored Methodist Episcopal (later, Christian Methodist Episcopal) Church organizes Paine Institute (later renamed Paine College) in Augusta, GA, with support from white Methodists Virginia State University is founded in Petersburg, VA, and becomes the first fully state-supported black college in the US Lane College is founded, Jackson, TN		Bishop Alexander Wayman's *Cyclopaedia of African Methodism* is published Rev. Alexander Crummell's *The Greatness of Christ*, a book of sermons, is published Rev. Walter H. Brooks (b Richmond, VA, 1851; d Washington, DC, 1945) becomes pastor of 19th Street Baptist Church, Washington, DC, where he remains until his death; Rev. Brooks is a noted temperance leader and poet
1883	George L. Ruffin is appointed judge of a municipal court in Charlestown, MA	Lucy Moten (b Fauquier Co., VA, 1851; d NYC, Aug 24, 1933) begins service as principal of Miner Normal School, later renamed Miner Teachers College, in Washington, DC; she serves for 17 years	The US Supreme Court rules that the Civil Rights Act of 1875 is unconstitutional The Maine and Michigan legislatures repeal laws banning interracial marriage	The Baptist Foreign Mission Convention of the US sends six missionaries to Liberia

1880

1881

| | Jack Haverly's* Colored Minstrels make their first European tour; the Colored Minstrels are the most famous and successful of all minstrel companies | Lewis Latimer and Joseph V. Nichols* patent an incandescent electric lamp with a filament | |

Following Reconstruction, industrial education and the manual arts were the primary emphasis for schools like Tuskegee Institute.

W. S. Campbell receives a patent for a self-setting animal trap

Norbert Rillieux receives a patent for an evaporating process for use with sugar beets

J. Wormley receives a patent for a lifesaving apparatus

Charles B. Purvis is the first physician to treat Pres. James A. Garfield* when the president is shot, Washington, DC; later this year he becomes the first black in charge of a civilian hospital, Freedman's Hospital

1882

Lewis Latimer receives patents for a process to manufacture carbon filaments made out of fibrous materials and for a globe supporter for an electric lamp

1883

George Washington Williams (1849–1891) publishes *History of the Negro Race in America from 1619 to 1880,* after researching over 12,000 books and thousands of pamphlets and newspa-

Jan E. Matzeliger (b Paramaribo, Surinam, 1852) receives a patent for a shoe-lasting "sole machine"; the first of its kind, this machine is bought by the United Shoe Machinery Co.

Edwin B. Henderson, pioneering physical education instructor and coach, b Washington, DC, Nov 24; he will organize the Negro Athletic Conference, Interscholastic Athletic Association and the Colored Inter-

	A. **General History**	B. **Education**	C. **Laws and Legal Actions**	D. **Religion**
1883		With the assistance of the American Baptist Home Mission Society, Hartshorn Memorial College for Women opens in the basement of Ebenezer Baptist Church, Richmond, VA; Hartshorn is intended to be a liberal arts college comparable to northern white women's schools—it deemphasizes industrial training Charles Henry Phillips serves as principal of Lane Institute until 1886		
1884	John R. Lynch, former US congressman, is elected temporary chairman of the Republican convention; he is the first black to preside over deliberations of a national political party At the International Conference, Berlin, Germany, representatives from various European nations divide African countries among themselves for colonial rule and exploitation; the new boundaries formed cause major disruptions among the many ethnic groups in Africa	Mary Ann Shadd Cary graduates from Howard University Law School at age 61 Bishop James A. Healy serves on a commission that plans and establishes the Catholic University of America, Washington, DC Francis L. Cardozo is appointed principal of the Colored Preparatory High School (later renamed M Street High School) until 1896 M. O. Ricketts, ex-slave, graduates with honors from the University of Nebraska College of Medicine Arkansas Baptist College is founded, Little Rock, AR		The African Methodist Episcopal Church licenses women to preach but restricts them to evangelistic work Rev. Richard De Baptiste, Baptist minister, founds the *Western Herald*, a religious journal The Third Plenary Council forms the Commission for Catholic Missions Among the Colored People and Indians, Baltimore, MD Zion Baptist Church is founded in Omaha, NE; it is the largest church in the state
1885		Hallie Q. Brown (b Pittsburgh, PA, Mar 10, 1845) begins service as dean of Allen University, Columbia, SC; she serves for two years Edward Brawley (b Charleston, SC, 1851; d 1923) founds and is the first president of Morris College, SC		African Methodist Episcopal bishop Henry McNeal Turner ordains Sarah A. H. and places her name on the list of male deacons; one year later the new presiding bishop removes her name from the book and declares that her "ordination was contrary to Church law" AME bishop Daniel Payne publishes *Treatise on Domestic Education* Mathilda Beasley (c1833–1903) begins Catholic communities of black sisters, first in Wilkes County and then in Savannah, GA

| | | William A. Hinton, b Chicago, IL; Hinton becomes a world renowned authority on venereal disease and develops the Hinton Test and the Davies-Hinton Test for the detection of syphilis | Collegiate Athletic Association | **1883** |

pers; the text will serve as a standard authority on the subject for more than 60 years

Rebecca Lee Crumpler, the first black woman physician in the US, writes *A Book of Medical Discourses in Two Parts* that gives advice to women who want to become doctors

W. Washington receives a patent for a corn husking machine

1884

The Philadelphia Tribune newspaper is founded

Alberry Whitman's "Rape of Florida," a narrative poem, is published

Businessman T. Thomas Fortune founds the *New York Age;* Fortune, an activist in the Republican Party, goes on to write several books

John E. Bruce (b Piscataway, MD, 1856; d 1924) begins the popular "Bruce Grit" column in the *New York Age* and the *Gazette* of Cleveland, OH; in his column, Bruce advocates self-help, economic development, and race pride among black Americans

Gussie Davis (1863–1899) writes "When Nellie Was Raking the Hay," a popular musical piece; he is the first black songwriter to succeed in Tin Pan Alley, New York City's commercial song-writing district that will become renowned 20 years later

Granville T. Woods (b Columbus, OH, April 23, 1856; d NYC, 1910) develops an apparatus for transmission of messages by electricity and patents a variation on the telephone transmitter that is bought by Bell Telephone; he also receives a patent for an improved steam boiler furnace

The Medico-Chirurgical Society of the District of Columbia is organized

John P. Parker invents a screw for tobacco presses; he later establishes the Ripley Foundry and Machine Company

W. Johnson receives a patent for an egg beater

Isaac Murphy wins the Kentucky Derby riding Buchanan, a horse trained by William Bird

Moses Fleetwood "Fleet" Walker, one of the first black major leaguers, signs as a catcher with the Toledo Blue Stockings, the champions of the Northwestern League of the American Association

---

1885

Gertrude Mossell's (b Philadelphia, PA, Jul 3, 1855) column, "Our Woman's Day," appears in the first issue of T. Thomas Fortune's newspaper, *Freeman*, Dec; Mossell, an early advocate for women's rights, writes several articles advocating women's suffrage and promotes career development, NYC

W. C. Carter receives a patent for an umbrella stand

Sarah E. Goode is the first black woman to receive a US patent; her invention is a folding cabinet bed

Granville T. Woods receives a patent for "telegraphony," an apparatus that combines the telegraph and the telephone; the device eliminates the need for Morse Code, making it possible for anyone to send telegraph messages

Erskine Henderson rides Joe Cotton to victory in the Kentucky Derby

Frank Thompson organizes the Cuban Giants, considered the first black professional baseball team; this team is so named with the hope that they will avoid prejudice against blacks; they also feign speaking Spanish to enhance the illusion and lead whites to believe they are not black Americans

The Cuban Giants team is one of the first salaried black professional baseball teams in the US

	A. General History	B. Education	C. Laws and Legal Actions	D. Religion
1885				Rev. Samuel David Ferguson is consecrated the first black priest in the Protestant Episcopal Church, New York
1886	Rev. Benjamin W. Arnett is elected to the Ohio legislature, where he helps to draft the bill that abolishes the state's "Black Laws"; Arnett is the first black elected representative to have a majority white constituency	Rep. Theophile T. Allain (R-LA) introduces a bill in the state legislature for a $20,000 appropriation to build Southern University Lucy C. Laney founds the Haines Normal and Industrial Institute in Augusta, GA (reorganized into a junior college in 1930) The first school of nursing for black students is organized at Spelman Seminary, Atlanta, GA Shorter College is founded, North Little Rock, AR Kentucky State University is founded, Frankfort, KY University of Maryland, Eastern Shore, is founded, Princess Anne, MD	New Mexico state legislature repeals the law banning interracial marriage	United Holy Church of America, Inc., is founded at Method, NC, by the Holiness Pentecostal Church Pres. Grover Cleveland* commissions Rev. Allen Allensworth (b Louisville, KY, Apr 7, 1842) chaplain of the 24th Infantry, a black regiment Louise "Lulu" Fleming (b Jan 28, 1862; d Philadelphia, PA, 1899) becomes the first black woman to be appointed and commissioned for career missionary service by the Woman's Baptist Foreign Missionary Society of the West; she serves as a medical missionary in the Congo (present-day Zaire) for about 10 years
1887	John H. Alexander (b Helena, AR, 1864; d Springfield, OH, Mar 26, 1894) graduates from the US Military Academy; he later reports to the all-black Ninth Cavalry Regiment at Fort Robinson, NE, and is promoted to first lieutenant in Oct 1893	Florida Agriculture & Mechanical (A&M) University is founded, Tallahassee, FL Central State University is founded, Wilberforce, OH	Ohio state legislature repeals a law banning interracial marriage The Georgia Supreme Court upholds the right of Amanda America Dickson, the daughter of wealthy plantation owner David Dickson* and his slave concubine Julia Dickson, to inherit her father's estate; this ruling allows Amanda to become one of the wealthiest women in Augusta, GA, and perhaps in the entire state	Edward Blyden's (b St. Thomas, West Indies, Aug 3, 1832) *Christianity, Islam, and the Negro Race*, in which he appeals to black men to convert to Islam, is published
1888	Henry P. Cheatham (b Henderson, NC, 1857; d Oxford, NC, 1935) (R-NC) is elected to the US Congress	Cornelia Bowen founds Mt. Meigs Institute, Mt. Meigs, AL St. Paul's College is founded, Lawrenceville, VA		Rev. Benjamin W. Arnett is elected a bishop of the African Methodist Episcopal Church; he serves the Seventh Episcopal District, SC, for four years

E. Literature, Publications, and The Black Press	F. The Arts	G. Science, Technology, and Medicine	H. Sports	
				1885
	George W. Chadwick's Second Symphony is published; it is the first symphonic work using black folksongs	Lewis Latimer receives a patent for a cooling and disinfecting apparatus M. Headen receives a patent for a foot-powered hammer J. Ricks receives a patent for a horseshoe Due to racial exclusion from the American Medical Association, Monroe Majors and 13 colleagues found the Lone Star State Medical Association (later the Lone Star State Medical, Dental, and Pharmaceutical Association), Brenham, TX	Frank Grant (b Pittsfield, MA) enters organized baseball as an infielder with the Meridian, CT, team of the Eastern League	**1886**
	Lewis Latimer, best-known for inventing carbon filaments for incandescent lamps, was also an accomplished artist and poet. (Schomburg)			
Charles W. Chesnutt's (1858–1932) short story "The Goophered Grapevine" is published in the *Atlantic Monthly*	Gussie Davis composes "The Lighthouse by the Sea"	A. Miles receives a patent for an elevator Granville T. Woods receives a patent for a railway induction telegraph system that allows messages to be sent between moving trains and from moving trains to rail stations; Woods organizes the Woods Electric Company, and the demand for his devices becomes so widespread that he closes the factory six years later in order to devote his time to inventing Archie Alexander (b Ottumwa, IA); despite limited opportunities for blacks, Alexander becomes one of the most successful engineers in the state of Iowa, where he constructs a million-dollar heating plant at the University of Iowa (d 1958)	Frank Peters founds a semiprofessional black baseball team, the Union Giants, Chicago, IL After the Meridian team disbands, Frank Grant joins the Buffalo team of the International League as a second baseman Isaac Lewis rides Montrose to win the Kentucky Derby	**1887**
William J. Simmons founds the magazine *Our Women and Children;* he hires several women journalists including Lucy Wilmot Smith, Mary V. Cook,	Sissieretta Jones (b Matilda S. Joyner, Portsmouth, VA, 1868; d 1933), opera singer, known as "Black Patti," makes her debut in New York City	Jan Matzeliger receives a patent for a mechanism that distributes tacks and nails A. B. Blackburn receives a patent for a railway signal	Shelby "Pike" Barnes wins the first Futurity Stakes, Sheepshead Bay, NY The Cuban Giants win the first Colored Championships of America, NYC	**1888**

	A. **General History**	B. **Education**	C. **Laws and Legal Actions**	D. **Religion**
1888	John Mercer Langston runs for a Virginia congressional seat as an Independent candidate after the Republican party refuses to nominate him The Savings Bank of the Grand Fountain United Order of True Reformers, the first black bank of the US, is founded in Richmond, VA Slavery is abolished in Brazil	The Virginia Seminary and College is founded, Lynchburg, VA Miles Vanderhurst Lynk (b near Brownsville, TN, June 3, 1871) founds the Louisville Medical College, Louisville, TN		AME bishop Daniel Payne publishes his memoirs, *Recollections of Seventy Years* Sarah Gorham (b Dec 5, 1832) is the first woman appointed by the AME Church to serve as a missionary to any foreign country
1889	Frederick Douglass is appointed US minister to Haiti Blanche K. Bruce begins service as Recorder of Deeds for Washington, DC; he serves until 1893 William Bush (b Clay County, MO, Jul 4 1832; d 1907), son of pioneer George Washington Bush, is elected to Washington's first state legislature; he serves two terms Thomas E. Miller (b Ferrebeeville, SC, 1849) (R-SC) is elected to the US Congress Oklahoma land is officially opened to settlers; about 10,000 blacks are among those staking claims The Mutual Trust Company, organized and owned by blacks, is established in Chattanooga, TN	Rev. Matthew Anderson and his wife, Dr. Caroline V. Still Anderson, found the Berean Manual Training and Industrial School in Kentucky Rev. Charles N. Grandison becomes the first black president of Bennett College in North Carolina and the first black president of a Freedman's Aid Society–funded school Maria "Mollie" Baldwin is the principal of Agassiz Grammar School, Cambridge, MA; she is one of the first black woman principals in Massachusetts and in the northeastern states		At the Philadelphia African Methodist Episcopal Conference Harriet Baker is appointed to take charge of the St. Paul's Church in the city of Lebanon, PA African Methodist Episcopal bishop Henry McNeal Turner founds the *Southern Christian Recorder*
1890	The Afro-American National League is founded in Chicago, IL; the League is the result of an idea conceived in 1887 by T. Thomas Fortune; the short-lived organization espouses agitation and revolution as means for securing rights for blacks; it also promotes industrial education, job training, and self-help; the League will go out of existence in 1893 The Colored Farmers' Alliance, founded in 1886 and dedicated to improving the economic condition of	Emma Frances Grayson Merritt (b Dumfries, VA, Jan 11, 1860; d Washington, DC, Jun 8, 1933), principal of the Garnet School, establishes the first kindergarten for black pupils in the US, Washington, DC Richard Robert Wright founds Savannah State College, Savannah, GA	The Mississippi state constitution restricts black suffrage through an "understanding" test In *Re Green,* the US Supreme Court confers control of elections to state officials, thereby weakening Federal protection for southern black voters; the Court also allows states to segregate public facilities Cong. Henry Cabot Lodge* sponsors a bill authorizing federal election supervisors to pass on the qualifications of excluded voters;	Rev. James A. Healy is promoted to the rank of Assistant at the Papal Throne Amelia E. Johnson's *Clarence and Corinne or God's Way* is the first book by a woman to be published by the American Baptist Publication and the first Sunday school book published by a black author

E. Literature, Publications, and The Black Press	F. The Arts	G. Science, Technology, and Medicine	H. Sports	
Ida B. Wells, and Ione E. Wood George Washington Williams's *The Negro in the American Rebellion* is published		Miriam E. Benjamin receives a patent for a gong and signal chair that is later used to signal pages in the US House of Representatives Granville T. Woods receives a patent for a tunnel construction for electric railways		**1888**
Ida B. Wells (later Barnett) (b Holly Springs, MS, Jul 16, 1862; d Chicago, IL, 1931) becomes part-owner and editor of the *Memphis Free Speech and Headlight,* a newspaper		William Richardson receives a patent for a baby carriage Purdy & Sadgar receive a patent for a folding chair Granville T. Woods receives a patent for an automatic safety cutoff for electric circuits	William Tecumseh Sherman Jackson and William Henry Lewis play on the varsity football team at Amherst College, MA; they are the first known black players at a predominantly white college or university; Lewis later plays for Harvard, MA	**1889**
Lewis Latimer's *Incandescent Electric Lighting* is published; it is the first book to be written about a lighting system Octavia R. Albert's (b Oglethorpe, GA, Dec 24, 1853; d c1890) *The House of Bondage* is published; the book consists of seven slave narratives collected by Albert, a former slave		Jan E. Matzeliger receives a patent for a tack separating mechanism William B. Purvis receives patents for a fountain pen F. J. Ferrell receives patents for steam engine valves and for a snow melting apparatus P. B. Downing receives a patent for an electric railroad switch D. McCree receives a patent for a portable fire escape	Shelby "Pike" Barnes rides the winning horse in the Belmont and Alabama stakes Joe Walcott "Barbados Demon" (b Barbados, Apr 7, 1872) wins the New England lightweight championship in both boxing and wrestling	**1890**

	A. **General History**	B. **Education**	C. **Laws and Legal Actions**	D. **Religion**
1890	black farmers, reaches membership of one million		the bill, aimed to help black male voters, fails	
	Janie Porter Barrett, a teacher, establishes the Locust Street Settlement House in Hampton, VA, one of the first black settlement houses in the US		Cong. Henry P. Cheatham (R-NC) is elected to the 52nd Congress	
	The Comite des Citoyens is formed in New Orleans, LA, by free people of color; this organization works to wage legal battle against discrimination			
	Pres. Benjamin Harrison* appoints Alexander G. Clark as US minister and consul general to Liberia			
	Monroe Majors (b Waco, TX, 1864; d Los Angeles, CA, 1960), the first black American to pass the California Board of Examiners, establishes the first black-owned drugstore in the southwest, Waco, TX			
	John Mercer Langston is the first black elected to the US House of Representatives from Virginia			
1891	At the Nationalist Populist Convention, southern white representatives attempt to segregate the delegates of National Colored Farmers' Alliance, Cincinnati, OH; their attempt is defeated	North Carolina Agriculture and Technical (A&T) State University is founded, Greensboro, NC		Bishop Daniel Payne's *History of the African Methodist Episcopal Church* is published
		West Virginia State College is founded, Institute, WV		
	Pres. Benjamin Harrison* appoints Minnie Cox (b Lexington, MS, 1869), educator and clubwoman, as postmistress of Indianola, MS	Delaware State College is founded, Dover, DE		
		Elizabeth City State University is founded, Elizabeth City, NC		
	Cong. Thomas E. Miller (R-SC) addresses the House in a rebuttal to Sen. Alfred H. Colquitt* of Georgia who attacks blacks as ''backward'' and ''uncouth''; Miller describes Colquitt's words as offensive and identifies white southerners as the culprits of the South's economic failures			
1892	Edwin C. Berry (b Oberlin, OH, Dec 10, 1854; d Athens, OH, Mar 12, 1931)	Hallie Q. Brown begins her one-year term as dean of		Bishop Henry McNeal Turner founds the *Voice of Missions*

		Granville T. Woods receives a patent for an egg incubator heated by electricity		**1890**
Julia Ringwood Coston edits and publishes *Ringwood's Afro-American Journal of Fashion,* the illustrated journal for black women; two years later Coston will publish *Ringwood's Home Magazine* Lucy Parsons begins publishing a newspaper, *Freedom: A Revolutionary Anarchist-Communist Monthly* I. Garland Penn's (b New Glasgow, VA, 1867; d 1930) best-known work, *The Afro-American Press and Its Editors,* is published	*The Creole Show*, a black musical comedy, opens; it is the first to feature a black female chorus and a female interlocutor and to deviate from traditional minstrel patterns The Onward Brass Band, a group from New Orleans, LA, travels to New York and wins wide attention and first place in a band contest	Daniel Hale Williams (b Hollidaysburg, PA, Jan 18, 1856; d Idlewild, MI, Aug 4, 1931) incorporates Provident Hospital, the first training hospital for black doctors and nurses in Chicago, IL, and the first interracial hospital in the US J. Standard receives a patent for a refrigerator P. B. Downing receives a patent for a street mail box	Isaac Murphy, riding Kingman, is the first three-time winning jockey of the Kentucky Derby	**1891**
Rev. William M. Alexander founds the *Afro-American*; in four years,	Sissieretta Jones, known as "Black Patti," performs before Pres. Benjamin	G. T. Sampson receives a patent for a clothes dryer	The first black college football game is played between Biddle College and	**1892**

	A. General History	B. Education	C. Laws and Legal Actions	D. Religion
1892	erects a 22-room hotel, The Hotel Berry, in Athens, OH; at the time of his retirement in 1921, he has a reputation as the most successful black small-city hotel operator in the US Outrage at the lynchings of three colleagues, Thomas Moss, Calvin McDowell, and Henry Steward, launches journalist Ida B. Wells into a lifelong crusade against racism; she starts the first phase of the antilynching movement with her articles and editorials in the Memphis *Free Speech* and the *New York Age* Dr. M.O. Ricketts begins service in the Nebraska state legislature George Washington Murray (b Sumter, SC, 1853; d Chicago, IL, April 21, 1926) (R-SC) is elected to the US Congress	women, Tuskegee Institute, Alabama Mary Holmes College is founded, West Point, MS Winston-Salem State University is founded, Winston-Salem, NC *Notable 19th-century African-American men, the majority of whom held political appointments during the Reconstruction.* (LC)		Russell Webb (d 1916), US consul to Manila and recent convert to Islam, returns to New York and attempts to convert other black Americans 
1893	Chris L. Rutt* hires Nancy Green to dress in costume (simple dress and head kerchief) and to flip pancakes to promote his pancake mix; five years later Rutt decides to mass market Green's character, naming her Aunt Jemima; she becomes one of the most enduring advertising trademarks in the US Florida Ridley, Josephine Ruffin, and Maria "Mollie" Baldwin found the Woman's Era Club that serves as a network between other women's groups; the club also organizes several kindergartens for black youth in Boston, MA, and one in Atlanta, GA George Murray (R-SC) is elected to the US Congress	Educators Anna Julia Cooper, Fannie Barrier Williams, and Fanny Jackson Coppin speak before the Women's Congress in Chicago, IL, addressing the theme, "The Intellectual Progress of Colored Women of the US since Emancipation" Clinton Junior College is founded, Rock Hill, SC Texas College is founded, Tyler, TX		The American National Educational Baptist Convention is organized under the National Baptist Convention of the USA The African Methodist Episcopal Church establishes the Women's Home and Foreign Missionary Society; it is the second organization geared specifically toward women in the denomination *The Autobiography of Amanda Berry Smith, AME evangelist* is published Russell Webb founds the Oriental Publishing Company and begins publication of the periodical *The Muslim World*
1894	Zeke Miller begins service as deputy marshal for the central district of Indian Territory (present-day Oklahoma)	Fanny Jackson Coppin opens the Women's Exchange and Girls Home, which gives instruction in domestic work (cooking,	US Congress repeals the Enforcement Act, making it easier for some states to disfranchise black voters	Rev. C. P. Jones of Selma, AL, leaves the Baptist faith to form the Church of Christ, Holiness USA

E. Literature, Publications, and The Black Press	F. The Arts	G. Science, Technology, and Medicine	H. Sports	
John H. Murphy, Sr., will buy the paper; it will become the largest black-owned publication on the East Coast Miles V. Lynk (b near Brownsville, TN, Jun 3, 1871) founds, edits, and publishes the *Medical and Surgical Observer,* the first black medical journal The Virginia Organization of True Reformers, a secret society, begins publishing a newspaper, *The Reformer;* it has a weekly circulation of 8,000 by 1900 Anna Julia Cooper's (b North Carolina, Aug 10, 1858; d Washington, DC, Feb 27, 1961) *A Voice from the South by a Black Woman of the South* is published Publication of the *Daily Crusade,* a daily newspaper, begins in New Orleans, LA Frances Ellen Watkins Harper's *Iola Leroy: or, Shadows Uplifted* is published	Harrison* at the White House, Washington, DC	Sarah Boone receives a patent for an ironing board S. R. Scottron receives a patent for a curtain rod	Livingstone College, Salisbury, NC The Calumet Wheelmen, an athletic club, is formed in New York City William Henry Lewis, of Amherst College (MA) and Harvard University (MA), becomes the first black American to play for the All-American Team when he is chosen as center-rush by Walter Camp*; Lewis later graduates from Harvard Law School and becomes the Assistant District Attorney in Boston, MA George Dixon is the world featherweight boxing champion; he holds the title from 1892 to 1900	**1892**

IDA B. WELLS.

Crusader Ida B. Wells-Barnett launched a national anti-lynching campaign and founded the Negro Fellowship League, the Alpha Suffrage Club, and several black women's clubs. (LC)

| Paul Laurence Dunbar's (b Dayton, OH, Jun 27, 1872; d Dayton, OH, Feb 9, 1906) first collection of poetry, *Oak and Ivy,* is published

Monroe Majors's *Noted Negro Women: Their Triumphs and Activities* is published | Gussie Davis composes "The Fatal Wedding"

The paintings of inventor George Washington Carver (b c1864; d Tuskegee, AL, Jan 15, 1943) are displayed at the Colombian Exposition, Chicago, IL

Henry O. Tanner (b Pittsburgh, PA, Jun 21, 1859; d Paris, France, May 25, 1937) paints *The Banjo Lesson,* the first of his short-lived black genre paintings; Tanner's work challenges white artists' stereotypical interpretations of black life | Provident Hospital is founded in Baltimore, MD, to provide medical care to migrating blacks and to offer training for black physicians

Daniel Hale Williams performs the world's first known open heart surgery at Provident Hospital, Chicago, IL

Granville T. Woods receives a patent for an electric railway conduit

T. W. Stewart receives a patent for a mop | Willie Sims (b Augusta, GA, 1870) rides the winning horse in the Belmont Stakes, New York

Tuskegee Institute of Alabama organizes the first major college track meet in the US, under the leadership of James B. Washington, sports director | **1893** |
| *Appointed,* by Walter Stowers and William H. Anderson, is published in Detroit, MI; this is the first black novel to reflect the | Ada "Bricktop" Smith, vaudevillian and saloon entertainer (b Alderson, WV, Aug 14); during the 1920s Smith will open a | Daniel Hale Williams is appointed chief surgeon of Freedman's Hospital, Washington, DC, Feb; Williams reorganizes the | Willie Sims rides the winning horse in the Belmont Stakes for the second consecutive year | **1894** |

	A. **General History**	B. **Education**	C. **Laws and Legal Actions**	D. **Religion**
1894		dressmaking, and home economics), Philadelphia, PA		Julia A. J. Foote, evangelist and missionary, becomes the first ordained deacon in the African Methodist Episcopal Zion Church
1895	The National Steamboat Company is organized, Washington, DC; the company sails a steamboat, the *George Leary*, between Washington, DC, and Norfolk, VA Booker T. Washington delivers his famous speech, ''The Atlanta Compromise,'' at the Cotton States International Exposition, Atlanta, GA A convention of women form the National Federation of Afro-American Women, Boston, MA	W. E. B. Du Bois (b Great Barrington, MA, Feb 23, 1868; d Ghana, Aug 27, 1963) receives the first doctorate degree awarded to a black from Harvard University, MA Mary Church Terrell (b Memphis, TN, Sep 23, 1863; d Annapolis, MD, Jul 24, 1954) is appointed to the District of Columbia Board of Education, becoming the first black woman to serve on the board The Fort Valley State College is founded, Fort Valley, GA Natchez Junior College is founded, Natchez, MS	Following the death of Frederick Douglass, Cong. George Washington Murray (R-SC) seeks to have Douglass's body lie in state in the rotunda of the Capitol; House Speaker Charles F. Crisp* (D-GA) rejects the request	Representatives from the Baptist Foreign Mission Convention, the National Baptist Convention, and the National Baptist Educational Convention meet in Atlanta, GA, and form the United National Baptist Convention of the US Rev. C. H. Mason leaves the Baptist church to form the first Holiness church, The Church of God in Christ, Lexington, MS William S. Crowdy, who believes that blacks are direct descendants from the 10 lost tribes of Israel, founds the Church of Christ in Lawrence, KS
1896	The National Federation of Afro-American Women and the National League of Colored Women merge to form the National Association of Colored Women; Mary Church Terrell is the first president; this women's self-help organization offers support programs geared specifically to black	Booker T. Washington receives the first honorary degree awarded to a black by Harvard University, MA The Colored Normal Industrial, Agricultural and Mechanical College (later renamed South Carolina State University) is	In *Plessy v. Fergerson*, the US Supreme Court rules that ''separate but equal'' facilities are constitutional	Rev. Richard Boyd founds the National Baptist Publishing Board, Nashville, TN Sarah E. C. Dudley Pettey (b New Bern, NC, 1869; d 1906) originates the woman's column in the *Star of Zion*, the weekly newspaper of the African Methodist Episcopal Zion Church

E. **Literature, Publications, and The Black Press**	F. **The Arts**	G. **Science, Technology, and Medicine**	H. **Sports**	
racism of "Jim Crow" practices of the 1890s; it treats peonage, convict-labor, lynching, disfranchisement, and segregation as aspects of systematic repression *The Woman's Era*, later to become the official communications organ of the National Association of Colored Women, begins publication Gertrude Mossell's *The Work of the Afro-American Woman* is published	Parisian nightclub, Bricktop's, that features American music and a high society clientele (d NYC, Jan 31, 1984)	hospital into separate medical and surgical departments, organizes pathological and bacteriological departments, and hires an interracial staff George W. Murray receives patents for his inventions of agricultural machinery, including a cotton chopper, a combined furrow opener, and a planter and fertilizer distributor reaper		**1894**
Paul Laurence Dunbar's *Majors and Minors*, a book of poetry, is published; it receives a favorable, full-page review by literary critic William Dean Howells* in *Harpers Weekly* Joseph Seamon Cotter, Sr.'s first work of poetry, *A Rhyming*, is published James Edwin Campbell's (c 1860–1895) *Echoes from the Cabin and Elsewhere*, a volume of poetry, is published Alice Ruth Nelson's (b New Orleans, LA, July 19, 1875; d 1935) first book, *Violets and Other Tales*, a collection of poetry, short stories and essays, is published; Nelson, who later marries poet Paul Laurence Dunbar, will become a noted clubwoman and advocate for women's rights	Eva Jessye, choral director, b Coffeyville, KS, Jan 20; Jessye will work as choral director of King Vidor's* *Hallelujah* and the original production of George Gershwin's* *Porgy and Bess* William Marion Cook (b Detroit, MI, Jan 27, 1869; d 1944), composer, makes his solo debut at Carnegie Hall, New York City; four of his most successful works are "Rain Song," "Swing Along," "Wid de Moon," and the adaptation to orchestra of a Negro sermon, "Exhortation" Gussie Davis wins second place for "Send Back the Picture and the Ring" in a contest sponsored by the *New York World* to find the 10 best songwriters in the nation Although her name is not on the official list of exhibitors, Harriet Powers (b Georgia, Oct 29, 1837), slave, is believed to have displayed her elaborate quilt *The Creation of Animals* at the Cotton States Exposition, Atlanta, GA	J. Lee receives a patent for a bread crumbing machine J. B. Allen receives a patent for a clothes line support J. Cooper receives a patent for an elevator device Purdy and Peters receive a patent for a design for spoons The National Medical Association, a professional organiztion of black physicians, is founded Nathan Mossell founds the Douglass Hospital, the first black hospital in Philadelphia, PA	James Perkins rides Halma to victory at the Kentucky Derby *Alice Dunbar-Nelson, former wife of poet Paul Laurence Dunbar, was accomplished in her own right as a public school teacher, journalist, poet, author, and clubwoman.* (Bethune) 	**1895**
W. E. B. Du Bois's *Suppression of the African Slave Trade*, the first title in the Harvard Historical Studies, is published Paul Lawrence Dunbar's collection of poems, *Lyrics of a Lowly Life*, is published; it wins national attention	Gussie Davis writes "In the Baggage Coach Ahead," which is later popularized by singer Imogine Comer;* more than one million copies are sold	Lewis Latimer receives a patent for a locking rack for hats, coats, and umbrellas C. B. Brooks receives a patent for a street sweeper W. D. Davis receives a patent for riding saddles	Willie Simms rides the winning horse in the Kentucky Derby	**1896**

	A. General History	B. Education	C. Laws and Legal Actions	D. Religion
1896	women; under Terrell's leadership, NACW establishes kindergartens, day care centers, and mothers' clubs; the organization also addresses political issues of the day, including suffrage and lynchings The Nickel Savings Bank of Richmond, VA, is established The Atlanta University Studies is inaugurated, conducted between 1896 and 1914; these studies deal with different phases of black life each year and represent "the first real sociological research in the South" George H. White (b Rosindale, NC, 1852) (R-NC) is elected to the US Congress	founded at Orangeburg, SC Booker T. Washington hires renowned scientist George Washington Carver to teach and conduct research at the Tuskegee Institute in Alabama Oakwood College is founded, Huntsville, AL		
1897	Victoria Earle Matthews (b Fort Valley, GA, May 27, 1861; d NYC, Mar 10, 1907) establishes the White Rose Missions in New York City to meet the needs of black women migrating from the South; the mission provides a social center and a shelter for young women Robert Adger organizes the Afro-American Historical Society, Philadelphia, PA Fannie M. Richards founds the Phillis Wheatley Home for Aged Colored Ladies, Detroit, MI Hon. Mifflin W. Gibbs becomes US consul at Tamatave, Madagascar; he serves until 1901 Henry P. Cheatham, former congressman, is appointed Recorder of Deeds for Washington, DC H. A. Rucker becomes the collector of internal revenue in Georgia	The American Negro Academy, an early scholarly society, is founded with help from Rev. Alexander Crummell and W. E. B. Du Bois; officers are S. G. Atkins, principal of the Slater Normal School, Winston-Salem, NC; L. B. Moore, dean of Howard University, Washington, DC; and W. H. Crogman, president of Clark University, Atlanta, GA; Anna Julia Cooper is the only woman elected to membership; the academy is the first body in the US that brings black intellectuals from all over the world together to foster scholarship The Colored and Normal University (later renamed Langston University in honor of John Mercer Langston) is founded in the Oklahoma territory Voorhees College is founded, Denmark, SC Lucy Hughes Brown (1863–1911), the first black woman physician in South Carolina, is instrumental in founding the Cannon Hospital and Training School for Nurses (later renamed McClennan-Banks Hospital)		The Lott Carey Baptist Home and Foreign Mission Convention of the US opens its first mission in Brewersville, Liberia

1896

Granville T. Woods invents a system to replace the bulky mechanical resistors that are used to dim the lights in theaters

Austin Curtis (1868–1938), surgeon, is invited to serve on the surgical staff of Cook County Hospital, becoming one of the first black Americans to work in an integrated hospital

---

1897

Willie Covan, tap dancer, b Atlanta, GA, Mar 4; he later appears in the original production of *Shuffle Along*

Playing jazz becomes a full-time profession rather than an avocation for solo pianists such as Ferdinand "Jelly Roll" Morton (b Philadelphia, PA, 1885; d Los Angeles, CA, 1941) as the Storyville district of New Orleans, LA, evolves

Andrew J. Beard invents the "Jenny Coupler," an automatic device that locks two railroad cars together by "bumping" them; Beard receives $50,000 for this invention, which reduces the number of injuries and deaths of railroad workers who manually couple railroad cars before this invention

J. L. Love receives a patent for a pencil sharpener

R. A. Butler receives a patent for a train alarm

A. L. Cralle receives a patent for an ice cream mold

C. V. Richey receives a patent for a railroad switch

J. W. Smith receives a patent for a lawn sprinkler

George Washington Carver reports for the first time in the US a new species of Taphrina (a fungus found to grow on red and silver and maple trees); the fungus is named after him—Taphrina Carveri

Willie Simms rides the winning horse at the Brighton Handicap

A. **General History**	B. **Education**	C. **Laws and Legal Actions**	D. **Religion**
1898	The battleship *Maine* is bombed, killing more than 250 officers and men, including at least 30 blacks, and igniting the US war against Spain		Louisiana originates the "grandfather clause," which qualifies males to vote if their fathers or grandfathers were eligible to vote on or before January 1, 1867; the provision excludes most blacks; by 1910, Georgia, North Carolina, Virginia, Alabama, and Oklahoma adopt the clause	Robert Turner is one of the first black Americans to embrace the Baha'i Faith; this world religion, founded in Iran in 1844, promotes racial harmony and equality between the sexes

During the Spanish-American War the 25th Infantry attacks the Spanish garrison in Santiago, Cuba; Pvt. Thomas C. Butler and Pvt. J. H. Jones are the first Americans to enter the fort and to capture the Spanish flag; they are forced to surrender the flag to a white man who, masquerading as an officer, receives official credit for the capture of the fort

John E. Bush (b Moscow, TN, c1856; d Dec 11, 1916), former slave and later teacher, is appointed receiver of the US Land Office in Little Rock, AR

S. W. Rutherford starts the National Benefit Insurance Company

John Merrick and Dr. A. M. Moore organize the North Carolina Mutual Life Insurance Company in Durham, NC

The appointment of a black postmaster in Lake City, SC, starts a riot; the postmaster and his family are murdered and their home burned to the ground

Illinois coal companies in Pana and Verden use southern blacks as strikebreakers; strike failure causes hostility between white and black members of the United Mine Workers

At least 25 black soldiers, members of the US 10th Colored Cavalry, participate in the famous charge up San Juan Hill, Cuba; this assault is a major engagement of the Spanish-American War; Edward Baker, Jr., is awarded the Congressional Medal of Honor for saving a wounded fellow soldier while under fire, San Juan Hill

E. **Literature, Publications, and The Black Press**	F. **The Arts**	G. **Science, Technology, and Medicine**	H. **Sports**	
Kate Drumgold's autobiographical narrative *A Slave Girl's Story* is published	Otis J. René, b New Orleans, LA, Oct 2; he and his younger brother Leon will establish Exclusive and Excelsior Records, Los Angeles, CA, in the 1930s; by the 1940s the brothers will be the leading independent record producers whose artists will include Nat "King" Cole, Herb Jeffries, and Johnny Otis		Willie Simms rides the winning horse at the Kentucky Derby and the Brighton Handicap	**1898**
	Concert pianist Thomas "Blind Tom" Bethune retires; he was said to have had a repertoire of 7,000 songs, 100 of which were his original compositions			
	Bob Cole's *A Trip to Coontown* is the first musical comedy written by a black for black actors			
	Will Marion Cook directs the musical comedy sketch *Clorindy, the Origin of the Cakewalk,* on Broadway, NYC; Cook composes music to lyrics written by poet Paul Laurence Dunbar			

	A. **General History**	B. **Education**	C. **Laws and Legal Actions**	D. **Religion**
1899	The Fanny Jackson Coppin Club, one of the first black clubs in the West, is established in Oakland, CA Maggie Lena Walker (b Richmond, VA, c 1867; d Dec 15, 1934), secretary-treasurer of the Independent Order of St. Luke, a mutual aid society in Richmond, VA, transforms the society into a successful financial complex that bolsters the black community in Richmond			
1900	Educator Booker T. Washington organizes the National Negro Business League, Boston, MA W. E. B. DuBois, scholar, is the secretary of the First Pan-African Conference in London, England; among the delegates, Anna Julia Cooper and Anna H. Jones are the only black women to deliver addresses	Coppin State College (named after educator Fanny Jackson Coppin) is founded in Baltimore, MD Following Robert H. Terrell's resignation as principal of M Street High School to become the first black municipal judge of Washington, DC, Anna Julia Cooper becomes the second black female principal of the school (Mary Jane Patterson was the first)		By this year, the African Methodist Episcopal church consists of 5,775 churches and 663,746 members Due to increased demands from its members, the African Methodist Episcopal Church establishes the position of deaconess exclusively for women; the position is not, however, part of the ordained ministry like the deacon position for men Nannie Helen Burroughs (b Orange, VA, May 2, 1879; d Washington, DC, May 20, 1961) is one of the founders of the Women's Convention, auxiliary to the National Baptist Convention, USA, Inc.; she serves as the corresponding secretary and delivers a historic speech, "How the Sisters Are Hindered from Helping"
1901	Booker T. Washington dines with Pres. Theodore Roosevelt* at the White House, Washington, DC; the dinner is met with criticism by many whites who view it as a marked depar-	Grambling State University is founded, Grambling, LA		African Methodist Episcopal bishop Henry McNeal Turner founds *Voice of the People*, a magazine

E. Literature, Publications, and The Black Press	F. The Arts	G. Science, Technology, and Medicine	H. Sports	
Sutton Griggs's *Imperium and Imperio* is published; now considered the first "black power" novel, it features a young militant who forms a secret anti-white society that aims to create a separate all-black republic in Texas

Charles W. Chesnutt's *The Conjure Woman,* a volume of stories, is published

Librarian Daniel Murray (b Baltimore, MD, 1852; d Washington DC, 1925) is asked to prepare a display on "Negro Literature" for the American Exhibit at the 1900 Paris Exposition; in preparation for the exhibit, Murray seeks the title of every book and pamphlet ever written by persons of African ancestry, eventually making him the leading authority on black bibliography | "Maple Leaf Rag" by Scott Joplin (1868–1917), a ragtime piece, is published; piano-rag music is an outgrowth of dance-music patterns developed among black folk during the antebellum period

Perry J. Lowery and his group perform with the Sells and Forepaugh Brothers Circus, Madison Square Garden, NYC: Lowery's is the first black vaudeville act in a circus; before this time, blacks were only allowed to play in the circus band | Joseph H. Dickinson invents and patents the pianola, an automatic player piano design still used today

George F. Grant, a dentist, invents and patents the golf tee

J. A. Burr receives a patent for a lawn mower

I. R. Johnson receives a patent for a bicycle frame

J. W. Butts receives a patent for a luggage carrier

R. Hearness receives a patent for a detachable car fender

Douglass Hospital is founded, Kansas City, KS; it is the first hospital west of the Mississippi River to admit people regardless of race | Marshall "Major" Taylor (b Indianapolis, IN, Nov 21, 1878) is the first black world bicycle champion | **1899** |
| Booker T. Washington's *Up from Slavery* is published; it is warmly received by many northern and southern whites for its nonvindictive attitude toward racism and slavery

Pauline Hopkins's *Contending Forces: A Romance Illustrative of Negro Life North and South* is published | The famed steam locomotive driven by John "Casey" Jones* collides with another train; Wallace Saunders, a member of the crew, is inspired to write a song, the "Ballad of Casey Jones," immortalizing Casey Jones, who died with his hand on the train's air brake

Brothers J. Rosamond (b Jacksonville, FL, 1873; d 1954) and James Weldon Johnson write the song "Lift Every Voice and Sing" for an Abraham Lincoln* birthday celebration; the song will become popularized as the "Negro National Anthem" | J. F. Pickering receives a patent for an airship | | **1900** |
| William Monroe Trotter (b Boston, MA, 1872; d 1934) founds the *Boston Guardian,* a militant newspaper | Bob Cole, J. Rosamond Johnson and James Weldon Johnson become the first black songwriters to sign a contract with a Broadway music company, Joseph W. Stern and Com- | | Encouraged by John J. McGraw,* manager of the Baltimore Orioles, Charlie Grant changes his name to Charlie Tokahama and declares that he is full-blooded Native American, | **1901** |

	A. **General History**	B. **Education**	C. **Laws and Legal Actions**	D. **Religion**
1901	ture from the "usual" racial etiquette			
1902	White citizens of Indianola, MS, protest the reappointment of Minnie Cox as postmistress, claiming that her reappointment permits "nigger domination"; Cox offers to resign, but Pres. Theodore Roosevelt,* in a show of support for black Americans, refuses the resignation and suspends postal service to the town; the next year Cox leaves Indianola but returns in 1904 after the controversy fades	Charlotte Hawkins Brown (b Henderson, NC, c 1883; d 1961) founds Palmer Memorial Institute, NC, and remains its president until 1952; Palmer is one of the oldest black preparatory schools in the US John D. Rockefeller,* philanthropist, founds the General Education Board, established to materially aid black education and to promote the training of black teachers for Southern schools; within six years, Rockefeller donates over $50 million to the Board	*Susie King, believed to be the first black nurse in the US Army.* (MSRC)  *Susie King Taylor.*	
1903	William Monroe Trotter, publisher, is arrested after heckling Booker T. Washington at the Columbus Avenue African Zion Church, Boston, MA; Trotter explains that he resorted to a public confrontation because Washington holds a monopoly on the American media and, consequently, opposing views on race relations are not heard Hon. Mifflin W. Gibbs is named president of Capital City Savings Bank in Little Rock, AR The Mississippi State Federation of Colored Women's Clubs is established When the Saint Luke Penny Savings Bank opens, financier Maggie Lena Walker becomes the first black woman bank president in the US Pres. Theodore Roosevelt* appoints Christopher Payne as consul general to the Dutch West Indies	William H. Crogman is elected president of Clark University (later renamed Clark College), GA Albany State College is founded, Albany, GA Utica Junior College is founded, Utica, MS Harriet Marshall (b Vancouver, British Columbia, Canada, Feb 18, 1868; d Washington, DC, Feb 25, 1941) founds the Washington Conservatory of Music and School of Expression for black students, Washington, DC		Harriet Tubman deeds a home for the elderly in Auburn, NY, to her African Methodist Episcopal Zion Church
1904	Boley, OK, an all-black town, is founded	Mary McLeod Bethune (b Mayesville, SC, Jul 10, 1875; d Daytona Beach, FL, May 18, 1945) founds the Daytona Normal and Industrial School (later renamed Bethune-Cookman College) in Florida		Virginia Broughton's *Women's Work, as Gleaned from the Women of the Bible* is published; Broughton's work examines biblical precedents for gender equality

E. Literature, Publications, and The Black Press	F. The Arts	G. Science, Technology, and Medicine	H. Sports	
	pany; this contract led to the popularization of their songs by white Broadway performers		thus subverting baseball's "color line"	**1901**
Susie King Taylor's *Reminiscences of My Life in Camp with the U.S. Colored Troops* is published Gwendolyn Bennett, poet, artist, and writer, b Giddings, TX, Jul 8; she will later become assistant editor of *Opportunity* and write a literary gossip column, "Ebony Flute," for the magazine (d May 1981)	Chicago's Local 208, a black musician's union, is incorporated into the American Federation of Musicians, becoming the first black union to join		Joe Gans (b Joseph Gaines, Baltimore, MD, Nov 25, 1874) KOs Frank Erne* in the first round and becomes the first native-born black American to win a world crown (lightweight)	**1902**
W. E. B. Du Bois's *The Souls of Black Folk*, a collection of essays, is published Benjamin J. Davis, Sr. (b Dawson, GA, May 27, 1870; d New York, NY, 1945) begins publishing a weekly newspaper, the *Independent*, which quickly becomes known as the most militant black newspaper in the South, GA; unable to obtain support from black- or white-owned businesses, the newspaper survives solely on subscriptions and the financial backing of the District Grand Order of the Odd Fellows, the wealthiest black fraternal organization in the South	The play *In Dahomey* travels to England where the company gives a command performance for King Edward VII* in London; by the time the cast is ready to leave eight months later, the cakewalk dance is as popular in England and France as it is in the US; *In Dahomey* is the first black American musical performed abroad N. Clark Smith and J. Berni Barbour establish the first black-owned music publishing company Wilbur Sweatman and his band are one of the first black groups to make a record when they record Scott Joplin's "Maple Leaf Rag," Minneapolis, MN		John "Jack" Johnson, (b Galveston, TX, Mar 31, 1878; d Raleigh, NC, Jun 10, 1946), considered by many the best black boxer in the US, defeats "Denver" Ed Martin for the Negro Heavyweight crown, Los Angeles, CA Dan McClelland pitches the first "no-hitter" (perfect game) by a black pitcher in professional baseball	**1903**
William Stanley Braithwaite's (1878–1962) *Lyrics of Life and Love*, a book of poetry in the tradition of the post-romantic British writers, is published			Samuel Ransom is one of the first blacks to play on a predominantly white college basketball team when he plays for Beloit College until 1908, WI	**1904**

A. **General History**	B. **Education**	C. **Laws and Legal Actions**	D. **Religion**
1905 W. E. B. Du Bois calls a conference of black leaders in Fort Erie, Canada; this group founds the Niagara Movement, dedicated to "aggressive action" on behalf of black freedom and growth; Du Bois serves as General Secretary until 1909	Mississippi Industrial College is founded, Holly Springs, MS		

The black community of Nashville, TN, launches a streetcar boycott in protest against newly imposed Jim Crow laws

The Committee for Improving Industrial Conditions of Negroes in New York City is organized

The National League for Protection of Colored Women is formed in New York

The constitution of the Industrial Workers of the World provides that "no working man or woman shall be excluded from membership in unions because of creed or color"

Ernest W. Lyon, US minister to Liberia, helps to create the New York Liberian Steamship Line to continue efforts to establish closer commercial relations between the US and Liberia

The Atlanta Life Insurance Company is founded by Alonzo F. Herndon, Atlanta, GA; Atlanta Life and North Carolina Mutual Insurance Company are the two largest black-owned companies in the US at this time

The Woman's Improvement Club opens an outdoor tuberculosis camp in Indianapolis, IN, reportedly the first in the US

Charles W. Anderson (1866–1938), former chief of the state treasury, is appointed collector of internal revenue for the second district of New York City; Warren Harding* appoints him for the third district in 1922

E. **Literature, Publications, and The Black Press**	F. **The Arts**	G. **Science, Technology, and Medicine**	H. **Sports**	
Robert S. Abbott (b St. Simons Island, GA, 1870) begins publishing his newspaper *The Chicago Defender*, Chicago, IL; by 1929 the *Defender* has a national circulation of over 250,000

W. E. B. Du Bois founds and serves as editor of *The Moon Illustrated Weekly*, a magazine

Frederick Moore (b Virginia, 1857; d New York City, 1943) becomes editor and part-owner of the *Colored American Magazine*, Boston, MA | Bob Motts founds Pekin Theater in Chicago, IL, the first permanent black theater in the US

The Philadelphia Concert Orchestra, the first black symphony in the North, is founded and incorporated; E. Gilbert Anderson is the first conductor

The Memphis Players, the first modern jazz band, makes its debut on a New York stage, with Abbie Mitchell singing and Ida Forsyne dancing | Lewis Latimer receives a patent for book supports | Edwin Henderson, W. A. Joiner, G. C. Wilkinson, R. N. Mattingley, and W. A. Decater found the Interscholastic Athletic Association to provide scholastic-athletic programs in the Washington, DC–Baltimore, MD area | **1905** |

	A. **General History**	B. **Education**	C. **Laws and Legal Actions**	D. **Religion**
1906	In the "Brownsville Incident," black soldiers accused of raiding the town, shooting to death a white bartender and wounding a white policeman are deprived of fair trial by court martial; more than 60 years later, the US Army clears the records of 167 soldiers who had been dishonorably discharged, Brownsville, TX Mary Church Terrell and William Monroe Trotter protest after Pres. Theodore Roosevelt* delivers a dishonorable discharge against three companies of black soldiers following the Brownsville, TX, riot Madame C. J. Walker (b Sarah Breedlove, Louisiana, Dec 23, 1867; d May 25, 1919) starts a black hair-care business in Denver, CO; she alters curling irons that were popularized by the French to suit the texture of black women's hair; at her death, she is considered the wealthiest black woman in America; she is arguably the first woman millionaire in the US Robert Church, Sr. (b Mississippi, Jun 18, 1839; d Aug 2, 1912), father of Mary Church Terrell and former slave, founds the Solvent Savings Bank and Trust Company in Memphis, TN, one of the fastest growing black-owned banks of the early 20th century; it is believed that by his death, Church is the first black American millionaire Chaplain Allen Allensworth is promoted to lieutenant-colonel, the highest rank held by a black in the military until Charles Young is promoted to colonel during WWI One hundred men and women gather at Harper's Ferry, WV, for the second meeting of the Niagara	John Hope (b Augusta, GA, 1868; d 1936) becomes the first black president of Morehouse College, Atlanta, GA; Hope denounces Booker T. Washington's "Atlanta Compromise Address" and is the only president of a black college to join the Niagara Movement		W. J. Seymour, Holiness preacher, starts the Pentecostal movement when members of the congregation receive baptism of the Spirit at a revival meeting in his home, Los Angeles, CA

| | | | | **1906** |
| J. Max Berber, journalist, founds the *Voice of the Negro,* which will become a leading periodical | Meta Vaux Warrick Fuller exhibits her sculpture *Portraits from Mirrors* at the 101st Annual Exhibition at the Pennsylvania Academy of the Fine Arts, Philadelphia, PA | | Joe Gans relinquishes the world lightweight title to gain the world welterweight title from champion Mike Sullivan* | |

Emancipation Day celebrations, commemorating the end of slavery, an annual and festive event in many Southern states. (LC)

A. **General History**	B. **Education**	C. **Laws and Legal Actions**	D. **Religion**
1906 Movement; they march in solemn procession to the site of John Brown's* raid The California black women's clubs create a State Federation of Colored Women's Clubs Alpha Phi Alpha, the first black Greek letter fraternity for undergraduates is founded at Cornell University, Ithaca, NY			
1907	Quaker heiress Anna Jeanes* establishes the Negro Rural School Fund, known as the Jeanes Fund, to improve rural schools for southern blacks; the trustees include Booker T. Washington, Andrew Carnegie,* Robert Moton, and James Dillard Alain Locke (b Philadelphia, PA, 1886; d 1954) graduates from Harvard College magna cum laude; he is selected as a Rhodes Scholar, becoming the first black to receive this award Kelly Miller (b Winnsboro, SC, 1863; d 1939) begins his tenure as dean of Howard University's College of Arts and Sciences and travels extensively throughout the US recruiting students; student enrollment increases 40% annually under his deanship Prentiss Normal & Industrial Institute is founded, Prentiss, MS Jesse Lawson founds Frelinghuysen University, Washington, DC, an institution for black adult education	The US Supreme Court rules that railroads may racially segregate passengers traveling between states, even when segregation is illegal in the states in which the train is traveling As special assistant to the Dept. of Justice, attorney James A. Cobb (b Arcadia, LA, 1876) begins prosecuting cases under the Pure Food and Drugs Act enacted in 1906; he serves in this position for eight years 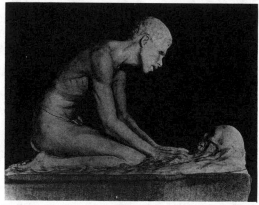 Talking Head *by Meta Vaux Warrick Fuller, one of the first black sculptors in the United States and the first black woman to receive a federal commission for her set of tableaux at the Jamestown Tercentennial Exposition.* (Schomburg)	
1908 The Woman's Day Nursery Association, which cares for the children of working black mothers, is formed in Los Angeles, CA Alpha Kappa Alpha, the first black Greek letter sorority, is founded, Howard University, Washington, DC	Morris College is founded, Sumter, SC		

1906

1907

Wendall P. Dabney establishes *The Union*, a newspaper in Cincinnati, OH

W. E. B. Du Bois is chief founder and editor of *Horizon: A Journal of the Color Line*; the journal advocates "Negro equality and human equality"

C. M. Hughes and Minnie Thomas begin publishing *Colored Woman's Magazine*; it will be one of the longest running periodicals under the control of black women

Kelly Miller's manuscript "The Education of the Negro" is published as chapter 16 in the US Bureau of Education's *Report for 1900–1901:* in the chapter, Miller, Howard University professor and noted sociologist, analyzes the impact of economic and social conditions on the progress of black education

Gladys Bentley, flamboyant lesbian entertainer, b Philadelphia, PA; during the Harlem Renaissance, Bentley, dressed in characteristic white tuxedo and top hat, becomes a cult star playing the piano and improvising risque lyrics to the melodies of popular songs (d 1960)

Meta Vaux Warrick Fuller becomes the first black woman artist to receive a federal commission when she is asked to craft 150 black figurines for the Jamestown Tercentennial Exposition; she later receives a gold medal for these works

Henry Minton, Eugene T. Hinson and Algernon B. Jackson establish Mercy Hospital, Philadelphia, PA; Mercy Hospital, along with Meharry and Howard Medical Schools, will train the majority of the country's black doctors

Jockey Jimmy Lee rides the winning horse in the Clipsetta Stakes, the Latonia Oaks, the Kentucky Oaks, and the Latonia Derby

Bill Pickett (b Williamson County, TX, 1870; d Oklahoma, 1932) signs a contract with the 101 Ranch Wild West Show, becoming one of its star performers; Pickett, who originates the "bulldogging" technique, will become internationally known

1908

Appointment of the first black bandmasters of the US Army: Wade Hammond (9th Cavalry), Alfred Jack Thomas (10th Cavalry), William Polk (24th Infantry), and Egbert Thompson (25th Infantry)

Alton A. Adams (b 1889) is the first black bandmaster of the US Navy

Fifty-two black graduate nurses meet at St. Mark's Methodist Church to address their inferior status as nurses and form the National Association of Colored Graduate Nurses; the group's activities include creating a national registry to help members find employment and campaigning to improve black-operated nursing schools

Jack Johnson defeats Tommy Burns* in the 14th round to become the first black American heavyweight champion of the world; prior to this match, blacks were allowed to compete in all other weight classes except for the heavyweight division

John Baxter "Doc" Taylor becomes the first black American Olympic gold

1908

1909

W. E. B. Du Bois and others, including whites, meet and advocate a civil rights organization to combat the growing violence against black Americans; this leads to the founding of the National Association for the Advancement of Colored People

Matthew Henson, accompanying Comdr. Robert Peary,* discovers the North Pole

William A. Attaway organizes the Mississippi Life Insurance Company, the first black legal reserve life insurance company

Nannie Helen Burroughs founds the National Training School for Women, Washington, DC (later renamed the Nannie Helen Burroughs School); today it operates as an elementary school and offers missionary as well as industrial training

Nannie Helen Burroughs, founder of the National Training School for Women and Girls in Washington, DC. (LC)

1910

George E. Haynes founds The Committee on Urban Conditions of Negroes to promote jobs and urban opportunities for blacks, New York City; the group will merge in 1911 with the National League for the Protection of Colored Women and change its name to the National Urban League; it will be incorporated three years later

Sara Winifred Brown and a group of friends, including clubwoman and activist Mary Church Terrell, found the College Alumnae Club in order to enable graduates of black colleges who are denied membership in the predominantly white Association of Collegiate Alumnae to enjoy the benefits of professional affiliation

Mary White Ovington* credits Kathryn Magnalia Johnson, former teacher, as the first field worker of

As of this year, Howard University, Washington, DC, and Fisk University, Nashville, TN, have graduated 514 black women; of the non-historically black colleges and universities, Oberlin College, Oberlin, OH, has graduated the largest number (66) of black women

North Carolina Central University is founded, Durham, NC

E. Literature, Publications, and The Black Press	F. The Arts	G. Science, Technology, and Medicine	H. Sports	
			medal winner after competing in the 1600-meter relay, London, England	**1908**
			Edwin B. Henderson begins the first serious city basketball competitions between New York City and Washington, DC	
Publication of the *Amsterdam News* begins in New York City	William Christopher "W.C." Handy composes "Mayor Crump Blues" for Edward Crump's* election campaign, Memphis, TN *Sambo* and *Rastus,* comedy shorts that depict black Americans in stereotypical childlike roles, become popular in movie theaters	Garrett A. Morgan (b Paris, KY, Mar 4, 1877) discovers and invents the first hair straightening chemical; he markets the product as G. A. Morgan Hair Refining Cream	Cumberland Posey organizes the Monticello Delaney Rifles, a basketball team, Pittsburgh, PA	**1909**
Publication of the *Crisis* magazine, the official organ of the NAACP, begins; W. E. B. Du Bois is its first editor Daniel Murray oversees the *Historical and Biographical Encyclopedia of the Colored Race Throughout the World,* an extensive 6-volume work			The Public Schools Athletic League (PSAL) in New York City sponsors the first large-scale indoor track meet ever organized by blacks Charles W. Follis, b Cloverdale, VA, Apr 5; Follis will become the first black American to play professional football Jack Johnson fights James Jeffries,* retired heavyweight champion; upon Jeffries's defeat, whites retaliate, injuring and killing several blacks; US Congress bans distribution of film clips of the fight across state lines for commercial purposes	**1910**

1910

the NAACP; over her career, Johnson works extensively in the South and the West establishing NAACP branches

Rev. Robert Bagnall (b Norfolk, VA, 1884; d Philadelphia, PA, 1943), an active member of the Detroit branch of the NAACP, over the decade spearheads efforts to persuade the Ford Motor Company to hire more black workers; he also fights against Jim Crow schools in Ypsilanti, MI, and campaigns against police maltreatment in Detroit

Ida B. Wells-Barnett, anti-lynching and civil rights crusader, becomes the first president of the Negro Fellowship League

Jesse E. Moorland (b Coldwater, OH, 1863; d New York City, 1940) raises $100,000 to renovate the oldest black YMCA building, Washington, DC; Moorland will travel extensively, raising funds for other YMCA buildings throughout the US

1911

Sarah M. Overton, suffragist, tours California to organize black support for the suffrage amendment

The National Negro Doll Company, founded by Rev. Richard Boyd, begins distributing black dolls

Marcus Garvey (1887–1940) establishes the Universal Negro Improvement Association, a grass-roots Pan-Africanist organization, in Jamaica

John E. Bruce, Arthur Schomburg, David Fulton, W. Wesley Weeks and William E. Braxton found the Negro Society for Historical Research to promote the study of black history and to collect books, photographs, letters and artwork pertaining to blacks

E. Literature,
   Publications, and
   The Black Press

F. The Arts

G. Science,
   Technology,
   and Medicine

H. Sports

1910

Scott Joplin's *Treemonisha* becomes the first black folk opera written by a black to be performed in any theater

The Interscholastic Athletic Association (ISAA) sponsors the first formal swimming meet among blacks, Washington, DC

William E. Kindle, the first black American soccer star, plays for Springfield College, MA

1911

A. **General History**	B. **Education**	C. **Laws and Legal Actions**	D. **Religion**
1911 Booker T. Washington is severely beaten for allegedly approaching a white woman, New York City			
1912 As keynote speaker at the National American Woman Suffrage Association convention, W. E. B. DuBois appeals to white delegates to admit black women as full and equal members	Tennessee State University is founded, Nashville, TN Jarvis Christian College is founded, Hawkins, TX		
1913 The Sojourner Truth Industrial Club, established to provide a home for orphans and unwed women, is founded in Los Angeles, CA As a delegate to the National American Woman's Suffrage Association's suffrage parade, journalist Ida B. Wells-Barnett refuses to march only with the other black delegates at the back of the procession; instead she marches with her white colleagues from Illinois as had been the tradition; the parade takes place in Washington, DC, on the eve of Woodrow Wilson's* first inaugural William Monroe Trotter confronts Pres. Woodrow Wilson* at the White House, accusing the president of lying when he denies responsibility for segregation in government cafeterias in Washington, DC Illinois is the first state east of the Mississippi river to enfranchise black women			Noble Drew Ali (b Timothy Drew, North Carolina, 1886; d 1929) founds the Moorish Science Temple, the first mosque in the US, in Newark, NJ; Ali advocates that true emancipation for blacks will come through their knowledge of their African heritage and by becoming Muslims

1911

1912

Charlotta Bass becomes owner and publisher of the *California Eagle*, a weekly newspaper

James Weldon Johnson's *The Autobiography of an Ex-Colored Man* is published

Monroe N. Work (b Iredell Co., NC, 1866; d Tuskegee, AL, 1945), director of records and research at Tuskegee Institute, publishes *The Negro Yearbook, Annual Encyclopedia of the Negro*

Sam Hopkins, guitarist and blues singer, b Centerville, TX, Mar 15

W. C. Handy's "Memphis Blues" is the first published blues composition

Under the direction of James Europe (b Mobile AL, 1881; d Boston, MA, 1919), 125 black symphonic musicians perform at Carnegie Hall, NYC, exposing many of the city's white residents for the first time to symphonies played by black musicians; Europe will go on to become an acclaimed jazz musician, noted musical director and bandmaster of the famed all-black 369th Infantry Band in World War I

Daniel Hale Williams is the first black appointed associate attending surgeon at St. Luke's Hospital, Chicago, IL; St. Luke's is the largest and wealthiest hospital in the city

Ernest E. Just (b Charleston, SC, 1883; d Washington, DC, 1941), premiere biologist and research scientist, publishes his first paper, "The Relation of the First Cleavage Plane to the Entrance Point of Sperm," in the *Biological Bulletin*; in 1915, Just will be awarded the NAACP's first Spingarn Medal for his accomplishments

Hampton University in Virginia is the first black college to have a varsity crew team

1913

William Stanley Braithwaite, poet and critic, publishes *Anthology of Magazine Verse;* this anthology is published annually until 1929

Fenton Johnson's (b Chicago, IL, May 7, 1888) first collection of poetry, *A Little Dreaming*, is published

Daniel Hale Williams is the first black member of the American College of Surgeons

Garrett A. Morgan founds the G. A. Morgan Refining Company, Cleveland, OH

John Shippen finishes fourth in the US Open; because of his light skin he is able to "pass" for white and play in the tournament when blacks are excluded

Jack Johnson fights Jim Johnson in the first world heavyweight match between two black contenders, Paris, France; the bout ends in a draw

	A. **General History**	B. **Education**	C. **Laws and Legal Actions**	D. **Religion**
1913	Pres. Woodrow Wilson* rejects Oswald Villard's* proposal to appoint a National Race Commission to study the social and economic condition of blacks			
1914	Spingarn Medal awards are instituted by Joel E. Spingarn, chairman of the board of directors of the NAACP, to distinguish merit and achievement of American blacks

Kelly Miller persuades Jesse E. Moorland, a Howard University alumnus and trustee, to donate his private collection of books on black America and Africa to Howard University as the first step of a proposed museum and library; the collection eventually grows into the school's current Moorland-Spingarn Research Center

Oscar Over, veteran of the Spanish-American War, is California's first black justice of the peace | | | Lucy Smith (b 1875), a member of the predominantly white Stone Church, Chicago, IL, receives a "calling" (speaking in tongues); Smith, who will later become an elder, will found the All Nations Pentecostal Church in the 1930s |
| **1915** | Carter G. Woodson (b New Canton, VA, Dec 19, 1875; d 1950) founds the Association for the Study of Negro Life and History; much of its early support comes from women

Southern blacks begin migrating to northern cities when war industries seek their services; between 1910 and 1930, almost one million blacks leave the South in what becomes known as the Great Migration | Following the death of Booker T. Washington, Robert Russa Moton is elected principal of the Tuskegee Normal and Industrial Institute in Alabama

Alain Locke petitions Howard University's board of trustees to teach a course on the scientific study of race and race relations; his petition is rejected; the Howard Chapter of the NAACP and the Social Science Club sponsors a two-year extension course of lectures by Locke entitled "Race Contacts and Inter-Racial Relations: A Study in the Theory and Practice of Race"

Maria "Mollie" Baldwin is appointed mistress of the Agassiz School, which is 98% white; she is the only black and one of two women to hold this position in Cambridge, MA | In *Frank Guinn and J. J. Beal v. United States*, the US Supreme Court declares that "grandfather clauses," used in southern states to disfranchise blacks, are unconstitutional

A South Carolina law prohibits factory owners from allowing blacks and whites to work in the same room and to use the same entrances, stairs, rest rooms, drinking cups, or water buckets | "Father Divine" (b George Baker, 1877–1965) establishes his first church, what will be known as the Peace Mission Kingdom; the Kingdoms will increase in popularity in the 1930s as members provide food, clothing, and shelter to others for little or no cost |

E. Literature, Publications, and The Black Press	F. The Arts	G. Science, Technology, and Medicine	H. Sports	
				1913
John W. Cromwell's *The Negro in American History* is published	*Darktown Jubilee* is the first film to star a black actor, Bert Williams	Garrett A. Morgan wins the First Grand Prize at the Second International Exposition of Sanitation and Safety for his invention, the smoke inhalator		**1914**
Carter G. Woodson's *The Education of the Negro Prior to 1861* is published

The Chicago *Defender* adopts the slogan "If you must die, take at least one with you," reflecting the increasing militant attitude found in the black community; sale of the paper is not permitted in many places outside Chicago, IL, and the slogan is modified to "An eye for an eye" the following year | The NAACP leads protests against D. W. Griffith's* film *Birth of a Nation;* based on the writings of Thomas Dixon,* the film features vicious racial stereotypes and glorifies the activities of the Ku Klux Klan | Booker T. Washington founds National Negro Health Week to increase awareness in the black community; it is the catalyst for the National Negro Health Movement that begins in 1932 | After seven consecutive years as champion, Jack Johnson loses the world heavyweight championship title when he is KO'd by Jess Willard* in the 26th round; Johnson later confesses to "throwing" the fight to gain an "additional percentage" of money from Willard's manager

Joseph E. Trigg of Syracuse University, New York, is the first known black athlete on a varsity crew team at a predominantly white college | **1915** |

215

	A. General History	B. Education	C. Laws and Legal Actions	D. Religion
1915		Under the leadership of president Janie Porter Barrett, the Virginia Women's Federation of Colored Women's Clubs raises money to build the Virginia Industrial School for Colored Girls (later renamed the Janie Porter Barrett School for Girls) near Richmond; the school provides a rehabilitation center for troubled black girls		
1916	Two black regiments serve with Gen. John J. Pershing* on Mexican punitive raids, which counter a raid across the border by Mexican leader Pancho Villa* Edward A. Johnson is the first black elected to the New York state assembly	Mary Ellen Cable (1881–1944), educator, institutes the first "fresh air" classroom for black children with tuberculosis at Public School 25 in New York City		As of this year, the Baptist Church constitutes not only the largest black religious group but the third largest of all religious groups in the US Because the Georgia state legislature seeks to prohibit white nuns from teaching black children, Ignatius Lissner, priest of the Society of African Missions, seeks to establish a community of black nuns
1917	US enters WWI; approximately 300,000 blacks serve during this conflict, and 1,400 blacks are commissioned as officers The Selected Service Act reopens Army enlistment of blacks; on registration day, approximately 700,000 blacks register for the draft	The first all-black officer training school is established by the US Army, Des Moines, IA	In *Buchanan v. Warley,* the US Supreme Court overrules a Louisville, KY, law that forbids blacks and whites from residing in the same neighborhood block	Father Ignatius Lissner and Elizabeth Williams (b Baton Rouge, LA, Feb 7, 1868) co-found a community of black nuns, the Franciscan Handmaids of the Most Pure Heart of Mary, Savannah, GA

The premiere issue of *The Journal of Negro History* is published; historian Carter G. Woodson is the editor	Lauretta Green (b Los Angeles, CA, Nov 6, 1881) opens the Butler Dance Studio, the first black-owned professional studio for children; although established primarily for blacks, Butler Studio also trains whites, including cast members of *Our Gang* and *The Little Rascals* films Charles A. Tindley's *New Songs of Paradise*, the first collection of gospel hymns by a black songwriter, is published James Van der Zee (b Lenox, MA, Jun 29, 1886) opens his photography studio; Van der Zee will become the premiere photographer of the 1920s, capturing prominent persons and themes of the Harlem Renaissance The NAACP presents Angelina Grimké's play *Rachel,* the first successful fully staged professional production of a work by a black playwright The Apollo Theater opens on 125th Street, Harlem, New York City; over the years many entertainers will get their start at the Apollo	Garrett A. Morgan and a rescue team use his gas inhalator to help save two dozen men trapped after a gas explosion in tunnel number five in Cleveland, OH; the city later awards Morgan a gold medal for heroism	The American Tennis Association is organized to promote tennis playing among blacks, Washington, DC Frederick "Fritz" Pollard of Brown University, Rhode Island, is the first black athlete to play in college football's Rose Bowl	**1916**
A. Philip Randolph (1889–1979) and Chandler Owen begin publishing *The Messenger;* the magazine champions the labor movement and the rise of socialism	Ulysses Simpson Kay, composer, b Tucson, AZ; Kay will become one of the first black classical composers in the US and one of the first to travel to the Soviet Union Evelyn Preer (b Vicksburg, MS, Jul 26, 1896; d 1932) makes her debut in *The Homesteader,* the first black	Louis Wright (b La Grange, GA, Jul 23, 1891; d NYC, Oct 8, 1952) enters the US Army as a first lieutenant in the medical corps; he introduces the method of vaccination for smallpox that is eventually adopted by the corps	Lucy Diggs Slowe (b Jul 4, 1885; d 1936) becomes the first black woman athletic champion when she wins the women's singles title at the American Tennis Association championships, Baltimore, MD	**1917**

1917

Whites react violently toward blacks who are hired in a factory that holds a contract with the federal government; a riot ensues, leaving 100 blacks killed or injured, E. St. Louis, MO

Following the East St. Louis, MO, riot, in a show of solidarity, approximately 10,000 black New Yorkers participate in the Negro Silent Protest Parade

The Central Committee of Negro College Men is organized to prove the willingness of blacks to fight in WWI, Howard University, Washington, DC

Eva D. Bowles (b Albany, OH, Jan 24, 1875; d Richmond, VA, Jun 14, 1943), pioneer social worker, is appointed head of the Colored Work Committee of the YWCA's War Work Council and given a $200,000 appropriation to build numerous recreational facilities for black girls throughout the nation; her work so impresses Theodore Roosevelt* that he donates $4,000 of his Nobel Peace Prize to be used under Bowles's direction

The 369th Infantry is the first black US combat unit overseas; in 191 days of action, the regiment never loses a man, a trench, or any ground; they become known to the Germans as the ''Hell Fighters''

Women organize the Circle for Negro War Relief to provide medical, recreational, and other services to black soldiers

Emmett J. Scott, former secretary to Booker T. Washington, is appointed special assistant to the US Secretary of War; Scott is to work for nondiscriminatory application of the Selective Training and Service Act

1917

silent film by producer/
director Oscar Micheaux;
Preer will star in other
successful silent films and
plays, including *Shuffle
Along* and *Lulu Belle*

	A. **General History**	B. **Education**	C. **Laws and Legal Actions**	D. **Religion**
1917	Lloyd A. Hall is named Assistant Chief Inspector of Powder and Explosives in the ordnance department of the US Army; he holds this position for two years			
1918	US soldier Henry Johnson attacks the German enemy with a bolo knife, freeing his captured friend Needham Roberts and forcing the Germans to retreat; both soldiers are awarded the highest French military award, the Croix de Guerre, the first Americans to be so honored			Edward T. Demby becomes the first black bishop of the Episcopal Church when he is consecrated suffragan bishop for the diocese of Arkansas and the province of the southwest
	"Secret Information Concerning Black-American Troops," a document describing the necessity for separating blacks and whites, is circulated by a French liaison officer among French soldiers; this document is used in an attempt to persuade French troops to adopt American racial attitudes			
	The National Liberty Congress of Colored Americans petitions the US Congress to make lynching a federal crime			
	The African Blood Brotherhood, a radical black nationalist organization, is founded			
	Frederick Madison Roberts, allegedly a descendant of former US president Thomas Jefferson* and slave Sally Hemings, is the first black elected to the California state assembly; he serves until 1934			
	The Women's Political Association of Harlem, New York, one of the first black organizations to advocate birth control, is organized by Cyril Briggs; it is a black auxiliary to the US Communist Party, NYC; membership is limited to persons of "African blood," although the organization is committed to an integrated fight against injustice			
	Hugh N. Mulzac becomes the first black to earn a shipmaster's license			

E. **Literature,**
Publications, and
The Black Press

F. **The Arts**

G. **Science,**
Technology,
and Medicine

H. **Sports**

1917

1918

Georgia Douglas Johnson's (b Atlanta, GA, Sep 10, 1877) *The Heart of a Woman* is published; this collection of poetry is her first book

Carol Brice, who will become one of the first black classical singers to record extensively, b Sedalia, NC, Apr 16

Pearl Bailey, entertainer, b Newport News, VA, Mar 29; she will receive a Tony award for her starring role in an all-black version of *Hello Dolly* and will later be named special advisor to the US mission to the United Nations

Actress Anita Bush (1883–1974) and Charles Gilpin found the Lafayette Players (or the Anita Bush Players), one of the first black theater troupes to perform nonmusical theater

Carol Brice, contralto soloist, one of the earliest African-American concert singers to record extensively. (Bethune)

Frederick "Fritz" Pollard is the first black All-American running back, Brown University, Providence, RI

	A. **General History**	B. **Education**	C. **Laws and Legal Actions**	D. **Religion**
1919	The famed 369th Regiment marches up Fifth Avenue in a grand celebration of the end of World War I, Harlem, New York City	Black residents in Pittsburgh, PA, refuse to send their children to a separate black school and force the school to close	In *State v. Young*, the West Virginia Supreme Court rules that a black man, sentenced to life in prison, was denied equal protection under law because his jury had no black members; the state subsequently admits black jury members	Elder Micheaux (b Buckroe Beach, VA, c 1885; d Washington, DC, 1968) organizes the Church of God movement, Newport News, VA, and begins broadcasting his services over a local radio station; by 1928 he will achieve national acclaim through his radio (later television) broadcasts and the *Happy News*, the church's official organ; Micheaux believes that blacks should create their own religion, rebuking Western religions for their racist practices
	W. E. B. Du Bois organizes the first Pan-African Congress at Grand Hotel, Paris	John W. Davis (b Milledgeville, GA, 1888) becomes president of West Virginia State College; during his 34-year tenure, Davis works to increase student enrollment and secure the school's accreditation by the North Central Association of Colleges and Secondary Schools		
	The Commission on Interracial Cooperation is formed to reduce racial tension after WWI (forerunner to the Southern Regional Council); Charlotte Hawkins Brown is one of the founders	Lucy Diggs Slowe becomes principal of Shaw Junior High School, the first black junior high in Washington, DC		
	Black soldiers returning from World War I service refuse to march at the back of a victory parade because a segregated parade seems contradictory to the principles they supposedly fought for, St. Joseph, MO			
	On behalf of the NAACP, W. E. B. Du Bois investigates racist treatment of black troops in Europe; the exposure creates an international sensation			
	After his application for a passport is denied, William Monroe Trotter obtains a job as a cook on a transatlantic ship in order to reach Europe for the Paris Peace Conference; at the conference he tries unsuccessfully to have the delegates at the conference outlaw racial discrimination			
	Major racial disturbances occur across the nation during what is later called the "Red Summer"; over 100 people die, and 1,000 are wounded			
	Marcus Garvey establishes the Black Star Line, a fleet of steamships, to link African descendants throughout the world			
	Georgia Hill Robinson is the first black woman police officer in the US, Los Angeles, CA			

1919

Delilah Beasley (b Sep 9, 1872; d San Leandro, CA, Aug 18, 1934), columnist, completes her only book, *The Negro Trail-Blazers of California;* the book is later nominated for inclusion in *Guide to the Best Books* because of its value to researchers

Claude A. Barnett (b Sanford, FL, 1899) founds the Associated Negro Press, Chicago, IL; the ANP assigns reporters throughout the US to more adequately cover items of interest regarding blacks

Mary Burrill's (1884–1946) play *They That Sit in Darkness* appears in the September issue of *Birth Control Review,* a monthly periodical that agitates for birth control rights; the play, possibly the first by a black woman that addresses a feminist theme, argues that every woman should have access to birth control

Lincoln Motion Picture Company, owned by Noble Johnson and Clarence Brooks, releases its first feature-length film, *A Man's Duty*

The National Association of Negro Musicians is founded under the leadership of Nora Douglas Holt

Oscar Micheaux's (b near Cairo, IL, 1884; d Charlotte, NC, 1951) first film, *The Homesteader,* is released by the Oscar Micheaux Corporation; Micheaux, who writes, directs and produces his own films, will become a pioneer in independent black filmmaking

Alice Parker receives a patent for a heating furnace that uses gas instead of coal for fuel

Fannie Elliott (b Knoxville, TN, 1882; d Mt. Clemens, MI, 1965) officially becomes the first black nurse to be recognized by the American Red Cross; "1A" is imprinted on the back of her Red Cross nurse's pin, indicating that Elliott is a "colored" nurse; the Red Cross does not stop this racial identification until after WWII

Louis Wright is the first black physician appointed to a predominantly white hospital staff; he is appointed clinical assistant visiting surgeon, the lowest rung of the medical ladder in Harlem Hospital, New York City

Andrew "Rube" Foster and a group of black baseball club owners form the National Negro Baseball League; the league's first game is played the following year in Indianapolis, IN

	A. **General History**	B. **Education**	C. **Laws and Legal Actions**	D. **Religion**
1919	Black delegates refuse segregated arrangements at the annual luncheon of the state convention of the American Legion; they stage a walkout in protest The federal government establishes a town exclusively for blacks at Truxton, near Portsmouth, VA			
1920	Zeta Phi Beta Sorority is founded on the campus of Howard University, Washington, DC; Zeta Phi Beta and Phi Beta Sigma become the first black Greek-letter sister and brother organizations Marcus Garvey's Universal Negro Improvement Association holds an international convention in New York; movement reaches its peak Audley "Queen Mother" Moore (b New Iberia, LA, Jul 27, 1898) during this decade organizes domestic workers in the Bronx and helps black tenants defy evictions by white landlords "Rent parties" become a common feature of black community life; to help pay their rent, many families hold parties where they sell food and play dance music, charging patrons 25 cents for admission The predominantly black women's International Council of Women and the Darker Races is founded Violette N. Anderson (b London, England, 1882; d 1937) graduates from the Chicago Law School; she later becomes the first black woman to practice law in Illinois		The 19th Amendment is ratified; it states "no person is to be denied the right to vote in the US or any state based upon sex"; only in two states—Tennessee and Kentucky—are black women equally enfranchised with whites for a brief period of time	Daniel T. Russell, Jr.'s *History of the African Union Methodist Protestant Church* is published
1921	Bessie Coleman receives a pilot's certificate from the Fédération Aéronautique Internationale, France; she is the first black woman to become a licensed pilot and is the first person of	Georgiana Simpson at the University of Chicago, Sadie Tanner Mossell Alexander (d Philadelphia, PA, Nov 6, 1989) at the University of Pennsylvania, and Eva Dykes at Rad-	At the request of southern white farmers, George Washington Carver speaks before the US House of Representatives Ways and Means Committee; he convinces the committee	The African Orthodox Church is founded by Archbishop George Alexander McGuire, formerly a Protestant Episcopal priest; although the church is associated with the Garvey

Marcus Garvey, founder and president of the Universal Negro Improvement Association (UNIA), led the most significant African-American social and political movement of the 1920s. (LC)

1920

Sally Wyatt Stewart, club woman, founds *Hoosier Woman*, a publication devoted to black women and their concerns

Anne Spencer's (b Annie Bethel, Henry County, VA, Feb 6, 1882) first poem "Before the Feast of Sushan" is published in *Crisis* magazine; Spencer's poetry is later included in every volume of black poetry from the 1920s through the 1940s

Vaudevillian Mamie Smith (1883–1946) records "Crazy Blues" for Okeh Records; the song is considered the first blues record

Emperor Jones opens, starring Charles Gilpin (1878–1930) in the title role at the Provincetown Theater in New York City

J. Rosamund Johnson sets to music James Weldon Johnson's song "Lift Every Voice and Sing"

Robert Nathaniel Dett, composer, arranger and conductor, is awarded Harvard University's Bowdoin Prize for an essay, "The Emancipation of Negro Music"

Otis Boykin, inventor, b; Boykin develops a range of electronic devices, one of which is a type of resistor used in most radios

David N. Croswait, Jr. (b Nashville, TN, 1898) invents and patents an automatic water feeder; he will later invent an automobile indicator (1921); a thermostat-setting apparatus (1928); a vacuum heating system (1929); and a vacuum pump (1930)

The Universal African Black Cross Nurses is organized as a female auxiliary of the Universal Negro Improvement Association; the nurses give public lectures on first aid, nutrition, and geriatric care

Walker Smith, Jr., later known as "Sugar" Ray Robinson, b Detroit, MI, May 3 (d California, Apr 12, 1989); Robinson will become a boxing champion, winning boxing titles in three different weight classes

The National Football League is formed and allows teams to sign black players

---

1921

Benjamin Brawley's *A Short History of English Drama* is published

Composer Eubie Blake (b Baltimore, MD, 1883) and Noble Sissle produce the musical *Shuffle Along*, the first of a popular series of musicals featuring all-black casts; actress Flo-

	A. **General History**	B. **Education**	C. **Laws and Legal Actions**	D. **Religion**
1921	any race or sex to receive an international pilot's license, enabling her to fly in any part of the world Jesse Binga (1865–1950) founds the Binga State Bank, Chicago, IL; the bank will flourish during the 1920s Mary B. Talbert's (b Sep 17, 1866; d Oct 15, 1923) invitation to speak at a National Woman's Party meeting is rescinded after Alice Paul,* NWP president, rules that Talbert, a representative of the NAACP, represents an organization that specifically advocates race, not gender, equality	cliffe College are the first black women in the US to receive PhDs	to vote in favor of a tariff to protect the peanut from foreign competition	movement from its inception, it does not become the official church of the Universal Negro Improvement Association The Ahmadiyya sect is established in the US; members of the organization, a variation of Orthodox Islam, believe that Hazrat Mirza Ghulam Ahmad* is the promised Messiah George E. Haynes (b Pine Bluff, AR, 1880; d 1960) helps organize and becomes the first executive secretary of the Department of Race Relations of the Federal Council of the Churches of Christ in America

Lucy Diggs Slowe, Howard University dean of women and co-founder of the Alpha Kappa Alpha sorority, also helped organize the National Council of Negro Women. (Bethune)

	A. **General History**	B. **Education**	C. **Laws and Legal Actions**	D. **Religion**
1922	Col. Charles R. Young (b Kentucky), one of the highest ranking blacks in the US Army, d Nigeria, Jan 8 Sigma Gamma Rho Sorority, Inc., is founded on the campus of Butler University, IN, the first black sorority founded on a white university campus A group of women delegates accuses the Universal	Lucy Diggs Slowe is named dean of women at Howard University, Washington, DC William Leo Hansberry (b Gloster, MS, 1894; d Chicago, IL, 1965), historian and lecturer at Howard University, offers the first course in African civilization at any American university; Hansberry teaches a seemingly radical perspective of African history,	An anti-lynching bill to make mob murder a Federal offense passes in the US House of Representatives but fails in the US Senate	Delegates at the Universal Negro Improvement Association convention propose that Islam become the organization's official religion; the group's leader, Marcus Garvey, however, does not act on the proposal due to the extreme popularity of the Ahmadiyya movement among several Garvey supporters

E. Literature, Publications, and The Black Press	F. The Arts	G. Science, Technology, and Medicine	H. Sports	
	rence Mills will achieve her first significant stage success in this comedy revue			**1921**
	The Sunday School Publishing Board of the National Baptist Convention publishes *Gospel Pearls,* a collection of 165 songs; these folk songs are not particular to any denomination			
	Thomas Dorsey (b Georgia, 1899) writes his first song "If I Don't Get There"; he is credited with coining the term "gospel song" to describe the church music of the black folk; the term does not have widespread use until much later			
	Charles Gilpin is the first actor to win the NAACP's Spingarn Medal for his portrayal of Emperor Jones in the Eugene O'Neill* play of the same name; he was also the cofounder and manager of the Lafayette Players Company, one of the earliest black stock companies in New York City			
	Harry Pace establishes Pace Phonograph Company to produce records on the Black Swan label; it is the first black-owned and -operated record company and will record blues, jazz, spirituals, and operatic arias			
	Anita Bush and Lawrence Chenault costar in *The Crimson Skull,* the first all-black Western movie in the US			
Claude McKay's (b 1889) volume of poetry, *Harlem Shadows,* is published	Bert Williams, theater legend, d NYC, Mar 4; in his lifetime Williams is considered the foremost black vaudeville performer, performing with George Walker in *In Dahomey* and later as a soloist with the Ziegfeld Follies		Harry Wills (b New Orleans, LA, May 15, 1892), boxer, becomes the first Colored Heavyweight Champion when he defeats Bill Tate	**1922**
	Louise Evans is the first black woman admitted to the United Scenic Artists Association for costume,			

	A. General History	B. Education	C. Laws and Legal Actions	D. Religion
1922	Negro Improvement Association of sexism, leading to the appointment of Henrietta Vinton Davis as fourth Assistant President General, Indianapolis, IN Mary B. Talbert receives the NAACP's Spingarn Medal for her efforts to purchase the Frederick Douglass Home as well as for her human rights activities; she is the first woman to receive the award Marcus Garvey and three associates are indicted for mail fraud after the Black Star Line goes bankrupt Violette N. Anderson is the first woman assistant city prosecutor in Chicago, IL The NAACP voices its opposition to US occupation of Hawaii	noting that Egypt derived its culture from the Cushite civilization to the south and also arguing that slave traders destroyed and supressed knowledge of African civilizations		
1923	A group of black intellectuals calling themselves a "Committee of Eight" sends an open letter to US Attorney General Harry M. Daughtery*; in the letter, Marcus Garvey is accused of "demagoguery, arousing ill feeling between the races, mismanagement, and inciting to violence" and Daughtery is urged to expedite Garvey's trial The US Department of Labor estimates that almost 500,000 blacks have left the South for the industrial centers in the North during this year	The first Catholic seminary for the education of black priests is dedicated in St. Louis, MO Virginia Proctor Powell is the first black woman to receive professional training in librarianship after completing the Carnegie Library School		Father George Hurley (b Reynolds, GA, Feb 17, 1884) founds the Universal Hagar's Spiritual Church, Detroit, MI; by the 1940s, Father Hurley establishes at least 37 other congregations; *The Aquarian Age* is the official church publication The Abyssinian Baptist Church moves to a $350,000 gothic structure on 138th St., Harlem, New York City
1924	Marcus Garvey organizes the Black Cross Navigation and Trading Company and acquires another ship; he dispatches a mission to Liberia in preparation for a		US Immigration Act limits the number of persons of African descent from entering the US, favoring persons from Western Europe over others	Howard University professor Thomas Wyatt Turner founds the Committee for the Advancement of Colored Catholics

E. Literature, Publications, and The Black Press	F. The Arts	G. Science, Technology, and Medicine	H. Sports	
	scenic, and lighting designers			**1922**
Opportunity: A Journal of Negro Life, the official organ for the Urban League, is founded; Charles S. Johnson is its first editor Jean Toomer's (b Washington, DC, 1894; d 1967) first and only novel, *Cane,* is published	Bessie Smith (1894–1937) records "Down Hearted Blues," written by Alberta Hunter and Lovie Austin; this single, the first that she records for Columbia Records, becomes a hit, selling 800,000 copies Elida Webb, the first known black professional choreographer in the US, choreographs *Runnin' Wild* on Broadway, New York City Willis Richardson's *Chip Woman's Fortune* is the first drama by a black author to be performed on Broadway, New York City Gertrude "Ma" Rainey (b Columbus, GA, 1886; d 1939), also known as the "Mother of the Blues," makes her first recording; although not the first blues singer, Rainey, and later Bessie Smith, will popularize blues music throughout the US	Garrett A. Morgan patents his automatic traffic signal invention; he later sells his patent to the General Electric Company George Washington Carver receives a patent for a woman's cosmetic; it is a thick cream consisting of mashed peanuts mixed with water, perfume, and a preservative; he will later receive the Spingarn Medal for his body of scientific work	The all-black Harlem Renaissance (Rens) professional basketball team is founded; it is considered the best basketball team of its time The Lincoln University (PA) team wins the one-mile relay at the prestigious Penn Relays, Philadelphia, PA; at this time black competitors are banned from most other track meets Fritz Pollard is named coach of the Akron Indians; he becomes the first black professional coach	**1923**
	Albert J. Cassell (b Baltimore, MD, 1895), architect, designs the gymnasium and athletic field for Howard University, Washington, DC; he	Mary Jane Watkins receives a Doctor of Dental Surgery degree and will go on to become the first woman dentist in the US military services	The Colored Intercollegiate Athletic Association holds its first track meet for predominantly black colleges	**1924**

	A. **General History**	B. **Education**	C. **Laws and Legal Actions**	D. **Religion**
1924	colonization plan that is later aborted

Mary Montgomery Booze (b 1877), club woman, is the first black woman elected to the Republican National Committee

Elizabeth Ross Hayes is elected to the National Board of the YWCA, becoming the first black woman board member | | | Bishop Ida Robinson establishes Mt. Sinai Holy Church of America, Inc., Philadelphia, PA |
| **1925** | Adelbert H. Roberts is the first black since Reconstruction to be elected to the Illinois state legislature

Marcus Garvey's conviction is upheld; he is imprisoned in Atlanta, GA

A. Philip Randolph organizes the Brotherhood of Sleeping Car Porters, the black Pullman porters' union

The Hesperus Club of Harlem (NY) is the first woman's auxiliary of the Brotherhood of Sleeping Car Porters

The newly revived KKK, whose membership is now restricted to native-born Protestants, stage a 40,000-man parade down Pennsylvania Avenue, Washington, DC

The National Bar Association is founded, the first professional organization for black lawyers | Alain Locke is fired from Howard University, ostensibly because of university reorganization but actually as part of an effort to balance black-to-white equity in faculty positions at the school

Xavier University is founded, New Orleans, LA

Mordecai Johnson, the first African-American president of Howard University. Considered to be the "capstone" of African-American education, Howard University became a fully accredited institution with several schools and colleges and an enrollment of more than 6,000 students. (Bethune) | | Charles Emmanuel Grace (Daddy Grace) founds and organizes the United House of Prayer for all People with congregations in approximately twenty cities on the East coast |

	will later design the school's College of Medicine (1926); three women's dormitories (1931); the chemistry building (1933); and Founders Library (1946)		
	Paul Robeson makes his screen debut in Oscar Micheaux's film, *Body and Soul*		
	Valaida Snow (b Chattanooga, TN, c1909; d 1956), musician, dancer, and actress, makes her Broadway debut in *Chocolate Dandies;* Snow will record more than 40 titles for several European record companies and will become internationally known as the "Queen of Trumpet"		
	Ruby Dee, actress, b Ruby Ann Wallace, Cleveland, OH, Oct 27; beginning her career in the early 1940s, Dee will become one of the foremost actresses in the US		

Rudolph Fisher's "The City in Refuge" appears in the *Atlantic Monthly;* this is the first of several short stories by Fisher that address the experiences of black southern migrants in northern cities	Max Roach, drummer, b New Land, NC, Jan 10; Roach will become an influential figure in the development of modern jazz, playing with Charlie Parker, Dizzy Gillespie, and Clifford Brown before forming his own groups in the 1950s	George Washington Carver receives patents for manufacture of paints and stains from clays and minerals	Ramon Herrera, a black Latino, plays baseball for the Boston Red Sox; he is one of several black baseball players who "passes" for white or another racial group during the 1888–1946 period in which blacks are banned from the major leagues
Arna Bontemps wins the Alexander Pushkin Award for "Golgotha Is a Mountain"	Garland Anderson's *Appearances* opens at the Frolic Theater; it is one of the first full-length plays written by a black to appear on Broadway, New York City		
Daniel Murray bequeaths his personal library of 1,488 volumes to the Library of Congress, which, for some time, becomes known as the "Colored Author Collection"	A plea in song for mercy wins prison inmate Huddie Ledbetter (b near Mooringsport, LA, 1885; d 1949), better known as "Leadbelly," a pardon from Texas governor Pat M. Neff*; Leadbelly will become an influential and widely imitated blues singer and musician		
	Lillian Evanti (b Lillian Evans, 1891; d Washington DC, 1967) makes her		

A. **General History**	B. **Education**	C. **Laws and Legal Actions**	D. **Religion**
1925 L. Marian Poe (b Aug 13, 1890) earns a law degree from Howard University (Washington, DC) and becomes one of the first black female attorneys in the South			
1926 Originated by historian Carter G. Woodson and the Association for the Study of Negro Life and History, the first "Negro History Week" begins; the celebration will be expanded to a month in 1976	Mordecai W. Johnson (b Paris, TX, Jan 12, 1890) becomes the first black president of Howard University, Washington, DC	Violette N. Anderson is the first black woman attorney to present a case before the US Supreme Court	

James A. Cobb becomes a judge of the Municipal Court of Washington, DC

Selena Sloan Butler founds the National Congress of Colored Parents and Teachers

The YWCA adopts an interracial charter at its national convention

Arthur Schomburg donates his personal collection of black literature to the Division of Negro Literature, the New York Public Library; the collection is named the Schomburg Collection of Black Culture, one of the most renowned repositories of black literature and photographs in the world

From top left: Arna Bontemps, Melvin Tolson, Jacob Reddick, Owen Dodson, Robert Hayden; from bottom left: Sterling Brown, Zora Neale Hurston, Margaret Walker, and Langston Hughes. The Harlem Renaissance, which flourished in the 1920s and lasted into the 1940s, manifested growing militancy, black pride, and the return of folk traditions among black artists, writers, and intellectual leaders. (Schomburg)

A group of black women, including Indiana Little, social worker, are beaten by election officials while attempting to register to vote, Birmingham, AL

1927 When her husband dies, Minnie Buckingham-Harper is appointed to fill her husband's unexpired term in the West Virginia legislature; she is the first black woman to serve in a US legislative body

Marcus Garvey's sentence is commuted by Pres. Calvin Coolidge;* Garvey is deported to Jamaica

Sadie Tanner Mossell Alexander serves as associate editor of the *Pennsylvania Law Review;* upon graduation from the University of Pennsylvania Law School, she becomes the first black

Annie Holland (b Dec 31, 1871; d Louisburg, NC, Jan 6, 1934), educator, founds the Parent-Teacher Association of NC

Ambrose Caliver (b Saltsville, VA, Feb 25, 1894) is the first black to be appointed dean of Fisk University, Tennessee

Citizens of Toms River, NJ, demand the dismissal of the local school principal because he discriminates against black students; the dismissal is upheld by the state supreme court

In *Nixon v. Herndon,* the US Supreme Court strikes down a law in Texas barring blacks from voting in the "white primary"

1925

	professional debut singing with the Paris Opera in *Lakmé*		

1926

Langston Hughes, Zora Neale Hurston, Wallace Thurman and others establish *Fire*, an avant-garde literary magazine; the premiere issue is the only issue to be published

Hallie Quinn Brown's *Homespun Heroines and Other Women of Distinction*, a collection of biographical sketches of notable black American women, is published

Langston Hughes's (b Joplin, MO, Feb 1, 1902; d 1967) first book, *Weary Blues*, a collection of poetry, is published

The Savoy Ballroom, nick-named the ''Home of Happy Feet,'' opens in New York City

Rose McClendon (b Greenville, SC, 1884; d New York City, 1936), one of the most popular black actresses of her time, wins rave reviews for her performance as Octavia in *Deep River*, an opera

Era Bell Thompson establishes five women's track records while a student at the University of North Dakota

Richard Henry, the first black prominent fencer, is named captain of the team at Springfield College, Massachusetts

The United Golfers Association, an all-black organization, is founded, Washington, DC

1927

Countee Cullen (b Baltimore, MD, May 30, 1903; d 1946) receives the Harmon Foundation's first gold medal for literature; Cullen is recognized for *Color*, a volume of poetry

James Weldon Johnson's *God's Trombones: Seven Negro Sermons in Verse* is published; the major work includes illustrations by Aaron Douglas

Charles Wesley's (b Louisville, KY, Dec 2, 1895) *Negro Labor in the United States, 1850–1925: A Study in American Economic History* is published

Florence Mills, one of the most popular actresses of her time, d Nov 1; with over 150,000 attendees, hers is the largest funeral in Harlem, New York, history

By this year Bessie Smith is the highest paid black artist in the world

William E. Harmon* establishes the Harmon Foundation to aid black artists

Thomas Dorsey travels throughout the Midwest and the South to peddle his gospel songs on printed texts; his are the first per

Tuskegee Institute, Alabama, establishes a women's track team and incorporates two track events especially for women—the 100-yard dash and the 400-meter relay—into the Tuskegee Relays for athletes at predominantly black colleges; Tuskegee is the only US college to have varsity competition for women at this time

Abe Saperstein* becomes manager of the Savoy Big Five basketball team, relocates the team to New York City, and renames them the Harlem Globe-trotters

	A. **General History**	B. **Education**	C. **Laws and Legal Actions**	D. **Religion**
1927	woman to enter the bar and practice law in the state of Pennsylvania; later she and her husband, Raymond Pace Alexander, enter private practice together as one of the earliest husband-wife legal teams in the US			
1928	Marcus Garvey tours Europe and petitions the League of Nations for redress of black grievances, urging creation of an independent black nation in Africa One hundred black spectators at the Republican National Convention Houston, TX, are segregated in the rear of the balcony—cordoned off by chicken wire	Alain Locke returns to Howard University during the administration of the school's first black president, Mordecai W. Johnson; Locke lobbies for an African Studies program (not institutionalized until 1954)		The Southern Methodist Episcopal Church declares that "Christ's teachings concerning human brotherhood demand equal justice and opportunity for all persons regardless of race, color, or sex" The African Muslim Welfare Society is incorporated as a religious body, Pittsburgh, PA; the organization, which consists mainly of Arab Muslims, makes a concerted effort to recruit blacks in the Pittsburgh area
1929	The Brotherhood of Sleeping Car Porters receives its charter from the American Federation of Labor The New York stock market crashes, signaling the beginning of the Great Depression; during the Depression blacks complain that they are "the last to be hired and the first to be fired" Albon Holsey of the National Negro Business League organizes the Colored Merchants Association; the group plans to establish stores and buy their merchandise collectively; the Depression forces these stores out of business within two years Francis E. Rivers is the first black admitted to the New York Bar Association	Numa Adams (1885–1940) is the first black dean of Howard Medical School, Washington, DC Anna Julia Cooper becomes the second president of Frelinghuysen University, Washington, DC		

1927

formances outside of a church to use the piano, as most church songs and spirituals are sung *a capella*

Laura Wheeler Waring (b Hartford, CT, 1887; d 1948), best known for portrait paintings, receives an award from the Harmon Foundation for her portrait of Ann Washington Derry

1928

Rudolph Fisher's first novel, *The Walls of Jericho,* is published

Georgia Douglas Johnson's *An Autumn Love Cycle* is published; this third book of poetry is considered her best work

Nella Larsen's (1891–1964) first novel *Quicksand* is published; the semiautobiographical novel explores intraracial and class conflicts within the black community

Monroe N. Work's *A Bibliography of the Negro in Africa and America* is published; it is one of the most comprehensive sources on black Americans

Archibald Motley is the first artist of any race to make the front page of the *New York Times*

Louis Wright becomes the first black police surgeon in New York City

1929

Wallace Thurman's (1902–1934) novel, *The Blacker the Berry,* is published

Walter White's *Rope and Faggot: A Biography of Judge Lynch,* a work written in protest of the lynching of blacks in the US, is published

Regina Andrews, Theophilus Lewis, Ira De Augustine Reid, Jessie Fauset, and Harold Jackson establish the Negro (Harlem) Experimental Theater in the basement of the New York Public Library, New York City

Hot Chocolates, with music by Fats Waller and lyrics by Andy Razaf, premieres at the Hudson Theater, New York City; the musical features the songs "Ain't Misbehavin' " and "Black and Blue"

Augusta Savage's *Gamin',* a sculpture of a black street urchin, wins Savage a Rosenwald grant; with this money she embarks on a trip to Europe to further her studies and work

Ernest E. Just is the first American invited to be a guest researcher at the Kaiser Wilhelm Institut für Biologie, Berlin-Dahlem, Germany

The Prairie View Bowl is established; it is the first black college post-season "bowl" football game

	A. **General History**	B. **Education**	C. **Laws and Legal Actions**	D. **Religion**
1929	Cong. Oscar DePriest (b Florence, AL, 1871; d 1951) (R-IL) is the first northern black to serve in the US Congress; during his term (1929–1935) he introduces a bill providing for a $75 monthly pension for ex-slaves Angry whites condemn Pres. Herbert Hoover* for inviting the wife of Cong. Oscar DePriest (R-IL) to the White House for dinner			
1930	*The New York Times* capitalizes the word "Negro" for the first time "in recognition of racial self-respect for those who have been for generations in the lower case" Fannie B. Peck organizes a group of women into the Housewives' League of Detroit; requirements for membership are "commitment to support black businesses, buy black products, patronize black professionals, and keep money in the black community"; four years later, membership has grown to 10,000 Librarian Dorothy Porter (b Warrenton, VA, May 25, 1905) begins to organize the Negro Collection into the Moorland-Spingarn Research Center at Howard University, Washington, DC; the center is now one of the largest and most comprehensive repositories of documentation on the history and culture of people of African descent in the US Writer George Schuyler founds the Young Negroes Cooperative League, New York City; the purpose of the group is to gain economic power through consumer cooperation	Ambrose Caliver becomes senior specialist on the education of blacks in the US Office of Education; he is promoted to specialist for higher education of blacks and advisor on related problems in the Office of Education in 1946	Pres. Herbert Hoover* nominates Judge John J. Parker* of North Carolina, a known racist, to the US Supreme Court; the NAACP leads a successful campaign against Parker's confirmation	W. D. Fard founds the Nation of Islam, a sect of the Moslem faith, Detroit, MI; the organization incorporates in its teachings a mixture of Koranic principles, the Christian Bible, Fard's own beliefs, and the beliefs of black nationalists Marcus Garvey and Nobel Drew Ali The Commandment Keepers of the Living God (the "black Jews" of Harlem, New York) is incorporated, led by Rabbi Wentworth A. Matthew
1931	Garrett A. Morgan, inventor, runs as an independent candidate for the Cleveland, OH, city council		Nine youths are arrested for allegedly raping two white women, Scottsboro, AL; they will be quickly	The Federal Council of Churches adapts these principles for its black delegates: no segregation of

E. Literature, Publications, and The Black Press	F. The Arts	G. Science, Technology, and Medicine	H. Sports	
				1929
	King Vidor* directs *Hallelujah,* the first major film musical with a black cast			
	Wallace Thurman's *Harlem* opens and runs for 93 performances			
Zora Neale Hurston (1891–1960) and Langston Hughes collaborate on *Mule Bone,* a comedy; the play is not finished or produced due to the authors' artistic differences	Richard "Blue" Mitchell, trumpeter, b Miami, FL, Mar 13; he later gains recognition while a member of Horace Silver's Quintet	A group of physicians, among them Louis Wright, organizes the Manhattan Medical Society; the Society opposes the Rosenwald Fund plan to build racially separate hospitals in the state of New York	The professional football leagues stop recruiting blacks until after WWII	**1930**
Nella Larsen is the first black to win a creative writing award from the Guggenheim Foundation	Ornette Coleman, musician, b Fort Worth, TX, Mar 19; he later becomes a noted avant-garde jazz saxophonist and composer			
	Richard B. Harrison stars as "De Lawd" in *Green Pastures* at the Mansfield Theater on Broadway, New York City			
	Caterina Jarboro becomes the first black to sing with a major opera company when she debuts as Aida at the Puccini Opera House, Milan, Italy			
Arna Bontemps's *God Sends Sunday* is published	Rudolph Fisher's *Conjure Man Dies* premieres on Broadway at the Lafayette Theater; the play is based	Dr. Virginia Alexander establishes the Aspiranto Health Home to provide pregnant women and their		**1931**

	A. General History	B. Education	C. Laws and Legal Actions	D. Religion
1931			convicted in a trial that outrages blacks and much of the nation; the case will be appealed, and the "Scottsboro boys" will be retried many times until all are free by parole, appeal, or escape by 1950	specific groups when it comes to assignments and no discrimination against any delegates when it comes to using church facilities
1932	Franklin D. Roosevelt* is elected US President, promising a "New Deal" for all Faced with agricultural distress and racial oppression in the South, a second major wave of black migration begins to the major industrial centers of the North and continues until 1940	Hartshorn Memorial College for Women merges with Virginia Union University, Richmond, VA *The Journal of Negro Education* begins publication, Howard University, Washington, DC		Thomas Dorsey, Sallie Morton, and Willie Mae Ford Smith organize the National Convention of Gospel Choirs and Choruses

E. **Literature, Publications, and The Black Press**	F. **The Arts**	G. **Science, Technology, and Medicine**	H. **Sports**

George Schuyler's first novel, *Black No More*, is published

Joel A. Rogers's *World's Greatest Men of African Descent* is published

on Fisher's short story, "Conjure-Man Dies: A Mystery Tale of Dark Harlem," considered the first detective fiction written by a black

Augusta Savage produces several sculptures this year, among them *Martiniquaise*, a carving in black Belgian marble; *After the Glory*, a plaster antiwar artwork; and *Envy*, a woodcarving

Oscar Micheaux's movie *The Exile*, the first "talkie" by a black-owned company, is released

Katherine Dunham (b Joliet, IL, Jun 22, 1909), modern dance performer, founds the Negro Dance Group, Chicago, IL

Edward Kennedy "Duke" Ellington (b 1899; d May 24, 1974) records "Creole Rhapsody"; the song is considered the first classic of modern dance music

Sam Cooke, singer, Clarkesdale, MS, b Jan 22; Cooke, best known for his recordings "You Send Me" and "Twistin' the Night Away," will become one of the most popular singers of the 1960s

children with health care information and facilities, Philadelphia, PA

Katherine Dunham, internationally renowned student and teacher of modern dance, founded her first professional dance company in 1939. (MSRC)

Sterling Brown's (b 1901; d 1989) *Southern Road*, a volume of poetry emphasizing social protest, is published; Brown's poetry is influenced by his admiration for the lives of blacks in the rural south

Bill "Bojangles" Robinson stars in *Harlem Is Heaven*, the first all-black talking movie

Thomas "Fats" Waller (1904–1943) records "Ain't Misbehavin'," his biggest hit

William E. Braxton, the first black artist to work as an expressionist painter, d

Richard B. Spikes, a mechanical engineer, perfects the gearshift, transmission and a contact trolley pole; Spikes is considered one of the first transmission experts

The New York Rens basketball team defeats the Boston Celtics, a predominantly white team, to win its first world championship; it is the first world championship for a black American team in any sport

Louise Stokes and Tydie Pickett become the first black women selected for a US Olympic team when they qualify in the 100-meter race, Los Angeles, CA; they are later replaced by two white athletes

Eddie Tolan wins a gold medal in the 100- and 200-yard dash, becoming the first black American to win a gold medal in a

A. **General History**	B. **Education**	C. **Laws and Legal Actions**	D. **Religion**
1932			
1933 Charles Alfred Anderson and Albert Forsythe are the first black civilian pilots to make a transcontinental flight Pres. Franklin D. Roosevelt* hires many black advisors who form the unofficial "Black Cabinet"	The NAACP begins to attack segregation and discrimination in education through legal suits; its first case is a suit against the University of North Carolina on behalf of Thomas Hocutt; the case is lost on a technicality		
1934 The average annual income for black tenant and wage laborers in the South is $278—the average for whites is $452 Delegates at the American Federation of Labor national convention reject A. Philip Randolph's resolution to end union discrimination; the organization's			*Spoken Word,* the first journal for the Peace Mission disciples, begins publication, Los Angeles, CA; the journal, which goes bankrupt in 1937, contains reprint transcripts of Father Divine's sermons, as well as announcements and editorials

E. Literature, Publications, and The Black Press	F. The Arts	G. Science, Technology, and Medicine	H. Sports	
			sprint event, Los Angeles, CA	**1932**
			Beginning this year and continuing through 1938, the Morgan State University, MD, football team, under the leadership of coach Edward Hurt, will be undefeated	
Elizabeth Lindsay Davis publishes *Lifting as They Climb*, the first history of the national black club movement	Paul Robeson plays the role of Brutus Jones in the film *Emperor Jones*, the first Hollywood production starring a black American with whites in supporting roles; it is Robeson's first starring movie role

Margaret Bonds (b Chicago, IL, Mar 3, 1913; d Los Angeles, CA, Apr 26, 1972) is the first black guest soloist with the Chicago Symphony Orchestra at the Chicago, IL, Worlds Fair; Bonds, also a noted composer, is commissioned by opera star Leontyne Price to write several spirituals for her

Hall Johnson's (b Athens, GA, Mar 12, 1888) *Run Little Chillun* is the first Broadway production of a Negro folk opera written by a black composer

The Public Works of Arts Project and the Federal Art Project of the Works Progress Administration are created to hire artists to adorn government office buildings, post offices, and public parks with their work; artists Jacob Lawrence, Aaron Douglas, Charles Alston, Richmond Barthé, Sergeant Johnson, Archibald Motley, Augusta Savage, and others benefit from this program | | | **1933** |
| Langston Hughes's first collection of short stories, *The Ways of White Folks*, is published | Louise Beavers (1908–1962) and Fredi Washington star in the popular film *Imitation of Life*

Legendary jazz singer Ella Fitzgerald (b Newport News, VA, Apr 25, 1918) is discovered after winning on the "Harlem Amateur Hour" | Louis Wright becomes the second black member of the American College of Surgeons

Percy Julian (b Montgomery, AL, Apr 11, 1899) presents two papers before the American Chemical Society; his work on the precursors of a drug known as physostigmine | Joe Louis (b Joseph Louis Barrow, Lexington, AL, May 13, 1914) wins the national light heavyweight tournament crown, St. Louis, MO; later this year Louis turns professional with an amateur record of 54 wins and 4 losses

The National Football League adopts an unoffi- | **1934** |

A. **General History**	B. **Education**	C. **Laws and Legal Actions**	D. **Religion**

1934

committee argues that no discrimination exists and supports the concept of separate unions for blacks and whites

Hilyard Robinson is appointed consulting architect to the National Capitol Advisory Committee and senior architect for the US Suburban Resettlement Administration

Arthur Mitchell (b Lafayette, AL, 1883) (D-IL) is the first black Democrat elected to US Congress, defeating Republican Oscar DePriest

W. E. B. Du Bois resigns from the NAACP because he feels the organization is dedicated to the interests of the black bourgeois and ignores the problems of the masses

Nation of Islam leader W. D. Fard disappears; Elijah Muhammad (b Elijah Poole, Sandersville, GA, 1897; d Feb 25, 1975) succeeds him and moves the organization's headquarters to Chicago, IL

The Pittsburgh Crawfords, 1935 champions of the Negro Leagues. (National Baseball Library, Cooperstown, NY)

1935

The National Council of Negro Women is formed in New York City; Mary McLeod Bethune is elected president, and Lucy Diggs Slowe is its first secretary

Blacks in Harlem, New York, protest Italy's invasion of Ethiopia

The First Negro Labor Conference convenes in Harlem, New York; the two principal speakers, A. Philip Randolph and Frank R. Crosswater call for solidarity of black and white labor, a 30-hour work week, condemnation of the failure of the New York state legislature to ratify the child labor amendment, and adoption of this amendment to the US Constitution

In *University of Maryland v. Murray* the Maryland Court of Appeals orders the University of Maryland to admit Donald Murray into its law school, Baltimore, MD

Charles Drew (b Washington, DC, Jun 3, 1904; d Burlington, NC, Apr 1, 1950) becomes an instructor in pathology at Howard University Medical School, where he later establishes a surgical resident training program for blacks

Eunice Hunton Carter (b Atlanta, GA, Jul 16, 1899; d Jan 25, 1970) begins work as the first black woman district attorney in the state of New York; she triggers the biggest organized crime prosecution in New York City in the late 1930s

Sadie and Raymond Alexander help draft the Pennsylvania state public accommodations law that prohibits discrimination in public places

Howard Thurman, a graduate of Morehouse College who achieves a national reputation as a preacher, leads a delegation of black Christians to Asia, where they meet with the members of the Student Christian Movement in India, Burma, and Ceylon

1936

Pres. Franklin D. Roosevelt* establishes the Office of Minority Affairs and names Mary McLeod Bethune its administrator; Bethune is also named director of Division of Negro Affairs of the National Youth Administration. Franklin D. Roosevelt's* reelection marks the first

The NAACP files the *Gibbs v. Board of Education* suit to eliminate pay differentials between black and white teachers and to equalize educational facilities

Shaw College at Detroit is founded, Detroit, MI

At this time, 62% of black congregations are in the rural South; 44% of black Americans claim membership in black churches

Father Divine's Peace Mission is at the height of its popularity; the official directory lists over 150 branches, of which more

E. Literature, Publications, and The Black Press	F. The Arts	G. Science, Technology, and Medicine	H. Sports	
	Gospel singer Mahalia Jackson (b 1912; d Evergreen Park, IL, Jan 27, 1972) makes her first record, including "God Shall Wipe Away All Tears"	attracts the attention of both American and European scientists	cial "gentleman's agreement" to ban black players in order to conserve jobs for whites during the Depression; the ban lasts for 12 years The Colored Intercollegiate Athletic Association is the only black college conference to offer wrestling	**1934**

Joe Louis, the "Brown Bomber." (Schomburg)

E. Literature, Publications, and The Black Press	F. The Arts	G. Science, Technology, and Medicine	H. Sports	
Zora Neale Hurston's *Mules and Men* is published	George Gershwin's* folk opera *Porgy and Bess*, starring Anne Wiggins Brown and Todd Duncan, premieres at the Alvin Theatre, New York City	George Washington Carver becomes a collaborator in the US Department of Agriculture's Bureau of Plant Industry Dr. Percy Julian makes his first major discovery when he synthesizes the drug physostigmine, which is used to treat glaucoma, an eye disease	John Henry Lewis (b Los Angeles, CA, May 1, 1914), boxer, defeats Bob Olin in 15 rounds in St. Louis, MO, to become the world's light heavyweight champion; Lewis defends the crown five times, then abdicates	**1935**
Dorothy Porter's *A Selected List of Books By and About the Negro* is published by the US Printing Office; this book is one of the first by Porter that will influence the field of bibliography and black American scholarship	*The Green Pastures* premieres at Radio City Music Hall in New York City; the movie features Eddie "Rochester" Anderson, Rex Ingram, and the Hall Johnson Choir Benny Goodman* becomes the first white bandleader to use black	Percy Julian is offered a job as chief chemist and director at the Glidden Company, one of the country's largest manufacturers of paints and varnishes; this is the first time a black person has the opportunity to direct a modern industrial lab; Julian's work is so successful that	Jesse Owens wins four gold medals in the Olympic Games, challenging Adolf Hitler's* notions of the superior Aryan race and the inferiority of black athletes, Germany Jackie Wilson, bantamweight boxer, wins a silver medal during the Olympic	**1936**

	A. **General History**	B. **Education**	C. **Laws and Legal Actions**	D. **Religion**
1936	time in US history that black Americans over-whelmingly vote for a Democratic president			than a quarter are located in New York State; the organization is the largest realty holder in Harlem; mission followers own several businesses, includ-ing grocery stores, barber-shops and cleaning stores
1937	William H. Hastie is ap-pointed the first black fed-eral judge in the US			Rev. Adam Clayton Pow-ell, Jr. (1908–1972), as-sumes the pastorate of the Abyssinian Baptist Church, NY
1938	Miriam Stubbs Thomas calls the first meeting of Jack and Jill of America in her home in Philadelphia, PA; the goals of Jack and Jill are to provide social, cultural, and educational programs to children of middle-class and profes-sional black families Crystal Bird Fauset (b Princess Ann, MD, 1894) (D-PA) is elected to the Pennsylvania House of Representatives, becoming the first black woman to serve in a state house of representatives A. Philip Randolph, presi-dent of the Brotherhood of Sleeping Car Porters, con-venes a meeting at which the Ladies' Auxiliary Or-der to the Brotherhood is formally founded, Chi-cago, IL	In *Missouri ex rel Gaines*, the US Supreme Court rules that a state must pro-vide equal educational fa-cilities for blacks within its boundaries; the plaintiff, Lloyd Gaines, mysteriously disappears following the Court's decision The International Sweet-hearts of Rhythm, an all-female swing band, is formed at Piney Woods Country Life School, Piney Woods, MS; the group performs throughout the US to raise money for the school	 *Billie Holiday's beautiful and unique voice made ''Lady Day'' one of the greatest jazz singers ever. (MSRC)*	

E. Literature, Publications, and The Black Press	F. The Arts	G. Science, Technology, and Medicine	H. Sports	
	jazzmen on a regular basis when he hires Teddy Wilson and Lionel Hampton	the company goes from a loss of $35,000 to a profit of $135,000 in one year	Games in Berlin, Germany; his loss in the finals to Ulderico Sergo* of Italy is celebrated by racists as an Aryan victory	**1936**
	Maud Cuney Hare's (b Galveston, TX, 1874; d Boston, MA, 1936) *Negro Musicians and Their Music*, which includes rare photographs of and biographical information on black musicians, is published		Joe Louis is KO'd by German Max Schmeling* in the 12th round; Adolf Hitler* and the Nazi regime in Germany call the defeat an achievement for the white race	
Benjamin Brawley's *Negro Builders and Heroes* is published	The Count Basie Orchestra, featuring vocalists Billie Holiday (b Eleanor Fagan, Baltimore, MD, Apr 7, 1915; d 1959) and Jimmy Rushing, opens at the Apollo Theatre in Harlem, NY	William Warwick Cardozo's (b Wahington, DC, Apr 6, 1905; d 1962) pioneer study, "Immunologic Studies in Sickle Anemia" is published in the *Archives of Internal Medicine*	Joe Louis KO's James Braddock* in Madison Square Garden, NY, to become the boxing heavyweight champion of the world; the fight is won in eight rounds before 45,000 fans, the largest audience to witness a fight to date	**1937**
Zora Neale Hurston's *Their Eyes Were Watching God* is published; it is one of her most revered novels			The first black-owned bowling alley is established, Cleveland, OH	
Charles Wesley's historical work *The Collapse of the Confederacy* is published			William "Dolly" King is the first black basketball player in the National Amateur Athletic Union (AAU) tournament	
Richard Wright's (b Natchez, MS, Sep 9, 1908) first book, *Uncle Tom's Children*, a collection of short stories, is published	Benny Goodman* leads a concert at Carnegie Hall; despite opposition from white racists, Goodman refuses to play without two black members of his band, Lionel Hampton, vibraphonist, and Teddy Wilson, pianist	Louis Wright contributes a chapter to Charles Scudder's* book *Treatment of Fractures*; Wright's expertise includes devising a brace for neck fractures and a special blade for surgical treatment of fractures above the knee joint	Joe Louis defeats German Max Schmeling* in a rematch of their 1936 bout; because of the German Nazi persecution of Jews in Europe and Adolf Hitler's* contempt for blacks, the fight takes on metaphoric proportions, with Louis seen by many as fighting to uphold democracy and the black race	**1938**
	The Harlem Suitcase Theater opens with Langston Hughes's play *Don't You Want to Be Free?* starring Robert Earl Jones, father of actor James Earl Jones		Oscar Robertson, b Charlotte, TN, Nov 24; "The Big O" will gain notoriety with the Milwaukee Bucks, winning a 1971 NBA championship with teammate Kareem Abdul-Jabbar	
	Billie Holiday is one of the first black vocalists to be featured with a white band when she performs with Artie Shaw*		Beginning this year through 1948, the Tuskegee Institute of Alabama's women's track team wins the Amateur Athletic Union indoor track title every year except 1943	
	"Sister" Rosetta Tharpe is the first gospel singer to record with a major record label		The Tuskegee Institute sponsors the first intercollegiate golf tournament	
	Owen Dodson's *The Divine Comedy* is produced at the Yale University Theatre in Connecticut			

	A. **General History**	B. **Education**	C. **Laws and Legal Actions**	D. **Religion**
1938				
1939	NAACP launches a drive to obtain one million signatures on an anti-lynching petition Mary T. Washington becomes the first black female certified public accountant after graduating from Northwestern University, Chicago, IL Jane Matilda Bolin (b Poughkeepsie, NY, Apr 11, 1908) is appointed a judge of the Court of Domestic Relations, in New York City, by Mayor Fiorello La Guardia;* Judge Bolin draws attention to the ways in which private schools and child care institutions in New York City discriminate against children because of race and color George W. Crockett (b Jacksonville, FL, 1909) becomes the first black attorney appointed to the US Department of Labor Under the leadership of attorney Charles Houston, the NAACP Legal Defense and Educational Fund is organized as a separate entity	West Virginia State College establishes the first black Civilian Pilot Training Program in peacetime	Sen. Theodore C. Bilbo* (D-MS) introduces a ''Back to Africa'' bill designed to ameliorate the race problem by a voluntary return of blacks to Africa	
1940	The US postal service issues the first stamp honoring a black American, Booker T. Washington Assistant Secretary of War Robert Patterson* issues a memo declaring the usual segregation policy among US troops, in direct opposition to the Selective Training and Service Act, which had just been issued to curb discriminatory practices in the Armed Forces	Charles Drew becomes the first black to receive a Sc.D. degree in the US, Columbia University, New York City	The US Congress passes a Selective Training and Service Act, containing an anti-discriminatory clause and a 10% quota system to ensure racial integration	

E. Literature, Publications, and The Black Press	F. The Arts	G. Science, Technology, and Medicine	H. Sports	
			among predominantly black colleges	**1938**
			Henry Armstrong (b St. Louis, MO, Dec 12, 1912; d 1988) wins the boxing lightweight championship and becomes the first fighter to hold three titles at one time	
	Langston Hughes establishes the New Negro Theater in Los Angeles, CA; Hughes's play *Don't You Want to Be Free?* is the company's first production	Charles Drew establishes a "blood bank" that allows him to study the physical, chemical, and biological changes that take place in the blood when it is stored, Presbyterian Hospital, Columbia University, New York City	The National Negro Bowling Association is established, Detroit, MI	**1939**
	Ethel Waters (b Chester, PA, Oct 31, 1896) plays the role of Hagar in *Mamba's Daughters,* becoming the first black woman to star in a leading role on Broadway		Simeon F. Moss of Rutgers University, New Jersey, is the first known black lacrosse player on a college team	
	Costar Hattie McDaniel (b Wichita, KS, Jun 10, 1895; d Oct 26, 1952) and other black cast members are barred from attending the premiere of *Gone with the Wind,* Atlanta, GA			
	The exhibit "Contemporary Negro Art" opens at the Baltimore Museum of Art, MD; the exhibit, which runs for 16 days, features works by Aaron Douglas, Jacob Lawrence, Richmond Barthé, and Archibald Motley, Jr.			
	Augusta Savage constructs "The Harp," a 16-foot structure commissioned by the World's Fair Corporation			
Robert E. Hayden's first book of poems, *Heart-Shape in the Dust,* is published	Abram Hill, Frederick O'Neal, and others found the American Negro Theater in New York City, where the careers of Harry Belafonte, Ruby Dee, and Sidney Poitier are launched	 *Richard Wright. His novel* Native Son *launched the career of this first African-American author to have a Book-of-the-Month Club selection. (MSRC)*		**1940**
Joel A. Rogers's historical work, *Sex and Race,* is published				
Richard Wright's landmark novel *Native Son* is published; the novel becomes the first literary work by a black American to become a Book-of-the-Month Club selection	The famous Cotton Club, known for showcasing major jazz talents such as Duke Ellington and Lena Horne, closes, Harlem, New York City			

A. **General History**	B. **Education**	C. **Laws and Legal Actions**	D. **Religion**

1940

Benjamin O. Davis, Sr. (b Washington, DC, 1877) is appointed brigadier general in the US Army, becoming the highest ranking black in the armed services

The Office of the Civilian Aide to the Secretary of War in Matters of Black Rights is created for William Hastie, dean of Howard University Law School; the position is similar to the one Emmett J. Scott held during WWI

The Virginia legislature chooses James Bland's (b Flushing, NY, Oct 22, 1854) ''Carry Me Back to Ole Virginny'' as Virginia's state song; the state legislators are not aware of Bland's race

1941

The 99th Pursuit Squadron, an all-black unit, is formed, and the Tuskegee Training Program is established; the 99th will fly more than 500 missions and more than 3,700 sorties during one year of combat before being combined with the 332nd Fighter Group

Ed Bradley, journalist, b Philadelphia, PA, Jun 22; Bradley will become a CBS news correspondent covering the Vietnam conflict and later a co-anchor for the television show ''60 Minutes''

The first all-black officered regular Army Infantry Regiment (366th) is activated

A race riot begins in East St. Louis, IL; after four days of rioting, one black is left dead

The first black tank battalion, the 758th, is activated

Pres. Franklin D. Roosevelt* holds an urgent meeting with A. Philip Randolph of the Brotherhood of Sleeping Car Por-

(Column C, 1941):

In a case brought by Cong. Arthur Mitchell (D-IL) the US Supreme Court rules that separate facilities on railroads must be substantially equal

Pres. Franklin D. Roosevelt* issues an executive order forbidding racial and religious discrimination in defense industries and government training programs; A. Philip Randolph calls off the planned march on Washington

Pres. Franklin D. Roosevelt* establishes a Fair Employment Practices Committee to monitor discrimination against blacks in defense industries

E. Literature, Publications, and The Black Press	F. The Arts	G. Science, Technology, and Medicine	H. Sports

1940

Horace Pippin (b West Chester, PA, 1888; d West Chester, PA, 1946), painter, had his first important one-man show, launching his career, Philadelphia, PA

Hattie McDaniel becomes the first black American to win an Oscar when she receives the Academy of Motion Picture Arts and Sciences Award for best supporting actress for her role in *Gone with the Wind*

Son of Ingagi, the first all-black horror film, is released

1941

The Negro Caravan, an anthology co-edited by Arthur P. Davis, Sterling Brown, and Ulysses Lee, is published

Charlotte Hawkins Brown's *The Correct Thing to Do, to Say, and to Wear* is published

Mary Cardwell Dawson founds the National Negro Opera Company, the first permanent black opera company in the US, Pittsburgh, PA

A. **General History**	B. **Education**	C. **Laws and Legal Actions**	D. **Religion**
1941 ters and other black spokespersons, urging them to cancel a planned march on Washington to protest employment discrimination and segregation in the national defense program; Randolph refuses			
The Integrated Officers' Candidate Schools opens			
Japanese forces attack Pearl Harbor; Dorie Miller, mess steward, mans a machine gun during the attack and downs four Japanese fighters; Miller will be awarded the Navy Cross for his heroic deeds			
Adam Clayton Powell, Jr., is elected to the New York City Council as an independent			
New York bus companies agree to hire black drivers and mechanics			
1942 The first black military police battalion (730th) is activated		The US Justice Department threatens 20 editors of black newspapers with sedition charges after several papers feature articles exposing segregation and injustices in the US military; many newspapers are unable to obtain newsprint until after they tone down their criticism	
Capt. Benjamin O. Davis, Jr., Second Lts. Mac Ross, Charles DeBow, L. R. Curtis, and George S. Roberts become the first five graduates of the Tuskegee Flying School; they will become part of the famous 99th Pursuit Squadron			
The 93rd Infantry, the first black division formed during WWII, is activated at Fort Huachuca, AZ			
The US Marine Corps begins the enlistment of blacks, Camp LeJeune, NC			
Bernard W. Robinson becomes a Naval Reserve ensign and the first black to earn a US Navy commission			
The Women's Army Auxiliary Corps is formed and accepts both blacks and whites			
Hugh N. Mulzac is the first black captain to command			

1942

Margaret Walker's (b Birmingham, AL, Jul 7, 1915) first book of poetry, *For My People*, is published; Walker becomes the first black American poet to be featured in Yale University's Series of Younger Poets

John H. Johnson begins publishing *Negro Digest*, a periodical containing news reprints and feature articles

Aretha Franklin, singer, b Memphis, TN, Mar 25; known as the "Queen of Soul," Franklin will earn 21 gold records

In recognition of the influence of so-called race music, *Billboard* creates its first ratings chart devoted to black music, *The Harlem Hit Parade*; the first number-one record is "Take It and Git" by Andy Kirk and His Twelve Clouds of Joy

Lena Horne makes her film debut in *Panama Hattie*

Hattie McDaniel, Olivia de Havilland,* and Bette Davis* star in one of the first Hollywood films to depict complex black characters, *In This Our Life*

Baseball pitcher Leroy "Satchel" Paige leads the Kansas City Monarchs to victory in the Negro World Series

1942

a US merchant ship, the *Booker T. Washington*

The *Pittsburgh Courier* endorses the "Double V," which stands for victory abroad and at home for black Americans; the slogan becomes increasingly popular in the black community

Charity Earley (b Kittrell, NC, Dec 5, 1918) is the first black commissioned officer in the Women's Army Auxiliary Corps

Cong. William Dawson (b Albany, GA, Apr 26, 1886; d Nov 6, 1971) (D-IL) is elected to the US Congress

1943

The Congress of Racial Equality stages the first successful sit-in demonstration at a restaurant, Chicago, IL

Eta Phi Beta, a black national business and professional sorority, is incorporated in Detroit, MI

The US Navy admits blacks into all branches of the service according to their percentage of the total population (10%)

The First Marine Depot is the first black unit to be sent overseas during WWII

Blacks in Detroit, MI, riot in protest of exclusion from civilian defense jobs; Federal troops are called in to control the violence, which results in 34 deaths

Dorie Miller, decorated Navy seaman, is lost at sea and presumed dead

W. E. B. Du Bois is the first black admitted to the National Institute of Arts and Letters

The dance hall license of the Savoy nightclub is revoked ostensibly to curb prostitution but actually as an effort to keep whites out of Harlem, New York City

Mercer Cook (b Washington, DC, 1903) becomes director of the English-teaching project in Haiti

Selma Burke, shown with one of her sculptures. (Schomburg)

E. **Literature,
Publications, and
The Black Press**   F. **The Arts**

G. **Science,
Technology,
and Medicine**   H. **Sports**

1942

Paul Robeson is the first black actor to play the title role in *Othello* on Broadway, New York City

George Gershwin's* *Porgy and Bess* opens on Broadway starring Anne Brown and Todd Duncan

Nat "King" Cole (b Nathaniel Coles, Montgomery, AL, Mar 17, 1919; d 1965), singer and piano player, records "Straighten Up and Fly Right" his first recording, which sells more than 500,000 copies

Selma Burke (b Mooresville, NC, Dec 31, 1900) is commissioned to create a profile of Pres. Franklin D. Roosevelt* after a national competition sponsored by the Fine Arts Commission in Washington, DC; the completed project, a plaque, is unveiled and installed at the Recorder of Deeds Building, Washington, DC

Lillian Evanti, internationally renowned opera singer, wins critical acclaim for her performance in *La Traviata* with the National Negro Opera Company, Washington, DC

Louis Wright becomes director of surgery at Harlem Hospital, New York City; five years later he is elected president of the Harlem Hospital medical board

Delegates at the Professional Golfers Association annual meeting vote to limit membership to whites only

1943

Political activist Paul Robeson was an exceptional student and athlete at Rutgers University, NJ, before he embarked on a successful theater, recording, and film career. (MSRC)

	A. **General History**	B. **Education**	C. **Laws and Legal Actions**	D. **Religion**
1943	Rev. Adam Clayton Powell, Jr. (D-NY), is elected to the US Congress			
1944	Thirteen blacks become the first commissioned as naval officers	Frederick Douglass Patterson, president of Tuskegee Institute, founds the United Negro College Fund	In *Smith v. Allwright,* the US Supreme Court rules that blacks cannot be denied the right to vote in primary elections	
	Charles F. Anderson becomes the first black in the US Marine Corps to be promoted to sergeant major, the highest noncommissioned rank among enlisted men			
	The US Secretary of the Navy orders all naval vessels integrated			
	The 320th Negro Anti-Aircraft Barrage Balloon Battalion assists in the D-Day invasion of Normandy, France			
	The US War Department forbids racial discrimination in recreation and transportation facilities on all US Army stations			
	Black stevedores refuse to return to work after an ammunition explosion at the docks near San Francisco, CA; the men are brought to trial and sentenced to 8-15 years' hard labor; Thurgood Marshall appeals the case and wins an acquittal in 1946			
	Black volunteers are integrated with white troops to fight the German "Bulge"; although US troops are successful, a new integration policy is not implemented			
	USS *Harmon* is the first fighting ship named for a black, Leonard Roy Harmon, who won the Navy Cross for heroism in a battle with Japanese forces			
	Bessie Garret is the first black woman in the US Navy's Women Accepted for Volunteer Emergency Service			
	Cong. William Dawson (D-IL) is the first black			

254

| E. **Literature, Publications, and The Black Press** | F. **The Arts** | G. **Science, Technology, and Medicine** | H. **Sports** |

1943

Harry S. McAlpin, reporter for the *Daily World* in Atlanta, GA, becomes the first black authorized to attend White House press conferences

Melvin B. Tolson's (b Moberly, MO, Feb 6, 1898) first volume of poetry, *Rendezvous with America*, is published

Diana Ross, singer and actress, b Diane Ross, Detroit, MI, Mar 26; as a member of the Supremes and as a solo artist, Ross will have more number one records than any other female artist in the history of the charts; she also receives a Tony Award for her Broadway show *An Evening with Diana Ross*

Dancer Pearl Primus makes her Broadway debut at the Belasco Theatre; she will become widely known for blending African and American dance traditions

Abram Hill's adaptation of the play *Anna Lucasta* premieres on Broadway, NYC, and runs successfully for 900 performances

Phillipa Duke Schuyler (b Aug 2, 1931), child prodigy, composes "Manhattan Nocturne," her first orchestral work, on her thirteenth birthday

Dizzy Gillespie begins to play at the Onyx Club, 52nd Street, New York City; it is believed that his style of music, "bebop," is first performed here

Charles Drew is appointed chief of staff at Freedman's Hospital, Howard University, Washington, DC; he is also appointed an examiner by the American Board of Surgery, becoming the first black to hold this position

Daisy Hill Northcross founds and becomes superintendent of Mercy Hospital, Detroit, MI

Jessie Abbott is Tennessee State University's first women's track coach

William Willis of Ohio State University is the first black player to start in the College All-Star Football game

1944

Dizzy Gillespie, innovative jazz trumpeter, helped to create bebop music during the 1940s. (MSRC)

	A. **General History**	B. **Education**	C. **Laws and Legal Actions**	D. **Religion**
1944	elected vice chairman of the Democratic National Committee A. Philip Randolph names Anna Arnold Hedgeman (b Marshalltown, IA, Jul 5, 1899; d Jan 17, 1990) executive director of the National Council for the Fair Employment Practices Commission			
1945	The 332nd Fighter Group stages a raid over Berlin, Germany; the Tuskegee Airmen, as this group is popularly known, later receive a Distinguished Unit Citation for bravery Col. Benjamin O. Davis, Jr., takes command of the 477th Composite Group of Godman Field, becoming the first black to command a US Army Air Force base Mary McLeod Bethune, representing the US State Department, attends the conference in San Francisco, CA, which establishes the United Nations	Thousands of white students walk out of classes in protest of integration, Gary, IN; this walkout will serve as a precedent for future integration resistance	New York is the first state to pass the Fair Employment Practices Commission law	The World Order of Congregational Churches designates voodoo as a bona fide religion

Mary McLeod Bethune, an educator by training, engaged in political, feminist, social, and civil rights activities. (MSRC)

	A. **General History**	B. **Education**	C. **Laws and Legal Actions**	D. **Religion**
1946	The first US coin honoring a black, Booker T. Washington, is issued Emma Clarissa Clement, mother of Atlanta University president Rufus E. Clement, is the first black woman named "Mother of the Year" by the Golden Rule Foundation Pres. Harry S. Truman* appoints William Hastie governor of the Virgin Islands The first group of black officers is integrated into the Regular US Army	Mississippi Valley State College is founded, Itta Bena, MS Charles S. Johnson, sociologist, is named president of Fisk University in Tennessee; Johnson, a noted scholar, has written several major works	In *Morgan v. Commonwealth of Virginia*, the US Supreme Court bans segregation in interstate bus travel Pres. Harry S. Truman* issues an Executive Order establishing the Committee on Civil Rights to investigate racial injustices and to make recommendations Cong. Adam Clayton Powell, Jr.'s (D-NY) "Powell Amendment" denying federal funds to any project where racial discrimination exists is first attached	

1944

1945

John H. Johnson's *Ebony* magazine, dedicated to black American life and culture, begins publication, Chicago, IL; the magazine is modeled after *Life* magazine

Gwendolyn Brooks's (b Topeka, KS, Jun 17, 1917) first book of poetry, *A Street in Bronzeville,* is published

Chester Himes's (1909–1984) first novel, *If He Hollers, Let Him Go,* is published; Himes, who also writes popular detective novels featuring the characters Coffin Ed Smith and Gravedigger Jones, will become one of the most prolific black novelists

Richard Wright's autobiographical *Black Boy* is published; the book becomes a best-seller

Eslanda Goode Robeson's *African Journey,* a diary of her trip to Africa, is published

Controversy ensues when John R. Sinnock's* engraving of Pres. Franklin D. Roosevelt* appears on the US dime; many accuse Sinnock of liberally borrowing from the work of sculptor Selma Burke

Sarah Vaughan (b Newark, NJ, Mar 27, 1924; d San Fernando Valley, CA, Apr 4, 1990) enters an amateur contest at the Apollo Theatre on a dare and is hired by Earl Hines as a result of her performance; she begins recording jazz tunes the following year, earning the name "The Divine One"

Nora Douglas Holt (b Kansas City, KS, 1885) becomes the first black person accepted into the Music Critics Circle of New York

1946

Ann Petry's (b Old Saybrook, CT, Oct 12, 1908) first book, *The Street,* is published; 1.5 million copies are sold

St. Louis Woman, based on a book by Arna Bontemps and Countee Cullen, opens on Broadway, NYC; the play brings wide attention to supporting actress Pearl Bailey, who stops the show nightly with her renditions of "Legalize My Name" and "A Woman's Prerogative"; Bailey will go on to win the Donaldson Award for Most Promising Newcomer

Camilla Williams is the first black woman to perform with the New York City Opera and to sign a

Holcombe Rucker begins summer basketball leagues in New York City that are the origins of public parks basketball games found in several major US cities; several professional players will get their start at these summer leagues

The Basketball Association of America, a professional league, is formed; the main objective of the BAA is to increase spectatorship for professional basketball; the league admits black players, hoping to encourage black attendance at the

	A. **General History**	B. **Education**	C. **Laws and Legal Actions**	D. **Religion**
1946	Margaret Roselle Hawkins and Sarah Strickland-Scott organize the Links, Inc., a public service, nonpartisan volunteer organization, in Philadelphia, PA		to the Flanagan Lunch Bill; when the bill passes both houses of Congress and is signed into law, Powell becomes the first black member of Congress to sponsor and see enacted a major civil rights law	
	Ralph J. Bunche (b Detroit, MI, Aug 7, 1904; d NYC, Dec 9, 1971) is named director of the division of trusteeships for the Secretariat of the United Nations			
	Mary Fair Burks, head of the Alabama State College English Department in Montgomery, founds the Women's Political Caucus as a means to promote voter registration and civic activism among black women			
	Charles W. Anderson (b 1907) is named Assistant Commonwealth Attorney of Kentucky, becoming the first black to occupy this position since Reconstruction			
	Paul Robeson co-founds the Progressive Party organized to exert pressure on the US Congress to exert constructive legislation			
1947	On behalf of the NAACP, W. E. B. Du Bois edits and presents to the United Nations an appeal against racism in the US	Texas Southern University is founded, Houston, TX	Rosa Lee Ingram, a Georgia tenant farmer, and two of her sons are convicted and sentenced to death for the murder of a white man whom Ingram alleges assaulted her; the case spurs a national defense and amnesty program that results in Ingram's pardon in 1959	
	The Journey of Reconciliation, sponsored by the Congress on Racial Equality, sends an interracial group on a bus trip through the South to test compliance with the *Morgan* (1946) decision; it is the precursor to the Freedom Rides of the 1960s			
	Ralph J. Bunche is appointed to the United Nations' Palestine Commission and works with Count Folke Bernadotte* on the Arab-Israeli dispute; after Bernadotte is assassinated, Bunche carries on negotiations and arranges an armistice in 1949			

1946

contract with a major opera company in the US

Osceola McArthy Archer (1890–1983), pioneering black director and actress, becomes resident director at Putnam County Playhouse, Mahopac, NY

Elizabeth Catlett completes her graphic series, "Negro Woman," Mexico

Richmond Barthé is commissioned to sculpt a bust of Booker T. Washington for the New York University Hall of Fame

Dinah Washington (b Tuscaloosa, AL, 1924) begins recording for Mercury Records; during the next 16 years she will place 45 songs on the *Billboard* R&B charts, causing her to be known as the "Queen of the Blues"

Gospel singer Mahalia Jackson records "Move on Up a Little Higher"; one million copies of the song will be sold

games and thus increase profits

The All-American Football Conference is formed and allows teams to sign black players

---

1947

John Hope Franklin's *From Slavery to Freedom: A History of Negro Americans* is published

Louis Lautier, Washington Bureau Chief of the Negro Newspaper Publishers Association, is the first black issued credentials for both the US Senate and House press galleries

Daisy Lampkin, shown here addressing the 1947 National Council of Negro Women Convention, is best known for her work as national field secretary for the NAACP. (Bethune)

Hattie McDaniel begins work on the radio program "Beulah"; she stars on the show until 1951

Jackie Robinson, (b Cairo, GA, Jan 31, 1919; d Stamford, CT, Oct 24, 1972) is the first acknowledged black American in the 20th century to be allowed to play in major league baseball when he joins the Brooklyn Dodgers

Dan Bankhead joins the Brooklyn Dodgers, becoming the first black pitcher in major league baseball

Wilberforce University in Ohio defeats Bergen College of New Jersey in the first football game between predominantly black and predominantly white colleges

Larry Doby becomes the first black to play in baseball's American League when he signs with the Cleveland Indians

	A. **General History**	B. **Education**	C. **Laws and Legal Actions**	D. **Religion**
1947	The President's Commission on Civil Rights attacks racial injustice in US in a formal report, *To Secure These Rights*			
1948	First Lt. Nancy C. Leftenant becomes the first black accepted into the regular Army Nurse Corps	In *Sipuel v. University of Oklahoma*, the US Supreme Court rules that a state must provide legal education for blacks at the same time it provides it for whites	In *Shelly v. Kraemer*, the US Supreme Court declares that courts cannot enforce segregated housing covenants	Martin Luther King, Jr., is ordained and at the age of 18 becomes the assistant pastor of his father's church, Ebenezer Baptist Church, Atlanta, GA

A. Philip Randolph forms the League for Non-Violent Civil Disobedience Against Military Segregation; Randolph tells a US Senate committee that he will advise black youths to refuse military induction unless segregation and discrimination are prohibited in the selective service system

Several southern white delegates walk out of the National Democratic Convention after a strong civil rights plank is adopted, Philadelphia, PA

W. E. B. DuBois is dismissed from the NAACP because of alleged pro-Russian and Communist Party sympathy

Pres. Harry S. Truman* appoints James C. Evans Civilian Assistant to the US Secretary of Defense to supervise the desegregation of the military

Ralph J. Bunche is appointed temporary United Nations mediator in Palestine

American Nurses Association elects the first black American to its Board of Directors

The Universal Declaration of Human Rights is adopted by the General Assembly of the United Nations; it states: "All human beings are born free and equal in dignity and rights. They are endowed with reason and conscience and should act towards one another in a spirit of brotherhood"; the Declaration provides an

Reserve Officers Training Corps (ROTC) units are established at Morgan State University, Florida A&M University, and Southern University

Denmark Technical College is founded, Denmark, SC

The Supreme Court of California rules that the state law prohibiting interracial marriages is unconstitutional

Pres. Harry S. Truman* issues Executive Order 9980 and Executive Order 9981, creating a Fair Employment Board to eliminate racial discrimination in federal employment; he also creates a Committee on Equality of Treatment and Opportunity in the Armed Services

The African Methodist Episcopal Church authorizes the ordination of women

A group of black ministers march on Capitol Hill and stage a prayer vigil; they urge legislation ensuring equality in education, work, and protection under the law

The Islamic Mission of America is established and incorporated as a religious institution, Brooklyn, NY; the organization promotes Orthodox Islam among blacks and is credited with establishing the first Islamic school in the US

W. E. B. Du Bois, scholar, author, and Pan-Africanist, eventually emigrated to Ghana, West Africa, where he became a citizen and was honored by President Kwame Nkrumah. (MSRC)

E. **Literature,
Publications, and
The Black Press**   F. **The Arts**

G. **Science,
Technology,
and Medicine**   H. **Sports**

1947

1948

Benjamin Quarles's first book, *Frederick Douglass,* is published

While working for the Associated Negro Press, Alice Dunnigan travels with Harry S. Truman,* covering his presidential election campaign

Doris Akers (b Brooksfield, MO, May 21, 1923) forms the Simmons-Akers Singers, a gospel group, with Dorothy Simmons; they later establish the Simmons and Akers Music House, which publishes and distributes their songs

Singer and pianist Bob Howard's television show premieres; it is one of the earliest television shows with a black host

Louis Wright organizes the Harlem Hospital Cancer Research Foundation, where he researches the effectiveness of chemotherapeutic agents in the treatment of cancer

Alice Coachman (b Albany, GA, Nov 9, 1921) is the first black American woman to win an Olympic medal when she defeats Britain's Dorothy Tyler* in the high jump competition, London, England; Coachman also sets an Olympic record for that event

Leroy "Satchel" Paige, formerly of the National Negro League, becomes the first black pitcher in American League baseball

Golfers Bill Spiller, Ted Rhodes, and Madison Gunter sue the PGA for racial discrimination; the suit is dropped after the "whites only" policy is rescinded

The National Committee for Fair Play in Bowling is established, and Minneapolis, MN, mayor Hubert Humphrey* is chairperson; the goal of the committee is to persuade the American Bowling Congress to repeal its "whites only" clause; ABC and the Women's International Bowling Congress admit blacks 18 months later

Marion Motley of the Cleveland Browns is the first player in professional football to lead in rushing yards

The Ladies Professional Golf Association is formed and bars blacks from membership, although no specific clause to that effect is written in the association's constitution

A. Philip Randolph, founder of the Brotherhood of Sleeping Car Porters, the Messenger *periodical, and the League for Non-Violent Civil Disobedience Against Military Segregation.* (Bethune)

	A. **General History**	B. **Education**	C. **Laws and Legal Actions**	D. **Religion**
1948	international forum for human rights			
	Edward R. Dudley (b Boston, VA, 1911) is appointed US ambassador to Liberia			
	William Thaddeus Coleman, Jr., is appointed the first black clerk of the US Supreme Court			
1949	Cong. William Dawson (D-IL) is elected chairman of the House Expenditure Committee, the first black to head a standing committee in the US Congress	Wesley A. Brown is the first black to graduate from the US Naval Academy, Annapolis, MD		
	The US Navy Department announces a policy of equality of treatment and opportunity to all persons in the Navy and Marine Corps	Coahama Junior College is founded, Clarksdale, MS		
	The US Army adopts a nondiscriminatory job policy	Southwestern Christian College is founded, Terrell, TX		
	At the Paris Peace Conference actor Paul Robeson makes the statement, "It is unthinkable that American Negroes could go to war on behalf of those who have oppressed us for generations against the Soviet Union, which in one generation has raised our people to full human dignity"			
	Dorothea Towles, the first black woman to earn a living as a professional model, begins her career in Christian Dior's* European showroom			
	As an assistant to an FSA administrator, Anna Arnold Hedgeman is the first black to hold a position in the Federal Security Agency Administration			
	Hon. William Hastie is nominated for the US Circuit Court of Appeals			
1950	Ralph J. Bunche receives the Nobel Peace Prize for his work as a mediator in the Palestine crisis, the first black to receive the honor	In *McLaurin v. Board of Regents*, the US Supreme Court rules against classroom and social segregation at the University of Oklahoma; this ruling is a	US Attorney General J. Howard MacGrath* and Solicitor General Philip Perlman* argue before the US Supreme Court for the reversal of the 1896 court	

E. **Literature, Publications, and The Black Press**	F. **The Arts**	G. **Science, Technology, and Medicine**	H. **Sports**

Frank Yerby's (b Augusta, GA, 1916) *The Foxes of Harrow* is published; this best-selling novel will become a successful movie	The popular music industry uses the term "rhythm and blues" rather than "race records" for the first time to refer to music performed by black Americans WERD-AM, the first black-owned radio station in the US, begins operation in Atlanta, GA William Still's *Troubled Island* becomes the first opera written by a black American that is produced by a major opera company when it premieres at the New York City Opera; singer Robert McFerrin makes his debut in this production The Charlie Parker Quintet, an innovative jazz group, begins playing music in a style that will become known as "the birth of cool" Dean Dixon (b NYC, 1915) is conductor of the Göteborg Symphony Orchestra, Sweden When the Howard Players of Howard University, Washington, DC, travel to Norway and other Scandinavian countries, they become the first undergraduate group to be invited by the US State Department and a foreign government to perform abroad	Charles Drew, appointed Surgical Consultant for the US Army's European Theater of Operations, is one of four physicians who tour hospital installations in occupied Europe to improve the quality of these hospitals	Ezzard Charles defeats Jersey Joe Walcott* to win the world heavyweight boxing championship Jackie Robinson of the Brooklyn Dodgers becomes the first black baseball player to win the major league's MVP Award The Harlem Globetrotters begin the transformation from serious professional basketball to entertainment after the team is denied admittance into the newly integrated NBA and ABA; by 1984 over 100 million people will have watched them play, and they will become the world's best-known sports team The Los Angeles Rams sign Paul "Tank" Younger of Louisiana's Grambling State University; he is the NFL's first player from a black college	**1949**
Gwendolyn Brooks is the first black American to win a Pulitzer prize in any category; she is recognized for her book of poetry, *Annie Allen*	Juanita Hall becomes the first black American to win a Tony award when she receives it for her portrayal of Bloody		At the NBA's annual players draft the Boston Celtics select Charles "Chuck" Cooper, making him the first black ever drafted by an NBA team	**1950**

	A. **General History**	B. **Education**	C. **Laws and Legal Actions**	D. **Religion**

1950

A. General History

Racial quotas are abolished in the US Army

Edith Sampson (b Pittsburgh, PA, Oct 13, 1901) is the first black appointed as alternate delegate to the United Nations

Paul Robeson recieves the "Champion of African Freedom" Award from the National Church of Nigeria

The American Medical Association seats its first black delegate

Helen O. Dickens (b Dayton, OH, Feb 21, 1909) is the first black woman admitted to the American College of Surgeons

Jesse Leroy Brown (b Hattiesburg, MS, Oct 13, 1926) is the first black American naval officer to lose his life in the Korean War

Audley "Queen Mother" Moore, along with Mother Langley and Dara Collins, found the Universal Association of Ethiopian Women; the group's major goals are to gain and promote economic reparations, cultural identity, and education for black Americans

W. E. B. Du Bois is a candidate from New York for the US Senate, on the American Labor Party ticket

US State Department revokes Paul Robeson's passport because he refuses to sign an affidavit that he has never belonged to the Communist Party

B. Education

result of actions taken after an otherwise qualified black student is denied admission to the all-white University of Texas Law School and a so-called Negro law school is hastily established on campus

In *Sweatt v. Painter*, the US Supreme Court rules that equality of education entails more than comparability of facilities, implying that "separate," by definition, is unequal

Mississippi Valley State University is founded, Ita Bene, MS

C. Laws and Legal Actions

ruling that upholds segregation

In *Henderson v. United States*, the US Supreme Court strikes down an Interstate Commerce Commission ruling requiring black passengers in railroad dining cars to eat behind a partition

Hazel Scott, musician, singer, and actress, became the first black woman to host her own nationally syndicated television program, "The Hazel Scott Show." (Bethune)

1951

A. General History

Gen. Douglas MacArthur* refuses to follow orders to desegregate the US Army and is removed from his command for insubordination; he is replaced by Lt. General Matthew B. Ridgway;* under Ridgway's command, 90% of all black soldiers in Korea are serving in integrated units by July 1953

C. Laws and Legal Actions

Racial discrimination is prohibited in New York's city-assisted housing projects

Pres. Harry S. Truman's* Executive Order 10308 creates the President's Committee on Government Contract Compliance to enforce the nondiscrimination clause for federal

D. Religion

Rev. John M. Burgess is named canon of the Episcopal Cathedral, Washington, DC

E. **Literature, Publications, and The Black Press**	F. **The Arts**	G. **Science, Technology, and Medicine**	H. **Sports**	
	Mary in the Broadway musical *South Pacific*		Jackie Robinson, baseball player, becomes the first black to appear on the cover of *Life* magazine	**1950**

Steveland Morris, songwriter, composer, and musician, b Saginaw, MI, May 13; Morris, better known as "Stevie Wonder," will become a musical and singing sensation at age 12 and go on to win 12 Grammy Awards and an Oscar for best song

Mahalia Jackson is featured in the first large-scale gospel concert, Carnegie Hall, NYC

Sidney Poitier (b Miami, FL, Feb 20, 1927) makes his Hollywood screen debut in *No Way Out*

Alice Childress's (b Charleston, SC, Oct 12, 1920) *Just a Little Simple* becomes the first play written by a black woman to be performed by unionized actors

Ethel Waters becomes one of the first blacks to star in a television series when she appears in "Beulah"

The "Hazel Scott Show" premieres, featuring Hazel Scott (b Port of Spain, Trinidad, Jun 11, 1920), jazz pianist; Scott is one of the first black women to host a musical variety television show

Gospel singer Mahalia Jackson was one of the first black female performers to gain national acclaim (MSRC)

Earl Lloyd is the first black to play in an NBA game when he plays with the Washington Capitols

Althea Gibson (b Silver, SC, Aug 25, 1927) becomes the first black American to play tennis at the US Open

Arthur Dovington of the Atlantic City Seagulls, Eastern Amateur League, is the first black to play organized ice hockey

Althea Gibson, the first African-American to win at Wimbledon, inspired the young Arthur Ashe, future world tennis champion. (MSRC)

E.	F.	G.	H.	
Anna Julia Cooper's *Personal Recollections of the Grimké Family* and *The Life and Writings of Charlotte Forten Grimké* are published Ethel L. Payne (b Chicago IL, Aug 14, 1911), known as the "first lady of the Black press," begins work as a reporter for the *Chi*	Janet Collins (b New Orleans, LA, Mar 7, 1923) becomes the first black prima ballerina in the US when she joins the Metropolitan Opera William Warfield and Muriel Rahn perform on "The Ed Sullivan Show"; they are among the first black concert artists to	Lloyd A. Hall, chemist, receives a patent for a bacon curing process that reduces the curing time from 15 days to a few hours	Althea Gibson is the first black American to play in the Wimbledon tennis tournament in England Sophronia Pierce Stent is the first black woman accepted into the Amateur Fencer's League of America	**1951**

A. **General History**	B. **Education**	C. **Laws and Legal Actions**	D. **Religion**

1951 Private William Thompson posthumously receives the Congressional Medal of Honor; it is the first such award given to a black American soldier since the Spanish-American War of 1898

Gov. Adlai Stevenson* of Illinois orders the National Guard to suppress a race riot, as more than 4,000 whites protest the attempt by a black family to occupy a home in an all-white neighborhood, Cicero, IL

The US Congress deactivates the 24th Infantry, the last all-black army unit

The US Marine Corps announces a plan to integrate its forces because under segregation the troop distribution scheme creates a shortage of men available for front-line fighting in the Korean War

Bernice Gaines Hughes (b Xenia, OH, 1904) is the first black woman to achieve the rank of lieutenant colonel in the US army

Arie Taylor is the first black Women's Air Force classroom instructor

Eslanda Goode Robeson is one of three protestors who disrupt the United Nations postwar conference on genocide; they argue unsuccessfully that violence against black Americans should be on the UN agenda

Florida NAACP Executive Secretary Harry Moore and his wife, both active in voter registration and antilynching campaigns, are killed by a bomb in their home; no arrests are made

C. Laws and Legal Actions:

agencies; agencies with government contracts cannot discriminate

Cong. William Dawson (D-IL) delivers an impassioned speech on the House floor that is primarily responsible for the defeat of the Winstead Amendment; the amendment would have allowed military personnel the option of choosing between all-white units and racially integrated ones

The US Justice Department indicts W. E. B. Du Bois as "the agent of a foreign principal" (Soviet Union), but he is acquitted; the same year, the US State Department denies Du Bois a passport until 1958

1952 Tuskegee Institute's Department of Records and Research reports 1952 as

cago Defender; two years later she becomes the paper's one-person bureau in Washington, DC

appear on a television show

"Sugar" Ray Robinson (b Walker Smith, Detroit, MI, May 3, 1920) defeats Jake La Motta* in the 13th round to win the middle-weight boxing champion-ship

1951

American-born entertainer Josephine Baker (b 1906; d 1975) adopted the New Look in Paris in the post-war years, a dramatic change from her famous banana costume in the 1926 Folies-Bergère, which won the heart of Europe.

Ralph Ellison's (b Oklahoma City, OK, Mar 1, 1914) first and only novel,

Canada Lee, actor, d New York, May 9; Lee is best known for his portrayal of

Floyd Patterson (b Waco, NC, 1935) wins the middleweight boxing gold

1952

1952

the first year in 71 years of tabulation that there are no reported lynchings in the US, AL

Paul Robeson is one of seven and the only American to receive the International Stalin Peace Prize, "a kind of counter-Nobel" awarded by the Soviet Union to honor citizens of any country who fight against war

Charlotta Bass, political activist and editor of *The California Eagle,* is the first black woman to run for vice president of the US (Progressive Party ticket)

At the Democratic National Convention, Cong. Adam Clayton Powell, Jr. (D-NY), insists that either the party take a stand on civil rights using the platform of presidential candidate Adlai Stevenson* or he will leave the party; after two months Stevenson agrees to Powell's demand

1953

Vivian Carter Mason (b Wilkes-Barre, PA, Feb 10, 1900) is elected president of National Council of Negro Women

The US Supreme Court bans segregation in restaurants in Washington, DC

Pres. Dwight D. Eisenhower* reactivates the Government Contract Compliance Committee to enforce the ban on antidiscrimination in government contracts

James Baldwin, prolific novelist and essayist. (MSRC)

Invisible Man, is published; Ellison wins the National Book Award for this literary work	Bigger Thomas in the Broadway play *Native Son* (1941) Ford's Theatre of Baltimore, MD, drops its segregation policy, which has been in effect since 1861 Paul R. Williams (b Los Angeles, CA, 1894) designs the Grave of the Unknown Soldier memorial at Pearl Harbor, Hawaii		medal in the summer Olympic Games; he later becomes the first gold medalist to win a world professional title	**1952**
Benjamin Quarles's historical work *The Negro in the Civil War* is published Gwendolyn Brooks's *Maud Martha,* an autobiographical novel, is published James Baldwin's (b NYC, Aug 2, 1924; d St. Paul de Vence, France, Dec 1, 1987) *Go Tell It on the Mountain* is published	Louis Peterson's drama *Take a Giant Step* opens on Broadway in New York City Mary Elizabeth Vroman, the first black woman to gain membership in the Screen Writers Guild, adapts her short story "Bright Road" into a screenplay "Big Mama" Thornton's "Hound Dog" stays at number one for seven weeks on *Billboard*'s R&B charts; Elvis Presley* will later sing and popularize the song for white audiences Black artists and teachers organize the National Conference of Artists, Florida A&M University, Tallahassee James Carter, Vivian Carter Bracken, and Calvin Carter found Vee Jay Records, Chicago, IL;		"Big Mo" Aldredge is the first black woman to make the national Amateur Athletic Union women's basketball team Toni Stone, a woman, signs to play professional baseball with the Indianapolis Clowns, the Negro American League champions	**1953**

A. General History	B. Education	C. Laws and Legal Actions	D. Religion
1953			
1954 Benjamin O. Davis, Jr. (b Washington, DC 1912), is the first black general in the US Air Force Charles H. Mahoney is the first black American appointed permanent delegate to the United Nations The US Department of Defense abolishes the remaining all-black units in the armed forces Cong. Charles C. Diggs, Jr. (b Detroit, MI, 1922) (D-MI), is the first black Congress member from Michigan Ralph J. Bunche is appointed Undersecretary of the United Nations; as such, Bunche is the highest ranking American official at the UN	The US Supreme Court rules in *Brown v. Board of Education of Topeka* that segregated schools are "inherently unequal" and thus unconstitutional, reversing *Plessy v. Ferguson; Brown* also establishes that other public facilities separated based on race are inherently unequal Massive school desegregation begins in the public schools of Washington, DC, and Baltimore, MD, this is the first attempt at widespread school desegregation since the *Brown* decision		Malcolm X (b Malcolm Little, Omaha, NE, May 19, 1925) is named minister of the Muslim New York Temple, No. 7, NYC Rev. Martin Luther King, Jr., is pastor of the Dexter Avenue Church, Montgomery, AL Rev. James Joshua Thomas is the first black pastor of the Reformed Dutch Church
1955 Pres. Dwight D. Eisenhower* appoints J. Ernest Wilkins Assistant Secretary of Labor Rosa Parks, seamstress, is arrested for refusing to yield her bus seat to a white man in Montgomery, AL; her arrest sparks the Montgomery bus boycott A. Philip Randolph and Willard Townsend are named vice presidents of	The US Supreme Court orders that the integration of schools proceed "with all deliberate speed" Willa B. Player (b Jackson, MS, Aug 9, 1909) becomes the first black woman to preside over Bennett College in North Carolina; she is also the first black woman in the US to be named president of a four-year women's college The Georgia Board of Education adopts a resolution	The US Supreme Court prohibits segregation of recreational facilities Interstate Commerce Commission bans segregation in buses, waiting rooms, and railroad coaches in interstate travel Executive Order 10590 establishes the President's Committee on Government Policy to enforce non-discriminatory policy in Federal employment	Rev. H. A. Batley becomes the second black president of the Methodist Conference on Christian Education

E. Literature, Publications, and The Black Press	F. The Arts	G. Science, Technology, and Medicine	H. Sports
	their clients include popular music stars the Dells, the El Dorados, the Impressions, the Staple Singers, and Jerry Butler; Vee Jay Records is the first US company to introduce the British rock group, the Beatles;* the company declares bankruptcy in 1966		
John Oliver Killens's (b Macon, GA, 1916; d Brooklyn, NY, Oct 27, 1987) first novel, *Youngblood,* is published Paule Marshall's (b Valenza Pauline Burke, Brooklyn, NY, Apr 9, 1929) first short story, "The Valley Between," is published in *Our World* magazine	Dorothy Dandridge (b Cleveland, OH, Nov 9, 1923) and Harry Belafonte (b NYC, Mar 1, 1927) star in *Carmen Jones,* one of the most publicized and commercially successful all-black films; Dandridge is nominated for an Academy Award for best actress, becoming the first black woman so honored The Chords, an all-male R&B group, records "Sh-Boom," regarded as the first rock and roll record in the US and one of the first R&B recording to reach number one on the Pop charts; the record is one of the first "covers," songs recorded by little-known black musicians which white groups duplicate; the duplicate versions usually outsell the originals Bill Haley* and the Comets record Joe Turner's "Shake, Rattle and Roll"; the song becomes a best-seller and a rock and roll classic National Negro Network, the first black-owned radio network in the US, begins broadcasting	Peter M. Marshall is president of the NY County Medical Society, the first American Medical Association unit with a black leader	Under the leadership of Coach John McLendon, Tennessee State University becomes the first black college team invited to play in the National Association of Intercollegiate Athletics basketball tournament The NBA adopts a rule requiring teams to attempt a shot within 24 seconds of inbounding; the new rule quickens the pace of NBA games and becomes more advantageous to those who play with the traditional "playground style" found in predominantly black urban areas

| | Marian Anderson becomes the first black to sing in the Metropolitan Opera House in New York City when she performs the role of Ulrica in Verdi's *The Masked Ball*

Alice Childress becomes the first black woman to receive an Obie Award when her play, *Trouble in Mind,* is named best off-Broadway production

Comedian Redd Foxx (d Los Angeles, CA, Oct 11, | | The National Collegiate Athletic Association doubles the width of the basketball foul lane from 6 to 12 feet—"The Russell Rule"—because player Bill Russell is so dominating; at 6'9", Russell is a great shot blocker and inside scorer; the Russell Rule is intended to limit his presence in the foul lane

Georgia governor Marvin Griffin* bans Georgia Tech University from playing in |

	A. **General History**	B. **Education**	C. **Laws and Legal Actions**	D. **Religion**
1955	the newly merged labor union AFL-CIO Emmett Till, a 14-year-old boy from Chicago, IL, is murdered in Leflore County, MS, because he allegedly whistled at a white woman Following the death of Walter White, Roy Wilkins (1901–1981) is elected executive secretary of the NAACP Lloyd A. Hall becomes a member of the national board of directors for the American Institute of Chemists; later he is the organization's first black councillor-at-large	that revokes the license of any teacher who teaches integrated classes	The US Court of Appeals for the 4th Circuit in Richmond, VA, declares in *Flemming v. South Carolina Electric and Gas Company* that intrastate bus segregation is unconstitutional	
1956	The home of Rev. Martin Luther King, Jr., is bombed in Montgomery, AL Paul Robeson appears before the House Committee on Un-American Activities, testifying at Congressional hearings to investigate "Communist sympathizers"; Robeson is called because he frequently visited the Soviet Union Robert N. C. Nix (b Orangeburg, SC, 1905; d Jun 1987) (D-PA) is elected to the US Congress The so-called Southern Manifesto is signed by 101 southern Congressional members, urging states to reject and resist the *Brown v. Board of Education* Supreme Court decision	After three and a half years of court action, the NAACP succeeds in forcing the University of Alabama to enroll its first black student, Autherine Lucy	A federal court rules that racial segregation on Montgomery, AL, city buses is unconstitutional, thereby ending the Montgomery bus boycott Following a six-month boycott, segregation is outlawed on buses in Tallahassee, FL In an attempt to undermine the efforts of the NAACP, the South Carolina legislature passes a law prohibiting city employees from affiliating with any civil rights organization	The Colored Methodist Episcopal Church changes its name to the Christian Methodist Episcopal Church Rev. Johnnie Coleman starts the Christ Universal Temple with 35 members; today, with 100,000 members, it is the largest black church in Chicago, IL

E. Literature, Publications, and The Black Press	F. The Arts	G. Science, Technology, and Medicine	H. Sports	
	1991) records the first of over 50 party records Charles "Chuck" Berry records "Maybellene," the first in a long string of rock and roll hits Antoine "Fats" Domino records "Blueberry Hill," which later becomes a rock and roll classic Following graduation from Barnard College of Columbia University in New York City in 1950, Norma Merrick Skalrek (b NYC, Apr 15, 1928) becomes the first black woman architect licensed in New York		the Sugar Bowl (New Orleans, LA) because their opponent, the University of Pittsburgh, has a black player; despite student outrage and protest, Georgia Tech does not play; it will be another 10 years before blacks are allowed to play in the Sugar Bowl	**1955**
Margaret Just Butcher's *The Negro in American Culture* is published; in the book the folk and formal contributions of blacks to American culture are traced	Nat "King" Cole is attacked by white men in Birmingham, AL, while he is performing at a concert featuring black and white performers before an all-white audience Nat "King" Cole's television series premieres Ruth Brown hits the pop charts with her first crossover hit, "Lucky Lips"; throughout the decade she will record so many hits for Atlantic Records that the company becomes known as "the house that Ruth built" James Brown (b May 3, 1933), who will become known as the "Godfather of Soul" and "Soul Brother Number One," releases his first hit song, "Please, Please, Please"		Nell C. Jackson serves as head coach of the US Olympic track and field team, becoming the first black head coach of any US Olympic team Ann Gregory becomes the first black American to play in an integrated women's amateur golf championship Earlene Brown wins the South Pacific Amateur Athletic Union title for the shotput and discus competition Charles Dumas, freshman at Compton College, CA, is the first high jumper to top seven feet Pres. Dwight D. Eisenhower* personally appeals to Bill Russell to play basketball for the US Olympic team; Russell consents and is the most popular choice for an All-American team Mildred McDaniel, high jumper, is the first black American female to set an Olympic and world record on the same day, Melbourne, Australia Floyd Patterson KO's Archie Moore in five rounds, becoming, at 21, the youngest heavyweight champion	**1956**

A. **General History**	B. **Education**	C. **Laws and Legal Actions**	D. **Religion**
1957 The Southern Christian Leadership Council is founded, Atlanta, GA; Rev. Martin Luther King, Jr., leaves Montgomery, AL, to head the group		Pres. Dwight D. Eisenhower* signs the first civil rights act since 1875; the Civil Rights Act of 1957 authorizes the federal government to bring civil suits on its own behalf to obtain injunctive relief where any citizen is denied or threatened in his or her right to vote; elevates the civil rights section of the Department of Justice to the status of a division, with an assistant attorney general leading it; and creates the US Commission on Civil Rights	Mother Charleszetta Waddles (b St. Louis, MO, Oct 7, 1912), Pentecostal minister, founds the Perpetual Mission for Saving Souls of All Nations, Detroit, MI

Rev. Martin Luther King, Jr., the NAACP, and others organize the Prayer Pilgrimage; the event, scheduled to coincide with the third anniversary of the *Brown v. Board of Education* decision, attracts a crowd of over 30,000 and is held on the steps of the Lincoln Memorial, Washington, DC

Ghana becomes the first African nation to achieve independence from colonial rule; Ghana is the first newly independent African country to join the UN

After fellow Nation of Islam member Hinton Johnson is beaten by New York City police while in jail, Malcolm X and a crowd of supporters stand outside the station and demand that Johnson be taken to the hospital

Blacks in Tuskegee, AL, boycott white merchants in protest of the state legislature's earlier efforts to thwart their quests for political power

Gov. Orval Faubus* orders units of the Arkansas National Guard to Central High School, Little Rock, on the first day of school; the nine black youths who are chosen to integrate Central High become known as the Little Rock Nine; they are led by NAACP member Daisy Bates

Pres. Dwight D. Eisenhower* sends 1,000 paratroopers from the 101st Airborne Division to Little Rock, AR, to enforce the *Brown* public school desegregation decision

Dorothy I. Height (b Richmond, VA, Mar 24, 1912),

Committed to public service and civil rights, Dorothy I. Height has distinguished herself as president of the National Council of Negro Women (NCNW) and of Delta Sigma Theta sorority. (Bethune)

			1957
Malcolm X founds *Muhammad Speaks,* a Muslim newspaper	William "Count" Basie's (1904–1984) band is the first US band to play a command performance for Queen Elizabeth II* of England and the first jazz band to play at the Waldorf Astoria Hotel in New York City		Althea Gibson is the first black American tennis player to win the singles and doubles titles at Wimbledon, England; she also is the first black woman to appear on the cover of *Sports Illustrated* magazine

James Brown (b St. Simon's Island, GA, Feb 17, 1936) becomes a member of the Cleveland Browns football team and is voted "Rookie of the Year" at the end of the season; the following year Brown is presented with the Jim Thorpe Trophy as the NFL's foremost star

Tennessee State University wins its first NAIA title, becoming the first black college to win a national basketball title

Bruce Davis wins the National Collegiate Athletic Association foil competition and becomes the first black fencer to win a national title

After losing the middleweight crown three times, "Sugar" Ray Robinson regains the championship title when he KO's Gene Fullmer* in the 5th round; Robinson becomes the first fighter in history to win the middleweight division title four times

| E. **Literature, Publications, and The Black Press** | F. **The Arts** | G. **Science, Technology, and Medicine** | H. **Sports** |

275

	A. **General History**	B. **Education**	C. **Laws and Legal Actions**	D. **Religion**
1957	former president of Delta Sigma Theta Sorority, Inc., assumes the presidency of the National Council of Negro Women Ebony Fashion Fair, a subsidiary of Johnson Publishing Company, a black-owned company, stages its first tour; it will grow into the world's largest traveling fashion show			
1958	At a summit meeting of national black leaders, Pres. Dwight D. Eisenhower* is criticized for urging blacks to "be patient" in their demands for full civil and voting rights Rev. Martin Luther King, Jr., is stabbed by a deranged black woman while autographing copies of *Stride Toward Freedom*, the story of the Montgomery bus boycott, Harlem, New York ABC airs a five-part, weeklong report by Mike Wallace* and Louis Lomax on the Nation of Islam; "The Hate that Hate Produced," featuring Malcolm X, is probably the first national exposure of the religious group Paul and Eslanda Robeson move to the Soviet Union to escape political persecution and racial discrimination in the US; they return five years later Due to philosophical differences, at the National Baptist Convention meeting, NBC president Joseph H. Jackson blocks the sale of Rev. Martin Luther King, Jr.'s book Clifton W. Wharton, Sr., becomes the first black to head a European embassy of the US when he is appointed ambassador to Romania	Ernest Green, the only senior among the Little Rock Nine, graduates from Central High School Interdenominational Theological Center is founded, Atlanta, GA		
1959	While visiting Africa, Malcolm X meets with Gamal Abdel Nasser,* the president of Egypt to establish a			

E. Literature, Publications, and The Black Press	F. The Arts	G. Science, Technology, and Medicine	H. Sports

1958

William R. "Cozy" Cole's "Topsy" is the first drum solo record to sell more than one million copies

Anita Baker, singer (b Toledo, OH, Jan 26); Baker's 1986 debut album *Rapture* will sell five million copies and earn her a Grammy Award in 1987

"Little Richard" Penniman records "Tutti Frutti"; over three million copies are sold, and the song is established as a landmark in rock and roll music

Choreographer Alvin Ailey (b Jan 5, 1931; d NYC, Dec 1, 1989) founds the Alvin Ailey Dance Theater; the troupe, which is later world-renowned, premieres in New York City

Bill Russell, center for the Boston Celtics, is named MVP of the NBA; he will be named again from 1961 to 1963 and in 1965

Prentiss Gault of the University of Oklahoma is the first black football player at a major southwestern white school

1959

Paule Marshall's *Brown Girl, Brownstones,* a semiautobiographical novel, is published

Lorraine Hansberry's (b Chicago, IL, 1930; d NYC, 1965) *A Raisin in the Sun* is the first play written by a

The integrated American Football League is formed; the league's nondiscrimatory policy serves as a ma-

A. **General History**	B. **Education**	C. **Laws and Legal Actions**	D. **Religion**
1959 diplomatic connection between Africans and African-Americans and to enlighten Egyptians on the United States's hypocritical civil rights policies Rev. Martin Luther King, Jr., and his wife Coretta visit India to study Gandhi's* nonviolent philosophy; they are received by Prime Minister Jawaharlal Nehru* W. E. B. Du Bois receives the Lenin Peace Prize Juanita Kidd Stout (b Wewoka, OK, Mar 7, 1919) is elected a county court judge, Philadelphia, PA			
1960 The modern "sit-in" movement, a civil rights protest method, begins when four black students from North Carolina A&T College sit at a "whites-only" Woolworth's lunch counter and refuse to leave when denied service, Greensboro, NC Blacks march to the Old Confederate Capitol building where they pray and sing the "Star-Spangled Banner" during a nonviolent demonstration against segregation, Montgomery, AL; the next day the state board of education expels nine participating students from Alabama State University San Antonio, TX, becomes the first major southern city to integrate lunch counters During a press conference, Pres. Dwight D. Eisenhower* states that he is "deeply sympathetic"		Pres. Dwight D. Eisenhower* signs the Civil Rights Act of 1960, which acknowledges the Federal government's responsibility in matters involving civil rights and reverses its customary "hands-off" policy	Elijah Muhammed, leader of the Nation of Islam, calls for the establishment of an all-black state; this later becomes a symbol and rallying cry among black nationalists Membership in the Nation of Islam reportedly reaches 100,000 nationally

E. Literature, Publications, and The Black Press	F. The Arts	G. Science, Technology, and Medicine	H. Sports	
	black woman to become a hit on Broadway; Lloyd Richards (b Toronto, Canada, Jun 29, 1922) directs this production of *A Raisin in the Sun*		jor draw for attracting black athletes	**1959**
			Elgin Baylor (b Washington, DC, 1936) is the first rookie to be named Most Valuable Player in an NBA All-Star game	
	Ruth Bowen (b Danville, VA, Sep 13, 1924) opens Queen Artists, a talent agency for black artists; by 1969 Queen Booking Corporation is the largest black-owned entertainment agency in the world; its talent roster includes Sammy Davis, Jr., Aretha Franklin, and Ray Charles		John McLendon is the first black coach of an interracial professional basketball team, the Cleveland Pipers	
	Dorothy Dandridge wins a Golden Globe Award for best actress in a musical for her role as Bess in *Porgy and Bess*			
	Berry Gordy (b Detroit, MI, Nov 28, 1929) founds Motown Records, Detroit, MI			
John A. Williams's first novel, *The Angry Ones*, is published	Harry Belafonte wins an Emmy award for his variety television special "Tonight with Harry Belafonte"; he is the first black to receive an Emmy; he is later fired by television sponsors because his integrated specials are considered too controversial		Floyd Patterson KO's Ingemar Johansson* in a rematch and becomes the first boxer to regain the heavyweight title	**1960**
			Track star Wilma Rudolph (b Clarksville, TN, Jun 23, 1940) is the first US woman to win three gold medals at the Olympic Games, Rome, Italy	
	Ike Turner (b Clarksdale, MS, Nov 5, 1931) and Tina Turner (b Anna Mae Bullock, Brownsville, TN, Nov 26, 1938) begin touring as the Ike and Tina Turner Revue, an R & B singing act		Fuller Gordy is the first black professional bowler; Gordy is a relative of Motown Records founder Berry Gordy	
	Chubby Checker (b Ernest Evans) records "The Twist," which spawns a nationwide dance craze		David Lucy of the University of Denver, is the first black skier on a college team, CO	
	While recording "Hallelujah, It's Done," Shirley Ceasar (b Durham, NC, Oct 13, 1938), of the gospel singing group the Caravans, ad-libs in the style		Ronnie Hobson wins the US Open for under-16s, under-13s, and the Junior Men's Doubles with teammate Bill Keim* to become the first black table tennis champion in the US	

1960

with the efforts of any group to enjoy constitutionally guaranteed rights; he calls for biracial conferences throughout the South to help solve racial problems

The Student Non-violent Coordinating Committee is founded on the campus of Shaw University, Raleigh, NC

The home of Z. Alexander Looby, Nashville, TN, council member and NAACP attorney, is bombed; several other homes in the neighborhood are damaged, and hundreds of windows are blown out at nearby Meharry Medical College, injuring several medical students; this act is reflective of the kind of violence perpetrated against civil rights activists throughout this decade

Paul Robeson speaks on behalf of the Aborigine Civil Rights Movement, bringing attention to the appalling conditions in which the Australian aborigines live; he receives the German Peace Medal for this accomplishment

Fifty blacks, among them Rev. Martin Luther King, Jr., are arrested for sitting in at the Magnolia Room of Rich's Department Store, Atlanta, GA; the others are released, but King is sentenced to four months of hard labor at the Reidsville State Prison; Sen. John F. Kennedy* (D-MA), Democratic presidential candidate, calls Coretta Scott King to express his sympathy; Kennedy's campaign manager and brother Robert calls the Georgia judge who sentenced King and pleads for his release;

E. Literature, Publications, and The Black Press	F. The Arts	G. Science, Technology, and Medicine	H. Sports

1960

of the black folk preacher
during the chorus; this
''song and sermonette''
technique will become
Ceasar's trademark

A. **General History**	B. **Education**	C. **Laws and Legal Actions**	D. **Religion**

1960   King is released the following day

The Pan-African Congress of South Africa organizes a protest to flood South African jails with racial pass violators; police in Sharpeville, near Johannesburg, fire on the protestors, leaving 72 persons dead and over 200 injured; the incident will become known as the Sharpeville Massacre

In the closest US presidential election of the century, Sen. John F. Kennedy* (D-MA) is elected president, defeating Vice President Richard Nixon*; a strong black voting bloc helped to determine the outcome

A. Philip Randolph founds the Negro American Labor Council, New York; the Council is an interracial group of Unionists who are dissatisfied with the AFL-CIO's inaction against racial discrimination

Suffrage has continued to be an important and significant privilege in the life of many African Americans. Thousands suffered threats, beatings, and even death while registering to vote. (LC)

1961   The "jail-in" movement starts when arrested students demand jail rather than fines, Rock Hill, SC

Robert C. Weaver is named administrator of the Housing and Home Finance Agency; he is the highest-ranking black in the Federal government at this time

James B. Parsons becomes the first black district court judge, northern Illinois

Sierra Leone gains its independence from Great Britain; Milton Margai becomes the first prime minister

Thirteen CORE-sponsored Freedom Riders begin a bus trip throughout the South to force desegregation of terminals; the bus

Four high schools are peacefully desegregated in Atlanta, GA; Pres. John F. Kennedy* praises the city, hoping it will set a new precedent

Cong. Adam Clayton Powell, Jr. (D-NY), becomes chairman of the Education and Labor Committee; during his tenure he sees all 50 of his legislative pieces enacted; they include expanded educational opportunities, job training, minimum wage protection, and school lunch program implementation

E. Literature, Publications, and The Black Press	F. The Arts	G. Science, Technology, and Medicine	H. Sports	
Leroi Jones's (later renamed Amiri Baraka) (b Newark, NJ, 1934) first book, *Preface to a Twenty-Volume Suicide Note*, is published	Leontyne Price (b Laurel, MS, Feb 10, 1927), opera singer, performs in Verdi's* *Il Travatore* at her Metropolitan House debut; Price will amass many operatic firsts, including the first black to sing opera on network television and the first to receive the Presidential Medal of Freedom	Frederick Jones, inventor of the first automatic refrigeration system for long-haul trucks, d; Jones accumulated over 61 patents in his lifetime, including an air-conditioning unit for military field hospitals, a portable X-ray machine, and a refrigerator for military field kitchens	Isiah Thomas b Chicago, IL, Apr 30; Thomas will become a basketball star, first for Indiana University and later for the Detroit Pistons, where he will lead the team to two NBA championships	**1961**
	Grace Bumbry makes her debut in Richard Wagner's* *Tannhauser* at the Bayreuth Festival, Bavaria, Germany; surrounded by controversy and protest because the role of Venus is played by a black woman, Bumbry receives 42 curtain calls during a 30-minute ovation		Boxer Cassius Clay (b Louisville, KY, Jan 17, 1942; later named Muhammad Ali) correctly predicts the round in which his opponent Alex Miteff* will fall; Clay, the most publicly outspoken black athlete since Jack Johnson, will identify in advance his opponents' knockout rounds in 13 out of 17 fights	
	Florence Ballard, Diana Ross, and Mary Wilson form a singing group, The		Ernie Davis, a Syracuse University, New York, running back, is the first black to win the Heisman Trophy, given annually to the nation's most out-	

	A. **General History**	B. **Education**	C. **Laws and Legal Actions**	D. **Religion**
1961	is bombed ten days later, and its passengers are attacked by whites near Anniston, AL			
	Thurgood Marshall (b Baltimore, MD, Jul 1908) is appointed to the Second Circuit Court of Appeals			
	Whitney M. Young, Jr. (1921–1971), is named executive director of the National Urban League; along with Rev. Martin Luther King, Jr., Roy Wilkins, and James Farmer, he will become one of the "Big Four" male leaders of the civil rights movement			
	W. E. B. Du Bois joins the Communist Party and takes up residence in Ghana as director of the Encyclopedia Africana project at the invitation of Ghana president Kwame Nkrumah			
	A group of black American demonstrators in New York disrupts the United Nations Security Council from the public gallery in protest of the assassination of Patrice Lumumba, prime minister of Congo (later Zaire)			
	Mercer Cook begins tenure as US ambassador to Nigeria; he serves for three years			
	Margaret and Charles Burroughs found the Ebony Museum of African American History (later the DuSable Museum of African American History and Art), Chicago, IL			
1962	Leroy Johnson is elected to the Georgia state senate, becoming the state's first black legislator since Reconstruction	Student protests at Southern University in Louisiana result in the closing of the institution, a precedent for handling future student disturbances	Pres. John F. Kennedy* prohibits racial discrimination in federally financed housing	Rev. W. E. Houston is the first black elected moderator of the United Presbyterian Church, NY synod
	Ann Roberts is appointed Federal Housing Administration Deputy Regional Administrator, the highest-ranking black woman in the federal housing field	The US Supreme Court orders the University of Mississippi to admit student James H. Meredith; Ross Barnett,* governor of Mississippi, tries unsuc-		With the support of Rev. Gardner Taylor of the Concord Baptist Church in Brooklyn, NY, a body of dissenters splits from the National Baptist Convention and forms the National Baptist Progressive Convention

E. **Literature, Publications, and The Black Press**	F. **The Arts**	G. **Science, Technology, and Medicine**	H. **Sports**	
	Supremes, Detroit, MI; under the auspices of Motown Records, the group will have 15 consecutive hit singles		standing collegiate football player	**1961**
	Motown Records has its first number one record with the Marvelettes' "Please Mr. Postman"			
	Dick Gregory fills in for an ailing comedian at the Playboy Club, Chicago, IL, and becomes an immediate success; he is later given special coverage in *Time* magazine			
	Amiri Baraka's play *The Dutchman* opens in New York City; Baraka will receive an Obie award for the best off-Broadway play for the 1963–64 season			
	Gail Fisher is believed to be the first black actress with lines to appear in a national television commercial			
	Quincy Jones (b Chicago, IL, 1934) joins Mercury Records and becomes the first black vice president of a white record company; while in this position he writes the score for several films and television shows, including the series *Roots*			
James Baldwin's *Another Country* is published	Mel Goode becomes the first black television news commentator when he begins broadcasting for ABC		Jackie Robinson is the first black inducted into the Baseball Hall of Fame and Museum, Cooperstown, NY	**1962**
Lerone Bennett, Jr.'s *Before the Mayflower* is published				
William Melvin Kelley (b 1937) wins the Richard and Hinda Rosenthal Foundation Award for his first novel, *A Different Drummer;* Kelley's novel	Louise Beavers, an actress who starred in more than 100 films, including *Imitation of Life, The Jackie Robinson Story,* and *Mr. Blandings Builds His Dream House,* d Los Angeles, CA, Oct 26		John "Buck" O'Neill is named coach of the Chicago Cubs, the first black coach of a major league baseball team	

	A. **General History**	B. **Education**	C. **Laws and Legal Actions**	D. **Religion**
1962	Edward Brooke (b Washington, DC, 1919) is elected Attorney General of Massachusetts, becoming the first black to hold the position Pres. John F. Kennedy* appoints Lloyd A. Hall to the American Food for Peace Council; Hall serves for two years Marjorie Lawson becomes the first black woman judge in Washington, DC Verda Welcome (b North Carolina, 1907; d 1990) (D-MD) is elected a Maryland state senator Augustus F. Hawkins (D-CA) is elected to the US Congress; one of his most notable accomplishments is the restoration of honorable discharges for the 167 black soldiers dismissed from the 25th Infantry Regiment of the US Army after being falsely accused of public disturbance in Brownsville, TX, in 1906	cessfully to block Meredith's admission		Rev. Frederick Eikerenkoetter, or "Rev. Ike," founds the United Church of Jesus Christ for All People, South Carolina; by 1976 he will have over 1,770 radio broadcasts and is the leading black religious figure outside the traditional black church in the 1960s and 1970s; Rev. Ike preaches the benefits of a positive self-image to his followers and emphasizes faith healing
1963	Civil rights demonstrators, led by Rev. Martin Luther King, Jr., are attacked by the Birmingham, AL, police force, led by Comm. Eugene "Bull" Conner*; the attack, which includes the use of high-powered water hoses and dogs, rouses sympathy and support for the protestors, especially in the North In a televised address, Pres. John F. Kennedy* makes an impassioned plea for an end to discrimination in the nation; the US Congress continues to take no action on the president's civil rights proposals Medgar Evers, field secretary for the NAACP, is killed outside his home in Jackson, MS John Lewis, head of the Student Non-violent Coordinating Committee, plans to deliver at the March on Washington a fiery speech	Vivian Malone and James Hood, accompanied by US Deputy Attorney General Nicholas Katzenbach,* attempt to register at the University of Alabama; they are met by Gov. George Wallace* who bodily blocks their entrance; when National Guardsmen return later in the day with Malone and Hood to enter the building, Wallace steps aside	In *Edwards v. South Carolina*, the US Supreme Court upholds the right to public demonstration, thereby allowing black Americans, and others, to continue their public protests for civil rights In *Johnson v. Virginia* the US Supreme Court reverses the contempt conviction of a black man who refused to obey a judge's order to sit in the "Negro section" of the courtroom	Rev. Benjamin J. Anderson, pastor of the Witherspoon Street Presbyterian Church, is nominated to become the first black to serve as moderator of the General Assembly of the United Presbyterian Church

				1962
examines the personal courage of Tucker Caliban, a former slave	Adele Addison (b NYC, Jul 24, 1925), soprano, is soloist at the opening concert of Philharmonic Hall at Lincoln Center, New York			

				1963
James Baldwin publishes a long essay, ''The Fire Next Time,'' in which he predicts the political and social unrest to come	Thirteen New York–based artists, among them Romare Bearden, Norman Lewis, Charles Alston, Richard Mayhew, and Hale Woodruff, meet to discuss their social responsibility as black artists; the group, later named Spiral, has a one-group show before disbanding four years later *Billboard* magazine stops publishing a separate Rhythm and Blues (R&B) best-seller music list because there are so many crossover singles on the Popular (Pop) charts; the R&B chart is revived 1965		Twenty-year-old Arthur Ashe (b Richmond, VA, Apr 10, 1943, d New York City, 1993) is the first black American to make the US Davis Cup tennis team	

1963 criticizing the Kennedy administration, but is admonished by older civil rights leaders; Catholic Archbishop Patrick O'Boyle threatens to withdraw if the program becomes too radical; Lewis reluctantly alters his speech

More than 200,000 marchers from all over the US stage the largest protest demonstration in the history of Washington, DC; the "March on Washington" procession moves from the Washington Monument to the Lincoln Memorial; Rev. Martin Luther King, Jr., delivers his celebrated "I Have a Dream" speech

Four girls—Addie Mae Collins, Denise McNair, Carole Robertson and Cynthia Wesley—are killed during Sunday school service when the Sixteenth Street Baptist Church is bombed by a group of white men in Birmingham, AL

Pres. John F. Kennedy* is shot and killed while campaigning in Dallas, TX

Following the assassination of Pres. John F. Kennedy,* Malcolm X refers to the killing as an example of "chickens coming home to roost"; Elijah Muhammad suspends Malcolm X from his duties and silences him

Pres. Lyndon B. Johnson* awards Ralph J. Bunche and Marian Anderson Medals of Freedom, the highest civilian decoration, for outstanding contributions to the ideals of freedom and democracy

Discrimination in building trades unions is protested in mass demonstrations at Harlem building sites

Gloria Richardson (b Baltimore, MD, May 6, 1922) and Inez Grubb of the

Malcolm X, who rose to prominence as a spokesman for the Nation of Islam, was an outspoken black nationalist and founder of the Organization of Afro-American Unity. (UPI/Bettmann)

E. Literature,
  Publications, and
  The Black Press   F. The Arts

G. Science,
  Technology,
  and Medicine   H. Sports

1963

E. Literature,
  Publications, and
  The Black Press   F. The Arts

G. Science,
  Technology,
  and Medicine   H. Sports

289

A. **General History**	B. Education	C. **Laws and Legal Actions**	D. **Religion**
1963 Cambridge Non-violent Action Committee lead protests, sit-ins, and demonstrations against segregation in Cambridge, MD; violence against the demonstrators leads to a conference in Washington, DC, with US Attorney General Robert Kennedy* and others			
Carl T. Rowan is appointed US Ambassador to Finland			
1964 Carl T. Rowan is named director of the US Information Agency, the highest Federal position ever held by a black; by virtue of his position, Rowan also becomes the first black to sit on the National Security Council		The 24th Amendment, which outlaws the poll tax requirement that was long used to disfranchise blacks, is ratified	Joseph H. Jackson, president of the National Baptist Convention, publicly condemns the practice of boycotting
Austin T. Walden becomes the first black judge in Georgia since Reconstruction		The US Congress passes the Civil Rights Act of 1964; the Act gives the US attorney general additional power to protect citizens against discrimination and segregation; forbids discrimination in most places of public accommodation; establishes a federal Equal Employment Opportunity Commission (EEOC); requires the elimination of discrimination in federally assisted programs, authorizing termination of programs or withdrawal of federal funds upon failure to comply; and authorizes the US Office of Education to provide technical and financial aid to assist communities in the desegregation of schools	Malcolm X makes a holy pilgrimage to Mecca and assumes the name Al Hajj Malik-El Shabazz
Malcolm X speaks at a CORE-sponsored meeting on "The Negro Revolt—What Comes Next?"; in his speech, "The Ballot or Bullet," he warns of a growing black nationalism that will no longer tolerate patronizing white political action			White Methodists hold a "kneel-in" at the Methodist General Conference, hoping to stir the denomination's conscience concerning racial segregation within the Methodist Church
Malcolm X officially splits with Elijah Muhammad and the Black Muslims and founds the Organization of Afro-American Unity			Jim Jones* establishes the Indianapolis People's Temple Full Gospel Church affiliated with the Disciples of Christ denomination, Indianapolis, IN; the group, which stresses racial equality, is harassed and threatened by white conservatives; the following year Jones and 100 members of the church move to Ukiah, CA
Charlotte Hubbard is appointed Deputy Assistant Secretary of State for Public Affairs, at this time the highest permanent federal position ever held by a black woman			
African National Congress leader Nelson Mandela is sentenced to life imprisonment for allegedly attempting to sabotage the white South African government		The US Congress passes the Economic Opportunity Act, which allows blacks to benefit from the Head Start program for preschoolers, the Upward Bound program for high school students, and the college work-study financial aid program	
The bodies of three slain civil rights workers—James E. Cheney, Michael Schwerner,* and Andrew			

			1964
Ralph Ellison's *Shadow and Act*, a collection of his essays and articles, is published	Louis "Satchmo" Armstrong's (1900–1970) "Hello Dolly" becomes the number one record on *Billboard*'s Top 40 Charts, replacing The Beatles' "I Want to Hold Your Hand"; it is Armstrong's first and only number one record	Samuel Kountz (b Lexa, AR, 1930), surgeon, and Roy Cohn* make medical history after they successfully transplant a kidney from a mother to a daughter; it is the first transplant between humans who are not identical twins	Cassius Clay KO's Sonny Liston in the seventh round to win the world heavyweight title in Miami Beach, FL; the next day he formally announces his conversion to the Muslim faith and changes his name to Muhammad Ali

Diana Sands makes theater history when she stars on Broadway in *The Owl and the Pussycat* in a role that is not written specifically for a black actress

George Harris, a member of the US Olympic judo team, is the first black to reach international competition in this sport

Thelonious Monk (b Rocky Mount, NC, Oct 10,1917), innovative jazz pianist and composer, is featured on the cover of *Time* magazine—only one of three jazz musicians so honored; Monk is considered one of the fathers of jazz improvisation and will play with such jazz masters as Coleman Hawkins, Art Blakey, John Coltrane, and Miles Davis

Amiri Baraka founds the Black Arts Repertory Theater School, a short-lived project that revolutionizes black theater and ushers in the Black Arts Movement; Baraka and others in the movement reject integrationist themes and emphasize arts grounded in the black folk experience

The Supremes have their first number one hit record, "Where Did Our Love Go"

Sidney Poitier wins the Academy of Motion Picture Arts and Sciences

1964

Goodman,* a college student—are discovered in a shallow grave on a farm outside Philadelphia, MS; the FBI accuses nearly two dozen white segregationists of complicity in the murders

Rev. Martin Luther King, Jr., receives the Nobel Peace Prize, Oslo, Norway; he divides his winnings among the Southern Christian Leadership Conference, the Student Nonviolent Coordinating Committee, the Congress on Racial Equality, the National Association for the Advancement of Colored People, the National Council of Negro Women, and the American Foundation on Nonviolence

The Mississippi Freedom Democratic Party is organized at the Democratic National Convention in Atlantic City, NJ

Constance Baker Motley (b New Haven, CT, Sep 14, 1921) is the first black woman elected to the New York State senate

Cong. John Conyers, Jr. (b Detroit, MI, May 16, 1929) (D-MI) is elected to the US Congress

Mercer Cook begins tenure as US ambassador to Senegal and Gambia; he serves for two years

Edith Sampson (d Chicago, IL, Oct 8, 1979) is the first black person to hold an appointment with the North Atlantic Treaty Organization; she is a member of the US Citizens Commission

Chevene "C.B." King (d San Diego, CA, Mar 15, 1988) is the first black to run for governor of Georgia since Reconstruction

Fair-skinned Donyale Luna is the first black model to be featured on the cover of a mainstream fashion magazine, *Harper's Bazaar*

Rev. Martin Luther King, Jr., was awarded the 1964 Nobel Peace Prize in recognition of his leadership of the civil rights movement. (UPI/Bettmann)

Award (Oscar) as best actor for his role in *Lilies of the Field;* this is the first time a black American wins an Oscar for a starring role

James Baldwin's play *Blues for Mr. Charlie* opens on Broadway starring Al Freeman, Jr., and Diana Sands

	A. **General History**	B. **Education**	C. **Laws and Legal Actions**	D. **Religion**
1964	Restaurateur Lester Maddox* closes his facility rather than integrate, Atlanta, GA; Maddox later uses his strong opposition to integration to win the governorship of Georgia			
1965	Rev. Martin Luther King, Jr., and Ralph J. Bunche, Undersecretary of the United Nations, lead about 200 persons in a 54-mile march from Selma to Montgomery, AL, in protest of racial oppression and segregation	Pres. Lyndon B. Johnson* delivers an address at Howard University's commencement, Washington, DC; Johnson pledges an all-out effort to bring blacks into the mainstream of American society		Bishop Prince A. T. Taylor, Jr., becomes the first black to assume the presidency of the Council of Bishops of the Methodist Church
	Malcolm X is assassinated at an Organization of Afro-American Unity meeting at the Audubon Ballroom, NY; actor Ossie Davis delivers the eulogy at his funeral six days later			
	Patricia Roberts Harris (1924–1985) is appointed ambassador to Luxembourg			
	Thurgood Marshall is appointed Solicitor General of the US			
	A clash between black residents and white police officers triggers the Watts rebellion, the most serious single racial disturbance in US history at the time, Los Angeles, CA; National Guardsmen are called in to quell the disorder which leaves 34 dead, 900 injured, more than 3,500 arrested, and property losses near $225 million			
	As of this year, black Americans account for 25% of all US casualties in the Vietnam War			
	Constance Baker Motley is elected Manhattan Borough President, the first woman to hold this position, the highest elective office held by a black woman, NYC			
	Pres. Lyndon B. Johnson* organizes the Council on Equal Opportunity, composed of cabinet officers			

E. Literature, Publications, and The Black Press	F. The Arts	G. Science, Technology, and Medicine	H. Sports

1965

The Autobiography of Malcolm X as Told to Alex Haley is published	Joan Murray becomes one of the first black women newscasters to join a major television station when she is hired by WCBS, New York		Ralph Boston breaks the world record for the long jump and becomes the first US track athlete to break a world record on six occasions
Claude Brown's *Manchild in the Promised Land* is published; the autobiography is a documentary of life in an urban community	Dorothy Maynor (b Dorothy Leigh Mainor, Norfolk, VA, Sep 3, 1910), former concert singer, founds the Harlem School of the Arts, NYC		
	The Alvin Ailey American Dance Theater begins one of the most successful European tours ever made by a US dance company; the troupe is held over in London, England for six additional weeks to accommodate ticket demands and receives an unprecedented 61 curtain calls in Hamburg, Germany		

	A. **General History**	B. **Education**	C. **Laws and Legal Actions**	D. **Religion**
1965	and heads of agencies with overall civil rights responsibilities, and appoints Vice President Hubert Humphrey* chair James M. Nabrit is named deputy chief of the US mission to the United Nations			
1966	The Student Non-violent Coordinating Committee is the first civil rights organization that officially denounces the Vietnam War Robert C. Weaver is appointed Secretary of Housing and Urban Development by Pres. Lyndon B. Johnson*; Weaver is the first black to serve in a US Cabinet Floyd McKissick (d Durham, NC, Apr 30, 1991) succeeds James Farmer as director of the Congress of Racial Equality; McKissick moves CORE organizationally away from its interracial, integrationist stance to a more militant, nationalist position Constance Baker Motley is appointed a judge in the federal district court of New York City, becoming the first black woman appointed to a judgeship in federal district court Pres. Lyndon B. Johnson* appoints Andrew Brimmer governor of the Federal Reserve Board, the first black to hold the position Milton Olive, Jr., is the first black to receive the Congressional Medal of Honor for bravery during the Vietnam War; he is honored for saving the lives of fellow soldiers by falling on a live grenade while participating in a search-and-destroy mission near Phu Coung Stokely Carmichael is elected chairman of the Student Non-violent Coordinating Committee	Merle James Smith, Jr., is the first black graduate of the US Coast Guard Academy, New London, CT	The Georgia House of Rep. refuses to seat Julian Bond because of his opposition to US involvement in the Vietnam War; he is seated almost one year later, after the US Supreme Court resolves the issue	Rev. Harold Perry is the first black Catholic bishop in the 20th century Rev. Joseph H. Jackson, president of the NBC, issues a statement disassociating himself from Martin Luther King's movement Rev. Martin Luther King, Jr., becomes co-chairman of the Clergy and Laymen Concerned about Vietnam

E. **Literature,**
   Publications, and
   The Black Press

F. **The Arts**

G. **Science,**
   Technology,
   and Medicine

H. **Sports**

1965

			1966

Jubilee, a novel by Margaret Walker is published

George "Hal" Bennett's first novel, *A Wilderness of Vines,* is published

Bill Cosby (b Philadelphia, PA, Jul 12, 1938), star of "I Spy," is the first black to win an Emmy for best actor in a dramatic series

Amiri Baraka's play *The Slave* wins second prize in the drama category at the First World Festival of Dramatic Arts, Dakar, Senegal

Meredith Gourdine (b Livingston, NJ, 1929), pioneer in the electrogasdynamic systems, is awarded by the US Department of Interior, Office of Coal Research, over $600,000 to perfect a model generator that uses low-grade coal to directly generate 80,000 volts of electricity

Bill Russell becomes the first black to coach an NBA team when he is named head coach of the Boston Celtics

Emmett Ashford becomes the first black major league umpire when he is named to the American League

Frank Robinson of the Baltimore Orioles is named MVP of the American League, becoming the only major league player to be voted MVP in both the American and National leagues (he was voted MVP of the National league in 1961 while playing for the Cincinnati Reds)

Frank Robinson is the first black baseball player to win the "triple crown"—finishing first in batting average, home runs, and runs batted in

1966   James Meredith is
wounded by a white sniper
during a Memphis, TN–
Jackson, MS voter registration march; Rev. Martin
Luther King, Jr., and other
civil rights groups continue
the march the next day
and register almost 4,000
blacks

Huey P. Newton (b Mon-
roe, LA, Feb 17, 1942; d
Oakland, CA, Aug 22,
1989) and Bobby Seale
found the Black Panther
Party in Oakland, CA; the
party organizes numerous
community programs in-
cluding free breakfast for
schoolchildren, free medical care, free clothing, and
free legal advice, among
other programs

A dispute between police
and black children over
the use of a fire hydrant
for recreation results in
rioting, Chicago, IL; Chicago mayor Richard
Daley* and Rev. Martin
Luther King, Jr., announce
new recreational programs
for Chicago's youth

Ruby Doris Smith-
Robinson (b Atlanta, GA,
Apr 25, 1942; d Oct 9,
1967), known for her cre-
ative protest tactics, succeeds James Foreman as
the executive secretary of
the Student Non-violent
Coordinating Committee

The "Black Power" con-
cept—which is generally
thought to mean that black
Americans should take a
more aggressive posture
toward obtaining civil
rights—is adopted by
CORE and the SNCC,
while the Southern Chris-
tian Leadership Confer-
ence shies away from the
idea and the NAACP disas-
sociates itself from the
concept entirely

Anna Pauline "Pauli"
Murray (b Baltimore, MD,
Nov 20, 1910), civil rights
activist, attorney and author, is one of the founding members of the newly

E. **Literature,**
   Publications, and
   The Black Press   F. **The Arts**

G. **Science,**
   Technology,
   and Medicine   H. **Sports**

1966

	A. **General History**	B. **Education**	C. **Laws and Legal Actions**	D. **Religion**
1966	established National Organization for Women Sen. Edward W. Brooke (b Washington, DC, 1919) (R-MA) is the first black since Reconstruction to be elected to the US Senate; while serving his second term he becomes the first senator to call publicly for the resignation of Pres. Richard M. Nixon* Robert C. Henry of Springfield is the first black to be elected a mayor in the state of Ohio Grace Hamilton (b Atlanta, GA, Feb 10, 1907) is the first black woman to serve in the Georgia state legislature Dorothy Brown, the first black woman surgeon to become a fellow of the American College of Surgeons, is elected to the Tennessee state legislature, becoming the first black woman to serve Comedian Dick Gregory makes an unsuccessful bid for mayor of Chicago, IL Pres. Lyndon B. Johnson* appoints Charles Rangel (b NYC, Jun 11, 1930) general counsel to the National Advisory Commission on Selective Service Barbara Jordan (b 1936) becomes the first black to serve in the Texas senate since 1883			
1967	Rev. Martin Luther King, Jr., announces his opposition to the Vietnam War at a press conference at the Overseas Press Club, New York, and also at the Riverside Church, New York City; he suggests the avoidance of military service "to all those who find the American course in Vietnam a dishonorable and unjust one" The worst summer of racial disturbances in US history occurs in major urban areas throughout the country, including Newark	Rev. Benjamin E. Mays retires as president of Morehouse College, Atlanta, GA; he is succeeded by Hugh M. Gloster, academic dean at Hampton Institute, VA In *United States v. Jefferson County,* the US Circuit Court, Fifth District, rules that "the only school desegregation plan that meets constitutional standards is one that works," thereby accelerating the desegregation process	The US House of Representatives votes to expel Cong. Adam Clayton Powell, Jr. (D-NY), from Congress based on allegations of misappropriated congressional funds; he sits out one full session and is later reelected overwhelmingly by his Harlem constituents; one year later the US Supreme Court rules that the House has no constitutional authority to deny Powell his seat The US Supreme Court rules unanimously that a Virginia law prohibiting	Rev. E. H. Evans is nominated for United Church of Christ national secretary, the first black to be nominated Rev. Joseph H. Jackson, president of the NBC, presides over a meeting of 100 clergymen who issue a manifesto categorically rejecting "Black Power"

E. **Literature,**
Publications, and
The Black Press   F. **The Arts**

G. **Science,**
Technology,
and Medicine   H. **Sports**

1966

Nikki Giovanni's first volume of poetry, *Black Feeling, Black Talk,* is published

John A. Williams's *The Man Who Cried I Am* is published

Ishmael Reed's (b Chattanooga, TN, 1938) first novel, *The Free-lance Pallbearers,* is published

Charley Pride (b Sledge, MS, Mar 18, 1939), the first black to become a successful country music star, debuts at the Grand Ole Opry

The Parliaments, a little-known group led by musician George Clinton, scores an R&B hit with ''(I Just Want to) Testify''; by the mid-1970s Clinton will build a veritable music empire that includes Parliament, Funkadelic, Bootsy's Rubber Band, Zapp, the Brides of Funkenstein, and Parlet

Renee Powell is the first black woman to join the Ladies Professional Golf Association tour

Harry Edwards, San Jose State sociology professor, forms the Olympic Committee for Human Rights to address the conditions of black athletes; six weeks later the group, later renamed the Olympic Project for Human Rights, issues a statement declaring that black athletes will boycott the 1968 Olympic Games; the boycott does not have widespread support

1967

A. **General History**	B. **Education**	C. **Laws and Legal Actions**	D. **Religion**

1967

NJ; Detroit, MI; and Chicago, IL

H. "Rap" Brown replaces Stokely Carmichael as chairman of the Student Non-violent Coordinating Committee.

Pres. Lyndon B. Johnson* appoints US Solicitor General Thurgood Marshall associate justice of the US Supreme Court; Marshall is the first black US Supreme Court justice

The Minority Officer Recruiting Effort is established at the Navy Bureau of Personnel, Washington, DC

Pres. Lyndon B. Johnson* appoints Walter E. Washington the mayor of Washington, DC; Washington is the city's first black mayor

Helen Jackson Claytor becomes the first black national president of the YWCA

Floyd McCree is elected mayor of Flint, MI

Carl B. Stokes is elected mayor of Cleveland, OH

Richard B. Hatcher is elected mayor of Gary, IN

Ida Van Smith (b Lumberton, NC, 1917), a licensed pilot, founds the Ida Van Smith Flight Clubs to teach children the career opportunities in aviation and space

Clara Adams-Ender (b Jul 11, 1939) is the first woman in the US Army to qualify for and be awarded the Expert Field Medical Badge

At the Black Power Conference held in Newark, NJ, delegates call for the "partitioning of the United States into two separate independent nations, one to be a homeland for whites and the other to be a homeland for black Americans"

C. Laws and Legal Actions: interracial marriage is unconstitutional, and subsequently nullifies laws in 15 other states

E. **Literature,**
Publications, and
The Black Press   F. **The Arts**

G. **Science,**
Technology,
and Medicine   H. **Sports**

The World Boxing Association and the New York State Athletic Commission strip Muhammad Ali of his heavyweight titles after he refuses draft induction

The Professional Rodeo Cowboy Association ranks Myrtis Dightman third in the country; Dightman is the first modern black rodeo performer

Thurgood Marshall, former attorney for the NAACP National Defense Fund and the first African-American Supreme Court justice. (LC)

	A. **General History**	B. **Education**	C. **Laws and Legal Actions**	D. **Religion**
1968	Lucius D. Amerson is the first black sheriff in the South since Reconstruction, Macon County, AL	Students take over the administration building at Howard University, Washington, DC, demanding the resignations of university officials and a stronger orientation toward black culture in the curriculum; it is the first of many college protests concerning black studies programs across the nation	Cong. John Conyers, Jr. (D-MI), introduces a bill that would establish the birthday of Rev. Martin Luther King, Jr., as a national holiday; the bill fails to reach the House floor for a vote	Author James Baldwin speaks before the World Council of Churches' convention in Geneva, Switzerland; he indicts the Christian church for its lack of support for blacks
	Rev. Martin Luther King, Jr., addresses a rally of striking garbage workers and their supporters, Memphis, TN		Pres. Lyndon B. Johnson* signs what will be known as the 1968 Housing Act, which outlaws discrimination in the sale, rental, or leasing of 80% of US housing; the bill also protects civil rights workers and makes it a federal crime to cross state lines for the purpose of inciting a riot	At the Fourth Assembly of the World Council of Churches meeting in Uppsala, Sweden, three blacks are elected to the Central Committee
	Rev. Martin Luther King, Jr., is assassinated in Memphis TN; during his funeral service in Atlanta, GA, over 30,000 people form a procession behind the coffin; Rev. Benjamin E. Mays delivers the eulogy; Pres. Lyndon B. Johnson* decrees a day of national mourning; widespread violence occurs in 125 cities, and 50,000 federal and state troops are called to duty all over the country	The first Naval ROTC at an historically black college or university is established at Prairie View A&M University in Texas		The Coordinating Committee of Black Lutheran Clergymen is formed by 56 of the 82 black ministers in the major Lutheran churches of the US
		The US Supreme Court rules that all public schools must present realistic desegregation plans immediately	Huey P. Newton, member of the Black Power Party, is convicted of manslaughter in California; he is later released after a California court finds procedural errors in the original trial	A group of Catholic priests form the Black Catholic Clergy Caucus; the caucus denounces the Catholic Church as "primarily a white racist institution" and demands that efforts be increased to recruit blacks for the priesthood
	The Poor People's March, led by Rev. Ralph D. Abernathy (b Linden, AL, Mar 11, 1926; d Atlanta, GA, Apr 17, 1990), begins as caravans from all over the country leave for Washington, DC, to protest poverty and racial discrimination	At the beginning of the school year, 20.3% of black schoolchildren in former Confederate states are in fully integrated schools; two years later, more than 90% of southern public schools are classified as desegregated		The National Black Sisters' Conference, an international gathering of black nuns, is organized
	Ruth A. Lucas is promoted to the rank of colonel in the US Air Force, the first black woman to achieve this rank	Elizabeth D. Koontz (b Salisbury, NC, Jun 3, 1919; d Jan 6 1989) is elected president of the National Education Association, the largest professional organization in the world		Rev. Albert B. Cleage, Jr., publishes *The Black Messiah,* which emphasizes the liberating and revolutionary aspects of Christianity
	Rev. Channing Phillips's name is submitted for the Democratic nomination for President; he receives only a small number of votes			
	Cong. Julian Bond (D-GA) is nominated for vice president on the Democratic Party ticket; he receives several votes before withdrawing his name because he is too young to serve			
	Dorothy Lee Bolden, community activist, organizes the National Domestic Workers Union, which successfully improves the wages and working conditions of domestic workers			

Alice Walker's (b Eatonton, GA, Feb 9, 1944) first volume of poetry, *Once*, is published

Ernest Gaines's (b Louisiana, 1933) *Bloodline*, a collection of short stories, is published

Eldridge Cleaver's *Soul on Ice* is published

Julius Lester's first book, *Look Out, Whitey! Black Power's Gon' Get Your Mama* is published; Lester also compiles *To Be a Slave*, a book consisting of selections from several slave narratives as well as sketches by Tom Feelings

Following the assassination of Rev. Martin Luther King, Jr., city officials consider canceling James Brown's music concert for fear of widespread violence and protest in Boston, MA; after reconsideration, the concert is broadcast live on public television stations and keeps many people off the streets

Henry Lewis becomes the first black to lead a symphony orchestra in the US when he is named director of the New Jersey Symphony

Ellen Holly becomes the first principal black actress on daytime television when she appears on ABC's "One Life to Live" as Carla, a black American "passing" for white

"Julia," a television situation comedy starring Diahann Carroll (b Carol Diahann Johnson, Bronx, NY, July 17, 1935), premieres

James Brown releases the song "Black Is Beautiful: Say It Loud, I'm Black and I'm Proud" and begins a tour of military bases in the Pacific for the USO

Barbara Teer (b East St. Louis, IL, Jun 18, 1937) founds the National Black Theatre Company, Harlem, NY

Julian M. Earls is named head of the Health Physics Section, becoming one of the youngest managers in NASA history

Hughenna L. Gauntlett is one of the first black women to obtain certification from the American Board of Surgery

Wyomia Tyus becomes the first person to win a gold medal in the 100-meter race in two consecutive Olympic Games, Mexico City

Medal winners Tommie Smith and John Carlos hold up their fists in a Black Power salute during the Olympic Games, Mexico City; their actions will come to symbolize the Black Power movement in sports and will result in their suspension from the games two days later; subsequently, Lee Evans, Larry James, and Ron Freeman, US track team members who finish first, second, and third, respectively, in the 400-meter dash, wear black berets and give the Black Power salute at the victory stand at the Olympic Games, Mexico City

Arthur Ashe wins the US Open tennis championships at Forest Hills, NY, and is ranked the number one player in the world

Wilt Chamberlain (b Philadelphia, PA, Aug 21, 1936) joins the Los Angeles Lakers basketball team; Chamberlain, also known as "the Stilt," is considered by many to be the greatest offensive player in the history of the game

Bob Foster knocks out Dick Tiger in four rounds to win the light heavyweight championship

O. J. Simpson is named the Heisman Trophy winner; he will play professional football with the Buffalo Bills and the San Francisco 49ers

Nearly all African nations and several Third World countries withdraw from the Olympic Games after South Africa is readmitted to participate

Marion Motley is the first player in the All-

1968

Naomi Sims (b 1949), fashion model, is the first black woman to appear on the cover of *Ladies' Home Journal;* the next year she is the first black woman on the cover of *Life* magazine

Clothilde Dent Brown is the first black woman colonel in the US Army

William Clay (b St. Louis, MO, 1931) (D-MO) is elected to the US Congress

Following riots in major US cities Pres. Lyndon B. Johnson* convenes the National Advisory Commission on Civil Disorders; the Kerner Commission report concludes that white racism is one of the fundamental causes of rioting in the US

Shirley Chisholm (b Brooklyn, NY, 1924) (D-NY) becomes the first black woman elected to the US Congress

A biracial coalition, led by state NAACP president Aaron Henry and composed of the major black organizations and a number of white liberals, mounts a challenge to the seating of Mississippi's predominantly white delegation to the Democratic National Convention, Chicago, IL; this predominantly black delegation, which eventually includes members of the MFDP, is recognized and seated by the national party as the Democratic party representatives for Mississippi

Barbara Watson, the first female Assistant Secretary of State, is the first woman administrator of the Bureau of Security and Consular Affairs of the US State Department

Elizabeth Koontz, president of the North Carolina Teachers Association and the first African-American president of the National Education Association. (Bethune)

1969

Rev. Ralph D. Abernathy leads a march of more than 700 striking hos-

Sixty-five black students at Brandeis University, Waltham, MA, invade

The US Supreme Court rules that cities cannot enact ordinances or char-

James Foreman, director of National Economic Development Conference,

E. **Literature, Publications, and The Black Press**	F. **The Arts**	G. **Science, Technology, and Medicine**	H. **Sports**	
			American Football Conference Hall of Fame	**1968**
			University of Texas at El Paso coach Wayne Vandenburg* dismisses six blacks from his team after they refuse to compete against Brigham Young University, a Mormon school; Mormons believe that blacks are damned by a biblical curse	
			Marlin Briscoe of the AFL's Denver Broncos is the first black quarterback to play regularly in professional football	
			Uriah Jones is the first black member on a US Olympic fencing team	
Sonia Sanchez's (b Birmingham, AL, Sep 9, 1934) *Homecoming*, her	James Earl Jones wins a Tony award for his portrayal of Jack Johnson		John B. McLendon becomes the first black coach in the American Basketball	**1969**

	A. **General History**	B. **Education**	C. **Laws and Legal Actions**	D. **Religion**
1969	pital workers, Charleston, SC	Ford Hall and barricade themselves in the building; their list of demands include an African studies department, year-round recruitment of black students by blacks, the hiring of black professors, the establishment of an Afro-American student center, and 10 full scholarships for blacks; university president Morris B. Abram* agrees to meet with the students	ter provisions that have the effect of establishing discrimination in housing	demands in ''The Black Manifesto'' that churches and synagogues pay $5,000,000 reparations to black people
	Alex Rackley, member of the Black Panther Party, is burned to death for alleged disloyalty to the Panther organization, New Haven, CT; party leader Bobby Seale is arrested for Rackley's murder		James Earl Ray* pleads guilty to the charge of first degree murder in the assassination of the Rev. Martin Luther King, Jr., and is sentenced to 99 years in prison	Washington Square United Methodist Church in New York City becomes the first predominantly white religious organization to give money to National Black Economic Development Conference; it gives director James Foreman $15,000
	Howard N. Lee is elected mayor of predominantly white Chapel Hill, NC	Harvard University moves to establish an Afro-American studies program, in addition to the already established African Studies program	The US Dept. of Labor issues guidelines, known as the ''Philadelphia Plan,'' which require contractors on federally assisted construction projects exceeding $500,000 to hire a specific number of minority workers	The Episcopal Church's House of Deputies votes to grant the National Economic Development Conference $200,000
	Charles Evers, brother of the late Medgar Evers, is elected mayor of Fayette, MS			
	Harlem Hospital in New York City is renamed Wright Hospital in honor of Louis Wright, the hospital's first black physician	Clifton Reginald Wharton, Jr., is appointed president of Michigan State University; he is the first black to head a major public university	After her membership in the Communist Party is revealed, Professor Angela Davis (b Birmingham, AL, Jan 26, 1944) is fired from her position at the University of California at Los Angeles; she challenges the dismissal in court and wins	
	Under instruction from Edward V. Hanrahan,* Cook County' state attorney, 15 Chicago, IL, policemen fire at and destroy the home of several Black Panther members, killing Panther leaders Mark Clark and Fred Hampton; in the following weeks several black members of Congress hold hearings and a Federal jury eventually indicts Hanrahan and 13 codefendants; Hanrahan, however, is acquitted	In *Alexander v. Holmes* the US Supreme Court rules that school districts must end racial segregation ''at once,'' overturning the 1954 decision which allowed districts to proceed with ''all deliberate speed''		
	Louis Stokes (b Cleveland, OH, 1925) (D-OH) becomes a US congressman	St. Clair Drake, sociologist and anthropologist, establishes and serves as director of the African and Afro-American Studies Program at Stanford University, Palo Alto, CA; the program will serve as a model for others across the nation		
	Coretta Scott King begins organizing the Martin Luther King, Jr. Center for Nonviolent Social Change in Atlanta, GA			
	Joseph Searles III, former aide to New York City Mayor John Lindsay,* becomes the first black proposed for a seat on the New York Stock Exchange	As dean of the Howard University Law School, Washington, DC, Patricia Roberts Harris is the first black woman to head a law school		
		Federal judge A. Leon Higginbotham, Jr., is the first black trustee of Yale University, CT		
	Pres. Richard M. Nixon* appoints Melvin H. Evans (b Christiansted, St. Croix, 1917) governor of the Virgin Islands	The Department of Health, Education and Welfare authorizes Antioch College to found an all-black studies program		

first volume of poetry, is published

Lucille Clifton's *Good Times* is published and is later chosen by *The New York Times* as one of the 10 best books of the year

Molefi Asante and Robert Singleton found the *Journal of Black Studies*, University of California at Los Angeles

Gwendolyn Brooks is named Poet Laureate of Illinois, succeeding Carl Sandburg*

in *The Great White Hope*

Gordon Parks's (b Ft. Scott, KS, Nov 30, 1912) *The Learning Tree* premieres; it is the first film directed by a black American for a major studio, Warner Brothers

Artists Romare Bearden, Ernest Crichlow, and Norman Lewis incorporate Cinque Gallery in New York City

Arthur Mitchell and Karel Shook* found the Dance Theater of Harlem, which makes its debut performance at the Jacob's Pillow Dance Festival

Undine Moore (b Jarratt, VA, Aug 25, 1905), composer, educator, and founder of the Black Man in American Music Program, founds the Black Music Center, Virginia State University, Petersburg, VA

The Jackson Five, a family act consisting of brothers Marlon, Michael, Jackie, Jermaine, and Tito, performs at a campaign benefit for the mayor of Gary, IN; among the guests at the benefit is singer Diana Ross, who is so taken with the boys' talent that she immediately introduces them to Berry Gordy of Motown Records; Gordy signs them to a recording deal, and the group scores the first of four consecutive number-one hits on the Billboard pop charts with "I Want You Back"

The Studio Museum in Harlem (under the direction of Edward Spriggs) is established for artists who need working space; the museum branches out into a cultural center and by 1972 becomes the premiere cultural center for New York City blacks

C. Edward Thomas founds the Afro-American Music

League when he signs a two-year contract with the Cleveland Pipers

Nell C. Jackson is the first black American to sit on the US Olympic Committee's board of directors; she is later inducted into the Black Athletes Hall of Fame

Tina Sloane-Green is the first black woman to compete on the US National Lacrosse team

Ruth White, who holds four national titles, is the youngest woman and the first black woman to win a national fencing championship

Stanford University of California announces a new policy honoring an athlete's "Right of Conscience"; this policy allows an athlete to boycott a sporting event without repercussions; although not heavily endorsed by other universities, the policy marks a breakthrough for black athletes who frequently boycott sporting events to protest racism and/or segregation practices

	A. **General History**	B. **Education**	C. **Laws and Legal Actions**	D. **Religion**
1969	Cong. Shirley Chisholm (D-NY) successfully fights against her appointment to the House Agriculture Committee, arguing that the committee is meaningless to her predominantly black and Puerto Rican constituents in Brooklyn's Bedford-Stuyvesant community James Farmer is appointed Assistant Secretary of Health, Education and Welfare; many in the black community are outraged at the appointment given the conservative views of the administration; Farmer resigns a short time later	Armed black students take over the main administration building at Cornell University, Ithaca, NY, to protest the limited presence of black students and faculty		
1970	Statistics released by the US Census Bureau confirm earlier reports that white families are fleeing the cities and moving to the suburbs, resulting in so-called white flight Coretta Scott King dedicates the Martin Luther King, Jr., Memorial Center, which is composed of King's birthplace, church, and crypt, Atlanta GA An army report ordered by Gen. William C. Westmoreland,* Army Chief of Staff, reveals that "all indications point toward an increase in racial tension" on US military bases throughout the world Cheryl A. Brown wins the Miss Iowa pageant and becomes the first black American to compete in the Miss America beauty pageant Kenneth Gibson is elected mayor of Newark, NJ, becoming the city's first black mayor and the first black mayor of a major eastern city A confidential memorandum from Daniel P. Moynihan,* domestic policy advisor to Pres. Richard M. Nixon,* is made public; in the memo, Moynihan	Gov. John Bell Williams* announces in a statewide telecast that he will seek to help build a Mississippi private school system as an alternative to public school desegregation Ohio State University students demonstrate and demand an end to ROTC programs and greater admissions for black students; the National Guard is called in to stop the widespread violence that ensues John S. Martin* superintendent of public schools in Jackson, MS, resigns, citing the pressures of school desegregation as his reason; Martin joins at least 200 other school superintendents in the South who have resigned in the past two years because of problems and tensions resulting from school desegregation Students at the all-black Jackson State College in Mississippi protest and throw rocks at white passers-by on their campus; police from the city of Jackson and the Mississippi State Highway Patrol open fire on unarmed students, killing two and injuring 12 others	The NAACP leads a successful campaign against the confirmation of Judge G. Harrold Carswell* to the US Supreme Court; Carswell's prosegregation record causes alarm among many in the black community and also members of the Senate A federal court orders that the Internal Revenue Service stop granting tax-exempt privileges to segregated schools in Mississippi Angela Davis is placed on the FBI's 10 most wanted list; she is charged with kidnapping, conspiracy, and murder in an attempt to link her with a planned getaway involving colleague Jonathan Jackson; after spending two months in hiding, Davis is found and put in jail without bail US District Court Judge Frank A. Kaufman* rejects the appeal of William H. Murphy, Jr., a member of the Nation of Islam, who requests exemption from military service as a conscientious objector; Kaufman rules that the Nation of Islam claims a political rather than religious objection to the war A federal judge orders a formerly all-white ceme-	Rev. Henry Jogner, Jr., becomes a minister of Calvary Methodist Church in Atlanta, GA; he is the first black minister to take the pulpit of an all-white southern parish of the United Methodist Church John M. Burgess is elected bishop in the diocese of Massachusetts; he is the first black suffragan bishop to serve a predominantly white diocese in the Episcopal Church in the US

Opportunities Association, Minneapolis, MN

Elizabeth Catlett's linocut *Malcolm Speaks for Us* receives wide critical acclaim

---

Publication of *Essence,* a magazine for black women, begins

Earl Graves's (b Brooklyn, NY, 1935) *Black Enterprise* magazine, dedicated to issues concerning economic development in the black community, begins publication

Toni Morrison's (b Chloe Anthony Wofford, Lorain, OH, Feb 18, 1931) first novel, *The Bluest Eye,* is published

I Know Why the Caged Bird Sings, the first book in the autobiographical series on the life of Maya Angelou (b Marguerite Johnson, St. Louis, MO, Apr 4, 1928), is published

Daddy Was a Numbers Runner, written by Louise Meriwether (b Haverstraw, NY, May 8, 1923), is published; Meriwether depicts the life of a black girl growing up in Harlem, NY, during the 1930s

The Black Woman: An Anthology, edited by Toni Cade Bambara (b NYC, 1939), is published; considered the first major work on contemporary black feminism, it includes poetry, short stories, and essays by well-known

"The Flip Wilson Show" starring comedian Clerow "Flip" Wilson, premieres on NBC; it is the first prime-time variety show starring a black man since "The Nat King Cole Show"

Madeline Anderson's documentary, *I Am Somebody,* is one of the earliest films by a black woman

Actor Frederick O'Neal is the first black elected president of the Actors Equity, a trade union for actors in the theater and film industry

Charles Gordon wins the Pulitzer Prize for his play *No Place to Be Somebody*

Effie O'Neal Ellis becomes special assistant for health services to the American Medical Association and the first black woman physician to hold an administrative office

Chris Dickerson becomes the first black to win bodybuilding's "Mr. America" title

College player Spencer Haywood signs a contract with three different professional basketball teams, although the NBA has a rule against signing college players before they have completed their four years of athletic eligibility; the following year a judge rules that the NBA rule is illegal, thereby allowing college players to turn professional anytime

Activist Angela Davis, after being cleared of second-degree murder charges in 1971, resumed teaching at San Francisco State University and has become a prolific writer and speaker. (Schomburg)

1970

A. General History

proposes that "the time may come when the issue of race could benefit from a period of benign neglect"; a week later a group of black civil rights leaders, authors, and educators issue a statement describing the memo as an example of the Nixon administration thwarting the efforts of civil rights progress

Clara McBride Hale (b 1904), known as Mother Hale, founds Hale House, a home for crack cocaine-addicted babies, New York City

Late in the year, Cong. Charles Diggs (D-MI) appoints a "shadow cabinet"— a group of black professionals knowledgeable about the government—to monitor the activities of top appointees of Richard M. Nixon*; every time a cabinet member or head of an agency presents a new program, his or her counterpart in the shadow cabinet responds, documenting the negative effects each proposal will have on the black community

Cong. Charles C. Diggs, Jr. (D-MI), requests a meeting between the Congressional Black Caucus and Pres. Richard M. Nixon* in order to discuss the growing alienation of the country's black population; two months later Nixon sends a rejection letter signed by a low-level White House staffer; in an unprecedented response, the CBC boycotts the president's State of the Union address

Charles Rangel (D-NY) is elected to the US Congress, defeating Cong. Adam Clayton Powell, Jr.

George W. Collins (b Chicago, IL, 1925; d Chicago, IL, December 1972) (D-IL) is elected to the US Congress

Ronald V. Dellums (b Oakland, CA, 1935)

B. Education

Robert H. Finch,* Secretary of Health, Education, and Welfare, estimates that as many as 400 private schools have opened in the South since the passage of the Civil Rights Act of 1964

Elliot L. Richardson,* who succeeds Robert H. Finch* as Secretary of Health, Education, and Welfare, announces a 30% increase in federal aid to predominantly black colleges

C. Laws and Legal Actions

tery in Ft. Pierce, FL, to accept the body of Poindexter E. Williams, a soldier killed in Vietnam; in reaction some angry whites threaten to remove the bodies of their relatives

The US Senate votes to extend the Voting Rights Act of 1965; among the provisions of the act is a ban on literacy tests as a qualification for voting and permission for one to vote in presidential elections if residency is established at least one month before election day

E. **Literature,
    Publications, and
    The Black Press**   F. **The Arts**

G. **Science,
    Technology,
    and Medicine**   H. **Sports**

1970

writers and women stu-
dents in the City College
SEEK program, NY

	A. **General History**	B. **Education**	C. **Laws and Legal Actions**	D. **Religion**
1970	(DCA), an outspoken opponent of US intervention in Indochina, is elected to the US Congress			
	Norma Holloway Johnson is confirmed to a seat on the US District Court, Washington, DC			
	Ralph H. Metcalfe (b Atlanta, GA, 1910; d Oct 1978) (D-IL) is elected to the US Congress			
1971	James A. Floyd is appointed mayor of Princeton Township, NJ, an affluent, predominantly white suburban community	The Newark (NJ) Board of Education votes to hang the Black Liberation flag in schools with a majority of black students; a NJ state court votes against the ruling	The Oregon Court of Appeals rules that mental anguish is one of the effects of racial discrimination and can be compensated for by a cash award	Dissension between white and black Catholics in the US peaks when the US Conference of Catholic Bishops omits funding for the National Office of Black Catholics
	The National Black Nurses' Association is founded; Lauranne B. Sams serves as its first president		Eight black federal employees file a suit in US Court, Washington, DC, claiming that the Federal Service Entrance Examination is "culturally and racially discriminatory"; the plaintiffs cite evidence of a "disproportionately low percentage" of blacks and other minorities passing the 1969 test	
	Rev. Leon Howard Sullivan is elected to the board of directors of General Motors Corporation			
	After a 12-month impasse, Pres. Richard M. Nixon* agrees to meet with the Congressional Black Caucus; during the meeting, CBC members deliver 60 policy recommendations to improve life for black Americans		The US Supreme Court rules that employers cannot use job tests that have the effect of screening out blacks if the tests are not related to the ability to do the work	
	Rev. Walter Fauntroy (b Washington, DC, 1933) becomes the first elected congressional representative from Washington, DC, since Reconstruction		The US Supreme Court upholds the constitutionality of closing Jackson, MS, swimming pools rather than integrating them	
	Fannie Granton serves as parliamentarian of the Washington (DC) Press Club, becoming the first black to hold office in that organization		In *Swann v. Charlotte-Mecklenburg,* the US Supreme Court rules that busing school children to achieve racial integration is constitutional	
	Representatives from the FBI and the local police raid the Republic of New Africa (RNA) headquarters to serve fugitive warrants on three RNA members, Jackson, MS; a 20-minute skirmish ensues and one police officer is killed; 11 RNA members are arrested and 7 of them (2 women, 5 men) are convicted two years later			

E. **Literature,**
   Publications, and
   The Black Press   F. **The Arts**

G. **Science,**
   Technology,
   and Medicine   H. **Sports**

1970

1971

Nikki Giovanni's autobiography, *Gemini: An Extended Autobiographical Statement on My First Twenty-five Years of Being a Black Poet,* is published

Ernest Gaines's *The Autobiography of Miss Jane Pittman* is published

Just Give Me a Cool Drink of Water 'fore I Diie, one of several volumes of poetry by Maya Angelou, is published; she will later be nominated for the Pulitzer Prize in poetry for this work

The Black Aesthetic, edited by Addison Gayle, is published; the book emphasizes the theories and ideas of the Black Arts Movement

"Contemporary Black Artists in America," an exhibit featuring the works of Betye Saar, Charles White, and Jacob Lawrence, among other artists, opens at the Whitney Museum of American Art in New York City

Gordon Parks directs *Shaft,* an action adventure starring Richard Roundtree; the film is a financial success that puts the struggling MGM studio back on its feet

Faith Ringgold (b NYC, 1934) is commissioned to paint a mural, *For the Women's House,* at the Women's House of Detention, Riker's Island; the mural portrays women engaged in various occupations and is intended to inspire the prisoners' rehabilitation

Sweet Sweetback's Baadasssss Song, directed and scored by Melvin Van Peebles, is released; the film ushers in a new era of black independent filmmaking and spawns a number of "blaxploitation" films

Baseball commissioner Bowie Kuhn* announces that Satchel Paige, veteran pitcher for the "Negro" and major leagues, will be given full membership in the Baseball Hall of Fame at Cooperstown, NY; it was originally intended that players in the Negro leagues be honored in a separate division

Joe Frazier defeats Muhammad Ali for the heavyweight championship title in a bout billed as the "fight of the century"

Willie Mays scores his 1,950th home run

After 14 years in the NBA, Elgin Baylor announces his retirement from the Los Angeles Lakers; Baylor has scored 23,149 points, the third highest in the league

Lee Elder (b Dallas, TX, Jul 14, 1934) is the first black to compete in the South African Professional Golfers Association Open

Boxing heavyweight champion Joe Frazier is the first black man since Reconstruction to address the South Carolina legislature

Leroy Walker organizes the Pan African Games at Duke University, North Carolina; black athletes from Africa and the US participate

1971 The "Black Expo," organized by Rev. Jesse Jackson, attracts almost one million people during its four-day run, Chicago, IL; the exposition was founded to expose the larger community to black-owned businesses

Following his departure from SCLC, Rev. Jesse Jackson founds Operation PUSH (People United to Save Humanity), Chicago, IL

Stephen Gil Spottswood, bishop of the African Methodist Episcopal Zion Church and board chairman of the NAACP, chastises the administration of Richard M. Nixon* for its policies toward blacks and refuses to retract his position, despite pressure from the Nixon administration

Amiri Baraka obtains approval of a $6.4 million mortgage for the construction of Kawaida Towers, a 16-story low- and middle-income housing project, Newark, NJ; Newark assemblyman Anthony Imperiale* unsuccessfully attempts to halt the construction

Aileen Hernandez is the first black president of the National Organization for Women

Parren J. Mitchell (b Baltimore, MD, Apr 29, 1922) is the first black elected to US Congress from the state of Maryland

Cong. Charles C. Diggs, Jr. (D-MI), is named the first chairman of the Congressional Black Caucus

Gov. Milton Shapp* appoints C. DeLores Tucker (b Philadelphia, PA, Oct 4, 1927) as Pennsylvania's Secretary of State

Adm. Elmo R. Zumwalt, Jr.,* Chief of Naval Opera-

E. Literature,
Publications, and
The Black Press

F. The Arts

G. Science,
Technology,
and Medicine

H. Sports

1971

	A. **General History**	B. **Education**	C. **Laws and Legal Actions**	D. **Religion**
1971	tions, announces the formation of a six-man team to oversee a five-year program to recruit more black officers and enlisted men for the US Navy			
1972	U.S.S. *Jesse L. Brown,* the first ship of the US Navy to be named in honor of a black naval officer, is launched at Westwego, LA Robert Wedgeworth is named director of the American Library Association, the first black to hold this position Maj. Gen. Frederick E. Davidson becomes the first black to lead an Army division when he is assigned command of the Eighth Infantry Division in Europe Benjamin Hooks, a Memphis lawyer and Baptist minister, is the first black named to the Federal Communication Commission; he works to improve the portrayal of and employment opportunities for blacks in the media Cong. Shirley Chisholm (D-NY) makes a bid for the presidential nomination of the Democratic party Frank Wills, a security guard at the Watergate office complex, discovers and detains a group of men installing surveillance equipment in the Democratic Party National Headquarters, Washington, DC; Wills calls the police and initiates the so-called Watergate scandal that leads to Pres. Richard M. Nixon's* resignation from office Charles Evers, mayor of Fayette MS, begins his campaign for governor of Mississippi; he is the first black since Reconstruction to seek the governorship Vernon Jordan (b Atlanta, GA, 1935), attorney, is named executive director	Approximately 2,000 black and white students from the University of Florida at Gainesville gather at the home of the university president Stephen C. O'Connell*; the students demand an end to the school's ''racist'' policies and call for O'Connell's resignation; following O'Connell's rejection of increased black recruitment, nearly 100 black students withdraw from the university James M. Rodger, Jr., of Durham, NC, becomes the first black to be honored as National Teacher of the Year, Washington, DC A National Education Association study reveals that blacks have lost 30,000 teaching positions since the 1954 desegregation decision  *Brooklyn congresswoman Shirley Chisholm became the first African-American woman in the Democratic Party to run for president of the United States.* (LC)	Angela Davis is acquitted of all charges at her trial, San Jose, CA Fleeta Drumgo and John Cluchette are acquitted by an all-white jury of the murder of a white guard at Soledad Prison; George Jackson, the third ''Soledad Brother,'' is killed in an alleged escape attempt The US Supreme Court overturns the 1967 draft evasion conviction of former heavyweight boxing champion Muhammad Ali	Rev. W. Sterling Cary is the first black president of the National Council of Churches

E. Literature, Publications, and The Black Press

Carl T. Rowan is elected to the prestigious Gridiron Club, an organization of Washington, DC, journalists; Rowan is the first black member

We Can't Breathe, Ronald L. Fair's semi-autobiographical novel of a nine-year-old boy trying to survive amid the injustice and racism of Southside Chicago, IL, is published

F. The Arts

Simon Estes (b Centerville, IA, Feb 2, 1938) famous operatic baritone, sings at the opening of the summer Olympic Games, Munich, Germany

Kathleen Battle (b Portsmouth, OH 1948), opera soprano, makes her solo debut in the German Requiem of Brahms, Spoleto, Italy

Berry Gordy of Motown Records produces *Lady Sings the Blues,* a semi-biographical film about the life of the late Billie Holiday, starring Diana Ross; Ross is nominated for an Academy Award for Best Actress

Elizabeth Courtney is nominated for an Academy Award for Costume Design for her work with *Lady Sings the Blues;* she is the first black woman nominated in this award category

Sue Booker, the first black woman to join the Directors Guild of America, wins an Emmy Award for producing *As Adam Early in the Morning*

Alma Thomas is the first black American woman to have an individual show at the Whitney Museum of Art, New York City

Faith Ringgold cofounds the Women Students and Artists for Black Liberation to pressure museums to exhibit the work of women artists

Betye Saar (b Pasadena, CA, 1926) creates *The Liberation of Aunt Jemima,* one of her more popular and political art pieces

Scott Joplin's opera *Treemonisha* makes its world premiere in Atlanta, GA

G. Science, Technology, and Medicine

Eighteen-year-old Hunter Nicolas is the first pre-college student in the US to deliver a paper before the American Federation for Clinical Research

Florence Gaynor, executive director of the New Jersey Medical School, College of Medicine and Dentistry, is the first woman to head a major teaching hospital

George Carruthers (b 1940), physicist, is one of two naval research laboratory scientists responsible for developing the Apollo 16 lunar surface ultraviolet camera/spectrograph that is placed on the lunar surface

H. Sports

Bobby Williams debuts at the Professional Bowlers Association US Open and is the first black to appear on the nationally televised bowling program

Wilt Chamberlain becomes the first player in the NBA to score 30,000 points when he plays in a game between the Los Angeles Lakers and the Phoenix Suns

During the anthem ceremony at the Olympic Games, Munich, West Germany, Vincent Matthews and Wayne Collett, winners in the 400-meter run, giggle and slouch while the US national anthem plays; the International Olympic Committee (IOC) considers their behavior disrespectful and bans the athletes from Olympic competition, though the men insist they were not protesting the US government

1972   of the National Urban League

Yvonne Braithwaite Burke (b Los Angeles, CA, Oct 5, 1932) (D-CA) is the first black woman from California elected to the US House of Representatives; as a member of the Public Works Committee, she attaches an amendment to the Alaska Pipeline Bill for a minority set-aside which results in hundreds of millions of dollars in contracts to black businesses

The first African Liberation Day Parade, organized by the African Liberation Support Committee, takes place in Washington, DC

The Black Soldier Statue, honoring all black American soldiers from all military branches, is dedicated in Baltimore, MD

Barbara Jordan (D-TX) is elected to the US Congress from Texas

The first National Black Political Convention, led by Cong. Charles Diggs (D-MI), Mayor Richard Hatcher of Gary, IN, and poet Amiri Baraka, convenes in Gary, IN

Angry over the racist political machine in Cook County, IL, black voters pool their support for the Republican candidate for Cook County prosecutor, Bernard C. Carey,* defeating Edward Hanrahan* and causing a major political upset

Cong. Yvonne Braithwaite Burke (D-CA) co-chairs the Democratic National Convention, becoming the first black person to chair a major party's national political convention

Pres. Richard M. Nixon* appoints Jewel Stradford Lafontant, the first black woman to serve as assistant US attorney, deputy solicitor general of the US

E. **Literature,
Publications, and
The Black Press**   F. **The Arts**   G. **Science,
Technology,
and Medicine**   H. **Sports**

1972

	A. **General History**	B. **Education**	C. **Laws and Legal Actions**	D. **Religion**
1973	Lelia Smith Foley becomes mayor of Taft, OK, the first black woman to be elected mayor of a US city Tom Bradley, veteran of the Los Angeles Police Department, is elected mayor of Los Angeles, CA Marian Wright Edelman (b Bennettsville, SC, Jun 6, 1939), the first black woman admitted to the bar in Mississippi, founds the Children's Defense Fund, Washington, DC The National Black Feminist Organization is founded to address the particular concerns of black women Cong. Cardiss Collins (b St. Louis, MO, Sept 24, 1931) (D-IL) is elected to fill the seat left vacant by her late husband, George W. Collins Cong. Charles C. Diggs, Jr. (D-MI), is elected chairman of the District of Columbia Committee; under his leadership, Washington, DC, residents obtain, for the first time in 100 years, the right to elect a mayor and city council Rev. Andrew Young (b New Orleans, LA, 1932) (D-GA) is elected to the US Congress	Upon her election as superintendent of schools for Washington, DC, Barbara Sizemore becomes the first black woman to head the public schools of any major US city	Imari Abubakari Obadali, President of the Legal Foundation of the Republic of New Africa, and Gaidi Obadele, attorney, submit legal documents in support of the Black Nation, the Republic of New Africa, before the US District Court, Mississippi	
1974	Grenada achieves its independence from Great Britain Beverly Johnson, one of the world's top fashion models, becomes the first black on the cover of *Vogue* magazine Jill Brown is the first black woman to qualify as a pilot in US military history Elaine Brown (b Philadelphia, PA, Mar 3, 1943),	Robert Dancz*, director of the University of Georgia marching band, announces that the University of Georgia Redcoat Band will not play "Dixie" at future university football games; Dancz considers "Dixie" offensive to the university's black student population	The House Judiciary Committee formally opens its impeachment hearings against Pres. Richard M. Nixon*; Cong. John Conyers, Jr. (D-MI), and Cong. Barbara Jordan (D-TX) are among the members of the committee; Jordan in particular distinguishes herself as an eloquent contributor to the hearings process	Rev. Alice Henderson becomes the first black woman chaplain in the US military

E. **Literature, Publications, and The Black Press**	F. **The Arts**	G. **Science, Technology, and Medicine**	H. **Sports**	
Elizabeth Carnegie is appointed editor-in-chief of the national journal *Nursing Research,* becoming the first black American to hold the position	*Raisin,* a musical adaptation of the Lorraine Hansberry play, opens on Broadway, NYC, and marks the debut of Debbie Allen; Allen will go on to become a successful choreographer, actress, and television producer Bernice Johnson Reagon, civil rights activist, forms the *a cappella* singing group Sweet Honey in the Rock; the internationally acclaimed all-women's group incorporates African themes in their music and revitalizes interest in traditional black spirituals, as well as folk songs Shirley Prendergast becomes the first black woman lighting designer on Broadway, NYC, when she joins the production of the Negro Ensemble Company's *The River Niger* Berry Gordy resigns as president of Motown Records to assume leadership of the new Motown Industries, which includes a record, motion picture, television, and publishing division Ten films with predominantly black casts, including *Sounder,* are nominated for Academy Awards Scott Joplin's music is featured in the film *The Sting,* igniting a revitalized interest in Joplin's work and ragtime music	Vernice Ferguson is the first black American nurse to become chief of the Nursing Department of the National Institutes of Health, Washington, DC		**1973**
Virginia Hamilton's (b Yellow Springs, OH, Mar 12, 1936) *M. C. Higgins, the Great* is published; it will be awarded the American Library Association's Newberry Medal, the National Book Award, the Lewis Carroll Shelf Award, and the International Board on Books for Young People Award Ann Allen Shockley's (b Louisville, KY, Jun 21, 1927) *Loving Her* is pub-	Cicely Tyson wins two Emmy awards for her role in *The Autobiography of Miss Jane Pittman* Richard Pryor wins an Emmy for his writing contributions on the Lily Tomlin* special ''Lily'' American Society of Composers, Authors and Publishers places a plaque honoring composer Scott Joplin at his grave site	Muriel Petioni (b Port of Spain, Trinidad, Jan 1, 1914) founds one of the first organizations for women doctors, the New York–area Susan Smith McKinney Steward Medical Society	Henry ''Hank'' Aaron (b Mobile, AL, Feb 5, 1934) of the Atlanta Braves breaks Babe Ruth's* record for most career home runs Lee Elder becomes one of the first black professional golfers after winning the Monsanto Open, Pensacola, FL Muhammad Ali KO's George Foreman in Zaire to regain the heavyweight	**1974**

	A. **General History**	B. **Education**	C. **Laws and Legal Actions**	D. **Religion**
1974	political activist, becomes the chairperson of the Black Panther Party, the highest position ever held by a woman in the BPP			
	Maynard Jackson (b Dallas, TX, Mar 23, 1938) begins service as mayor of Atlanta, GA; he is reelected in 1982 and 1990			
	Harold E. Ford (D-TN) is elected to the US Congress			
	Comedian Redd Foxx is named police chief of Taft, OK, an all-black town			
1975	Pres. Gerald Ford* appoints William T. Coleman Secretary of Transportation	Educator Marva Collins (b Monroeville, AL, Aug 31, 1936) founds the Westside Preparatory School, an alternative educational institution for black children in Chicago, IL; the school will serve as a model for other alternative education institutions throughout the nation; Presidents Ronald Reagan* and George Bush* will offer Collins appointments to serve as US Secretary of Education, but she will decline the offers	JoAnne Little is acquitted of murder charges after she kills in self-defense a prison guard who had raped her while she was incarcerated, Beaufort, NC; the case will become nationally known as the issues of sexual abuse against black women and the extent to which civil rights apply to prisoners are highlighted	Upon the death of Elijah Muhammad, founder of the Nation of Islam, his son, Wallace D. Muhammad, succeeds him and begins to change the leadership, organizational structure, and doctrine to more closely adhere to orthodox Islam; Muhammad changes the name of the Nation of Islam to the World Community of Al-Islam
	James B. Parsons becomes a chief judge of a Federal court, the US District Court in Chicago, IL			
	After studying recently discovered artifacts, archaeologists announce that Africans, rather than Christopher Columbus* or the Vikings, were the first outside explorers in the "New World"			
	The Combahee River Collective, named after the river in South Carolina where Harriet Tubman, during the Civil War, led the only military campaign in US history that was planned by a woman, is founded in New York City; the Collective, one of the first modern black feminist organizations, plays a key role in raising the issue of homophobia in the black community			
	Daniel "Chappie" James is the first black four-star general in US history			
	Gloria Randle Scott is the first black woman to become national president of the Girl Scouts, USA			
	Cong. Cardiss Collins is the first black and first			

E. Literature, Publications, and The Black Press	F. The Arts	G. Science, Technology, and Medicine	H. Sports	
lished; it is the first known novel by a black woman with a lesbian protagonist Chester L. Washington, the first black reporter for the *Los Angeles Times*, becomes head of the Central News-Wave Publications in California; under his leadership the organization grows to become the largest black newspaper operation in any single metropolitan area			crown in a fight billed as "the Rumble in the Jungle"; the bout is the first heavyweight title fight held in Africa Frank Robinson is named manager of the Cleveland Indians and becomes the first black manager of a major league baseball team Gloria Jean Byard is the first black to play field hockey on the US National team	**1974**
	Adam Wade becomes the first black game show host when he hosts "Musical Chairs," a nationally televised show Ntozake Shange's play *For Colored Girls Who Have Considered Suicide When the Rainbow Is Not Enuf* premieres in New York City WGPR-TV, the first black-owned and black-operated television station in the US, begins operations in Detroit, MI Donna Summer's disco anthem "Love to Love You Baby" hits number two on the *Billboard* Pop charts; because of this song and subsequent releases, Summer is dubbed the "Queen of Disco" Beah Richards's (b Beulah Richardson, Vicksburg, MS, c1933) one-woman show, "A Black Woman Speaks," is broadcast on television; this production later wins Richards an Emmy Award	Donna P. Davis becomes the first black woman physician in the US Navy medical corps	Muhammad Ali successfully defends his world heavyweight crown by defeating contender Chuck Wepner* Kareem Abdul-Jabbar (b Ferdinand Lewis Alcindor, NYC, Apr 16, 1947) begins playing for the Los Angeles Lakers; one of the finest players in NBA history, Abdul-Jabbar will become the leading scorer in the NBA and will lead the Lakers to five NBA championships Arthur Ashe wins the Wimbledon Singles Championship and the World Championship Tennis Singles, London, England Lee Elder becomes the first black to play in the Masters Golf Tournament, Augusta, GA Moses Malone becomes the first player to go directly from high school into professional basketball Morgan State University in Maryland achieves a ranking of number 10 in the lacrosse college division; becoming the first black college to achieve national prominence in the sport	**1975**

	A. **General History**	B. **Education**	C. **Laws and Legal Actions**	D. **Religion**
1975	woman to be appointed as Democratic whip-at-large Mervyn Dymally (b Cedros, Trinidad, May 12, 1926) becomes lieutenant governor of California			
1976	Hector Petersen, a 13-year-old Soweto boy, is the first to die in what will become known as the "Children's Crusade," the first nationwide black South African uprising of the decade Kenneth Gibson, mayor of Newark, NJ, becomes the first black president of the US Conference of Mayors In a private conversation at the Republican National Convention, US Secretary of Agriculture Earl L. Butz* accuses blacks of laziness and shiftlessness; as a consequence he is forced to resign Cong. Barbara Jordan (D-TX) is the keynote speaker for the Democratic National Convention; she is the first black to deliver the keynote address for a major political party's national convention Unita Blackwell, a founding member of the Mississippi Freedom Democratic Party, becomes the first black woman mayor in the history of the state of Mississippi; she is elected mayor of Mayersville Under the leadership of Alma Rangel, wife of Cong. Charles Rangel (D-NY), spouses of Congressional Black Caucus members organize the Congressional Black Caucus Foundation; the primary goal of the foundation is to provide congressional internship opportunities and legislative training for blacks Jimmy Carter,* former Georgia governor, is elected US President, defeating Gerald Ford;* more	The US Army reorganizes part of its college scholarship program in an attempt to double the number of black officers in the ROTC program While Mary Frances Berry (b Nashville, TN, Feb 17, 1938) technically becomes the first black woman to head a major research university when she is named chancellor of the University of Colorado at Boulder, she actually does not serve in the position; instead, she accepts the appointment and serves as Assistant US Secretary of Education Clara Adams-Ender becomes the first woman to be awarded an M.A. in military science from the Command and General Staff College, Ft. Leavenworth, KS		Pauli Murray is ordained the first black female priest of the Episcopal Church The congregation of President-elect Jimmy Carter's* Baptist church votes to drop its 11-year ban on blacks, Plains, GA

1976

Alex Haley's (d Seattle, WA, Feb 10, 1992) *Roots* is published; more than 1.6 million copies are sold in the first six months after publication, and the autobiography is translated into 22 languages; later this year Haley receives a special Pulitzer Prize for the book

Michael Schultz's *Car Wash,* which features a predominantly black cast, premieres; the film is a popular and financial success

William Lucas, former player, is named director of personnel for the Atlanta Braves; it is the highest position ever held by a black in professional baseball

"Sugar" Ray Leonard (b Ray Charles Leonard, Wilmington, SC, May 17, 1956) wins an Olympic Gold medal for boxing; Leonard will go on to have a successful professional boxing career, winning titles in both welterweight and middleweight divisions

Linda Jefferson leads the Toledo Troopers to the National Women's Football League championship

Evie Dennis is named the first black woman officer of the United States Olympic Committee

Anita DeFrantz wins an Olympic bronze medal in rowing

	A. **General History**	B. **Education**	C. **Laws and Legal Actions**	D. **Religion**
1976	than 90% of all black voters support Carter Cong. Yvonne Braithwaite Burke (D-CA) is the first woman to chair the Congressional Black Caucus			
1977	Armed black Muslims take hostages at three different sites in Washington, DC; the gunmen demand, among other things, that the premiere of *Mohammad, Messenger of God* be canceled because the film ridicules Elijah Muhammad The Afro-American Historical and Genealogical Society is founded in Washington, DC The oldest known identified photos of African slaves in the US are published in *American Heritage* magazine; the photos were discovered in an attic at Peabody Museum, Harvard University in Massachusetts Bernadine Denning (b Detroit, MI, Aug 17, 1930) is appointed director of the Office of Revenue Sharing for the US Department of the Treasury; while in this position, she administers a fund of $9 billion and also enforces civil rights laws prohibiting federal funds from going to any unit practicing racial discrimination Under the leadership of chairperson Elaine Brown, the Black Panther Party encourages voter registration which results in the election of Lionel Wilson, the first black mayor of Oakland, CA Clifford Alexander, Jr., is named the first black Secretary of the Army Muriel Petioni organizes the Medical Women of the National Medical Association, the first female physician's group officially admitted as a component of the NMA	Civil rights activist and scholar Mary Frances Berry is appointed assistant secretary for education in the Department of Health, Education, and Welfare		Louis Farrakhan, international spokesman for the World Community of As-Islam, defects and decides to lead a group of Nation of Islam members in the tradition of Elijah Muhammad

E. **Literature, Publications, and The Black Press**	F. **The Arts**	G. **Science, Technology, and Medicine**	H. **Sports**

1976

1977

Toni Morrison's *Song of Solomon* is published; the novel sells over three million copies and becomes only the second book by a black author chosen as a Book-of-the-Month Club selection

Mildred Taylor (b Jackson, MS, 1943) wins the Newberry Medal for *Roll of Thunder, Hear My Cry*

Errol Garner, pianist and composer (d Los Angeles, CA, Jan 2); Garner is considered the best-selling jazz pianist in the world; he is best known for his work "Misty"

Roots, a television miniseries based on the book by Alex Haley detailing his African-American genealogical beginnings, airs on ABC; 130 million Americans watch over eight nights; *Roots* sweeps the Emmy awards, with actor Louis Gossett, Jr., receiving the Best Actor award

Muriel Petioni organizes the Medical Women of the National Medical Association, the first female physician's group officially admitted as a component of the NMA

Reggie Jackson (b Wyncote, PA, May 18, 1946) of the New York Yankees is the first baseball player to hit three home runs in a World Series game; Jackson, who becomes known as "Mr. October," will lead the Yankees in their defeat of the Los Angeles Dodgers to capture the World Series title

Gale Sayers (b Wichita, KS, May 30, 1943), running back for the Chicago Bears, is elected to the Football Hall of Fame, Canton, OH; he is the youngest player to receive the honor

The Women's Basketball League, patterned after the NBA, is organized

Lusia Harris is the first black American woman to be drafted by an NBA team, but declines offers from the New Orleans Jazz and Milwaukee Bucks

Donna Lynn Mosley is the first black American to compete in the US Gymnastics Federation Junior Olympic Nationals

	A. **General History**	B. **Education**	C. **Laws and Legal Actions**	D. **Religion**
1977	Pres. Jimmy Carter* appoints Eleanor Holmes Norton (b Washington, DC, Jun 13, 1937) to chair the Equal Employment Opportunity Commission; Norton is the first woman to head the organization Pres. Jimmy Carter* appoints Hattie Bessent (b Jacksonville, FL, Dec 26, 1926) to the Presidential Task Force for the Friendship Treaty to China and to the Presidential Commission on Mental Health; Bessent, a psychiatric nurse, is the first black nurse in Florida to receive a doctorate and the first black dean of the Graduate School of Nursing, Vanderbilt University, TN Pres. Jimmy Carter* appoints Patricia Roberts Harris US Secretary of Housing and Urban Development; she then becomes the first black woman to serve in a presidential cabinet Andrew Young is named US Ambassador to the United Nations			
1978	Benjamin Hooks assumes leadership of the NAACP, succeeding Roy Wilkins The first stamp of the US Postal Service's Black Heritage Series honors Harriet Tubman Maxima Corporation, a computer systems and management company, is incorporated; it will become one of the largest black-owned companies in the US Louis Martin becomes special assistant to the president and the first influential black on the White House staff Faye Wattleton (b St. Louis, MO, Jul 8, 1943) is the first black, first woman, and the youngest person (at 25) to serve as president of Planned Par-	The US Supreme Court decides that the University of California at Davis's affirmative action policy is the equivalent of reverse discrimination and orders that Allan Bakke* be admitted to the school's Medical College	Pres. Jimmy Carter* signs into law the Humphrey-Hawkins Full Employment Bill cosponsored by Sen. Hubert H. Humphrey* (D-MN) and Cong. Augustus Hawkins; the bill calls for effective remedies to unemployment	Wallace D. Muhammad announces that the World Community of As-Islam in the West will drop its separatist philosophies Cult leader Jim Jones* leads his religious followers in a mass suicide, Guyana, South America; the majority of the 910 people who die are black The Church of Jesus Christ of Latter-day Saints (Mormons) reverses its 148-year-old policy that excludes black men from the priesthood Rev. Emerson Moore, Jr., becomes the first black monsignor of the Catholic Church

E. **Literature,
Publications, and
The Black Press**   F. **The Arts**   G. **Science,
Technology,
and Medicine**   H. **Sports**

1977

E. Literature, Publications, and The Black Press	F. The Arts	G. Science, Technology, and Medicine	H. Sports	1978
James Alan McPherson, Jr., wins the Pulitzer Prize in fiction for his volume of short stories, *Elbow Room*	*Roots—The Next Generation,* a mini-series based on the life of Alex Haley, is televised	Guion S. Bluford, Jr., Frederick D. Gregory, and Ronald E. McNair join the NASA space program and begin training as astronauts; they are the first black Americans ever admitted to the program	Leon Spinks defeats Muhammad Ali, the defending champion, and gains the World Boxing Association title in one of the biggest upset matches in heavyweight history	

Toni Morrison's *Song of Solomon* wins the National Book Critics Circle Award

Sharon Harley and Rosalyn Terborg-Penn's *The Afro-American Woman: Struggles and Images* is published and becomes the first anthology of black women's history

Sonia Sanchez wins the American Book Award for her book of poems *I've Been a Woman*

Robert E. Hayden's *American Journal,* a book of poems commemorating the achievements of black Americans, including Phillis Wheatley and Paul Laurence Dunbar, is published

Larry Holmes defeats Ken Norton to win the WBC heavyweight title in Las Vegas, NV

Muhammad Ali regains the WBA heavyweight title after defeating Leon Spinks in New Orleans, LA; Ali becomes the first heavyweight boxer to win a championship title three times

Larry Doby becomes baseball's second black manager when he signs with the Chicago White Sox

Eddie Robinson, Grambling State University

A. **General History**	B. **Education**	C. **Laws and Legal Actions**	D. **Religion**
1978 enthood Federation of America			

Karen Farmer is the first black member of the Daughters of the American Revolution; she traces her ancestry to William Hood, a soldier in the patriot army

Bennett Stewart (b Huntsville, AL, 1912) (D-IL) is elected to the US Congress to fill the seat left by the late Cong. Ralph Metcalfe

Cong. Julian C. Dixon (b Washington, DC, 1934) (D-CA) is elected to the US Congress

Melvin H. Evans, former governor of the Virgin Islands, is elected to the US Congress as a non-voting delegate, representing the Virgin Islands

George "Mickey" Leland (D-TX) is elected to the US Congress, replacing Barbara Jordan

| **1979** The Association of Black Women's Historians is founded | Singer Lou Rawls launches the Lou Rawls Parade of Stars, an annual telethon to benefit the United Negro College Fund | | Walter Dennis is consecrated suffragan bishop of the diocese of New York in the Episcopal Church |

The National Archives for Black Women's History and the Mary McLeod Bethune Memorial Museum opens in Washington, DC

Audrey Neal is the first woman of any race to become a longshoreman on the US eastern seaboard

The US Department of Commerce awards the WCIW, a firm owned by the World Community of Al-Islam in the West, a $22 million contract; WCIW provides precooked combat rations for the US military; this is the largest amount ever awarded to a black firm

Amalya L. Kearse is the first woman and the second black appointed to the US Court of Appeals for the Second Circuit

E. Literature, Publications, and The Black Press	F. The Arts	G. Science, Technology, and Medicine	H. Sports	
			coach, is invited to interview for a head coaching position with the Los Angeles Rams; he is the first black coach to be seriously considered for any NFL team	**1978**
Barbara Chase-Ribaud wins the Janet Heidinger Kafka prize for her novel *Sally Hemings*, a historical romance based on an alleged relationship between US President Thomas Jefferson* and one of his slaves

Lucille Clifton (b Thelma Lucille Sayles, Depew, NY, Jun 27, 1936) is named Poet Laureate for the state of Maryland

Robert Maynard is the first black editor-publisher of a daily newspaper with a predominantly white readership, *The Oakland Tribune-East Bay Today;* he renames the paper *The Oakland Tribune* | Max Robinson (d Nov 20, 1988) is the first black network news anchor when he appears on ABC's "World News Tonight"

The Sugar Hill Gang's "Rapper's Delight," the first rap record with national airplay, is released; the single marks the beginning of a new musical genre that will grow into a national phenomenon over the next decade | | Sugar Ray Leonard KO's Wilfredo Benitez* in Las Vegas, NV, during the 15th round to win the world welterweight boxing title | **1979** |

	A. **General History**	B. **Education**	C. **Laws and Legal Actions**	D. **Religion**
1979	Franklin A. Thomas becomes the first black to head a major US charitable organization when he is named president of the Ford Foundation Frank E. Peterson is named the first black general in the US Marine Corps The first of several black youths is found murdered, Atlanta, GA; by the following year, 29 victims are found, igniting what will be known as the Atlanta Child Murders case; Wayne Williams, entertainment talent scout, is convicted of two of the murders Rev. William H. Gray III (b Baton Rouge, LA, 1941) (D-PA) is elected to the US Congress Marcella Hayes becomes the first black woman pilot in the US armed forces Rev. Jesse Jackson travels to the Middle East and meets with President Hafez al-Hassad* of Syria and Yasser Arafat,* head of the Palestine Liberation Organization (PLO), to discuss long-term peace settlements between the Palestinians and Israel; the talks outrage many pro-Israeli Americans			
1980	Hazel W. Johnson (b 1927) becomes the first black woman in US history to hold the rank of brigadier general, the US Army Nursing Corps Mervyn Dymally (D-CA) is elected to the US Congress Cong. George W. Crockett (D-MI) is elected to the US Congress Gus Savage (b Detroit, MI, 1925) (D-IL) is elected to the US Congress Pres. Jimmy Carter* appoints Norma Holloway Johnson, the first black	Marian Wright Edelman, director of the Children's Defense Fund, becomes the first black and second woman to chair the board of trustees of Spelman College, her alma mater The first annual Black College Day is organized, Washington, DC; more than 18,000 black students attend the conference and hear speeches on the preservation of black colleges and universities	The US Supreme Court rules that intentional discrimination must be proven in order to declare a local election unconstitutional; the ruling stems from a Mobile, AL, case (*City of Mobile v. Bolden*) that highlights the fact that while blacks represent 35% of the city's total population, black candidates never win in the city's elections	Many black religious organizations, including the Progressive National Convention, take official stands against the Moral Majority movement

E. Literature, Publications, and The Black Press	F. The Arts	G. Science, Technology, and Medicine	H. Sports
Lucille Clifton is nominated for a Pulitzer Prize for *Two-Headed Woman*, a book of poetry	Robert L. Johnson establishes Black Entertainment Television (BET), a cable television company that begins broadcasting from Washington, DC	Levi Watkins, Jr. (b Parsons, KS, Jun 13, 1945) performs the first surgical implantation of the automatic implantable defribrillator, a battery-operated heart-regulating device, Johns Hopkins U. Hospital, Baltimore, MD	Willie Davenport and Jeff Gadley, the first black Americans to represent the US in the winter Olympics, place 12th in the four-man bobsled competition
Toni Cade Bambara receives the American Book Award for *The Salt Eaters*	Billy Thomas, actor (d Los Angeles, CA, Oct 11); he is most notable as the third child to portray Buckwheat in the *Our Gang* television series		Maury Willis is named manager for the Seattle Mariners, becoming the third black major league manager
	Sidney Poitier directs *Stir Crazy* starring Richard Pryor and Gene Wilder;* as of this year, the film is the largest grossing movie by a black American director		Larry Holmes KO's Muhammad Ali in the 11th round for the world heavyweight boxing title
			Earvin "Magic" Johnson (b Lansing, MI, Aug 14,

1980

woman to graduate from Georgetown Law School (1962), to the US District Court

Angela Davis runs for vice president of the US on the Communist Party ticket; she runs again in 1984

Pres. Jimmy Carter* names Hannah Diggs Atkins, Oklahoma state legislator, delegate to the 35th Assembly of the United Nations

The National Black Independent Political Party is founded; its charter requires equal female-male representation in all leadership positions

Harold Washington (b Chicago, IL, 1922; d Nov 25, 1987) (D-IL) is elected to the US Congress

Ronald Reagan* is elected US President, soundly defeating Jimmy Carter*; Carter carries 90% of the black vote

1981

One hundred thousand marchers rally in Washington, DC, in support of designating the birthday of Martin Luther King, Jr., a Federal holiday

Pres. Ronald Reagan* appoints Samuel Pierce, Jr., Secretary of Housing and Urban Development; Pierce's leadership will be questioned when in 1989 an estimated $2 billion is lost due to fraud and mismanagement

The US Air Force Academy ends its ban on applicants with the sickle-cell trait

Following talks with Rev. Jesse Jackson of Operation PUSH, the Coca-Cola Company agrees to spend $14 million with minority vendors and sets a goal to increase the number of blacks on its management staff from 5% to 12.5%; similar agreements will be made with Kentucky Fried

Morehouse School of Medicine is founded, Atlanta, GA

Toni Morrison, former student and instructor at Howard University, is one of the most celebrated African-American authors of the twentieth century. In 1993, Morrison will win the Nobel Prize for Literature. (Schomburg)

1980

1959) joins the Los Angeles Lakers basketball team; Johnson will become one of the best point guards in the NBA

1981

Washington Post reporter Janet Cooke wins the Pulitzer Prize for "Jimmy's World," a profile of an eight-year-old drug addict; three days later the prize is withdrawn after Cooke confesses that the story is fabricated

Kitchen Table: Women of Color Press begins publishing

Toni Morrison's *Tar Baby* is published and becomes an instant commercial success, appearing on *The New York Times* best-seller list less than one month after it is published

Pamela Johnson is named publisher of the *Ithaca* (New York) *Journal* and becomes the first black female publisher since Julia Ringwood Coton (1891)

Bryant Gumble is named co-anchor of NBC's "Today"

Lena Horne: The Lady and Her Music opens on Broadway and becomes the longest running one-woman show on Broadway; the show later wins a Tony Award, a Drama Desk Award, and a Drama Critics Circle citation

Byllye Avery founds The National Black Women's Health Project

Zina Garrison is the first black American player to win the junior singles tennis championship at Wimbledon, England

Boxer Sugar Ray Leonard is named Sportsman of the Year by *Sports Illustrated* magazine

Earvin "Magic" Johnson signs a 25-year, $25 million contract with the Los Angeles Lakers basketball team; this is the largest total sum in team sports history

1981 Chicken, the Southland Corporation, Anheuser-Busch, 7-Up, and Burger King

Jewell Jackson McCabe (b Washington, DC, Aug 2, 1945) founds the National Council of 100 Black Women

Harriet "Liz" Byrd (b Cheyenne, WY, Apr 20, 1926), former teacher, is the first black legislator from Wyoming

Pres. Ronald Reagan* appoints Cong. Melvin H. Evans (d 1984) ambassador to Trinidad and Tobago

Edolphus "Ed" Towns (b Chadbourn, NC, 1934) (D-NY) is elected to the US Congress

Rev. Andrew Young, former US congressman and ambassador, is elected mayor of Atlanta, GA

Pres. Ronald Reagan* appoints William M. Bell chairman of the EEOC, replacing Eleanor Holmes Norton; Bell's appointment is met with disappointment by many in the black community and civil rights groups because of his apparent lack of experience and credentials in civil rights; Reagan later withdraws the nomination

Pres. Ronald Reagan* replaces Arthur S. Flemming, chairman of the US Commission on Civil Rights, with Clarence Pendleton, a conservative Republican; this is the first time a president has removed a standing chairman from the commission

Arnetta R. Hubbard is the first woman president of the National Bar Association

Lenora Cole-Alexander is the first black woman to head the US Labor Department's Women's Bureau

E. Literature,
   Publications, and
   The Black Press   F. The Arts

G. Science,
   Technology,
   and Medicine   H. Sports

1981

	A. General History	B. Education	C. Laws and Legal Actions	D. Religion
1982	Pres. Ronald Reagan* announces that he will nominate Rev. B. Sam Hart of Philadelphia, PA, to the US Commission on Civil Rights; he eventually withdraws Hart's name following vigorous protests from those who question Hart's conservative philosophies Pres. Ronald Reagan* appoints Patricia Roberts Harris as US Secretary of Health and Human Services Alan Wheat (b San Antonio, TX) is elected to the US Congress; the following year he becomes one of only three freshman members ever to serve on the Rules Committee		The US Congress votes to extend the Voting Rights Act of 1965, despite a 10-day delay by Sen. Jesse Helms* (R-NC)	
1983	Cong. Charles Hayes (b Cairo, IL, Feb 17, 1918) (D-IL) is elected to the US Congress, succeeding Harold Washington Harold Washington is the first black mayor of Chicago, IL Rev. Jesse Jackson announces his bid for the presidency Rev. Jesse Jackson travels to Syria to plead with President Hafez al-Hassad* for the return of Lt. Robert Goodman, a navigator-bombadier who was taken prisoner after his plane was shot down over Syria; President Hassad turns Goodman over to Jackson Major Robert Owens (b Memphis, TN, 1936) (D-NY) begins service in the US Congress Vanessa Williams is crowned Miss America, becoming the first black to win in the history of the pageant; 10 months later she concedes the title to		Cong. Katie Hall (D-IN) is elected to the US Congress; while still a freshman, she introduces a bill that will designate the birthday of Rev. Martin Luther King, Jr., a federal holiday; Pres. Ronald Reagan* signs the legislation into law Cong. Julian C. Dixon (D-CA) writes the first economic-sanctions law against South Africa; four years later he authors an emergency appropriations bill to provide humanitarian aid to southern Africa	Nelson W. Trout is elected Bishop of the American Lutheran Church's South Pacific District; he becomes the first black ever elected to full-time office in the North American Lutheran Church

E. **Literature, Publications, and The Black Press**	F. **The Arts**	G. **Science, Technology, and Medicine**	H. **Sports**	
All the Women Are White, All the Blacks Are Men, but Some of Us Are Brave, edited by Gloria T. Hull, Patricia Bell Scott, and Barbara Smith, is published; the work is a pioneering text in black women's studies	Charles Fuller wins the Pulitzer Prize for *A Soldier's Play* Louis Gossett, Jr., (b Brooklyn, NY, May 27, 1936) wins an Academy Award as Best Supporting Actor for his role in *An Officer and a Gentleman,* becoming only the third black American to win an Academy Award Quincy Jones (b Chicago, IL, Mar 14, 1933) wins five Grammy awards for *The Dude,* including producer of the year Kathleen Collins is the first black woman to direct a feature-length film, *Losing Ground* Michael Jackson (b Gary, IN, Aug 29, 1958), formerly of The Jackson Five, releases *Thriller;* over 40 million copies are sold		Julius "Dr. J" Erving leads the Philadelphia 76ers to the NBA championship finals; Dr. J electrifies NBA crowds with his slam dunks	**1982**
Alice Walker is awarded the Pulitzer Prize for her novel *The Color Purple* Gloria Naylor (b Brooklyn, NY, Jan 25, 1950) wins the National Book Award for her novel *The Women of Brewster Place*	Eubie Blake, pianist and composer (d NYC, Feb 12); Blake, known for his song "I'm Just Wild About Harry," composed the first all-black musical *Shuffle Along* Independent filmmaker Julie Dash directs *Illusions;* Dash will receive numerous awards and nominations, including the Black American Film Society Award, Cable ACE Award in Art Direction nomination (1988), and the Black Filmmaker's Foundation's Best Film of the Decade Award (1989) The two-hour television special "Motown 25—Yesterday, Today, and Forever" airs on NBC; the show features several highlights including reunions of the Jackson Five, the Miracles, and the Supremes; it will become one of the most watched variety specials in the history of television	Guion S. Bluford, Jr. (b Philadelphia, PA) becomes the first black American astronaut in space when he serves as a mission specialist for STS-8 Orbiter Challenger *Alice Walker won the Pulitzer Prize and the American Book Award for* The Color Purple. *(Schomburg)* 	Herschel Walker, Heisman Trophy winner, signs with the New Jersey Generals of the US Football League; at $8 million for three years, it is the largest contract in football history NCAA Proposition 48 seeks to impose mandatory academic minimums for all scholarship athletes, requiring a C average in high school courses and a combined score of 700 on the SAT exam or a 15 on the ACT exam; the proposal is controversial within the black community because the SAT is considered racially biased against ethnic minorities	**1983**

	A. **General History**	B. **Education**	C. **Laws and Legal Actions**	D. **Religion**
1983	Suzette Charles, first runner-up, after *Penthouse* magazine publishes a series of compromising photos taken when Williams was 18 years old			
1984	W. Wilson Goode is the first black mayor of Philadelphia, PA			Rev. Leontine T. C. Kelly (b Washington, DC, Mar 5, 1920) is elected bishop of the United Methodist Church in the San Francisco, CA, area; she is the first black woman bishop of a major religious denomination
	In an off-the-record interview with a reporter from the *Washington Post*, Rev. Jesse Jackson refers to New York City as "Hymie Town," which many consider a racial slur against Jewish Americans			
	Pennsylvania Supreme Court Justice Robert N. C. Nix, Jr., is inaugurated as chief justice, the first black to head a state Supreme Court			
	At the time of the Democratic National Convention, Rev. Jesse Jackson has garnered approximately 300 delegates			
	Blacks across the nation vote in record numbers due largely to the candidacy of Rev. Jesse Jackson			
	Although he wins 17% of the actual vote, Rev. Jesse Jackson is given only 10% of the delegates at the Democratic party's national convention; consequent dissatisfaction with the DNC's methods for distributing convention delegates causes Jackson to reluctantly support the eventual Democratic nominees for president and vice president, Walter Mondale* and Geraldine Ferraro,* respectively			
	Washington, DC, delegate to Congress Walter Fauntroy, TransAfrica executive Randall Robinson, and civil rights activist Mary Frances Berry are arrested after holding a sit-in at the South African embassy; their protest is the catalyst for nationwide grass roots movements to influence the policies of Pres. Ronald Reagan* toward South Africa			

E. **Literature,
   Publications, and
   The Black Press**   F. **The Arts**

G. **Science,
   Technology,
   and Medicine**   H. **Sports**

1983

1984

Octavia Butler (b Pasadena, CA, Jun 22, 1941), the first black woman to gain popularity and critical acclaim as a science fiction writer, wins the Hugo Award for excellence in science fiction writing

Linda Beatrice Brown's *Rainbow Roun Mah Shoulder* is published; it is later the unanimous choice for first prize in a literary contest sponsored by the North Carolina Cultural Arts Coalition and Carolina Wren Press

Prince, producer, songwriter, and composer, rose to superstardom with the box-office smash ''Purple Rain.'' The film's soundtrack earned him an Oscar and several Grammy awards. (Paisley Park Enterprises)

Purple Rain, a semi-autobiographical film based on the life of rock musician Prince (b Prince Rogers Nelson, Minneapolis, MN, Jun 7, 1959), premieres; some critics hail it as the best rock movie ever made; Prince later receives an Oscar award for best original sound score and soundtrack album

''The Cosby Show'' premieres on NBC; starring Bill Cosby and Phylicia Ayers-Allen (later Rashad), the series becomes one of the most popular shows in the US and the most watched situation comedy in the history of television

Wynton Marsalis (b New Orleans, LA, Oct 18, 1961), jazz trumpeter, is the first musician to win Grammy awards for jazz and classical music recordings simultaneously

Tina Turner's *Private Dancer* is released, eventually reaching multiplatinum status and marking Turner's comeback; Turner will win three Grammy awards for this album

Clara Adams-Ender is named chief of the Department of Nursing at Walter Reed Army Medical Center, Washington, DC, the first black nurse to hold that position

The Georgetown University Hoyas basketball team wins the NCAA championship, making coach John Thompson the first black coach to win the title

Evelyn Ashford wins a gold medal in the 100-meter race, Edwin Moses wins a gold medal in the 400-meter hurdles, and Carl Lewis wins gold medals in the 100- and 200-meter dash, long jump, and 400-meter relay at the summer Olympic Games, Los Angeles, CA

The women's US Olympic basketball team features Lynette Woodward, Pam McGee, and Cheryl Miller; Miller is hailed as the best female player in the history of the sport

Peter Westbrook wins a bronze Olympic medal in the saber competition; it is the first fencing medal of any kind won by the US since the 1960 Olympics

Diane Durham, the first internationally ranked black American female gymnast, injures herself just before the Olympic Games and does not compete

A. **General History**	B. **Education**	C. **Laws and Legal Actions**	D. **Religion**
1984 Rev. Jesse Jackson leads the 25th Anniversary March on Washington, Washington, DC			
Shirley Chisholm founds the National Political Caucus of Black Women			
Joseph E. Lowery, president of the Southern Christian Leadership Conference, make an unsuccessful bid for the Democratic Party nomination for US President			
1985 Libyan leader Muammar el-Qaddafi,* speaking at the Nation of Islam International Savior's Day convention, Chicago, IL, calls on black Americans to leave the US military and join him in creating an independent black state; blacks, among them Nation of Islam minister Louis Farrakhan, reject Qaddafi's proposal		Cong. John Conyers, Jr.'s amendment to prohibit the export of any nuclear materials, technology, equipment, and information and to preclude authorization of technical personnel to work in or for South Africa, which is a part of the Anti-Apartheid Act, passes in the US House of Representatives	
Mayor Wilson Goode authorizes police involvement after neighbors file several complaints against the black radical group MOVE; 11 members, including 4 children, are killed after a state police helicopter drops a bomb on the group's house in Philadelphia, PA; community residents file suit against the city because 300 persons are left homeless as a result of the explosion			
Sherian Cadoria (b Marksville, LA, Jan 26, 1940) is promoted to brigadier general, becoming the first woman in the regular US Army to achieve this rank			
Cong. William H. Gray (D-PA) is elected chairman of the House Budget Committee			
Reuben V. Anderson is the first black to be appointed a judge on the Mississippi Supreme Court			
Donnie Cochran is the first black pilot to fly with the US Navy's elite squadron, the Blue Angels			

E. **Literature,**
   Publications, and
   The Black Press   F. **The Arts**

G. **Science,**
   Technology,
   and Medicine   H. **Sports**

				1985

Gwendolyn Brooks is appointed poetry consultant to the Library of Congress, becoming the first black woman to hold the position

Rita Dove (b Akron, OH, 1952) wins the Pulitzer Prize for *Thomas and Beaulah,* a collection of poetry inspired by and devoted to her grandparents

"We Are the World" is released as a single; the song, whose proceeds benefit African famine efforts, is written by Lionel Ritchie and Michael Jackson and is produced by Quincy Jones

The Apollo Theater reopens to celebrate its 50th anniversary; businessman Percy Sutton spearheads the $10 million renovations

Leontyne Price, opera diva, in her farewell appearance with the Metropolitan Opera, sings in the role of Aida

Whoopi Goldberg and Danny Glover star in the film adaptation of Alice Walker's *The Color Purple;* the NAACP protests the film's allegedly stereotypical representations of black family life

Russell Simmons (b 1957), rap music promoter and manager, founds Def Jam Records and Rush Productions; within a short period Def Jam becomes the home of rap's biggest artists, including Run DMC, Public Enemy, and LL Cool J

Under the leadership of Coach Vivian Stringer, the University of Iowa plays Ohio State University in front of the largest crowd to ever see a women's basketball game

Bo Jackson (b Bessemer, AL, Nov 30, 1962) wins the Heisman Trophy; he later becomes one of few professional athletes to play in two sports, football and baseball

Eddie Robinson of Grambling State University (LA) becomes the winningest football coach in history

	A. **General History**	B. **Education**	C. **Laws and Legal Actions**	D. **Religion**
1985	Sharon Pratt Kelly (b Washington, DC, Jan 30, 1944) becomes the first woman to serve as treasurer of the national Democratic Party			
	The US version of *Elle* magazine becomes the first white fashion magazine to consistently use black models			
	The National Organization of Black Elected Legislative Women is founded in Philadelphia, PA			
1986	Sidney Barthelemy is elected mayor of New Orleans, LA, succeeding Ernest Morial			
	Edward Perkins is appointed US Ambassador to the Republic of South Africa, the first black to hold the position			
	Rev. Floyd Flake (b Los Angeles, CA, 1945) is elected to the US Congress from the state of New York			
	The space shuttle Challenger explodes after lift-off at Cape Canaveral, FL; all seven crew members, including physicist Ronald McNair, are killed			
	One black man is killed and two others are injured when a gang of white youths attack them in Howard Beach, a predominantly white section of Queens, NY; the black men, who experienced car troubles, were confronted by the whites after they stopped in a pizza parlor to call for help; Michael Griffith was hit by a car and killed while trying to escape his attackers, and Cedric Sandeford was severely beaten by a baseball bat			
	Coretta Scott King travels to South Africa to meet with Pres. P. W. Botha* and Chief Mangosuthu Buthelezi; following criticism, she cancels the meeting and instead meets with African			

1985

1986

F. The Arts

The Capital Repertory Theater performs Toni Morrison's *Dreaming Emmett*, written in honor of the first national observance of the Martin Luther King, Jr., holiday; the play is based on the life of Emmett Till, slain at age 14 by white southerners for whistling at a white woman

John Wilson's bronze bust of Martin Luther King, Jr., is on display at the US Capitol Building, Washington, DC; it is the first statue of a black American to stand in the halls of Congress

Oprah Winfrey is the first black woman to host a nationally syndicated talk show, "The Oprah Winfrey Show," based in Chicago, IL

Run DMC's "Walk This Way" is number one on the *Billboard* Pop Charts, becoming the first rap song to achieve mass crossover success

Salt-N-Pepa's debut album *Hot, Cool and Vicious* sells one million copies, making them the first female rappers to go platinum

H. Sports

Debi Thomas wins first place in the World Figure Skating Championship

Martin Blackman is the first black male to win the national 16 and under event of the US Tennis Association, Kalamazoo, MI

George Branham wins the Brunswick Memorial World Open, becoming the first black American to win a Professional Bowlers Association title

James "Bonecrusher" Smith KO's Tim Witherspoon to become the first black with a college degree to win the heavyweight boxing championship

Lynette Woodard is the first female member of the Harlem Globetrotters basketball team

Boxer Mike Tyson defeats Trevor Berbick and becomes, at age 20, the youngest heavyweight champion

	A. **General History**	B. **Education**	C. **Laws and Legal Actions**	D. **Religion**
1986	National Congress leader Winnie Mandela Coretta Scott King awards Bishop Desmond Tutu, leader in the struggle against apartheid in South Africa, the Martin Luther King, Jr., Non-Violent Peace Prize on behalf of the King Center for Non-Violent Social Change John Lewis (b Troy, AL, 1940) (D-GA) is elected to the US Congress; he is the chief sponsor of legislation to establish a national African American museum in Washington, DC William Lucas makes an unsuccessful bid for governor of Michigan on the Republican Party ticket			
1987	Rioting occurs when a young black man dies from a police choke hold, Tampa, FL Kurt Schmoke is elected the first black mayor of Baltimore, MD Cong. Mike Espy (b Yazoo City, MS, 1953) (D-MS) is the first black congressman from Mississippi since Reconstruction Cong. Harold E. Ford (D-TN) is named Child Advocate of the Year by the Child Welfare League of America for his leadership in crafting a welfare reform bill Kweisi Mfume (b Frizell Gray, Baltimore, MD, 1948) (D-MD) is elected to the US Congress; he is the author of the Minority Business Development Act Carrie Saxon Perry (b Hartford, CT, Aug 10, 1931) is elected mayor of Hartford, CT	Johnetta B. Cole is appointed president of Spelman College, Atlanta, GA; she becomes the first black woman to lead the all-female institution in its 106-year history Niara Sudarkasa is appointed the first woman president of Lincoln University in Pennsylvania, the nation's oldest black college	Cong. Gus Savage's (D-IL) 5% set-aside provision in the Defense Authorization Bill of 1987 results in substantial contracts for minority-owned and -controlled businesses	
1988	Juanita Kidd Stout becomes an associate justice	Bishop College of Dallas, TX, at one time the largest	Pres. Ronald Reagan* vetoes a civil rights bill that	Eugene Marino (b Biloxi, MS) is appointed arch-

E. Literature, Publications, and The Black Press	F. The Arts	G. Science, Technology, and Medicine	H. Sports

1986

1987

The critically acclaimed Broadway production *Fences* wins four Tony awards: Best Play (August Wilson), Best Director (Lloyd Richards), Best Performance by an Actor (James Earl Jones), and Best Performance by a Featured Actress (Mary Alice), and the Pulitzer Prize for drama

Bo Diddley is inducted into the Rock and Roll Hall of Fame

Aretha Franklin becomes the first woman inducted into the Rock and Roll Hall of Fame

Willie D. Burton is the first black American to win an Oscar for sound when he receives the award for the movie *Bird*

The National Aeronautics and Space Administration selects Mae Jemison (b Decatur, GA, c1957) as an astronaut, making her the first black woman astronaut

Clara Adams-Ender is appointed chief of the Army Nurse Corps, becoming the second black woman to hold the position

Benjamin Carson (b Detroit, MI, Sep 18, 1951), neoursurgeon, surgically separates a pair of West German infant twins who were born joined at the backs of their heads; the landmark operation in Baltimore, MD, lasts 22 hours

Walter E. Massey is the first black to serve as president of the American Association for the Advancement of Science, the largest general science organization in the country

Los Angeles Dodgers executive Al Campanis* is fired for racially biased comments about the managerial potential for blacks

1988

Forty-eight black authors write an open letter to *The*

Motown Records is sold for $61 million to an in

Washington Redskins quarterback Doug

	A. **General History**	B. **Education**	C. **Laws and Legal Actions**	D. **Religion**
1988	of the Supreme Court of Pennsylvania, the first black woman to serve on a state supreme court Rev. Jesse Jackson places second in the Democratic presidential primary, losing to Massachusetts Governor Michael Dukakis*; Jackson delivers an electrifying speech at the Democratic National Convention, Atlanta, GA Lee Roy Young is the first black Texas Ranger in the 165-year history of this famed state police force Colin Powell (b NYC, Apr 5, 1937) is promoted to four-star general; in 1989 he will become the first black Chief of Staff for the US Armed Forces Following a seven-month investigation by a New York State grand jury, it is concluded that 16-year-old Tawana Brawley "fabricated" her story of abduction and sexual abuse by a gang of white men in Wappingers Falls, NY, in November 1987; Brawley was found nude in a garbage bag covered with feces and racial slurs Marcelite Harris (b 1943) is the first black woman to earn the rank of brigadier general in the US Air Force The Black Women Mayor's Caucus is organized at the National Conference of Black Mayors Lenora Fulani of the New Alliance Party is the first black and the first woman presidential candidate to get on the ballot in all 50 states	black college in the West, closes due to bankruptcy Comedian and television star Bill Cosby and his wife Camille donate $20 million to Spelman College, Atlanta, GA Temple University is the first university in the US to offer a doctorate degree (Ph.D.) in African-American studies; Philadelphia, PA	would restore protections invalidated by the US Supreme Court's 1984 ruling in *Grove City v. Bell;* the US Congress overrides the veto less than one week later Donald M. Payne (b Newark, NJ, 1934) (D-NJ) is elected to the US Congress; he later successfully secures passage of legislation to highlight illiteracy and the establishment of National Literacy Day; Pres. George Bush* signs the resolution into law in 1990	bishop of Atlanta, GA, becoming the first black archbishop in the American Roman Catholic Church

General Colin Powell, first African-American Chairman of the Joint Chiefs of Staff.

	A. **General History**	B. **Education**	C. **Laws and Legal Actions**	D. **Religion**
1989	Ronald H. Brown, former campaign manager for Rev. Jesse Jackson, becomes chairman of the Democratic National Committee, the first black to hold this position	Students from Howard University, Washington, DC, take over the school's administration building as a protest of the selection of Lee Atwater,* chairman of the Republican National	In *City of Richmond v. J. A. Croson Co.,* the US Supreme Court invalidates the city's minority set-aside program	Barbara Harris (b Philadelphia, PA, Jun 12, 1930) becomes the first woman to be consecrated a bishop in the Episcopal Church

E. Literature, Publications, and The Black Press	F. The Arts	G. Science, Technology, and Medicine	H. Sports	

New York Times Book Review protesting the failure to award the National Book Award to Toni Morrison for the novel *Beloved*

Toni Morrison is awarded the Pulitzer Prize for *Beloved*

Former tennis great Arthur Ashe publishes *A Hard Road to Glory*, a comprehensive three-volume series that documents the accomplishments of black American athletes

vestment group that includes a venture capital firm, record executive Jheryl Busby, and others

Once accused by black artists of racism, Music Television (MTV), the 24-hour cable music channel, premieres "Yo! MTV Raps" which showcases rap music and hip-hop culture; it will become one of the station's most popular programs

Mississippi Burning, a film about the modern civil rights movement, receives criticism from the black community for its focus on white FBI agents and not the blacks who actually initiated the movement

Carole Simpson (b Chicago, IL, Dec. 17, 1940) is named anchor of ABC's "World News Saturday"

Williams is named MVP after leading his team to victory over the Denver Broncos in Super Bowl XXII; Williams is the first black quarterback to start in a Super Bowl game

Debi Thomas, world class figure skater, is the first black American to win a medal in the winter Olympic Games; she wins the bronze medal in Calgary, Canada

Florence Griffith-Joyner wins three gold medals and one silver medal in the summer Olympics, becoming the first US woman to win four medals in one Olympic Game, Los Angeles, CA

CBS TV fires football commentator Jimmy "the Greek" Snyder* for making racist remarks; in an interview with a local Washington, DC, reporter, Snyder comments that blacks' athletic superiority is a result of selective breeding during US slavery

Lynette Love wins an Olympic gold medal in *tae kwondo*, a martial arts sport

Anita DeFrantz, past Olympic rowing winner, becomes the first black woman to serve on the International Olympic Committee

Heavyweight champion Mike Tyson defeats contender Michael Spinks in only 91 seconds and wins an impressive $22 million purse

"The Arsenio Hall Show" premieres; Hall is the first black to host a regularly scheduled late night talk show

Bill White (b Lakewood, FL, c 1933) becomes president of the National Baseball League, becoming the first black to head a major sports league

	A. **General History**	B. **Education**	C. **Laws and Legal Actions**	D. **Religion**
1989	Pres. George Bush* nominates William Lucas assistant attorney general for civil rights; the Senate vote for Lucas's confirmation results in a tie, thereby rejecting the nomination	Committee, to the Howard University board of trustees; Atwater resigns four days later	The Georgia Supreme Court declares the Atlanta Minority-Female Business Enterprise program unconstitutional; the program had set a 35% "minority participation goal" in all city contracts	Rev. Joan Campbell is elected moderator of the Presbyterian Church, USA, becoming the first black woman to head the Church
	Louis Sullivan (b Atlanta, GA, Nov 3, 1933) is confirmed as Secretary of Health and Human Services	Twenty students at Morris Brown College, Atlanta, GA, take over the school's administration building, demanding a Pan-African studies program, "a more lenient delinquent fees policy," better campus services, and an upgraded physical plant	The US Senate tries US District Court Judge Alcee Hastings on charges of fraud, corruption, and perjury stemming from a 1981 bribery conspiracy case; Hastings is convicted and impeached in October; Hastings is the first judge to be impeached even though he has previously been acquitted by a jury	Disputes over the inclusion of more African culture into the Catholic Church and other issues cause Rev. George Stallings to leave the Church and establish Imani Temple, Washington, DC
	Cong. William H. Gray (D-PA), chairman of the House Democratic Caucus, is elected Democratic Whip of the House of Representatives	Oprah Winfrey, national talk show host, receives a Doctor of Humane Letters degree from Morehouse College, Atlanta, GA, and donates $1 million to the school's scholarship fund; Winfrey requests that the money be used to fund the education of at least 100 black men		Rev. Rodney Patterson founds the New Alpha Missionary Baptist Church, the first predominantly black church in the state of Vermont
	A confrontation between police officers and black college students results in four injuries and 160 arrests in Virginia Beach, VA; the National Guard is called in to quell the disturbance and to prevent further looting of local businesses	Due to increasing financial problems, Atlanta University and Clark College merge to form the new institution, Clark-Atlanta University, Atlanta, GA		
	David Dinkins is elected mayor of NYC, defeating incumbent mayor Ed Koch* and becoming the first black to ever hold the office			
	Kenneth Chenault (b Long Island, NY, Jun 2, 1951), attorney, is named the president of the Consumer Card and Financial Services Group of American Express and becomes one of the highest ranking blacks in corporate America			

E. **Literature, Publications, and The Black Press**	F. **The Arts**	G. **Science, Technology, and Medicine**	H. **Sports**	
	Ruth Brown, Cholly Atkins, Henry LeTang, Frankie Manning, and Fayard Nicholas win Tony awards for the musical *Black and Blue*		Art Shell (b Charleston, SC, Nov 26, 1946) is named head coach of the Los Angeles Raiders and becomes the first black head coach in the NFL	**1989**
	Ernest Dickerson wins the New York Film Critics Circle best cinematography award for filmmaker Spike Lee's *Do the Right Thing*		Bertram Lee and Peter Bynoe lead a group of investors to buy the Denver Nuggets and become the first blacks to own an NBA team	
	Barbara Brandon's (b NYC, 1958) comic strip, "Where I'm Coming From," first appears in the *Detroit Free Press;* when it is acquired by Universal Press Syndicate two years later, Brandon becomes the first black female cartoonist to be syndicated in the mainstream white press		Andre Ware of the University of Houston (TX) is the first black quarterback to win the Heisman Trophy	
	When Oprah Winfrey buys Harpo Productions, she becomes the first black woman and only the third woman in the US to buy a television and movie production studio		Frank Robinson of the Baltimore Orioles is named manager of the year by both the AP (Associated Press) and UPI (United Press International)	
	Gordon Parks's film *The Learning Tree* is selected among the first films to be registered by the National Film Registry of the Library of Congress; the National Film Registry is formed in 1988 by an act of Congress to recognize films that are "culturally, historically, or aesthetically significant"		Comer Cottrell (b Mobile, AL, Dec 7, 1931) is the first black to co-own a major baseball team, the Texas Rangers	
	Judith Jamison, dancer, becomes director of the Alvin Ailey American Dance Theater			
	Jennifer Lawson (b Fairfield, AL, 1946) is named executive vice president of national programming for the Public Broadcasting System; during Lawson's first year, PBS records *The Civil War,* a five-night series that becomes the most watched show in PBS history			

	A. **General History**	B. **Education**	C. **Laws and Legal Actions**	D. **Religion**
1990	L. Douglas Wilder is inaugurated as governor of Virginia, the first black to be elected governor of any state	Students at Tennessee State University, Nashville, TN, stage sit-ins and marches protesting the school's "poor conditions"	In an FBI undercover sting operation, Washington, DC, mayor Marion Barry is arrested for allegedly purchasing and smoking crack cocaine in a Washington, DC, hotel room; he is later convicted and sentenced to prison	Rev. George Stallings is excommunicated when he declares that Imani Temple is totally independent of the Catholic Church; he later is ordained the first bishop of the African-American Catholic Church by six white bishops from the Independent Old Catholic Churches of California
	Nelson Mandela, leader of the African National Congress, is released from prison after being held for 27 years without a trial by the South African government	Walter H. Annenberg,* former publisher of *TV Guide,* pledges $50 million to the United Negro College Fund, the largest single donation ever offered to the group	Abjuda Abi Naantaabuu files a $10 million suit against Ralph Abernathy and Harper & Row, the publishers of his autobiography, *And the Walls Came Tumbling Down;* in the book Abernathy alleges that Naataabuu and Rev. Martin Luther King, Jr., had an extramarital affair	Harold I. Bearden, minister and civil rights leader (d Atlanta, GA, Mar 19); Bearden (b Atlanta, GA, May 8, 1910) served as pastor of the Big Bethel African Methodist Episcopal Church, Atlanta, GA, and bishop of the AME Church
	Carole Gist is the first black to be crowned "Miss USA," Wichita, KS	Comer J. Cottrell, President of Pro-Line Corporation, pays $1.5 million in a bankruptcy auction for Bishop College campus, an historically black college, Dallas, TX	A Gwinnett County, Georgia, state court judge rules that a 39-year-old law prohibiting members of the Ku Klux Klan from wearing hooded masks in public is unconstitutional	Thea Bowman, Catholic educator (d Jackson, MS, Mar 30); Bowman was the only black member of the Franciscan Sisters of Perpetual Adoration and encouraged black Catholics to express their cultural heritage within the Church
	A group of black leaders meet with Secretary of State James A. Baker III* to request an increase in aid to Namibia	Marguerite Ross Barnett (1942–1992) is appointed president of the University of Houston becoming the first woman president of that university and also one of the few to head any school that is not historically a women's college	Two 19-year-old white youths are sentenced to prison for the murder of Yusuf K. Hawkins; the youths shot Hawkins because they believed he was visiting a white girl in Bensonhurst, a predominantly Italian neighborhood in New York City	
	A *New York Times*/CBS Network News Poll reveals that blacks have given Pres. George Bush* "the highest level of sustained approval" of any Republican president in 30 years		The Americans with Disability Act, led by Cong. Major Owens (D-NY), chairman of the Subcommittee on Select Education, is signed into law	
	Gov. L. Douglas Wilder (D-VA) directs state agencies and institutions to divest themselves of all business investments in South Africa			
	Joseph E. Lowery, president of the SCLC, holds a two-hour workshop on race relations with four members of the Ku Klux Klan; the men were sentenced to participate in the meeting for their participation in a racial disturbance in Decatur, AL, in 1979			
	Nelson Mandela arrives in Washington, DC, to begin a five-day speaking tour; Mandela, accompanied by his wife Winnie, meets with several influential Americans, including Randall Robinson, head of TransAfrica, Jacqueline Kennedy Onassis,* widow of former US President John F. Kennedy,* and Pres. George Bush*			
	Theo Mitchell, state senator, wins the Democratic primary contest for gover-			

E. **Literature, Publications, and The Black Press**	F. **The Arts**	G. **Science, Technology, and Medicine**	H. **Sports**	
Walter Mosley's *Devil in a Blue Dress* is published; the novel's realism and strong black American characters will earn its author praise and a nomination for best novel by the Mystery Writers of America	Quincy Jones receives the French Legion of Honor for his contributions to music as a trumpeter, composer, arranger, and record producer	Roselyn Payne Epps is the first black woman to serve as president of the American Medical Association	Elaine Weddington becomes assistant general manager of the Boston Red Sox baseball team	**1990**
Charles Johnson (b Evanston, IL, Apr 23, 1948) wins the National Book Award for his third novel *Middle Passage;* he is the first black man since Ralph Ellison to win the award	August Wilson's *The Piano Lesson* wins the Pulitzer Prize for drama		James "Buster" Douglas KO's champion Mike Tyson in a major upset in boxing history, Tokyo, Japan	
	Ernie Singleton is named president of MCA Records' Black Music division; Singleton, Jheryl Busby, president of Motown Records, Sylvia Rhone, president of Atco EastWest Records, and Ed Eckstine, president of Mercury Records, are the highest-ranking blacks in the record business		Bernadette Locke becomes the first female on-court coach of a men's team when she is named assistant coach of the University of Kentucky's men's basketball team	
	Sammy Davis, Jr., entertainer (d Beverly Hills, CA, May 16); Davis is best known for his songs "The Way You Look Tonight" (1946), "That Old Black Magic" (1955), and "The Candy Man" (1972)		The NFL withdraws its plan to hold the 1993 Super Bowl in Phoenix, AZ, because the state refuses to honor Rev. Martin Luther King, Jr.'s birthday	
	Jonathan A. Rodgers is named president of CBS's Television Stations Division, making him the highest-ranking black in network television			
	Quincy Jones wins a Grammy Legend Award, making him the most nominated artist in Grammy history with 76 nominations and 25 wins			
	Denzel Washington (b Mt. Vernon, NY, Dec 1954) wins the Academy Award for Best Supporting Actor for his performance in *Glory*			

1990

nor of South Carolina; Mitchell loses the general election in November to incumbent Governor Carroll Campbell*

Harvey Gantt loses the North Carolina senatorial election to Republican incumbent Jesse Helms*

Flossie M. Byrd (b Sarasota, FL, Aug 8, 1927) receives the Distinguished Service Award from the American Home Economics Association in honor of more than four decades of outstanding teaching and leadership and leadership in home economics

Richard Parsons (b NYC Apr 4, 1942) is named chief executive officer of Dime Savings Bank, the first black CEO of a large, non-minority US savings institution

Eight black Americans are among the 130 delegates from around the world who found the Institute of the Black Peoples, the first comprehensive international African think-tank, Ouagadougou, Burkina Faso

Pres. George Bush* names Arthur Fletcher chair of the US Commission on Civil Rights

Sharon Pratt Kelly becomes the first woman mayor of Washington, DC

LA state senator William J. Jefferson (b Lake Providence, LA, Mar 14, 1947) (D-LA) is elected to the US Congress

Eleanor Holmes Norton is elected US congressional delegate from Washington, DC

Craig Washington (D-TX) is elected to the US Congress, replacing his friend, the late Cong. "Mickey" Leland

Maxine Waters (b St. Louis, MO) (D-CA) is

E. Literature,
   Publications, and
   The Black Press   F. The Arts   G. Science,
                                        Technology,
                                        and Medicine   H. Sports

1990

E. Literature,
   Publications, and
   The Black Press   F. The Arts   G. Science,
                                        Technology,
                                        and Medicine   H. Sports

357

	A. **General History**	B. **Education**	C. **Laws and Legal Actions**	D. **Religion**
1990	elected to the US Congress from the state of California			
	Cong. Barbara Rose-Collins (b Detroit, MI) (D-MI) is elected to the US Congress			
	Cong. Gary Franks (b Waterbury, CT, Feb 9, 1953) (R-CT) is elected to the US Congress			
1991	US Congress grants Pres. George Bush* the authority to wage war against Iraq; many black Americans feel that the deepening economic recession at home is a more immediate problem and are four times less likely than whites to support the war	Jean Camper Cahn, co-founder of the Antioch School of Law, Washington, DC, and founder of the Urban Law Institute, George Washington University, Washington, DC, d Jan 7	College Professor Anita Hill appears before a US Congressional Committee that is hearing testimony for the confirmation of Judge Clarence Thomas to the US Supreme Court; Hill charges Thomas with sexual harassment and ignites a national debate concerning the issue	Chester Talton is consecrated as suffragan bishop of the Episcopal Diocese of Los Angeles, CA
	Ronald Burris is named Attorney General for the state of Illinois; he is the first black to hold this position	Alan Page, former defensive lineman for the Minnesota Vikings football team is awarded the Friend of Education Award, the National Education Association's highest honor		Bishop Smallwood E. Williams, founder of the Bible Way Churches Worldwide, d Washington, DC, Jun 30; his ministry claims over 100,000 members
	Speaker of the House Thomas S. Foley* (D-WA) names Cong. John Lewis (D-GA) Democratic deputy whip	Former Cong. William II. Gray (D-PA) is elected president of the United Negro College Fund		
	Members of the Harlem Hell Fighters, one of the oldest and most renowned black National Guard units in the US, report that their unit has been broken up, stripped of its equipment, and moved to the front line without proper preparation and training for the Persian Gulf War	Hampton University of Hampton, VA, students stage a silent protest against the commencement address of Pres. George Bush* to highlight their opposition to his civil rights policies		
	Adrienne Mitchell is the first black woman to die in combat in the Persian Gulf War			
	Rev. Emmanuel Cleaver is elected mayor of Kansas City, MO, the first black to hold this position			
	Maryann Coffey is elected the first woman and first black co-chairperson of the National Conference of Christians and Jews			
	Wellington Webb is elected mayor of Denver, CO, the first black to hold this position			

Shelby Steele's *The Content of Our Character*, a book on affirmative action, wins the National Book Critics Circle Award

Toni Morrison is commissioned to write the lyrics for the operatic piece *Honey and Rue* performed by Kathleen Battle in Carnegie Hall

Rev. James Cleveland, pianist, singer, composer and producer (d Los Angeles, CA, Feb 9); Cleveland was the first gospel artist to receive a star on Hollywood's Walk of Fame

A bronze sculpture of civil rights activist Rosa Parks goes on display at the National Portrait Gallery, Washington, DC

New Jack City, directed by Mario Van Peebles and produced by George Jackson and Doug McHenry, premieres

Whoopi Goldberg wins an Academy Award for best actress in a supporting role for *Ghost*

Ethel L. Payne, newspaper reporter, journalist, and first black woman commentator employed by a national broadcast network, d Washington, DC, May 28

Russell Williams II wins an Academy Award for sound in the film *Dances with Wolves*

Lloyd Richards, the first black artistic director of a major US theater, announces his retirement from Yale Repertory Theater

Arthur Jafa wins the Best Cinematography award at the Sundance Film Festi-

The *New England Journal of Medicine* reports that blacks are at least three times more likely to suffer kidney failure than whites, but do not get as many transplants or donate as many kidneys

A study in the *Journal of the American Medical Association* reveals that higher rates of high blood pressure found in black Americans may be due more to living with racial discrimination than to genes

Astronaut Mae Jemison is mission specialist for the June shuttle Discovery flight Spacelab-5

Tennis star Althea Gibson becomes the first woman to win the Theodore Roosevelt Award, the NCAA's highest honor

James "Cool Papa" Bell, a prominent player for several Negro League teams (d St. Louis, MO, Mar 7); Bell, who is widely regarded as the fastest man ever to play baseball, never played in the major leagues because of the ban on black players

Ricky Henderson of the Oakland A's steals his 939th base, breaking Lou Brock's* record

Willy T. Ribbs becomes the first black American driver to qualify for the Indianapolis 500; during the race, which occurs the following week, Ribbs is forced to drop out due to engine failure

Hal McRae is named manager of the Kansas City Royals, becoming one of two black managers in major league baseball

Baltimore Orioles manager Frank Robinson is named general manager of the club

Reggie Waller is appointed director of scouting for the San Diego Padres baseball team, becoming the team's first black executive

1991

Hon. Thurgood Marshall, the first black Supreme Court justice, announces that he is retiring from the court on the advice of his wife and doctor

1992

Former tennis star Arthur Ashe announces that he has contracted the HIV virus as a result of receiving contaminated blood when he underwent surgery several years previously

Police officers of the Los Angeles Police Department are accused of brutally beating motorist Rodney King and are found not guilty; riots and looting ensue, resulting in many deaths, injuries, and over $1 billion in property damage

Earvin "Magic" Johnson resigns from the National Commission on AIDS after criticizing Pres. George Bush's* lack of commitment to the cause

Lucien Blackwell (b Aug 1, 1931) (D-PA) is elected to fill the US Congressional seat left vacant by Cong. William H. Gray

Former Cong. Barbara Jordan (D-TX) is the keynote speaker at the Democratic National Convention, NYC

Carol Moseley Braun (b Chicago, IL, Aug 16, 1947)

According to the Department of Education, an admissions policy that gives special treatment to University of California, Berkeley, minority candidates violates federal law

An American Council of Education study reveals that black college enrollment has made significant gains between 1988 and 1990, after several years of regression

DeWitt Wallace,* publisher of the *Reader's Digest*, donates $37 million to Spelman College, Atlanta, GA—the largest gift ever to an historically black college

val, Utah, for filmmaker Julie Dash's *Daughters of the Dust,* the first film by a black American woman to have a national release

Michael Jackson signs an unprecedented $1 billion multimedia contract with Sony Records

Patrice Rushen (b Los Angeles, CA, Sep 30, 1954), composer and popular music artist, becomes the first woman musical director of a network television show when she joins "The Midnight Hour" on CBS

Black Americans receive a record seven Emmy Awards; James Earl Jones wins two awards (for the series "Gabriel's Fire" and the made-for-television movie *Heatwave*)

Pearl Stewart is named editor of the *Oakland Tribune,* becoming the first black woman to edit a daily newspaper in a major US city

Terry McMillan's (b Port Huron, MI, Oct 18, 1951) *Waiting to Exhale* is published; the novel remains on *The New York Times* best-seller list for months

In an unprecedented act of black economic solidarity, entertainers Bill Cosby, Janet Jackson, Oprah Winfrey, Prince, Magic Johnson, Michael Jordan, and philanthropist, Peggy Cooper Cafritz come to the aid of Spike Lee, who runs over budget while filming *Malcolm X*

Michael Davis, Derek Dingle, Denys Cowan, and Dwayne McDuffie of Milestone Media launch a deal with DC Comics, publisher of "Batman" and "Superman," to distribute nationally comic books that feature multiethnic heroes and villains

John Singleton is the first black American director to be nominated for an Academy Award for best director, and his film, *Boyz N the Hood,* is the first by a black American to be nominated for best screenplay

Branford Marsalis (b New Orleans, LA, Aug 26, 1960) becomes the musical director for the "Tonight Show" hosted by Jay Leno*

Astronaut Mae Jemison travels as a science mission specialist aboard the space shuttle Endeavor

Michael Jordan is named the NBA's MVP after leading the Chicago Bulls to a 67-15 record, the best in franchise history

Jackie Joyner-Kersee becomes the first woman to repeat as Olympic heptathalon champion when she defeats Irina Belova* of the Unified Team, Barcelona, Spain

Ron Dickerson is named coach of the Temple University football team, becoming the first and only black to head a Division I-A team, Philadelphia, PA

Barry Bonds of the San Francisco Giants signs a $43.75 million contract for six years and becomes baseball's highest paid player

Lusia Harris is inducted into the Basketball Hall of Fame

Mike Tyson, former boxing heavyweight champion, is convicted of rape and sentenced to six years in prison

Barbara J. Jacket is the head coach of the US wom-

1992 of Illinois is the first black woman Democrat elected to the US Senate

Pres. George Bush* nominates Edward Perkins as ambassador to the United Nations

Former federal judge Alcee Hastings (D-FL) is elected to the US Congress

Carol Moseley Braun is the third African American and the first African-American woman to serve in the US Senate. (US Congress)

E. **Literature,
Publications, and
The Black Press**

F. **The Arts**

G. **Science,
Technology,
and Medicine**

H. **Sports**

en's track and field team at the Olympic Games, Barcelona, Spain, the second black woman to hold this position

When Vivian L. Fuller is named athletics director at Northeastern Illinois University, she becomes the first black female athletics director in the history of Division I sports

Dominique Dawes becomes the first black woman gymnast on a US Olympic team; teammate Jair Lynch is the third black male gymnast to compete

INDEX

Orthodox Church,
1921D
frican Presbyterian Church,
1834A
African Union Church, 1813D,
1850D, 1866D
African Union First Colored
Methodist Protestant
Church, 1805D, 1866D
African Union Meeting House,
1820A
African Union Methodist Church,
1814D
African Union Society, 1783D,
1787A
African Wesleyan Methodist
Episcopal Church, 1818D
Afro-American, 1892E
Afro-American Historical and
Genealogical Society, 1977A
Afro-American Historical Society,
1897A
Afro-American Music Opportuni-
ties Association, 1969F
Afro-American National League,
1890A
*Afro-American Press and Its Editors,
The* (Penn), 1891E
Afro-American Woman, The
(Harley and Terborg-Penn),
1978E
After the Glory (Savage), 1931F
Agassiz Grammar School, 1889B,
1915B
Agriculture Department, U.S.,
1935G
Ahmad, Hazrat Mirza
Ghulam,1921D, 1922D
Ahmadiyya sect, 1921D, 1922D
Aida (Verdi), 1985F
Ailey, Alvin, 1958F, 1965F,
1989F
"Ain't I A Woman?" (Truth),
1852A
"Ain't Misbehavin'" (Waller),
1929F, 1932F
Aird, James, 1782F
Air Force, U.S.:
black officers in, 1954A,1968A,
1988A
blacks serving with distinction
in, 1945A
women in, 1974A, 1979A,
1988A
Air Force Academy, U.S., 1981A
Akers, Doris, 1948F
Akron, Ohio, 1852A
Akron Indians, 1923H
Alabama:
black politicians in, 1870A,
1872A, 1874A
black sheriffs in, 1968A
education in, 1867B, 1868B,
1875B, 1876B, 1878B,
1881A, 1881B, 1888B,
1892B, 1893H, 1896B,
1915B, 1927H, 1938H,
1952B, 1956B, 1960A,
1963B
in entering Union, 1819A
migration to, 1881A
opening of public lands in,
1866C
preachers in, 1833C
selling alcohol in, 1863C
settlement of, 1540A
voting rights in, 1819C, 1898C,
1980C
Alabama, University of, integration of, 1956B, 1963B
Alabama Stakes, 1890H

Alabama State Agricultural and
Mechanical College for Ne-
groes, 1875B
Alabama State University, 1874B,
1946A, 1960A
"Alarm Gun Quadrille, The"
(Hazzard), 1804F
Alaska Pipeline Bill, 1972A
Albany, N.Y., 1820D, 1822D
Albany Enterprise Academy,
1863D
Albany State College, 1903B
Albert, Octavia R., 1890E
*Album Littéraire, Journal des Jeunes
Gens, Amateurs de la Littéra-
ture, L'*, 1843E
Alcinder, Ferdinand Lewis, *see*
Abdul-Jabbar, Kareem
Alcorn State University, 1871B
Aldredge, "Big Mo," 1953H
Aldridge, Ira Frederick, 1824F,
1825F, 1833F, 1858F,
1865F
Alexander, Archie, 1887G
Alexander, Clifford, Jr., 1977A
Alexander, John H., 1887A
Alexander, Raymond Pace,
1927A, 1935C
Alexander, Sadie Tanner Mossell,
1921B, 1927A, 1935C
Alexander, Virginia, 1931G
Alexander, William M., 1892E
Alexander v. Holmes, 1969B
Alexandria, Va., 1876E
Ali, Muhammad (Cassius Clay),
1961H, 1964H, 1967H,
1971H, 1972C, 1974H,
1975H, 1978H, 1980H
Ali, Noble Drew (Timothy
Drew), 1913D, 1930D
Alice, Mary, 1987V
Alienated American, 1852E
Allain, Theophile T., 1869B,
1886B
All-American Football Confer-
ence, 1946H
Allegheny, Pa., 1864A
Allen, Debbie, 1973F
Allen, Ethan, 1775A
Allen, J. B., 1895G
Allen, Macon B., 1845A
Allen, Peter, 1830F
Allen, Richard, 1780D, 1786D,
1816D, 1817D, 1820D,
1827D, 1832D
on abolition of slavery, 1799C
The African Church organized
by, 1791D
African Masonic Lodge and,
1798A
American Colonization Society
and, 1817A
Bethel AME Church estab-
lished by, 1794D
black mutual aid group
founded by, 1787D
conversion of, 1777D
education and, 1795B, 1804B
Free African Society and,
1793A
hymns and, 1801D, 1818D
Methodist Episcopal Church
Conference and, 1784D
monument to, 1876A
ordained as deacon, 1799D
on sin, 1808D, 1809A
and War of 1812, 1812A
Allen, Sarah, 1827D
Allen, William Francis, 1867E
Allen, William G., 1842E,
1853E

Allen's Brass Band, 1850F
Allensworth, Allen, 1886D,
1906A
Allen University, 1870B, 1871B,
1885B
Alliance, 1812F
All Nations Pentecostal Church,
1914D
*All the Women Are White, All the
Blacks Are Men, but Some of Us
Are Brave* (Hull, Scott, and
Smith), 1982E
Alpha Kappa Alpha, 1908A
Alpha Phi Alpha, 1906A
Alsdorf, Dubois, 1827F
Alston, Charles, 1933F, 1963F
Alto California, 1851A
Alton, Ill., 1837A
Alvin Ailey American Dance
Theater, 1935F, 1958F,
1965F, 1989F
Amateur Athletic Union (AAU),
1937H, 1938H, 1953H
Amateur Fencer's League of
America, 1951H
AME Church, *see* African Meth-
odist Episcopal Church
American and Foreign Anti-
Slavery Society, 1840A
American Anti-Slavery Society,
1833A, 1838E, 1839A,
1840A, 1842B, 1851A,
1868A
American Association
(baseball),1884H
American Association for the Ad-
vancement of Science,
1987G
American Baptist Free Mission
Society, 1849B
American Baptist Home Mission-
ary Society, 1867B, 1870B,
1873B, 1874B, 1883B
American Baptist Missionary
Convention, 1840D, 1858D,
1859D
American Baptist Publication,
1890D
American Basketball Association
(ABA), 1949H
American Basketball League,
1969H
American Board of Surgery,
1944G, 1968G
American Bowling Congress
(ABC), 1948H
American Chemical Society,
1934G
American Church for Negroes,
1741D
American College of Surgeons,
1913G, 1934G, 1950A,
1966A
American Colonization Society,
1876A
Liberia and, 1817A, 1820A,
1822A
opposition to, 1817A, 1831D,
1852A
purpose of, 1816A
state endorsements of, 1829A
American Convention of Dele-
gates from Abolition Soci-
eties, 1794A, 1804A
American Council of Education,
1992B
American Equal Rights Association, 1869A
American Express, 1989A
American Federation for Clinical
Research, 1972G

American Federation of Labor,
1929A, 1934A
see also AFL-CIO
American Federation of Musi-
cians, 1902F
American Food for Peace Coun-
cil, 1962A
American Football League (AFL),
1959H, 1968H
American Foundation on Nonviolence, 1964A
American Freedmen's Aid Commission, 1862A
American Heritage, 1977A
American Home Economics Association, 1990A
American Institute of Chemists,
1955A
American Journal (Hayden),
1978E
American Labor Party, 1950A
American League (baseball),
1947H, 1948H, 1966H
American League of Colored La-
bourers, 1850A
American Legion, 1919A
American Library Association,
1972A, 1974E
American Lutheran Church,
1983D
American Medical Association
(AMA):
blacks banned from, 1870G,
1886G
first black delegate of, 1950A
first black officers of, 1954G,
1970G, 1990G
American Missionary Associa-
tion, 1860B, 1861B, 1866B,
1867B, 1868D, 1874B
American Moral Reform Society,
1835A
American National Baptist Con-
vention, 1880D
American National Educational
Baptist Convention, 1893D
American Negro Academy,
1897B
American Negro Theater, 1940F
American Nicodemus Town
Company, 1877A
American Nurses Association,
1948A
"American Polka Quadrilles"
(Connor), 1850F
*American Prejudice Against Color,
The* (Allen), 1853E
American Red Cross, 1919G
"American Slavery as It Is"
(Weld), 1839E
American Society of Composers,
Authors and Publishers,
1974F
Americans with Disabilities Act,
1990C
American Tennis Association,
1916H, 1917H
American Union Methodist
Church, 1865D
American Woman Suffrage Asso-
ciation, 1869A
Americas:
Christianizing of Africans in,
1540D, 1608D
first black bishop in, 1715D
immigration from Spain to,
1517A
slave trade and, 1517A, 1518A,
1550A, 1562A, 1600A,
1618A, 1619A, 1621A,
1624A, 1626A, 1634A,

...wn, Ronald H., 1989A
...rown, Ruth, 1956F, 1989F
Brown, Sara Winifred, 1910A
Brown, Scipio, 1778F
Brown, Solomon G., 1833A
Brown, Sterling, 1932E, 1941E
Brown, Wesley A., 1949B
Brown, William, 1798A
Brown, William Wells, 1842A,
   1843A, 1847E, 1849A,
   1849F, 1851E, 1853E,
   1858F, 1863A, 1863E,
   1867E, 1867E, 1874E,
   1880E
Brown and Latimer, 1874G
Brown Fellowship Society,
   1790A
Brown Girl, Brownstones (Mar-
   shall), 1959E
Brownington, Vt., 1829B, 1829D
Brownsville, Pa., 1859A, 1865A
Brownsville, Tex., riots in,
   1906A, 1962A
Brown University, 1764B,
   1916H, 1918H
*Brown v. Board of Education of
   Topeka*, 1954B, 1956A,
   1957A
Bruce, Blanche K., 1864B,
   1870A, 1874A, 1879A,
   1881A, 1889A
Bruce, John E., 1884E, 1911A
Brunswick Memorial World
   Open, 1986H
Bryan, Andrew, 1773D, 1779D,
   1788D, 1790D, 1794D,
   1800D, 1802D, 1813D
Bryant's Minstrels, 1853F
Buchanan, James, 1847C
Buchanan v. Warley, 1917C
Buckingham-Harper, Minnie,
   1927A
Buffalo, N.Y., 1843A
Buffalo baseball team, 1887H
Buffalo Bills, 1968H
Buffalo Musical Association,
   1851F
Buffalo Soldiers, 1869A
Bulge, Battle of the, 1944A
Bumbry, Grace, 1961F
Bunche, Ralph J., 1946A, 1947A,
   1948A, 1950A, 1954A,
   1963A, 1965A
Bunker Hill, Battle of, 1775A,
   1775F
Bureau of Education, 1907E
Bureau of Refugees, Freedmen,
   and Abandoned Lands,
   1865C
Burgess, John M., 1951D, 1970D
Burke, Selma, 1943F, 1945F
Burke, Yvonne Braithwaite,
   1972A, 1976A
Burkina Faso, international Afri-
   can think-tank in, 1990A
Burkins, Eugene, 1874G
Burks, Mary Fair, 1946A
Burlington, Vt., 1850A
Burma, 1935D
Burns, Anthony, 1854A, 1860D
Burns, Tommy, 1908H
Burr, J. A., 1899G
Burrill, Mary, 1919E
Burris, Ronald, 1991A
Burroughs, Charles, 1961A
Burroughs, Margaret, 1961A
Burroughs, Nannie Helen,
   1900D, 1909B
Burton, Willie D., 1987F
Busby, Jheryl, 1988F, 1990F
Bush, Anita, 1918F, 1921F

Bush, George:
   AIDS and, 1992A
   black appointees of, 1975B,
      1989A, 1990A, 1992A
   black support for, 1990A
   civil rights and, 1989A, 1990A,
      1991B
   National Literacy Day and,
      1988C
   Persian Gulf War and, 1991A
Bush, George Washington,
   1844A, 1855A, 1889A
Bush, John E., 1898A
Bush, William, 1889A
Butcher, Margaret Just, 1956E
Buthelezi, Mangosuthu, 1986A
Butler, Benjamin F., 1838A,
   1861A
Butler, Charles, 1822D
Butler, Jerry, 1953F
Butler, John "Picayune," 1864F
Butler, Mary, 1771C, 1787C
Butler, Octavia, 1984E
Butler, R. A., 1897G
Butler, Selena Sloan, 1926B
Butler, Thomas C., 1898A
Butler, William, 1771C, 1787C
Butler Dance Studio, 1916F
Butler University, 1922A
Butts, J. W., 1899G
Butz, Earl L., 1976A
Byard, Gloria Jean, 1974H
Bynoe, Peter, 1989H
Byrd, Flossie M., 1990A
Byrd, Harriet "Liz," 1981A
Byrd, T. J., 1872G, 1874G
Byrd, William, 1758D

Cabeza de Vaca, Álvar Núñez,
   1527A
Cable, Mary Ellen, 1916D
Cable ACE Award, 1983F
Cadoria, Sherian, 1985A
Caesar (comic actor), 1771F
Caesar, John, 1835A
Cafritz, Peggy Cooper, 1992F
Cahn, Jean Camper, 1991B
Cain, Richard H., 1859D, 1862D,
   1865D, 1866E, 1872A,
   1873D, 1880D
Calhoun, John C., 1816A, 1842C
California:
   black-owned newspapers in,
      1851A, 1912E, 1974E
   black politicians in, 1918A,
      1962A, 1970A, 1972A,
      1975A, 1976A, 1978A,
      1980A, 1983C,1990A
   black women's clubs in, 1906A
   campaigns for women's suf-
      frage in, 1911A
   colonization of, 1538A
   discovery of passage to, 1844A
   education in, 1874B, 1956H,
      1969B, 1969H
   and emancipation of slaves,
      1856C
   in entering Union, 1850C
   entertainers in, 1854F
   first black justice of the peace
      in, 1914A
   first Christian burial in, 1771D
   fugitive slave laws of, 1852C
   Independent Old Catholic
      Churches of, 1990D
   on interracial marriages,
      1948C
   judicial rights in, 1862C,
      1863A
   Newton's trial in, 1968C
   number of blacks in, 1850A

   religious organizations in,
      1964D
   slavery outlawed in, 1849C
   U.S. rule of, 1845A
   voting rights in, 1854A
California, University of:
   at Berkeley, 1992B
   at Davis, 1978B
   at Los Angeles, 1969C, 1969E
California Eagle, 1912E, 1952A
California State Federation of
   Colored Women's Clubs,
   1906A
Caliver, Ambrose, 1927B, 1930B
Callioux, André, 1863A
"Call to Rebellion" (Garnet),
   1843A
Calumet Wheelmen, 1892H
Calvary Episcopal Church, 1848D
Calvary Methodist Church,
   1970D
Cambridge, Mass., 1776E, 1915B
Cambridge, Md., 1963A
Cambridge Nonviolent Action
   Committee, 1963A
Camp, Walter, 1892H
Campanis, Al, 1987H
Campbell, Carroll, 1990A
Campbell, Israel, 1861E
Campbell, James Edwin, 1895E
Campbell, Joan, 1989D
Campbell, Robert, 1859A
Campbell, W. S., 1881G
Camp LeJeune, N.C., 1942A
Camp Moultrie Treaty, 1823C
Canaan, N.H., 1835B
Canada:
   black immigration to, 1783A,
      1815A, 1829A, 1830A,
      1831D, 1842A, 1851A,
      1852E, 1854A, 1860C
   black-owned newspapers in,
      1851E
   Morrill's plot and, 1690A
   Olympics in, 1988H
   religious organizations in,
      1930D, 1937D, 1940D
Canadian Rebellion, 1837A
"Candy Man, The," 1990F
Cane (Toomer), 1923E
Cannon, Noah C. W., 1833D,
   1842D
Cannon Hospital and Training
   School for Nurses, 1897B
Canterbury, Conn., 1833B,
   1834B
Capers, William, 1829D, 1844D
Capital City Savings Bank, 1903A
Capital Repertory Theater, 1986F
Capitana, 1502A
Captain Wyatt's Company,
   1830F
Caravans, 1960F
Cardoza, Thomas W., 1873B
Cardozo, Francis L., 1864D,
   1865B, 1868A, 1870A,
   1872A, 1884B
Cardozo, William Warwick,
   1937G
Carey, Bernard C., 1972A
Carey, John, 1852D
Carey, Lott, 1813D, 1815D,
   1819D, 1821D, 1822A,
   1826A, 1897D
Carlos, John, 1968H
Carmantee, slaves of, 1712A
Carmen Jones, 1954F
Carmichael, Stokely, 1966A,
   1967A
"Carnaval Waltz" (Brady),
   1854F

Carnegie, Andrew, 1907B
Carnegie, Elizabeth, 1973E
Carnegie Hall, 1895F, 1912F,
   1938F, 1950F, 1991F
Carnegie Library School, 1923B
Carney, William H., 1863A
Carolinas, 1663A, 1715A, 1729A
   see also North Carolina; South
      Carolina
Carolina Wren Press, 1984E
Carrington, T. A., 1876G
Carroll, David, 1841D
Carroll, Diahann, 1968E
Carruthers, George, 1972G
"Carry Me Back to Ole Virginny"
   (Bland), 1940A
Carson, Benjamin, 1987G
Carswell, G. Harrold, 1970C
Carter, Aaron, 1786A
Carter, Calvin, 1953F
Carter, Eunice Hunton, 1935C
Carter, Jack, 1818H
Carter, James, 1953F
Carter, Jimmy:
   black appointees of, 1977A,
      1978A, 1980A
   election of, 1976A
   on employment, 1978C
Carter, W. C., 1885G
Carver, George Washington:
   Congress addressed by, 1921C
   government posts of, 1935G
   honors and awards of, 1923G
   paintings of, 1893F
   patents of, 1923G, 1925G
   scientific work of, 1897G
   teaching posts of, 1896B
Car Wash, 1976F
Cary, Mary Ann Shadd, 1852E,
   1853E, 1855A, 1864A,
   1871A, 1880A, 1884B
Cary, W. Sterling, 1972D
Cassell, Albert J., 1924F
"Caste Schools" (Reason), 1850E
Catechism School, 1704B, 1712A
Catholics, *see* Roman Catholic
   Church
Catholic University of America,
   1884B
Catlett, Elizabeth, 1946F, 1969F
CBS, 1951A, 1965F, 1988H,
   1990F, 1991F
Ceasar, Shirley, 1960F
Cenelles, Les, 1845E
Census Bureau, U.S., 1970A
Centenary Biblical Institute,
   1869B
Central Committee of Negro Col-
   lege Men, 1917A
Central High School, Little Rock,
   Ark., 1957A, 1958B
Central News-Wave Publications,
   1974E
Central Presbyterian Church,
   1844D
Central State University, 1887B
Central Tennessee College,
   1876B
Cesar (slave), 1792G
Ceylon, 1935D
Chadwick, George W., 1886F
Chaffin's Farm, Battle of, 1864A
Chains and Freedom (Lester),
   1838E
Challenger explosion, 1986A
Chamberlain, Wilt, 1968H,
   1972H
Chambersburg, Pa., 1859A
Charles, Archduke of Spain,
   1517A
Charles, Ezzard, 1949H

National Association for the Advancement of Colored People (NAACP) *(cont.)*
civil rights and, 1956C
DuBois and, 1909A, 1910E, 1934A, 1947A, 1948A
films protested by, 1915F,1985F
first field worker of, 1910A
founding of, 1909A
Howard Chapter of, 1915B
Legal Defense and Educational Fund of, 1939A
on lynchings, 1939A
MFDP and, 1968A
NWP and, 1921A
on occupation of Hawaii, 1922A
officers of, 1955A, 1971A, 1978A
Prayer Pilgrimage and, 1957A
publications of, 1910E
school integration and, 1933B, 1936B, 1956B, 1957A
Spingarn Medal of, 1912G, 1914A, 1921F, 1922A, 1923G
support for, 1964A
Supreme Court nominees and, 1930C, 1970C
theatrical performances presented by, 1916F
World War I and, 1919A
National Association for the Relief of Destitute Colored Women and Children, 1865A
National Association of Baseball Players, 1867H
National Association of Colored Graduate Nurses, 1908G
National Association of Colored Women (NACW), 1894E, 1896A
National Association of Intercollegiate Athletics (NAIA), 1954H, 1957H
National Association of Negro Musicians, 1919F
National Baptist Convention (NBC), USA, Inc.:
on Black Power concept, 1967D
founding of, 1880D
King and, 1958A, 1966D
subconventions of, 1893D, 1895D, 1900D, 1962D
Sunday School Publishing Board of, 1921F
National Baptist Educational Convention, 1895D
National Baptist Progressive Convention, 1962D
National Baptist Publishing Board, 1896D
National Bar Association, 1925A, 1981A
National Basketball Association (NBA):
All-Star games in, 1959H
championships in, 1938H, 1961H, 1975H, 1982H
college players and, 1970H
first blacks in, 1950H, 1966H, 1989H
MVPs in, 1958H, 1992H
record holders in, 1971H, 1972H
24-second rule and, 1954H
WBL and, 1977H

National Benefit Insurance Company, 1898A
national black club movement, first history of, 1933E
National Black Feminist Organization, 1973A
National Black Independent Political Party, 1980A
National Black Nurses Association, 1971A
National Black Political Convention, 1972A
National Black Theatre Company, 1968F
National Black Women's Health Project, The, 1981G
National Book Awards, 1952E, 1974E, 1983E, 1988E, 1990E
National Book Critics Circle Awards, 1978E, 1991E
National Capitol Advisory Committee, 1934A
National Church of Nigeria, 1950A
National Collegiate Athletic Association (NCAA), 1955H, 1957H, 1983H, 1984H, 1991H
National Colored Farmers' Alliance, 1890A, 1891A
National Commission on AIDS, 1992A
National Committee for Fair Play in Bowling, 1948H
National Conference of Artists, 1953F
National Conference of Black Mayors, 1988A
National Conference of Christians and Jews, 1991A
National Congress of Colored Parents and Teachers, 1926B
National Conscription Act, 1863C
National Convention of Colored Citizens of the U.S., 1834A, 1855A, 1864A
National Convention of Gospel Choirs and Choruses, 1932D
National Council of Churches, 1972D
National Council of Colored People, 1853A
National Council of Negro Women, 1935A, 1953A, 1957A, 1964A
National Council of 100 Black Women, 1981A
National Domestic Workers Union, 1968A
National Economic Development Conference, 1969D
National Education Association, 1968B, 1972B, 1991B
National Emigration Board, 1855A
National Federation of Afro-American Women, 1895A, 1896A
National Film Registry, 1989F
National Football League (NFL), 1920H, 1934H, 1949H, 1957H, 1978H, 1989H, 1990H
National Freemen's Relief Association, 1865A
National Institute of Arts and Letters, 1943A
National Institutes of Health, Nursing Department of, 1973G

Nationalist Populist Convention, 1891A
National Labor Union (NLU), 1866A
National Lacrosse team, U.S., 1969H
National League (baseball), 1966H, 1989H
National League for the Protection of Colored Women, 1905A,1910A
National League of Colored Women, 1896A
National Liberty Congress of Colored Americans, 1918A
National Literacy Day, 1988C
National Medical Association (NMA), 1895G, 1977A
National Negro Baseball League, 1919H, 1948H, 1991H
National Negro Bowling Association, 1939H
National Negro Business League, 1900A, 1929A
National Negro Catholic Congress, 1837D
National Negro Convention, 1843A
National Negro Doll Company, 1911A
National Negro Health Week, 1915G
National Negro Network, 1954F
National Negro Opera Company, 1941F, 1943F
National Office of Black Catholics, 1971D
National Organization for Women (NOW), 1966A, 1971A
National Organization of Black Elected Legislative Women, 1985A
National Philanthropist, 1828A, 1828E
National Political Caucus of Black Women, 1984A
National Portrait Gallery, 1991F
National Race Commission, 1913A
National Reformer, 1838E
National Security Council, 1964A
National Steamboat Company, 1895A
National Teacher of the Year, 1972B
National Training Schools for Women, 1909B
National Urban League, 1910A, 1923E, 1961A, 1972A
National Watchman, 1842E
National Woman's Party (NWP), 1921A
National Woman Suffrage Association, 1869A, 1876A
National Women's Football League, 1976H
National Youth Administration, 1936A
Nation of Islam:
all-black state and, 1960D
draft laws and, 1970C
founding of, 1930D
International Savior's Day convention of, 1985A
leaders of, 1930D, 1934D, 1975D, 1977D
Malcolm X and, 1957A, 1958A, 1964A
number of members of, 1960D

Native Americans:
in attempted uprisings, 1727A
in attending church, 1730D
black immigration to settlements of, 1783A
black missionaries to, 1785D, 1816D, 1819D
blacks claiming to be, 1901H
blacks in battles with, 1729A, 1735A
British missionaries to, 1701D
Buffalo Soldiers and, 1869A
in burning owners' homes, 1658A
buying or receiving goods from, 1693C
Christianization of, 1540D, 1660D, 1682D
curfews for, 1690C, 1703C, 1723C
education of, 1751B
employment of, 1715C
entertainment of, 1703C, 1723C
firearms carried by, 1712C
Fort Donnelly attacked by, 1788A
home ownership by, 1712C
in interracial marriages, 1691C
judicial rights of, 1705C, 1827C
in military service, 1652A, 1660C
Morrill's conspiracy with, 1690A
murders and, 1708C, 1718C
office holding by, 1705C
as property, 1705C
rapes by, 1770C
religious instruction for, 1724D
restrictions on meetings of, 1685C
runaway slaves and, 1828C
selling alcohol to, 1750C
settlement of Africans among, 1526A
slave trade and, 1639A, 1712C
Texas raids of, 1839A
threat of attacks by, 1708A
travel rights of, 1682C
voting rights of, 1778C
and War of 1812, 1812A
wrongful enslavement of, 1772C
see also specific Native American groups
"Natives of America, The" (Plato), 1841E
Native Son (play), 1952F
Native Son (Wright), 1940E
"Nat King Cole Show, The," 1970F
Naval Academy, U.S., 1872B, 1949B
Naval Office, R.I., 1712C
Navigation Acts, 1697C
Navy, Confederate, 1861A, 1862A
Navy, Union, 1861A, 1861C, 1862A, 1863C, 1864A
Navy, U.S.:
black bandmasters in, 1908F
black officers in, 1942A, 1944A, 1950A, 1972A
black recruitment program of, 1971A
black scientists in, 1972G
blacks in, 1789A, 1803C, 1842C, 1941A, 1942A, 1943A, 1944A, 1950A
blacks serving with distinction in, 1941A, 1943A, 1944A
Blue Angels of, 1985A

Photographs not otherwise credited are courtesy the following sources: Bethune: Bethune Museum and Archives. LC: Library of Congress. MSRC: Moorland Springarn Research Center, Howard University. Schomburg: Photographs and Prints Division, Schomburg Center for Research in Black Culture, The New York Public Library, Astor, Lenox and Tilden Foundations.